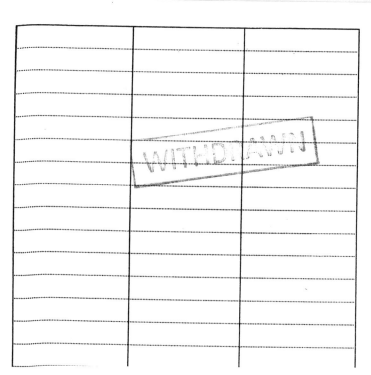

Selected Letters of Michael Tippett

Selected Letters of Michael Tippett

Edited by
THOMAS SCHUTTENHELM

With a Foreword by
DAVID MATTHEWS

faber and faber

First published in 2005
by Faber and Faber Limited
3 Queen Square London WC1N 3AU

Typeset by Faber and Faber Limited
Printed in England by Mackays of Chatham plc, Chatham, Kent

A CIP record for this book
is available from the British Library

ISBN 0–571–22600–0

2 4 6 8 10 9 7 5 3 1

Contents

The Letters

List of Illustrations

1 Michael Tippett (photo Axel Poignant)
2 MT's mother
3 MT's home in Wadhurst
4 With Jessica Minchinton and his mother, 1951
5 MT at Corsham
6 With Karl Hawker
7 With John Minchinton, August 1955
8 With Benjamin Britten on Tippett's sixtieth birthday, January 1965 (photo Eric Auerbach)
9 With John Amis
10 With William Glock (photo Mike Evans/Lebrecht)
11 With Howard Hartog
12 MT and Michael Tillett at Dartington for a performance of *The Vision of St Augustine*
13 With Meirion Bowen, Berlin 1989 (photo Michael Haring)
14 With Colin Davis (photo Mike Evans/Lebrecht)
15 MT conducting, probably at Morley College
16 With Colin Davis and Meirion Bowen at rehearsals for the première of *The Mask of Time* in Boston (photo Florence Montgomery)
17 With Jessye Norman in a performance of *Child of our Time* at the BBC Proms, 1979

The publishers have made every effort to research dates and trace copyright owners and we will be glad to hear from those that we have been unable to locate or have inadvertently omitted, to whom we extend our apologies.

Acknowledgements

This book would not have been possible without the support and initiative of the Tippett Estate, specifically Meirion (Bill) Bowen. His generosity, assistance and friendship were essential. And to Nick Wright who steered it all to the finish line.

A special mention must be reserved for Sally Groves from Schott who provided some behind the scenes direction, and the necessary encouragement in the most delicate of times. In particular I would like to thank Polly Fallows for her immeasurable editorial contributions on improving the text and preparing the letters for publication, and Alison Latham for the timeline.

Throughout this project I was assisted by numerous librarians and their staff: Jeanette Casey from Northwestern University, the librarians at the William Ready Division of Archives and Research at MacMaster University, Julie Snelling from the BBC Written Archives Centre, John Newman at the Minet Library, and especially all those from the Rare Books and Music Room at the British Library. Two in particular, Steve Cork and Nicolas Bell, assisted me with research and gathering materials, and became good friends in the process.

A sincere thank you to all those who have so generously placed their correspondence with Tippett at our disposal, in particular Sophie Bowness, who provided me with the letters to Barbara Hepworth; Rachel O'Higgins, who brought the Bush collection to my attention; and to Gwyn Rhhyderch and Paul Crossley from the Tippett Foundation (and John Brackband who kept up the correspondence between Mr Crossley and myself). Also to Stephen Pettitt for his kindness and friendship and David Matthews for his assistance in uncovering a new letter to Benjamin Britten, and for providing the Foreword.

A very special thank you to Eric Seddon who turned my indecisions into a focused plan, and whose suggestions were key to improving the book. To my parents, friends, and family who endured the long silences while I was consumed with work, your support and loyalty has been a great comfort to me.

To Caroline, whose companionship and belief in ideals kept me always looking higher.

Foreword

There are some composers – for instance Bruckner – who have communicated virtually nothing about their music, so that our knowledge of it depends solely on the evidence of the notes themselves. Others – Wagner is a notable example – have devoted much energy and time to expounding their work and their ideas. Michael Tippett is firmly in the second category. Throughout his long life he felt a compelling need to explain himself and what he was trying to do, whether in the three books he published during his lifetime (*Moving Into Aquarius*, 1959; *Music of the Angels*, 1980; and his autobiography *Those Twentieth Century Blues*, 1991), or in his many letters to friends and colleagues, of which this book contains about a fifth of the approximately 2500 that survive.

The letters paint a vivid self-portrait of a man constantly absorbed with ideas that will nourish his overriding concern, his music. He was unashamedly self-centred, although perhaps no more so than many other great artists. Besides, Tippett's self-obsession was of an especially engaging kind. When I first met him in 1974 I wrote in my journal: 'He talked for $2^{1}/_{2}$ hours with hardly a stop, about an enormously interesting composer called Tippett & his equally interesting music.' I wasn't being facetious; it was just that he seemed to have a wonderful ability to talk quite objectively – and fascinatingly – about himself. The letters demonstrate this. Those from the 1930s especially reveal the probing depths of his mind, as he moved away from involvement with left-wing politics – he was one of the first intellectuals to see through the false hopes of communism – towards a kind of pantheistic religious view which asserted the value and beauty of life without embracing any particular faith. They also display the astonishingly wide range of his interests.

We learn a great deal about Tippett's music from these letters, much more about the earlier works – in particular *A Child of Our Time* and *The Midsummer Marriage* – than the later ones. There is virtually nothing about the last two operas, or *The Vision of St Augustine* and

The Mask of Time. This is partly because of his deteriorating eyesight and his increasing reliance on the telephone, so that there is no equivalent in the later years of the long, elaborate letters from the 1930s and 1940s. Undoubtedly the most interesting letters in this collection are those to his closest friends of that period – such as David Ayerst, Francesca Allinson and Douglas Newton (also a lover) – to whom Tippett uninhibitedly confessed everything that was currently on his mind, including remarkably frank details about his sexual life. Then there are his composer friends, Benjamin Britten and Alan Bush, to whom he gave accounts of his work in progress and occasionally (as in his letter about *The Rape of Lucretia*) telling criticism of theirs; and a few of his close collaborators such as Barbara Hepworth, who designed the sets for the first production of *The Midsummer Marriage* and who received a series of obsessive letters about that opera.

The correspondence with Britten, most of which is included here, is a particularly valuable one. In the 1940s they were close friends, each recognising the other as the only other living British composer who really mattered; both of them actively involved in the revival of pre-Classical music, above all Purcell; both soon devoting their main energies to opera. For a few years Tippett almost took the place that Auden had played in Britten's life, as a kind of wise older brother; while for Tippett, Britten was 'the most purely musical person I have ever met and I have ever known', as he recorded in the obituary he wrote for the *Listener*. Britten's letters to Tippett, sadly, have not survived: whereas Britten assiduously kept everything sent to him, Tippett (like Auden) was careless with the letters he received. He was never a hoarder: his house contained relatively few books, considering the vast number he read. He lived very much in the present, and cast aside anything that had ceased to be useful to him.

There are some notable gaps in Tippett's own correspondence: no letters to his parents; no contemporary ones to Wilfred Franks that might have illuminated his first and most serious love affair (though we do learn a lot about this from some of his letters to David Ayerst); nothing to Karl Hawker, his companion for seventeen years. There are compensations for these losses, however: for instance in the many letters to Francesca Allinson, which show Tippett at his most intimate. Theirs was a loving relationship, though not a sexual one: despite his attractiveness to women, Tippett seems to have been exclusively homosexual in practice. Fresca was also a lesbian, so their idea of marriage and having children, often discussed, came to nothing. Her suicide in 1945 affected him perhaps more than anything in his life. It can also perhaps be seen as a turning point, a further confirmation of the change that had followed the Jungian analysis he undertook at the end of the 1930s, at the painful conclusion of his affair with Wilfred Franks. This had started under the brilliant but maverick analyst John Layard, and continued, at Layard's suggestion, with Tippett analysing his own dream material. This analysis had given him more confidence to continue as an artist, but also suggested to him that from now on he should live a life free of intense emotional involvement. One consequence was the sense of detachment evident in the later letters.

Although Tippett's need to communicate was compulsive, communication for him sometimes took the form of a monologue. 'Don't be worried by these rows of letters. I get into the habit of writing a whole batch to someone and then stop for a bit', he writes, a little disconcertingly, to Alan Bush, almost implying that 'someone' could be anyone. Many of the letters to colleagues and collaborators are understandably concerned for the most part with practical matters, but even when he draws closer to a collaborator such as Barbara Hepworth, we learn little about her concerns or their relationship. There is a contrast here with Britten, who liked to treat his friends as an extended family. Tippett kept himself more aloof; yet every letter too contains glimpses of his natural warmth, as well as his infectious enthusiasm.

My own personal memories of Michael Tippett start from the day I went to lunch with him at Nocketts, his home near Calne in Wiltshire, to discuss the short book on him I was intending to write. He seemed extraordinarily youthful, at least fifteen years younger than his actual age, with quick, expressive movements and energetic step. I remember him bounding upstairs, singing the theme from the slow movement of the Concerto for Double String Orchestra. A few weeks later I spent a weekend in Cambridge with him and his biographer Ian Kemp, and we made an expedition to his childhood home at Wetherden, which Tippett had not seen since his parents had sold it in 1919. We had been taken aback to discover that the woman who had bought it from the Tippetts was still living there, and had hardly altered the house at all, so it was like stepping back into the past. We asked to see the barn, where Tippett had often played with his brother, and were given a rusty key; we had to clear away many years' growth of ivy from the door before we were able to unlock it, and then an ancient interior was revealed by shafts of sunlight streaming through the dormer windows, the dilapidated timber looking as if it was just about to collapse. Tippett was very moved; a little later he pointed out a tree in the garden under which he remembered standing when he heard the news that the First World War had begun.

Over the next twenty years I saw him quite often at concerts, the last time at his 90th birthday celebration at the Wigmore Hall, when he was so affected by a performance of *The Heart's Assurance* – the piece he had written in memory of his beloved Fresca – that he could hardly speak. He was then quite frail; yet I thought he would see out the century and witness the Millennium, as he hoped, so his death in January 1998 came as a shock. He was such a central figure in our musical life that his absence is still strongly felt, not simply as a composer but as a man whose integrity and conviction were evident in everything he said and did. The publication of these letters will at least help to reclaim some of those qualities for us.

David Matthews

Introduction

Throughout his life, which spanned almost the whole of the twentieth century, Michael Tippett was a prolific letter writer. In 1944, writing to Douglas Newton, his friend and one-time collaborator on the libretto for the opera *The Midsummer Marriage*, Tippett remarked, 'I never seem to write 1 letter but I write 3.' That a huge amount of this correspondence has survived and is already housed in major libraries around the world is itself indicative of its importance. Taken as a whole it reveals a side of the composer that until now has been largely unknown.

Tippett's letters show a powerful, fertile mind struggling with the relevance of diverse and sometimes conflicting ideologies in an attempt to shape a universal artistic expression embodying the aspirations of humanity. His music, in which are combined poetic metaphors, historical archetypes and the driving forces of the human spirit, has a complexity equalling that of its creator's character – a complexity manifest in the letters written in parallel with his compositions. These place the reader at the composer's side, within the historical moment, as a witness to the creative process. They allow the reader to observe his reactions to shifts in aesthetics and style and reveal an intimate and vulnerable side of a man keenly aware of the inner sensibilities of the human psyche.

In his landmark study *Tippett: The Composer and His Music* (1984) Ian Kemp writes that Tippett, in a letter to his parents, was unusually and innocently explicit about sexual practices at Fettes College, where he was sent in 1918. While the particulars of that incendiary document have been lost, a thread of uninhibited openness – whether about musical, political, sexual, poetic or personal matters – runs through these letters. From the bombing of his cottage in Oxted, Surrey, to the ecstasy of a breakthrough that led to progress on a new composition, each event and accomplishment is documented with clarity and urgency. With hindsight we can measure the cumulative effect of those seemingly insignificant, even trivial encounters that had profound and far-reaching consequences for the composer.

The letters extend far beyond the 'shop talk' one might expect from a prominent composer. Tippett casts his net wide over diverse topics, from social, political, economic and artistic issues to personal affairs, down to the most mundane details of everyday life. His correspondence highlights his capacity to synthesise ideas from across the disciplines and integrate them into his composition.

Tippett's instinct to protect the inner world of his imagination from practical realities comes through clearly in his letters. Ever aware of the need to balance his desire for external stimuli with the contemplative life of a composer, and with tranquillity in mind, once his student days were over he chose to remove himself from urban to rural surroundings. Throughout his life he was aided by a succession of 'protectors' and mediators, most notably Francesca Allinson, Karl Hawker and Meirion Bowen, who helped to insulate him from the distractions that might interfere with his creative momentum. Each was unique to specific stages or periods in Tippett's life, corresponding roughly with his main places of residence – respectively Oxted (1929–51); Tidebrook Manor, Wadhurst, Sussex (1951–60), then Parkside, Corsham, Wiltshire (1960–70); Nocketts, Calne, Wiltshire (1970–96) – and each played a distinct but crucial role in his development.

Francesca Allinson, who helped Tippett financially while he was living at Oxted, understood his artistic temperament and offered emotional support when required. The bond between them remained strong throughout her short life, and the letters testify to the most sustained outpouring of love in Tippett's career. The painter Karl Hawker appears to have helped the composer with his correspondence and business affairs during their seventeen-year companionship. In the mid-1970s Meirion Bowen, the composer's partner for the rest of his life, positioned himself as Tippett's assistant and manager.

Tippett's Life in Letters

The details of Tippett's family history, childhood and development to maturity have been well documented by writers associated both personally and professionally with the composer. The studies by Meirion Bowen (*Michael Tippett*, 1982) and Ian Kemp in particular have a comprehensiveness due to their authors' access to Tippett, whose autobiography, *Those Twentieth Century Blues*, contains further information about specific events and moments. (For a Chronology of his life and works, see p. 439.) But the processes of fact gathering, analysis and recollection can provide only a narrative and, at best, a partial understanding of past events. A profound curiosity remains about the origins of Tippett's ideas, the motivation for his behaviour, and the influences and susceptibilities that lay behind his multifaceted music. The present volume of letters – to friends and lovers; professional colleagues in music performance, publishing and broadcasting; poets, dramatists and critics, and figures with whom he engaged in lively discussion of politics, pacifism and social affairs – goes some way towards satisfying that curiosity. Together with the current biographies, the autobiography and the music, the correspondence chronicles the life and times of a composer whose personal trials and accomplishments mirror the principal cultural developments of the twentieth century.

While Tippett's letters, even in combination with his other writings, do not add up to a broad philosophy of music or define a specific aesthetic doctrine, they do articulate his individual compositional routine, placing him in a long tradition of composers who have written about the intricate and sometimes mysterious creative process. The letters in this selection shed new light on the effort Tippett put into the texts for his vocal music and, most particularly, his opera librettos. Still denounced on occasion as 'confused' or 'obscure', these continue to be divorced by unsympathetic critics from the music for which they were intended, despite Tippett's assertion that they should not be read as literature.

His retreat to the countryside, where he could work undistracted by the highly charged atmosphere of London, made letter writing a necessity. His friendships and professional affairs, conducted long-distance, needed constant attention and updating. Tippett dealt with this chore as quickly as he could, as can be seen from his flyaway handwriting, his use of abbreviations and other short cuts, and his frequent references to matters being dispatched in haste. He would often use train journeys as an opportunity to write letters so as not to waste his precious time at home, which was reserved for composition. As his eyesight deteriorated owing to the macular dystrophy he inherited from his mother's side of the family, he found it increasingly difficult to read and write without a magnifying glass or secretarial help. But it was the distraction from writing music that he resented most. As he wrote in 1973, 'The more I write (letters) – tiddlypom – the more I write. And the more I regret writing. And it distracts *me* from where I am *now* and what I am having to do *now*.' (Quoted in Kemp, p. xi.)

Tippett's reaction to the dissolution of his family in his childhood manifested itself in adult life in a determination to create a stable home that would be both a sanctuary where he could work undisturbed and an inviting meeting place for his friends. He also wanted to indulge his enjoyment of the countryside, as welcome relief from the rigours of composition.

While still a student at the Royal College of Music, Tippett became involved with amateur music making in Oxted. He moved there from London in 1929 and set up his first long-term home, in a new redbrick bungalow, in 1938. Far removed from the distractions of the capital, he quickly settled into a gentler pace of life, living simply and frugally with no telephone and only the barest of furnishings. At the RCM he had turned down an opportunity to study with Vaughan Williams, and his decision to leave London was consistent with his determination to avoid the influence of any individual or institution as he concentrated on finding his own voice. Tippett structured his life to accommodate his musical interests, specifically the sixteenth-century madrigalists (a repertory then largely unexplored by the mainstream musical institutions), as well as his growing interests in literature, psychology and socio-political movements. Although he had no official commissions, or even any performances in prospect, he worked single-mindedly at composition. During his two decades at Oxted he came of age as a composer, producing a series of important works that included three string quartets, the Concerto for Double String Orchestra, the oratorio *A Child of Our Time*, his first Symphony and two acts of his first opera, *The Midsummer Marriage*.

Despite his voluntary isolation, the cottage at Oxted was a hub of activity. Tippett alternated between entertaining such colleagues as Priaulx Rainier and providing a weekend getaway for 'the boys' (John Amis, Douglas Newton, David Ayerst et al). His home was a refuge for conscientious objectors and struggling artists where his friends could escape the pressures of working in London and avoid the wartime bombing, where phonograph recitals were held, books and poetry were discussed, new ideas for works tested, and recently completed ones shared. It also afforded Tippett the freedom and privacy to pursue his romantic interests. During this time he experienced his first mature love affair, with the painter Wilfred Franks. Although Tippett was completely at ease with his sexuality, he seems to have been unprepared for the extremes of emotion that accompany falling in and out of love, and the relationship ended abruptly when Franks announced his decision to marry.

By this time Tippett had long since rejected the traditional notions of religion and its institutions, and while he was a firm believer in the power of humankind to control its destiny, he laid himself open to the workings of chance. 'My artistic life has been full of accidents', he wrote in his autobiography (p. 11). The letters included here chronicle some of these 'accidents' and their often advantageous outcome.

The years surrounding the Second World War proved particularly grim, with little prospect for Tippett of a productive future as a composer. In desperation he writes to David Ayerst, 'It seems to be going over the edge. I lose all my jobs in London. Composition isn't a social possibility in war.' The war did, however, offer Tippett an opportunity to gain wider recognition within England's cultural landscape as BBC radio broadcasts replaced live events. His first radio talk, *Stravinsky and the Dance*, was a turning point in his career, bringing him into contact with influential programme producers and others able to disseminate his music through broadcasts. After the Third Programme was launched in 1946 Tippett was regularly invited to give talks and appear in discussion programmes. His letters to Anna Kallin, the producer with whom he worked most closely, show how seriously he took such opportunities to establish a basis from which to promote his music.

In 1951, with financial assistance from his mother, Tippett bought a large, dilapidated house, Tidebrook Manor, near Wadhurst, Sussex. Although he had successfully combined composition with hospitality to his friends at Oxted, he had long desired a stable partnership like that enjoyed by his friends Benjamin Britten and Peter Pears, John Amis and Olive Zorian, and David and Larema Ayerst. This move was symbolic in that it allowed Tippett to restore his broken home with his mother and in due course to make a new home with Karl Hawker. Earlier in the year he had resigned from his post as music director of Morley College, and to help offset the expense of living at Tidebrook he began to explore other sources of income, such as investing in forestry and cultivating the land nearby, while continuing to give talks for the BBC. Allowing his imagination free rein to finish *The*

Midsummer Marriage during the year after the move undoubtedly contributed to the change in his style that followed shortly on completion of the opera.

In 1960, Tippett decided to leave Tidebrook for the small country town of Corsham, Wiltshire. Moving his mother to Maldon in Essex, he and Hawker took over the rental of Parkside, a Georgian house in the High Street, from David Ayerst's brother in-law Bryan Fisher. Backing on to Corsham Park, it was ideally placed for Tippett's daily routine of a long walk after a morning's composing. The town was home to the Bath Academy of Art, where Tippett was engaged as music adviser and external examiner. Eventually he established a connection with the Festival of Music in the city of Bath itself: in 1969 he became one of a triumvirate of directors, alongside Colin Davis and Jack Phipps. He assumed sole direction of the festival the following year and remained in that position until 1974.

The period between 1960 and 1970 was a turbulent one for Tippett. His work began to gain public recognition, and many new pieces were commissioned. Besides being knighted he was awarded honorary doctorates and made frequent appearances as a speaker and conductor. It was during this time that relations with Karl Hawker deteriorated and Meirion Bowen established himself as the primary figure in the composer's life. The passionate but secretive beginnings of their relationship are documented in the letters, and Tippett's vitality and exuberance even in his sixties are clearly evident.

As Tippett grew in popularity and status, demands for his work increased, and the time he spent composing and attending to the public's call reduced his availability to his wider circle of friends, while his core of loyal friends and advisers became more restricted. Despite increasing publicity, Tippett remained fiercely committed to composition. Although the residency at Corsham was one of his shortest and generated the fewest letters, it was a time of intense productivity, during which four major works were completed: Piano Sonata No. 2, the Concerto for Orchestra, *The Vision of Saint Augustine* and his third opera, *The Knot Garden*. Tippett's association with some of the best performers and institutions allowed a degree of creative freedom, but he was always concerned with the practicalities of performance and remained attuned to the difficulties of his music.

In 1970, with money inherited from his mother, Tippett bought Nocketts Hill Farm, a modern house with an indoor swimming pool in the country outside the small town of Calne, Wiltshire. The correspondence from the next twenty-six years consists mostly of short notes and postcards, the main reason for the reduction in letters being his macular dystrophy, which was formally diagnosed in 1970. Tippett had grown used to writing his music on enlarged manuscript paper and to reading with a magnifying glass, but as the symptoms became ever more pronounced it was difficult for him to respond to the growing volume of correspondence.

After Tippett's separation from Karl Hawker in the mid-1970s, he and Meirion Bowen were free to appear together in public. In 1979 Bowen, recognising a need for someone to organise the composer's increasingly busy professional life, persuaded him to centralise his public activities by setting up an office in London, first near Covent Garden, then at Schott's. The office handled correspondence and contractual negotiations, and in general acted as a mediator, controlling Tippett's contacts with the press and public by diverting and screening most of his telephone calls and establishing a private direct line to the composer. While this number was supposed to remain confidential, Tippett was notorious for leaking it to his friends. The office facility and the convenience of the telephone contributed further to the drop in correspondence in the Nocketts period.

While thus freed to compose and to contemplate new works, Tippett was left more isolated than ever. With most of the business being handled on his behalf, his daily diversions were limited to television and the occasional phone call that was allowed through; most of his visitors had to be cleared by the office, with proper arrangements made to accommodate his demanding composition and commission schedules.

In October 1987, having been diagnosed with colon cancer, Tippett reduced the number of his public engagements. Despite his relatively fragile health and failing vision he continued to compose, but after he had finished the String Quartet No. 5 his energy began to diminish significantly, and in 1993, with the completion of *The Rose Lake*, he announced his retirement. With the exception of *Caliban's Song*, written for the tercentenary commemoration of Purcell's death, he ceased writing music entirely. In April 1996 he sold Nocketts and moved to a rented house in Isleworth, Middlesex. In September that year he suffered a mild stroke, but although his speech was slightly impaired, he remained mentally alert. His last letters were written to Colin Davis just a few months before the end of his life, after he had had another stroke and was living with a young married couple, both trained carers who provided round-the-clock support and attention. On 8 January 1998 he died peacefully at home.

Editor's Note

My first task as editor was to become acquainted with Tippett's style and script. This alone presented a formidable challenge, as his handwriting is notoriously difficult to read. The letters tend to the colloquial, and are even wild compared to the more polished and elegant prose of his autobiography and essays. They abound in abbreviations, elisions, misspellings, and accidental or deliberate omissions that result in made-up words. Tippett did this for poetic or comic effect, and occasionally made a point of commenting on his disregard of the conventions of English usage. Adept at reading and conversing in modern languages, he would also sprinkle his letters with German, Italian and French expressions, not to mention the occasional phrase in Latin or Greek.

Thankfully, Tippett was concerned more with capturing his fleeting thoughts than with proper form, but his unconventional use of punctuation combined with fragmented but lengthy sentence structure may present the reader with some initial difficulty. He preferred a dash to a comma to mark a sudden shift of thought, an editorial insertion, or a parenthetical remark or idea that may continue for paragraphs, only to return to the original sentence after a page or more. While preserving his idiosyncratic style and some colourful misspellings, I have in most cases, for ease of comprehension, substituted the full word for the abbreviation (wld, cld and shld are rendered as would, could and should; & as and; tho and altho as though and although; yr(s) as your(s); pr'aps as perhaps; abt as about, and agin as against), made minor adjustments to the punctuation and silently corrected some misleading errors in proper names.

Many of Tippett's letters begin with phrases that can be understood only as part of a continuing exchange, for example 'Yes, I agree.' Where such a phrase is pertinent to the subject I have explained, where known, the context in which the letter was written. Where it is of no relevance I have inserted an editorial ellipsis: [. . .]. Such ellipses are also used to eliminate obscure references and repetition.

During the Second World War paper was scarce, and in an effort to conserve materials Tippett would frequently reply on the back of a letter sent to him. Sometimes, when he wanted the recipient to see a specific concert notice, news clipping or article, he would simply write his letter on the object in question. He was also in the habit of using all the available space, so when he reached the end of the page he would turn it sideways and write in the margin. If he ran out of room on the page and did not want to start another sheet, or if a further thought occurred to him after he had sealed the envelope, he would continue writing on the envelope itself, occasionally adding a non sequitur as yet another idea struck him: 'How about a go with a W. African Negro dancer. Want music arranged (?*Child?*) for 2 pfs and 4 tom-toms!!'

Each group of letters in this selection is ordered chronologically. Some of the people with whom Tippett mixed and corresponded are famous, others unfamiliar. In order to give maximum space to the letters and to keep footnotes and explanatory material to a minimum I have sketched a profile of the recipient, outlining his or her connection to Tippett, at the head of each collection; the Biographical Appendix (p. 433) gives, where possible, brief biographical details of the less well known figures mentioned. By thus limiting footnotes in the letters themselves I have aimed to keep Tippett's unique delivery and style intact. My primary concern has been to preserve the integrity of his reasoning and thought processes, thereby demonstrating his remarkable ability to engage in critical debate on a variety of topics.

Fortunately, Tippett provided dates or locations, or both, for most of his letters. The dates assigned to each letter here are taken either directly from the letter itself or, failing that, from the postmark. Some of the undated letters have a date provided by the recipient, which I have retained. Where no date appears in the letter, I have provided an approximate one based on internal evidence or corroborated by a letter in another collection and placed the letter among others with similar general content. If I have been unable to make more than a tentative guess, the date is given in square brackets. I have included the place of origin only when Tippett was not writing from home.

The objection I have encountered most frequently while preparing the letters for publication has been that Tippett 'wouldn't have wanted this'. While that argument has some validity, it must be said that the composer himself included a number of letters (some of which are reprinted here with corrections) in his autobiography. Eric Walter White's *The Operas of Michael Tippett* (1979) contains many examples, while others were published in Tippett's lifetime without his permission (e.g. the correspondence John Ardoin included in an article for *Opera Annual*); and after his death, with the agreement of his executors, a sequence of letters written to the BBC early in his career was included in a symposium contribution by Lewis Foreman. That the publication of his letters enables Tippett to speak for himself is ultimately its own justification.

Thomas Schuttenhelm

The Letters

Adrian Boult

One of the leading British conductors of his day, Adrian Boult (1889–1983) was best known as a champion of English music, giving first performances of major works by Holst, Bliss and Vaughan Williams among others. He began teaching at the Royal College of Music in 1919 and conducted the first orchestra during Tippett's years there. In order to deepen his knowledge of the orchestra and how to compose for it, Tippett regularly attended rehearsals, eventually joining Boult on the rostrum and thus acquiring through practice his own approach to conducting, rehearsal techniques and orchestration. The first letters in this selection were written to Boult in his capacity as music director and founder conductor of the BBC Symphony Orchestra between 1930 and 1950, during which time he introduced much new music from abroad, most notably Berg's Wozzeck, *Busoni's* Doktor Faust *and Hindemith's* Trauermusik. *The letters are characteristic of Tippett's habit of writing sporadically, yet with enough regularity to maintain contact. The long periods between some of them may be explained by the composer's deteriorating eyesight and his increasing use of the telephone for communication; it is also possible that others are missing or lost. The deferential tone of those chosen for inclusion here is representative of Tippett's style and manner when writing to professional associates.*

26 October 1931

Dear Dr Boult

I have presumed to send you the accompanying score [Psalm in C: *The Gateway*] because I know you must be sympathetic in your heart to all young composers. David [Moule-]Evans 'did' it for me with my choral society a year and a half ago when I tried out a show of my own stuff and it seemed to please [Frank] Howes of *The Times*. But I felt it was the only work worth revising, and that it needed it. So I have eventually completed it in the version I am sending you, in the hope that you could help it towards a 'try-out' at the BBC if you like it enough.

If my own very inexpert performance of it on the piano would save you the bother of attacking the score I can come up to see you any afternoon after 3.30. Mornings except for Sat. I have to attend school.

It plays just under 15 minutes. Please forgive me if this makes an infernal bother for you. I hate doing it, but I'm badly in need of some hearing other than in this small neighbourhood.

Yours Sincerely
Michael Tippett

21 April 1943

Dear Sir Adrian,

I have been advised to write you on my own behalf – which I do with some reluctance – by Cyril Smith, Benjamin Britten *entre autres*. It's about the problem that has arisen between me and the Ministry of Labour. A year ago, about, I was granted conditional exemption by C.O. [Conscientious Objector] Tribunal – unconditional exemption being refused – the condition, among others, being work on the land. Frankly I have not seen my way to accept the condition, really because I have always had a sense of vocation about music and teaching.

So strongly that it is tied up with matters of conscience and I can't divorce them. However that is not the gist of the matter at this present moment. A friend of mine, a Colonel [David] Ayerst of the War Office, is much concerned that quite apart from matters of conscience the Ministry of Labour should see fit to consider the work I do as composer, as musical director of Morley College, as better in all respects than to be a farm labourer. But the Ministry have not taken this view, though it has taken them a year to come to final decision – Ayerst has the opinion that the Ministry have looked at the thing purely quantitatively and not seen fit to find out in any way how it seems to workers of my own profession with ability and standing to judge. He therefore urges me before it is too late to ask responsible members of the profession if they feel able to write the Ministry of Labour, either direct or via me, stating that in their opinion it is better that I should be employed as a musician rather than as a farm labourer – for this is the only matter in dispute.

I feel just about able to write you in this way because I know you will believe me when I say I should have no distress at all if you had to decline for any reason whatsoever – or for more. And I feel too that I can be quite sure I am not putting you in any false position. Benjamin Britten, who is much concerned as a colleague, is taking it on himself to write Bax – and [Edward] Sackville-West of the BBC is seeing Bliss for me.

Please do not misjudge these moves. I can't help feeling that honestly it is a fact that I am better used in one capacity than the other, quite apart from my own uncompromising attitude on the matter. In fact I do not intend to go on the land in this way and will prefer to do my time in Wormwood Scrubs. But that is not the matter in dispute. It is the feeling that the Ministry might see reason if they were given means to make a fresh judgment. Otherwise we come to the queer position that instrumentalists, like Cyril Smith for instance, get deferment, while the composers, even if in teaching, get no such exemption – a matter which Cyril himself feels strongly about. However as I have said, I shall not worry in any way if you think it not the thing to do. But should you do so it is a question of a limited time, and the point at issue is that in the opinion of musicians of standing I am better employed at the present moment as musician and teacher than as an agricultural labourer, which would be a misuse of ability and sensitiveness culturally. And if you do wish to write such a letter, either to send it direct to the Ministry of Labour, Head Office, or to me personally.

With kind regards.
Yours Sincerely
Michael Tippett

February 1958

Dear Adrian,

I should have written before a big *Danksagung* to you for all the work and tribulation of the Symphony [No. 2].* But I've been dilatory – and also much snowed up with a fairly considerable mail in consequence of the performances.

Anyhow, I do it now – and with pleasure.

I found this is *nur unter vier Augen gesagt* [said just between ourselves]. Paul Beard at his most unhelpful this time. It's an odd com-

---

* The first performance, on 5 February 1958, had broken down because of Paul Beard's interference with the orchestral parts.

parison to set his unwillingness besides the willingness of a youngster like [John] Minchinton. It's temperamental and circumstantial I know – but it leaves something unhappy behind it. I'm going off to Germany in a week for a big performance of *A Child of Our Time*, and however will recoil from German life back to my native home and country. I shall almost certainly get a different treatment from the leader of the orchestra there. But still – it's a very old story – and in the long run of no consequence. In the short it's annoying. And I was annoyed for you also. There just isn't all that difficulty there. Technical problems – yes. And big demands. But problems that are solvable with good will and technical ingenuity, as I'm quite certain in the end they will be. The odd thing was that the long high violin passages at the recapitulation in the first movement had been bowed and fingered in my presence by Barbirolli! I could not say this at the time because I wouldn't want to start Beard off on another attack. But Barbirolli hadn't done this in any case over the earlier difficult passages. They wouldn't have come more in tune without better precision, but they would have sounded brilliant and then leggiero, if P.B. hadn't refused to do the bowing set down to produce that effect. I think next première I have with him I shall come armed with a tame fiddler!

Still I didn't mean to moan about a mere matter of unhelpfulness. I'd meant just to thank you – as I do again.

Yours –
Michael Tippett

1974

My dear Adrian,

I did not realise it was your 85th birthday till turning on the radio this evening – some recordings of yours. So not a congratulatory telegram but a letter. One of the pieces played was Brahms 3. You won't remember (though I do, as it were yesterday) my standing beside you at the rostrum at the RCM [Royal College of Music] during a term's training of that piece. (The cellos always had trouble with 2nd subject of the finale!) It's a long time ago. But what I learnt, as a composer, through those 4 years of Fridays at your side is nobody's business. A belated thank you – and for much beyond. But please don't reply.

Yours –
Michael

BBC Collection

The most diverse collection in this volume, Tippett's letters to the BBC cover a period of thirty-five years and discuss details of his broadcast talks, performances of his music, and commissions for new works. By the outbreak of the Second World War, BBC radio had become the central source for news and entertainment nationwide. It also made cultural experience available to the public at a time when concerts, lectures and other events were frequently curtailed or cancelled because of bombing. In 1941 Tippett was engaged to give his first BBC radio talk, Stravinsky and the Dance. *This was the start of a fruitful and life-long collaboration between composer and broadcasting organisation and an opportunity to engage with a wider public.*

The launch of the Third Programme in 1946 was the most significant expansion of radio broadcasting in the post-war era: every evening it offered concerts, opera, drama, talks and features that were not determined by popular taste. From its inception, Tippett received regular invitations to contribute talks and take part in discussion programmes (see also the letters to Anna Kallin, p. 360). His place in English culture was largely determined by his dealings with the BBC, and to that end he tailored his approach to suit each of the many different personalities with whom he corresponded. The letters show how he negotiated with one of Britain's foremost cultural institutions in fostering the development of his career.

21 June 1937

Dear Mr [Clarence] Raybould,

I have just got back the score from my copyist of a new work which I believe would really suit the BBC. It is a short choral work, setting for chorus and orchestra of a poem of Blake's, 'A Song of Liberty', out of 'The Marriage of Heaven and Hell'. I've been at work on it for a year and a half, though it only plays about 15 minutes.

It is very forcible and ejaculatory, like Blake's words, ending finally on something peaceful – the moods are very fast so that only a trained crowd of people could really pull it off, but I believe for that reason the effect would be all the more exciting and novel. Anyhow it is, for me, the best work I have done and meant months of concentration. May I bring it to you do you think – I am always in London on Thursdays till 5 p.m. – preferably in the morning. But if that weekday were inconvenient I could come up specially, as from after this week – I do really think (though it is not my place to say so) that here is something which would reward a BBC performance, being short and direct and in an underived idiom!

Yours Sincerely,
Michael Tippett

15 June 1938

Dear Mr Raybould,

After finishing a new work for piano solo [Fantasy Sonata (Piano Sonata No. 1)], I have just at last carried out the alterations to the middle movement of the Symphony [in B flat], which I have had in mind to do for a long time. I am now going to make the score and parts correspond. May I come in to Broadcasting House tomorrow Thursday about 12.30 or so and get the score of the symphony which you have there? It is actually the only one in existence.

I do feel that you are very much the right person to do a broadcast of the symphony at one of the early evening concerts that you do. I should be very reassured if it was in your hands. When I have had the score put straight and the parts to correspond, would you consider the possibility again sometime? I should be very grateful. The symphony is a very lyrical expression of things and gets across to an audience fairly naturally. I believe (though perhaps I oughtn't to suggest it) that you would enjoy yourself doing it!

Many thanks and kind regards.
Yours sincerely
Michael Tippett

4 December 1942

Dear Alec [Robertson],

Thanks for your letter of the 27th last. The 31st of Jan. is alright, provided I am at large then. I'll keep you informed immediately of anything untoward if it were to happen.

I've been thinking over lots of ideas, but rather come back to *Stravinsky and the Dance* or some such title. I would like to show how deep-seated is his feeling for dance and movement and rhythm – and to exemplify his unconscious, perhaps, or attitude by playing a few moments from a Bali gong orchestra and then Stravinsky himself, a few moments, playing his own *Piano Rag Music*. And so to lead through (or to) *Petrushka* and the Russian dance towards some final piece to be played complete, either a portion of the *Symphony of Psalms*, or *Les Noces* (the final scene) – or a (living) 2-piano version of the *Dumbarton Oaks* concerto, 1st movement. The great point about Stravinsky is that the initial musical experience for him and for his listeners thereof, is abruptly physical and immediate. Played properly it is gay and unsentimental, exhilarating.

By the way, I'm using the weekend to look at his new Symphony [in C] before the score goes to the BBC. Stravinsky's publisher is mine too! All by accident. So what with my natural interest, I have good opportunity to get hold of all I want.

Will you let me know sometime soon if this strikes you as the right idea and then I'd like to get a script out to you and vet as soon as possible.

I had tea and supper with Ben [Britten] and Peter [Pears] last Saturday. Showed them my magnum opus, an oratorio, called *A Child of Our Time*. The text is my own, with advice from T. S. Eliot, and the whole work is modern, and contemporary, but religious without being in the cult. Sometime I want to show it you. Ben has just written me on a p.c. that 'what a grand work the oratorio is and a performance must be arranged soon'. Easier said than done! But meanwhile Schott's are going to bring out a piano vocal score as the first move. If you're interested I must try and get hold of a text for you. There were some prints made, but I'm short on them. One, by the way, went to Raybould and must be buried in the corporation – wish you could recover it.

[. . .] Excuse the rigmarole. I'm feeling very gay as I've finished the new 4tet [String Quartet No. 2] and it looks like a performance at Wigmore in Feb.

Please let me have a word on the Stravinsky thing – and shall I try my hand at a script?

Yours
Michael

29 April 1946

Dear [Victor] Hely-Hutchinson

I see from various programmes that the BBC have had a fair number of the Continental radio conductors over here, and I fancy you had in particular Franz André of Brussels. I would very much like to recommend to you insofar as I am competent to do so the young Flemish conductor, Léoncé Gras, who conducted the *Child of Our Time* for me there in January, because he seemed to me to be more than competent and in some degree worthy of being given a chance to become known outside his own country. You may have heard of him already. He is one of the young men around Paul Collaer, and he was first of all a light music conductor, then choral conductor for the Flemish Radio, and is now used for all sorts of other work. He took immense trouble over the *Child of Our Time* and gave a quite exceptional performance of it. I have since listened in to performances of classical works by him, and in my opinion he is very good. I thought, therefore, I should bring at least his name to your notice.*

Yours sincerely

Michael Tippett

8 February 1947

Dear Hely-Hutchinson,

[. . .] If you mean by 'new', written here and now, so to speak, there is nothing except a little piece for strings [*Little Music for String Orchestra*], written especially for [Reginald] Jacques. Whether Jacques hopes to give its first broadcast himself, I don't know. It's not a big work, as its title indicates. If 'new' has a slightly wider use, then I should suggest the work which was strictly new, when I answered your similar letter a year ago: the Symphony [No. 1] (1945), as my publishers call it – as far as I know this hasn't come on the English ear, though it has been suggested that it will do so on March 7th, when we do it in a Morley College concert. But there is nothing definite. In any case that is of course the BBC Orchestra etc – and so, if I may, I would like to commend it to you once again, in the hope it won't be regarded as a 'known' work – for it clearly isn't as yet. However it may not suit your book at all.

* Tippett sent copies of this letter to David Webster of Covent Garden and Adolph Borsdorf of the London Philharmonic Orchestra.

A score is due off the press in a week or so – or a month maybe – and a copy goes automatically I imagine to the corporation. It's 35 minutes – and usual orchestra – double w-wind, 4 horns, 3 trumpets, etc. Anyhow, all that gets dealt with by Schott & Co.

Thank you very much for your kindness in writing to me as you have done.

Yours sincerely
Michael Tippett

7 April 1948

Dear Mrs [Grace Wyndham] Goldie,

I have got back from my walk in the hills and am quite recovered – and think I see more clearly the way towards the talk.*

I feel I should like a very broad title – something like *A Composer Looks at Life* – but as you will see in a moment that won't really do because it won't give the right clue to the train of thought.

I'm certain now that I want to enter the subject by means of some simple consideration and description of what art and music does to the recipient – and then what happens inside the maker, the artisan. The mysterious process by which the usual and the daily life becomes material for the more durable artefacts which one knows as works of art. The nature of this durability, its quality, and its value. Its relation to the everyday material and on the other hand its relation to necessity of the imaginative and spiritual life. The balance in any given society between material and imagination. What is happening now.

I feel I shall need to use metaphors from most of the arts, but naturally always with especially more personal reference to music. Whether with actual music I can't see till I get down to the script proper. [. . .]

Yours sincerely
Michael Tippett

If we can find a reasonable title the 'subtitle' might run something like: a talk in which a composer speaks of the imaginative life and its relation to everyday things.

Perhaps a possible title could be: *A Composer's Point of View.*

If all the above is tolerably suitable, including the last suggestions for title, etc, then please go ahead and fix any date, including May 2nd if still open.

* Broadcast under the title *A Composer's Point of View* on Sunday, 2 May 1948.

20 November 1948

Dear Herbert [Murrill],

There seems to have been a bit of muddle with the announcements to the 'baby' music [*Suite for the Birthday of Prince Charles*] – or rather, on getting back from Holland, the usual comment to me has been that people heard the name but not the music! Fresh from the usual Dutch attacks on myself as responsible in some way for the hopeless reception of the Third, can I ask you to see if it were possible later to play the music on one of the stations with coverage? I do this partly because I have indeed had two letters from actual hearers. One from a simple person blessing me for writing simply – the other from a distinguished, indeed famous, Hungarian mathematician resident here [Paul Dienes], contemporary and friend of Bartók, great amateur of music with an uncompromising taste, in which he says, 'I enjoyed your suite from beginning to end. It's lovely and healthy like Mozart; fresh, clear like a brook in the mountains.' While discounting the great name of Mozart, it gives me at least the confidence that I didn't disgrace myself, even if the music can be also comprehended by the people. So, if the BBC can see their way to letting it come out to its potentially wider audience, I'd be grateful. For if my wretched tough Symphony [No. 1] is properly for the Mind, this new music is for all. Can you give it a chance to cross that frontier from Third to somewhere less restricted in reception and type of listener? But if you can't then that's just too bad, and I shan't worry.

Child of Our Time was as usual horribly moving. The Dutch have taken it up rather excessively – as it seems to me. [. . .]

Ever Yours
Michael

29 October 1949

Dear Herbert,

I've at last received today the original score of Birthday Suite [*Suite for the Birthday of Prince Charles*] back from Mainz so that I can correct proofs of the new printed scores and material. This all reminds me that I should have written to you some time back thereabout. For the great haste in which the piece was done for you all, this time last year, meant that the last, 5th movement didn't seem to me to stand properly. First of all I wrote a completely new one, which [Walter] Goehr tried out in March or so – but I didn't think it suited. So I returned to the original, making a cut of 20 bars or more from the 'exposition' (rather naive setting of Helston Furry) and writing something fresh in its place (material based on 'Early One Morning'). This change also affected the reprise. I think therefore you'd better have from us a new score, because the original is in a mess. And either let us put the 5th movement straight in your official set of parts, or do that yourselves, or buy the piece. I am really only concerned with my duties, responsibility to the corporation arising out of the original commission.

The opera [*The Midsummer Marriage*] is going well. I'm over the half way and moving I think a bit farther at last!

Yours sincerely,
Michael Tippett

4 April 1950

Dear Sir Steuart [Wilson],

We are all so known to each other that often the obvious gets left unsaid, so I'm writing to you rather formally, just to put on record that the last two big performances I have received at the hands of the BBC have been so splendid. This seems to be due, as I see it, to the fact that Goehr has treated the music with as much care and responsible consideration as for any composer dead or alive. I must say honestly that apart from Continental thoroughness and courtesy (which I am slowly getting used to!) from Goehr alone in this country have I received, without asking for it, just this unfailing effort and pains. And I do believe, from seeing some of his work on other music for my own concerts, that it is not only because he holds me in personal esteem. The performance of *A Child of Our Time* on Saturday was magnificent. The score has never been heard like that before in Germany. It was for me, as for many others, a revelation – and all obtained by hard work and the authority of knowing the score in every detail. May I say as a mere composer, say that for us, this means more than gold – at this time, when rushed rehearsals and tired, bored and supercilious conductors leave us often wishing we'd never written a note! So through you, to the corporation a sincere 'thank you'.

Yours ever
Michael Tippett

14 August 1952

Dear Christopher [Holme],

I've been meaning to write you since we met at Glyndebourne, because that reminded me. You know that I shall finish *The Midsummer Marriage* about October 1st. It will have been 5 and a half years' work, during which I've pondered and pondered over the eternally fascinating problems of opera. I've got a lot of material in my head that I think Third Programme stuff, of quite general interest to some, and under some such generic title as 'Music and Theatre'. It's about renaissance ideas of the Greeks, and 18th-century ideas, and contemporary ideas (with a glance at Wagner – whose *Oper und Drama* taught me so much). That's the more general literary side – the musical side goes complementary with it – i.e. changing 'costumes' and metaphors to accomplish the changes in attitude.

Would this interest you for, say, a couple of talks? I can't digest it sensibly into one.

I go away for 3 weeks on Monday – so this letter is only to make suggestions for something ahead if and when Third felt like it. (But I'd prefer to be looked after by Niouta [Anna Kallin].)

All good wishes
Michael

7 January 1953*

Dear Leonard [Isaacs],

I've realised afterwards that you might have meant our other Christopher [Holme] than Christopher Fry. So I've written off to John Morris by the post and he wrote to me.

I won't repeat my distress. And I didn't confuse you with what I said about Schott's. You see composers are wilful people and so get at cross-purposes with their publishers – who indeed always feel they know best! I rang you in the first place, before Christmas, when I had promised to consult with Howard [Hartog] beforehand. And what seems to have set the inside off was his making me realise, when I did eventually tell him what I'd done, that the commission for Edinburgh was to be finished by May [*Fantasia Concertante on a Theme of Corelli*]. At once I began to count the days and hours and try to work

* Reply to a letter requesting a work of 20–25 minutes' duration, using text by Christopher Fry, for Kathleen Ferrier to sing at a concert on 6 June 1953.

14

at pace, but this afternoon I felt it was madness. The decision I then took had of course nothing to do with copyright problems – and they don't really interest me – so long as Schott's, who are very good and generous to me, feel reasonably alright. But I shall continue to feel that I have my own relations direct with you – and with Malcolm [Sargent] or any other. Schott's, no doubt like the other publishers, feel they know best what works should go here or there, or be played by him or her. I do find that often I am very wrong in my own judgment – but I shall go on making it, I'm sure. Though I trust Schott's, because they trust me. And I stick by their problems as they stick by mine. I must with generosity take the rough with the smooth, as they with generosity accept the popular and the peculiar. This all is no concern of yours, dear Leonard – you have plenty of problems of your own – public and more important. The long rigmarole is merely a very roundabout way of saying I speak always to you – and to many others – in a confidence that occasionally strays out of the natural confidence between publisher and composer. I wanted to take your advice on Prom matters. Is an older or a newer work the right thing? Schott's are again differing I think. But I also think I must learn, as indeed I almost have, to leave those things to settle themselves. I'm so looking forward to hearing the Ritual Dances – after 20 long years' labour.

Love –
Michael

1954

Dear Mr Fiske,

Many thanks for your letter. I need to think it over and take counsel, if I may. I wonder therefore if you can select what seems to you the appropriate broadcasting space, while I consider what I myself would feel the best to be done? For I would very much have liked at any rate to hear the *Troilus* [*and Cressida*] talk first before deciding things. As you know I care a lot about radio and have given this vexed question of radio opera a lot of consideration. *The Midsummer Marriage* has no leitmotivs, and it is as extravagant in strange goings-on as *The Magic Flute*. Probably all that can be given ahead is the tradition from which it springs – and some sense of the story. The music will be easier for broadcast listening than *Turn of the Screw* because it has arias in plenty, and the Ritual Dances themselves are 1/5th of the opera. I'll write you again very soon.

Michael

13 December 1955

Dear Douglas Cleverdon,

But that I only finished the horn piece [Sonata for Four Horns] yesterday (concert next Tuesday!) I would have written you before. As luck would have it the script came on the day I had to go and see the Belgian Radio Orchestra, and I got caught up in a BBC reception for them. (I had the script with me to read on the train.) There I received or was offered a commission for an orchestra work, here and now, for Third Programme anniversary, which, while leaving me very short of time, did exactly tune in with my composer's desire to write a second symphony. So after a lot of consideration I accepted, later in the week.

I am afraid this puts the Barker script right out.* I could never do them both. I shall write to Barker to explain and confirm.

My mother, who is an inveterate listener, was very struck and impressed by the [David] Gascoyne–[Humphrey] Searle 'script' [*Night Thoughts*]. Unluckily hadn't time to hear it. It seems to have given Searle opportunities for adventuring in sound-cum-music. It's on this side of things that I'd like to meet you one day and talk. Something where the composer was also in from the start, almost. What do you think?

Michael

August 1957

Dear Leonard [Isaacs],

I exploded on the fatal day like a *mitraillette*; and I hope it did good. In fact I'm sure it did. With what I felt in myself, and what I knew, it had to be taken note of.

Now I'm back finishing the Symphony [No. 2]. Have just written Boult to say I'm glad he's doing it.

Tell Maurice [Johnstone] (he will be amused, only not for general use of course yet) that I've just had a commission from Koussevitzky Foundation [eventually resulting in *King Priam*] for a choral–orchestra work 20–30 minutes long – at a fee. Well, BBC can hardly compete!

However it's rather exciting; and quite an honour I feel.

Michael

* Cleverdon had requested music for George Barker's radio morality play *The Seraphina*.

16

14 November 1957

Dear Rudy [Rudolf Schwarz],

I have wanted to write you but didn't dare desert my desk until the Symphony [No. 2] was finished: yesterday! I had wanted to say that I'd been at the first half of your concert in Festival Hall. That I was quite ravished by the sounds in the Schubert Unfinished. I felt a period of 'slap-dashery' in the orchestra was giving way to care and quality. And I admit I was selfishly pleased – because I realised how advantageous this is to my coming première! But please don't think my emotions were only egotistical. That isn't true either.

I think I told you that I'm strangely excited by my new work. It seems to me to be a new marriage in my oeuvre between conciseness and imagination. The nearest I have come to a long-standing ideal – the classical ideal of variety in unity. You will be there won't you? I want you to hear it, and see what you think. It is orchestrally difficult – in that it asks for precision and subtlety, as well as the usual substance that symphonies have. I ran into Boult at the British Council last Monday, and he seemed very inclined to ask you whether he could have the piece read through once, a fortnight or so before the proper rehearsals. This was partly my idea, but chiefly his – from his own past experience. I personally feel the benefit would very much outweigh the short time needed – if you follow me. It's a matter of the players seeing what is on the plate – and then having just a little time to adjust to the demands made. I know I would be more than grateful if this was possible, and would willingly come and do the job myself if Adrian were unable to fit in the precious time allotted.

I think you'll be interested in a quite different context that I'm going in March to Germany to attend the first public performance of *Ein Kind unserer Zeit*, to use its German title. The piece (especially the BBC transcription tape with [Schmidt-]Isserstedt) has been booming – both professionally and going now into the small amateur societies. But Germany had always broken down over the matter of the 'story'. Now, with the new feeling since the *Diary of Anne Frank*, it is to be given publicly at Wuppertal in good proper Lutheran circles. I am going over chiefly to make certain it is seen as a humanitarian document and work of art, not a political manifesto, even against Germany.

Incidentally, the RPO [Royal Philharmonic Orchestra] have now recorded the work, after a public performance, at Liverpool – with

Pritchard. The Liverpool people and a good cast of soloists. And again weeks back we put the Ritual Dances from *The Midsummer Marriage* (Covent Garden Orchestra) onto the 4th side. The strange thing was the extraordinary unity in style of the Dances, and the effect of a tremendous stream of music. I don't think it had quite come out like that before.

I'm sorry – this letter has gone a long way astray from the beginning to tell you of my enjoyment of the Schubert.

Michael

12 March 1958

My dear Richard [R. J. F. Howgill],

Now that all the dust is settling, I think you'd like to hear a bit more of the story of your piece [Symphony No. 2]. I had to go to Germany a week ago and Minchinton went up to Manchester for me to take Barbirolli's score, and violin parts, and disc of the 2nd BBC performance. They had a tremendous session – playing the disc 6 times, with the score – and they travelled back in the evening together to London. Sir John [Barbirolli] was very worried by the technical difficulties (for conductor) of the scherzo – and his own extremely hard-pressed schedule.

Yesterday, as I got back from Germany, a letter came from him, most generous, preferring not to conduct himself, but suggesting either myself or Minchinton – with 9 hours' rehearsal, after he, Sir John, had taken nine reading sectional rehearsals.

So Minchinton it is to be. I believe now in the future of that young man (Lennox Berkeley wants to send him to America for his Symphony) and I believe the generous gesture to a fierily conscientious young artist is the proper one.

You must try and get up to either 1 or 2 if you can. Will be extremely interesting. I have a great personal success at Wuppertal, very moving.

Yours ever,
Michael

9 May 1958

Dear Richard,

I've been meaning to write you since the Collegium Musicum broadcast – but I've been away (a sudden desperate necessity to break for 8 days, after overworking) and now I'm back again trying to finish off my piece [*Crown of the Year*] for the [Badminton] Girls' School centenary, and being nagged all the while by the boiling up of a new opera [*King Priam*]. So letters have got piled up and forgotten.

But I oughtn't to forget the excellent broadcast. You see, it all is in fact very interesting. I had to do the first performance of Fantasia Concertante [on a Theme of Corelli] with BBC Orchestra's strings at Edinburgh, and then the subsequent Prom. Yet, with all the great good will of the orchestra, I don't think I brought the piece really over. Anyhow it got generally panned for complexity, etc, etc. Pritchard then did I'm afraid (and as he knows himself) a rather poor studio performance of it, with Boyd Neel Orchestra. (It was at the time that he knew his scores less well – and before he'd conducted *The Midsummer Marriage*.) Then Scherchen did a truly execrable, if not scandalous, performance with the LSO [London Symphony Orchestra]. And all I'd ever heard that really triumphed was a wonderful tape of the NDR [Norddeutscher Rundfunk] strings under [Schmidt-]Isserstedt. So it was interesting enough to see how John M[inchinton] would manage. And in my opinion it triumphed too. Under all the careful, indeed impeccable rehearsal of detail, came through in the end the musical structure, in such a way that the work seems to have spoken without embarrassments of any kind. The exciting thing for me especially is that I did not go to any of the rehearsals at all till the play-through.

So I must thank whoever in the BBC put it into his head to perform the piece, for I did no such thing myself.

It strikes me that technically the great gain to my music is just this ability to see immediately what is decoration and what is structure. I can of course see this myself – but I don't think I can ever obtain either the exact performance of the detailed decoration, or the relations of the details into the piece as a whole structure. It's what is really missing from Boult, Symphony No. 2 performance. Only please don't think I'm being difficult again about Adrian. That is all over. I'm just commenting technically. I use a 'layers of sound' technique sometimes that needs just that extra stylistic presentation that Fantasia Concertante got. And allied to the 'layers of sound' is the going in and out of nearer chamber music within the orchestra texture. A Stravinsky technique perhaps. Anyhow I've got great hopes now of John, though I think his way will be hard and slow. Because his gift lies in the unusual rather than the hackneyed. So he will have less quick public support.

All good wishes
Michael

8 December 1958

Dear Maurice [Johnstone],

I hope Rudi [Rudolf Schwarz] told you how well the Piano Concerto went on last Saturday with [Ilona] Kabos. It really did. A real triumph. I was extremely pleased. Kabos was quite the right choice, as it turned out. The whole piece glowed with colour from the orchestra and as someone has written to me: 'it all seemed so clear now'. I'm going up to Manchester to hear the performances there. I hope Rudi was pleased too? He deserves to be. And I think he doesn't regret the labour he's given to the piece, at Brum [Birmingham] and London. For the music began to express its lyricism as the initial troubles cleared away and it began to sound natural and easy. It's going to turn out an acceptable and accessible piece in the end. As it was always meant to be.

I've taken a private disc for myself. So glad I did.

Many thanks. Also I believe some of the minor 'personal' troubles for me with some of the orchestra were charmed away.

Yours
Michael

2 March 1959

Dear Maurice,

I've been meaning in a vague way to send you this since I got it some weeks ago. Because of its sentence about the BBC – which is a bit unclear anyhow. These are a set of 4 folk song settings, 'English', 'Irish', 'Scottish' and 'Welsh', that I did on commission for a Festival of European Folksong in Bremen. But they weren't performed – though they paid the small commission. (They're published by Schott's, Mainz.) They've been done only so far on the French and Belgian Radio though an English choir (London Bach Group)* – not in England yet at all.

* The first performance, at the Royaumont Festival in July 1958, was conducted by John Minchinton.

[Eric] Blom wrote a first letter telling me of his coming tape-recording and that he found the songs 'extremely beautiful and extremely difficult'. I replied saying I thought the latter only relative (the England choir sang them apparently with fair ease, and much success – I haven't heard them though), and depended on style. I suspect the German chorus and even professional groups are just less adaptable. If the tape comes over at all, I'd welcome a chance to hear it – I haven't heard the pieces at all yet.

Michael

April 1959

Dear Howard [P. H. Newby],

A personal request. The symphony of mine (No. 2) commissioned by Third Programme for 10th birthday, but which ran into difficulties in performances (Boult and BBC Orchestra), has been scheduled in the Liverpool Philharmonic winter season for Dec. 29th – conducted by Pritchard [who], as Howgill agreed, should really have given its première. I would very much like to see Pritchard and the Royal Liverpool who are doing so well for British music and new music generally, helped and myself helped by a finer performance by a relay on the Third. Can you help about it, if you concur? I find it difficult to write to Glock, just because I know him so very well. I feel he needs to be left quite alone for the moment, as to botherations from the outside. So I'm asking you to mediate the request for me, or advise. Shall Pritchard 'apply' if that's the right term? I mean, of course the Royal Liverpool Philharmonic Society.

Did Routledge send you the book [*Moving Into Aquarius*]? Niuta [Anna Kallin]; personal copy – get off to her from here tomorrow.

Yours ever –
Michael

28 August 1961

Dear Eric Warr,

Getting the BBC concert folder has reminded me of my intention to write to you. I want to plead once again for the idea of a small group, ensemble, to do [Divertimento on] 'Sellinger's Round' with me – if possible out of the full rehearsal schedule and not therefore involving Paul Beard. The string body is something like 5,4,4,4,2 I guess (players not desks of course). Or 4,3,3,4,2 (on the whole I like very good cello body) – so it could be 4,3,3,3,2. But you know more about Festival Hall acoustics than I do. We can always scale the ground down, but not up. So let's not cut them too far.

Then, please (but I know you won't) don't unsuspectingly feel that the small ensemble means the piece is easier to rehearse; rather the contrary! Give me plenty of time. I want to do a top-notch show for you.

I'm writing this letter ahead, because otherwise I should put it off and off and never do it. (I'm on the final scene of *King Priam*.)

Yours Sincerely,
Michael Tippett

31 March 1966

Dear Philip [Moore],

Just off for a week away – London, Leeds, Leicester (where I do my annual concert with the Leicester CYO [Children's Youth Orchestra, i.e. Leicestershire Schools Symphony Orchestra]). The 'Musicale' proposal in Lacock [Abbey, Chippenham, Wiltshire] sounds nice – and could do. I have all September free. Rehearsals as you suggest.

But – can you have the LSO horns with Barry Tuckwell for the Sonata [for Four Horns]? Point 1, they are much above the Civil 4tet and do a perfectly incredible performance in their virtuosity. 2, they'll probably have recorded it by then as fill-up to LSO doing Symphony No. 2. So all in all they're the boys!

Michael

28 July 1972

Dear Robert [Ponsonby],

Thank you for your letter, which I found on my return from Canada. I performed there at the National Arts Centre Ottawa, *A Child of Our Time*. The work had its usual profound effect. I've heard from Colin [Davis] that your project for performances and recording of the piece is well under way. That is very nice.

I am honoured by your suggestion that I collaborate with you in the 1974 Prom season, but I fear it would be irresponsible of me as a composer to agree, because, as the 3rd Symphony showed all over again, the kind of works I want to write are totally demanding of time and energy, at a period when I have to count the remaining active years of my life. I can tell you confidentially that I am getting out of the Bath Festival in the first year I decently can. No more commitments!

The problem of the Proms is surely to retain their magnificent vitality and width of appeal without adding further gimmicks. Any Prom season now is surely the most extraordinary festival of music-making in the world. But with many audiences. I'm sure it cannot be the same people, or should be, that fill the Albert Hall for *Iolanthe* and 2/3 fill it for *Moses and Aaron*. So it would seem risky, except subjectively to oneself, to constrain this marvellous variety of music into a theme. It might be laying a dead hand on a hugely alive organism. Please, dear Robert, do not do that.

Might I suggest however, since the matter of British music is in general very near my heart, that we have a talk about it over lunch, when you are settled in the south. I have ideas on this theme, that is, what kind of voice our national music is, at its best, and how it can find its true place in the general variety of our Western musical experience. I mean, why the Tallis 40-part motet is probably the most extraordinary piece of European music of its period; what can be successfully performed of Purcell in the concert hall; the real gap in the English tradition during the 18th and 19th centuries; why, at the return, Elgar is a great creative genius and Bax is second rate; what is the core of Vaughan Williams? and earlier of Delius? and so on.

These are merely the sort of signposts I erect for myself to steer a way between the Scylla of dismissing all English music as provincial and the Charybdis of countering such an opinion by doing performances of the English second rate, just because the greatest festival of Western music takes place in London.

I am sure you are looking forward to your new job and I should have written to congratulate you on the appointment much earlier on. However I do now.

Yours Sincerely,
Michael Tippett

Schott Collection

Schott was Tippett's lifelong and exclusive publisher, and the majority of his letters are addressed to the head of the firm in Mainz, Willy Strecker. On the outbreak of the Second World War, a few of Tippett's compositions had recently been accepted for publication. Although the firm then decided to suspend activities until the war was over, relations with Tippett were resumed shortly afterwards and immediately bore fruit. The correspondence deals not only with the background and technical details of publication of Tippett's music, but also with such topics as the progress of his work, forthcoming premières, and the financial problems of a composer in the twentieth century.

9 July 1939

Dear Mr Strecker,

It's some time since you replied to my original letter on April 14th, and so courteously invited me to take my time about sending you my scores. I am posting you tomorrow the 5 scores mentioned in Scott Goddard's article in the *Musical Record* which I believe I sent you.* I have put the dates at the end of each of them.

I think myself the best work is the latest, the Concerto for Double String Orchestra, and the one preceding it, the Piano Sonata [Fantasy Sonata/Piano Sonata No. 1], is the point where I began at last to feel sure of my own style. But I am not probably a good judge of my own works. Yet I was genuinely sure enough of the piano sonata to feel very much I should have liked to see it in print. And the dedicatee [Francesca Allinson], a woman musician friend of mine, felt and feels still so sure of it, that she had offered me financial help towards the cost of engraving for publication if such a thing was permitted. I am not au fait with the conventions on this point but realising the hopelessly uncommercial nature of the sort of music I have got to write I

* 'The Younger English Composers: IX. Michael Tippett', *Monthly Musical Record* 69 (March/April 1939), 73–6.

had often wondered if the composer himself was ever justified in helping to make his own work available in printed form. I feel this strongly about the string concerto I have just finished, where there's a
considerable chance of its being an attractive work to the numerous
new string orchestras in England, America and elsewhere. The Piano
Sonata and the Concerto for Double String Orchestra are the two children I should most like to launch into this fierce world! And I have just
finished a composing and conducting commission for a municipality
which gives me a small financial amount above my usual limited
income.

I am preparing work now for a modern oratorio for which I am trying to get the co-operation of T. S. Eliot. I have just sent him a typescript of the idea, at his request, but he may not find time or
inclination for it – though it's just possible he may. I think you will be
interested in it if I bring it off. I am using Negro spirituals in the same
sort of way as the *Gemeinde* chorale of the German passion music.
That is to say three levels of expression – the dramatic chorus, the contemplative aria and the *Gemeinde* chorale; and in a quite real sense. I
have chosen about 5 spirituals to fit the particular situations – the subject is a modern religious one.

By the way, I have a private disc of the piano sonata taken from a
broadcast which I could send over to you if you liked. It's very soft,
but excellently played.

Hoping the scores reach you safely.

Yours Sincerely,

Michael Tippett

15 October 1950

Dear Willy,

I thought you'd like to know that I have not only finished the cuts
and improvements to Act 1 [of *The Midsummer Marriage*], but finished the music and score to Act 2. So I'm very cheerful, though tired.
I'm going away tomorrow to stay for a week (at least) with Britten, to
have a complete rest, before I gather myself together to imagine the
pre-final draft of Act 3, i.e. the text. This is always the better, the more
I can imagine at least the main shapes of the music at the same time,
so that the words are ready material for the music when it comes.

Act 2 comes to be 31 minutes. So that's not too bad.

I'm glad you heard Act 1. It did me quite a lot of good. For sometimes in the extreme *Wagnis* of such a long undertaking, one almost loses confidence. And it is so hopeless trying to explain verbally what one is creating – especially when it is of such a character.

Actually, I have deep down not only a confidence in the work itself, but even in a measure of success. Though that will take time. I have a notion that Schott's won't do so badly by it, even financially, in the end, seeing how I stand with the BBC etc. The opera may not gain money so quickly as the *Child* did, but despite the bigger outlay it will all the same I think.

While Act 3 text is being considered and looked at, I shall finish the little song cycle [*The Heart's Assurance*] for next year's Festival [of Britain]. When I have eventually settled down, as I hope to do soon in a new and more comfortable home with my mother, then the composer's life will be lived *par excelsis*! I feel I have so much to do, little enough time to do it, so that it is 'now or never'. But I think it will be 'now'. When once at last the opera is finished!

Yours
Michael

29 October 1950

Dear Willy,

[Walter] Goehr came here yesterday and we had the first playthrough of Act 2 [of *The Midsummer Marriage*]. He was very pleased with it and thinks it to be many times better than the music to Act 1. I only hope he is right! However it was at least reassuring. What he felt meanwhile about the suite of dances (as an orchestral pieces) was, what I originally told you was my own guess, that the most likely exactly proper ending to them (i.e. to the 3 existing ones in Act 2) will prove to be the 4th dance (Fire in Summer) which comes at the climax of Act 3, indeed the climax of the whole opera. And he feels that even if it will be accompanied by singing, we can deal with that on the lines of the Prince Igor dances of Borodin: versions with and without a choir. Goehr made this suggestion after I told him the 'story' of Act 3. I am fairly certain that he is right. In any case we have decided (in Schott's, London) not to consider a première of the dance suite till after the Festival of Britain, because by great good luck Goehr has a performance of *Child of Our Time* with Morley College, in the

Festival Hall on an early and good date in the Festival, and he did not want *Child* to be prejudiced by any *Aufführung* – which is quite reasonable. It is much better to be represented in the Festival by the big work. So that by then it is quite possible that the music to the 4th dance will be being written anyway.

Seiber came here a few days ago quite unannounced and persuaded me to play him Act 1, from the full score. I did this with such unexpected verve that he was more than delighted with it all – I think quite genuinely. While I was doing so I had *einen guten Einfall* about the cuts I have made (dutifully!) to the second verse of King Fisher's aria. I suddenly realised that if I retained the cuts in the music but did not cut the words, I could, by giving the voice more words per bar, keep the proper dramatic sense of his appealing to the girls a different argument from that which he uses to the men, and also give the music of the second verse a new slant by this means. So that one makes a virtue out of necessity. As Goehr said when I told him, one cannot see all possibilities of play between words and music in opera all at once. What this means simply is that this week I will post you a fresh copy of the pf. score to King Fisher's second verse i.e. from where the cuts begin – in order that the copyist can see exactly how the new voice part reads. That seems to me the clearest and easiest. There is no need for you to hold up the work for this, because he can't get there for some time.

Otherwise I think [Howard] Hartog has written to say that the *Zettel* in the *Noten* with suggested cuts in the first scene should not have been there. *Es sind nur Vorschläge* [they are only suggestions] – which I discussed with Goehr that day we said goodbye in Schott's – and the suggestions for cutting the first scene were set aside. The copyist has only to copy what is before him observing the few cuts (in ink or pencil) made.

But the success in cutting King Fisher has made me feel that one of the other cuts were better left optional. It refers to Scene 2. After the little March, there is a dance (in 3/8) which originally is shown to be repeated (dramatically to produce the effect of a continuous ritual practice) and Mark only runs on to the stage at the end of the second time. (This was written out of course as you can see in the score, with first- and second-time bars, and repeat mark.) In my haste to cut anything I could I decided to cut the repetition of this dance. Now I feel that it may really be dramatically a mistake, and that what we should do is merely to indicate that it can be cut if thought better by the producer. For if the producer really wanted the dance twice (for the effect I describe above) then it will be most annoying to put it back if a first-time bar has been taken away. Do you think you could just direct the copyist to copy the first- and second-time bars as they were, underneath my pencil (or ink) erasure of the former? I think you will see my point – and the question of repetition is quite appropriately an *ad libitum* matter, in my opinion. There will be nothing invidious in putting a note in to that effect. And certainly I am much less sure that it is a gain to cut any of the more formal pieces of music at the start of the opera when, as always, there is so much explanatory recitative to get through. I have compressed that indeed to the point of approaching incomprehensibility, and my instinct was all the time to balance the recitative by aria, ensemble or formal dance, or whatever, immediately any argumentative recitative were completed. However I admit it's not a very serious matter perhaps, in this case of the dance. So do what seems best.

Act 2 had only 2 very short scenes of recitative, an aria, a duet, chorus song, and dances – so that musically it was much simpler to unify it all rather more obviously. It has come out to be a bit like a more elaborate [*Prélude à*] *L'Après-midi d'un faune*. More impressionistic and dreamlike, as I had intended.

Act 3 of course is to be musically and dramatically the *wichtigsten* – though it won't run to the length of Act 1.

I have already written 1/2 the proposed text for Act 3, and will finish in a day or two. Then it will go to be typed and with copies for various people to criticise etc. As you have seen so many texts in your time, would you like to see a copy? Or is it too far away (in space) to be of much use, do you think?

As I told you – while the text is being discussed I hope to finish the other 2 songs of the little cycle [*The Heart's Assurance*] for [Peter] Pears to sing in the Festival next year.

Britten told me, by the way, when I was at Aldeburgh, that he and Pears have decided at last to record *Boyhood's End*. That's very good news indeed, it seems to me.

Excuse this immense letter! All good wishes, and to Hugo [Strecker].

Yours
Michael

3 March 1951

My dear Willy,

The above [Tidebrook Manor] is my new address where I have set-tled, or am trying to settle down, with my mother in another part of the house. It has a fine music room and (externally) absolute tran-quillity.

This letter is chiefly to apologise for not letting you have Act 2 pf. score sooner [*The Midsummer Marriage*]. Unfortunately I did not imagine the circumstances in which you would need it quickly, so I did not hurry [Michael] Tillett, who has been ill, and now that I have just done so (by letter and telegram) most of it has come to hand but in much less careful, accurate and legible form and I don't like you to have it now until I can correct it and rewrite if necessary some of the passages. Otherwise it will not be fair on your copyist. Also – this gives the chance (*hoffentlich*!) to have a proper session and play through with Goehr, similar to that of Act 1. I don't think the delay will be very long, except that Goehr is so busy and leaves very soon for Israel and Greece (probably playing Tippett) and so I may have to dispense with him and trust entirely to my own judg-ment.

Act 2 is more of a piece than Act 1, so that the formal problems are less intricate. Goehr already thinks it much better than Act 1, but I myself am a bit worried over the shape of the 3 dances, which, as you pointed out from the text, are similar. I need this formal sim-ilarity to some extent to give the effect of a ritual i.e., in this case, of a possible capture and sacrifice in different disguises. I have to keep the ground similarity while using as much musical art as pos-sible to give variety by every other means. The first 2 dances are alright. The difficulty is over the 3rd. Or rather it is here that I would like Goehr to get to know it well enough to help me make a final judgment. I would rather not hurry this or even forgo it, if Goehr delays visiting me, unless you feel that you ought to have it all willy-nilly.

There will in any case be a considerable gap before Act 3 pf. score is available, as the music itself will not be finished till Christmas and after. Is it possible, do you think, to give me a little more time to pre-pare Act 2, so that I can send it you in total (instead of piecemeal) with no misgivings? If you feel the matter of your good copyist very urgent then I shall understand and would be grateful for a word either direct to me or via Hartog.

I've already written and scored the first scene of Act 3 and revised the whole text except for the short finale, which is still giving me pause. As soon as I've got Act 2 ready for you, and indeed immediately, I shall do the 5th and last song of my song cycle [*The Heart's Assurance*]. Four have already gone to press.

I am working very hard and once this opera is out of the way, new compositions will flow more rapidly from the pen. I have so many in mind.

Greetings,
Michael

5 October 1951

Dear Willy,

[. . .] These last 3 days I have been doing the proofs of Act 1 of the opera [*The Midsummer Marriage*] which I will take to London on Monday, for sending back to Mainz. They will be complete but for 1 page that seems to have been mislaid, and the portion which had to go back to the copyist.

I am working hard at Act 3. You can guess how thankful I shall be to finish it. It often depresses me. Not only for myself, but for you. I know of course that there is something of value in it, but it has so much *Problematik* in it, addressed to perhaps an audience that hardly exists yet. So it may prove only something on which others will build. Yet, with opera you can never tell. Not being fashionable, or journalistic, or even avant-garde, it may be just a matter of time. So I want to finish it and get on quickly to some pieces which will do something to make up my publisher's losses!

I have corrected the proofs with immense care.

Ever Yours
Michael

20 March 1952

Dear Jack [Avshalomoff],

[. . .] You ask for a few words about the *Child*. About the work, probably the best even now is the very first programme note we wrote for the work and which is reprinted in the leaflet I enclose.

After all that has been written one way and another about it I still think something on these lines is the best we can do, unless you have anything personal to add. I went in December to Switzerland to conduct the first Italian performance of it for Radio Lugano and by one of those accidents which do happen it seems likely that it will get done in December in Rome by Karajan, so that is its news up to date!

As to myself, I am just about to finish my 5¹/₂ years labour of the opera *The Midsummer Marriage* which, as you can guess, am more than relieved to have done with it. As I think I must have said at one time or another it is a kind of complement to *A Child of Our Time*, on the light as against the dark side.

All that you say about the conditions in which you are going to do the work on April 25th [at Columbia University, New York] I find most exciting. I do wish I could have been there because I can't imagine a nicer occasion for the kind of work the oratorio really is and you can be certain that I shall be present in spirit when the day comes.

In any case, give my best wishes for a successful performance to everyone concerned, not least including yourself.

If you could have a recording taken do so because it would be fascinating to hear. There is no recording this side of the water.

Yours
Michael Tippett

[January 1953]

[To Howard Hartog]

I've plunked now for: Fantasia Concertante for String Orchestra on a Theme of Corelli [as the title for the Edinburgh Festival commission]. And I'll send you before Wed. a note for [Ian] Hunter (with a copy to make for yourself as it goes by). Then I'll also give you a schedule for the opera proofs (John [Minchinton] and I are busy on some back from Tillett now) i.e. where to send and to whom. So that if possible the whole of Acts 2 and 3 are ready to return to Mainz by end of Feb. Act 1 has already gone back. Presumably we (in England) collect up the whole of an act (2 or 3) before any more is returned to Mainz? Could you ask Hugo?

M.

5? February 1953
Schönenberg, Pratteln, Basle*

Dear Howard,

First rehearsal went this morning – very well. S[acher] clearly likes the piece and thinks it a probable success (I merely feel that everything of value has been said hundreds of times before and that's all we're any of us good for). So he's keeping his score, which he's marked and translated and covered with instructions to himself. No trouble is too much.

Then he had given *vorher* the *Observer* article to Willi Reich who is coming over to see me to suggest I assemble my writings so that he can translate them and publish them in Zürich in a little book. Also, in the friendliest way possible, Sacher seems to be saying that if Schott's want it, from a business point of view, or whatever, he thinks Zürich good for the opera première, in the summer festival next year. That though he's glad I don't sell my wares as blatantly as [Rolf] Liebermann (sic!) he nevertheless thinks they ought to be sold and that the name is good enough. So I fancy he would be a kind of *Vermitteler* if we wanted. I'll see how I get on with Reich; and *gelegentlich* talk to Paul [Sacher] a bit more explicitly.

He performs Double Conc. [Concerto for Double String Orchestra] in the Tonhalle at Zürich in March, and he does not expect it to be broadcast. There is no connection. He'd had Pritchard's name for the first time before him, recommended by Philips (recording). Asked me all about him. Thought, incidentally, Beromünster would welcome Tippett if John P. wishes that. The general standing of T. is here good!! . . .

But the disagreeable thing is only that little John [Minchinton] was right. The orchestra have complained like mad over some of the parts and some have had to be done again. I had my nose rubbed in it all this morning and was given a long lecture about the lack of business acumen in publishing parts which wasted orchestral time, lost goodwill and *could* be different and good. The Swiss written parts are like Mainz work. You'll see them maybe. Anyhow I sit down on the beautiful score and do my best for 'my house' – and have some practical suggestions to make later – and if need be will earn a bit and pay for. You see, it's chiefly certain pages and certain parts, and anyhow some of these parts have been done again already – one or two by the players themselves –

* Home of Paul Sacher, where Tippett stayed during preparations for the première of the Ritual Dances from *The Midsummer Marriage*.

others by professional men because the orchestra struck.

Also – and this is *ehrlich gesprochen* I hope – I'll produce the next piece so on time that we are not rushed. Though it was not altogether anyone's special fault in this last instance.

Anyhow, the gains are considerable. I *think* Sacher does like the piece (and Tippett generally) and will do it elsewhere. And he's ready to say good words and act good deeds on my behalf. And it all helps to build the *renommée* that eventually makes all losses good. [. . .]

herzlichst

M.

7 February 1953
Schönenberg, Pratteln, Basle

Dear Howard,

I'm feeling better in every way – just need your advice. What's good is that I am resting and in good health – that they all like the piece – and that by dint of careful work and much goodwill the 2nd rehearsal began to make the music sing everywhere – and it is most exciting. The players are beginning to give over rubbing my nose in the mess of the material (and in any case have the very bad spots now done afresh for them) but Sacher is clearly unwilling to let the material go back to Mainz at all! He has fallen for the piece and wants to have it in his repertoire for next season – and it's his habit (with Schott's Mainz at any rate) to keep his own material on such occasions and pay over the fees after his use of them – or so Willy once explained to me. So I'm a bit unsure what to do: because I don't want to *froisser* him, when he's got so far – and he really does conduct around and about more than we realise – *ausser Frankreich*. It's a *big* step, in *my* opinion, when a conductor wants to take a piece into repertoire, rather than give it a once-over in some series. So I personally would like to come as far to meet him in his wishes as you will let me.

Now – as to the notational mistakes in the parts, I have noted so far 6, which are real and serious. But probably 4 of them would come out in the wash anywhere at rehearsals. However I can write them down and give them to Goehr – and post to you for Hans. That I will do in any case, for the other materials. It's only 5 minutes to correct the parts, as they are so easy and obvious – but helpful to the ear! Send me your opinion on the question of Sacher's retention of material, if he persists, either by return letter, or *mündlich* by Johnny [Minchinton].

Anyhow – whatever the Basel press will think, Sacher feels it's a success work – *très réussi* as he put it – and again *eine ganz neue Welt* from the string piece. It's his cup of tea, and seems to appeal to him.

I've spoken with Walter and he came Tuesday to rehearsal and to spend the day with me. *Wieder aüsserst freundlich*. So I'm mighty pleased. I think he'll do his best and that it will succeed with him too.

But seeing how much the music has begun to appear only after careful rehearsal etc etc, I'm wondering again about Hamburg. Ought I to go to rehearsals? after all. Can you in any case get Hans to a Goehr rehearsal if humanly possible – and I'll send you in a day or two a letter for him in which I'll try and say the essentials in simple language! But if you have his ear, it's come out in the wash very clearly, that this score is the most carefully marked and orchestrated that I have ever done, and that once the dynamic's markings (as in Mahler!) are obtained the music speaks. That is point 1, the purely musical point. Point 2 is that it is pictorial music for the first 3 dances and best played and understood under that sign – while Dance 4 is a big *musical* ensemble, of canons and what have you, where the problem for the conductor is to release the canonic pattern (having no solo voices) from within the web of sound.

Put it this way – it seems it may be a good piece – and while I doubt if other conductors will take it up like Sacher intends to (because there must be some personal extra-musical things operating there I think) I really am ready to fly to Hamburg and back for the rehearsals, if you or Hugo think enough depends on it. Perhaps you could explain my misgivings about my possible dereliction of duty to Hans when you see him, and see how he reacts. And then leave me instructions for my return.

[Conrad] Beck came to dinner Friday. Lots about Oslo and my own position vis-à-vis the ISCM [International Society for Contemporary Music] – which I'll discuss when we meet. Otherwise it had the advantage to bring Fricker's name up in discussion and I guess Sacher will get there soon. It's clear that the English school is beginning to have standing. Britten is *still* regarded as an outstanding talent with some good and real works to his credit. Beck dislikes Henze violently! They only have regard for Hartmann and Fortner. *Very* amusing stories of the latter and his habits – viz. his dress, his spitting, his washing. Much what we all know – but friendly as well as malicious.

What is odd is that Beck regards Isaacs as the word of god. He takes everyone and everything Leonard tells him or recommends him. He puts Ritual Dances on tape of course. Sacher is going to make records in Vienna for Philips!

The Karajan *Child* has done good in the press sense of *renommée*. So that all in all it's well.

I'm drunk with Klee.

M.

11 February 1953
Schönenberg, Pratteln, Basle

[To Howard Hartog]

PS. Meeting with Goehr has been extremely friendly and good. And by means of the rehearsal I think everything augurs well for London. I forgot to give him the 6 important corrections for the material (which matter is settling a bit) so I may have to send them you for him. I think you will find him in good spirits and anxious to see you all. It's crystal clear that if a conductor can hear the actual music once beforehand he can take all and everything in immediately. So I'm much less worried about Hans – at least if he hears *Band* or rehearsal.

In any case he'll do it well I think and maybe I'm a bit in too good opinion of the piece (and myself!). It makes one impatient for the great opera day when it comes as it will in its time.

M.

[1953]
en route to London

Dear Howard,

I managed to get the 1st m[ovement] of the Serenade [probably *Divertimento on 'Sellinger's Round'*] done this morning – so ²/₅th are ready, when they're transcribed to ink, for the copyist. I hope to go back in Oct. to the Pf. Conc., but can finish the other ³/₅th of the Serenade at any time needed. We'd simply prefer to get a movement of the concerto done first.

The points that I haven't or can't settle ahead are these:

1. BBC. You should receive (as all letters will come to you) monies as per the 2 contracts: and surely something for rehearsals? There were 2 in London, 1 in Edin[burgh], and 1 again in London – last 2 just run-throughs. So don't let them diddle me. But you'll have to hold the cheques, I suppose.

Can you, on the plea of settling my affairs for me in absence, find out if *Music Magazine* [radio programme] expected to pay anything for Sun. last – or was it just unpaid interview – if the former, which I hold it should be, then sign the contract for me. D[itt]o if you get one from Halpern for the 3 1/2 m[inute] American stint. For I shall be stony broke when I return! Suggested recording morning of 7th.

2. Munich. Have written Willy to say that I'd suggest going to Mainz Oct. 13, stay the night, go to Munich 14–15–16. And can you ask the latter about the radio talk (German script should come to you from Beate [Ruhm von Oppen]) – and see for a hotel?

3. Liverpool. Herewith correspondence, answered, to date – so that you can see how it goes. Can you get Ashton, the travel agent, to book a 1st class sleeper for Liverpool–London, night of 6–7th. Provided I can get on it late enough after concert. If I can't of course, then BBC recording date must be afternoon. And please, a room at Adelphi for the 5th *angeblich* – I wrote [Hugo] Rignold last that I suggested coming up Mon. 5th, but could come Sun. 4th if preferred – to let you know – so that Adelphi booking turns on that.

So sorry to leave all this with you, but I hadn't information to do it myself before I went.

Don't lose my letters!

Am full of beans. Will send you a can.

Who's Who, to return as per Hugo [Strecker]'s additions and my alteration.

herzlichst

M.

Corelli. Can you confirm that Hugo sent Amaducci of Lugano Radio a score? Can you let Boyd Neel have one with my recommendation. And I promised Priaulx [Rainier] one! but have failed to send her – c/o Trewyn Studio, St Ives.

[1953]

Dear H[oward] and H[ugo],

Herewith the clean (and final) copy [of the libretto of *The Midsummer Marriage*], i.e. final in all senses, I think. I should imagine, after a copy has been made, that it would be more sensible now to have it leisurely set up in print, against the day of release? That would save expense of further typing. I haven't checked all the conventional

36

things e.g. R., or right (?), L., or left (?), for stage directions etc –
because I've never had much to do with letterpress stage play printing.
I think though we might agree on 'midsummer-day' (no capital but
hyphen) for the actual day of June 24, and 'midsummer day' (no capital or hyphen) for a day in midsummer.

There are some horrid trivial lines in it on re-reading, but many less
than I feared. And the manner and matter on the whole clearly stated.
I am much less disturbed by the latter now than I used to be. In print
it will have even more authority.

Some librettos (e.g. *Mathis* [*der Maler*]?) have names of characters
printed above their words, instead of beside.

Yours
M.

[1953]

Dear Howard,

Sorry to bother Miss Simmons; but can she correct her file copy as
per enclosed, and let me have 2 clean copies of the corrected one. I did
make most of these corrections before it went to Hunter – but didn't
refer them back to the file; which clearly is uncorrected and should not
go out as it stands.

It will be that the Fantasia [Concertante on a Theme of Corelli]
should suit both small and large orchestra. I will work out a minimum
'registration' for Concertino Grosso e Armonico. I want it playable by
all the usual small string bodies and ensembles, at least those used to
playing the standard 18th-cent. concerti grossi.

I think the 4 horrible days at the proofs tired me excessively. I am
only slowly recovering and getting back to work. Return to the music
of the opera is still rather like the return of dog to vomit.

Yours
M.

[1953]

Dear Howard,

If you've already sent the madrigal proofs [*The Source, The
Windhover*] to Stainer & Bell, can you phone them the following information?: forgotten and accidentally remembered yesterday evening!

It's the metronome marks – for which they have left space, but I had forgotten to fill. They are 2:

1. Allegro (Tempo Primo) ♩ = 120±

(This is at the very start)

2. Pochissimo meno Allegro (Tempo Secondo) ♩ = circa 108

(This is 37 bars later.)

If you've still got the proof sheets at Schott's, you could put them in for me (red ink!).

On Wed. next I may not have easily time to reach Schott's before I get to Covent Garden – so would have been glad of a full score Ritual Dances, if you can have it posted.

Maybe, on second thoughts, *News Chronicle* man is right: 'the ballet that followed the play looked to my untutored eye exactly like a Morris dance by a member[s] of a Fabian summer school to celebrate the opening of one of the new towns.'

Very good journalism! And I'm inclined to agree.

Yours

M.

20 April 1953

Dear Willy,

I opened your letter with anxiety and trepidation and was more than *erleichtert* when I read it. So that is at last that.

I agree with you about Biennale and Sacher. And hope in any case to find means of offering the latter the Fantasia Concertante on a Theme of Corelli. This I am designing for large or small orchestras. So that it can be played successfully, not only by the usual string bodies of big orchestras, but also by the smaller bodies that play the 18th-cent. concerti grossi. I notice that they are everywhere becoming a feature of modern musical life, and economically can get more around. E.g. the Boyd Neel here in England, that tours America and the Commonwealth as well as Europe. And there are good bodies in Holland and Italy that I know of.

As to the Biennale, I answered their letter a month ago, and that seems to the usual end. But whether they do answer or not I shall write the Piano Concerto next because I have its warm sounds now in my head. The more astringent piece (for Sacher) [*Divertimento on 'Sellinger's Round'*] I shall do later. [. . .]

Yours,

Michael

[early summer 1953]

Dear Howard,

John [Minchinton] and I have done the corrections of the [Fantasia Concertante on a Theme of] Corelli sent to date. Very little problem. John is bringing it in. I also send my BBC contract so that you can manage (I hope) to wrestle with it. Only facts that matter are: a) my single fee for Prom 2 years ago was £25; b) there is no mention to date of anything for Edinburgh.

My plan, if Glyndebourne, Thurs., transpire, is to come back to town and come into Schott's on Fri. morning. I need to settle one or 2 organisational matters about dates and lodgings etc. And ask Hugo more advice about Purcell – which isn't so easy as it seems.

There are 2 matters of scores that need, if you could, getting straight, in case of subsequent loss.

1. To obtain score of *Fanfare for the Four Corners* [Fanfare No. 2, for four trumpets] from – Flight Lt Alison, RAF Station, St Mawgan, nr Newquay, Cornwall. (And the other fanfare back to be destroyed!!)

2. To obtain score (for copying and file) of Sellinger variation from, Miss Elizabeth Sweeting, Festival Office, High St, Aldeburgh, Suffolk. (Because they have unfortunately my pencil score as well: and I've a good idea for a better, more profitable use, of this little piece.)

Sonata [for Four Horns] is ready to go to town with, more or less. Will bring it Friday.

Michael

24 June 1953

Dear Willy,

I have been through the clean vocal score of Act 3 [of *The Midsummer Marriage*], and the number of final corrections is very small. So few pages are involved that I am posting them to you by letter post, so that there is no further hold-up for printing the whole vocal score. And I will post on the other pages of Act 3 later, so that you will have again a complete Act 3 for the copyist of the full score. Because he will need a correct vocal score for the words and notes of the voice parts and all stage directions. (Some of the latter I forgot to write into the full score MS.) My next job will be to get the full score Act 3 ready to send out to Mainz. Then, when we have printed vocal scores, I will prepare a final libretto, to be set up in print against the great day of release.

[. . .] I saw *Gloriana*. It is another thin opera. Whatever else happens, *The Midsummer Marriage* will seem musical wine to the water of B.B.'s [Britten's] last 2 efforts. I think everyone who is not prejudiced will be secretly thankful and pleased. *Ma – bisogna avere cantor e cantatrice buonissimi. Dover.* [But – the need to have an excellent male and female singer. Essential.] No half-baked singing, if we can avoid it.

Am gay and cheerful. All goes well.

Michael

24 August 1953
4 Crabbe St, Aldeburgh, Suffolk

Dear Willy,

I am here with Britten for a weekend, resting before I go to Edinburgh to conduct (and to see *The Rake's Progress*!). This letter is just to report that we had the first full rehearsal of the Corelli Fantasia Concertante last week and that the piece turns out to be 'bigger and better' than I expected. It plays 17 minutes, and suits a big body of strings. So that it may turn out to be less useful to the smaller bodies I spoke of in my last letter [see also letter of 20 April 1953]. (Clearly, z.B. [*zum Beispiel*] Virtuosi di Roma are unable to tackle it.) Hugo [Strecker], who heard the end of the rehearsal, spoke of it as a new, different, Concerto for Double String Orchestra – placing it in a bigger category, you see. Anyhow he'll tell you what he thinks sometime. He was pleased, meanwhile.

Love
Michael

[mid-November 1953?]

Dear Howard,

I'm sending the £2 for Miss Luker, because I'm getting so short it had better be done now. By the New Year I shall be stony broke again and borrowing from Max [Steffens] – or someone. However – 2 questions to resolve – a) if I don't pay up my subs to the Composers' Guild I become a 'lapsed member'. Shall I? b) if I don't pay 2 gns by Nov. 30 I cease to be a member of IMA club. As I go only about 3–4 times a year in all, it seems an expensive toy. *Nicht wahr?*

Third question is: did I ought to write a nice little note to Royal Phil. – and is that the man with the white beard? (Ritson-Smith?) He offered me spare programmes. Maybe I should have taken them. For the notes with notes could be very useful. Should Schott's ask for a few to file?

Slowly returning to Pf. Concerto. It was difficult to get the [Ritual] Dances and the opera [*The Midsummer Marriage*] out of my mind. But I'm extremely pleased inside.

Yours

M.

25 November 1953

My dear Willy,

[. . .] I was absurdly excited by the Ritual Dances concert here; because it really made its impression and augurs so well for the whole opera. And the whole atmosphere and press seemed to be a kind of vote of confidence in Tippett in my home country. Having never been 'officially' backed like Rawsthorne or Rubbra, by some one influential section or other, or had the kind of clique that Britten suffers from, I felt that nevertheless the music itself was obtaining slow but steady recognition. So that when the opera comes in full, it may well be a landmark in one's public career. As you can see from this letter, I am still a trifle light-headed!

[. . .] I am a bit behind-hand with *Korrekturen*, but I will get ahead again soon. The amanuensis, John Minchinton, who helps me, and is so good at it, has been too busy on his own affairs.

[. . .] I am working very hard at my Piano Concerto. Also at Divertimento [on 'Sellinger's Round'] for chamber orchestra for Sacher; Basel, Jan. 1954 (along with Bartók, Viola Concerto, and Stravinsky, Symphony in 3 Movements).

Yours

Michael

22 December 1953

Dear Willy,

[. . .] My new work (Piano Concerto) moves very slowly. And yet the music seems to be always and ever simpler and further and further from the complications of even a Hartmann let alone a Boulez. You must not let me get spoilt and made soft (if that could ever happen to me) by success. It's such a strange period that mere thinking about artistic (and social) problems won't provide certainty – so that one has to trust the creative instinct, and that is also suspect, if allowed to be just subjective. What strikes me a bit about my present music (since the opera) is that I am playing with many traditional and inherently simple musical ideas, and which are only not exhausted by the skin of their teeth (to mix all the metaphors). It's for me a very 'traditional' period (as suppose it is even for the greats like Hindemith and Stravinsky). I have been wanting for some time to talk to you at length about it. Maybe the Toronto course, which is to be contemporary music, will after all help keep my creative instincts disciplined to their proper objective function. And then the opera on the stage will permit a clearer judgment.

Belated Christmas Greetings
Michael

[summer 1954?]

Dear Howard –

[. . .] I bit Joyce Faulkner's head off – but really because of [Edgar] Hunt. In future we must have things put down on paper. It's that Hunt told Joyce to let Barkwith copy both the solo piano part and the (unready) second piano part. Whereas we had all agreed that he was to be asked to do the former only, but in such a way that it could be used both in the full score and the edition for sale. However: a) as it isn't the making of hire material it is not a matter of the 'costs of production', but a matter of E.H., maybe, wasting Schott's money; b) it may not be very serious, in that I don't think there will in fact be many changes to make at all. Most of the second piano part will, I guess, stand as it is now. (The minor changes and pedalling which [Julius] Katchen himself may feel good for piano solo part will only appear in the final version for sale.)

You will have heard all about Katchen's sudden appearance etc. I've sent a letter off to him at Piccadilly Hotel asking for a visit here or there – and informing him that 1) first movement copy went to Singapore. If he must have another, to ring you at once, so that a pull can be made from Barkwith's new traces (just in) – which I will correct on the dye-line itself for notes.

2) Second movement already being pulled for a copy for him (will correct for notes on the dye-line).

3) Last movement only just finished. But expect J.M. [John Minchinton] can transcribe solo part at least straight away, and can be sent to Paris early Sept. (Katchen wants to use first 3 weeks of Sept. to learn the piece: a movement a week one supposes!)

I've written all this out at length and labour so that, so far as is possible, everything is known to all first hand . . .

Lastly – I'm writing a hymn tune (to be called *Wadhurst*) for the local Salvation Army Band!!! (Those exclamations because it's sacred.) Just in case it got around, can copyright be held through Schott's?

Am beginning opera things today, as I've finished all the ink copying of the concerto.

M.

March/April 1954

Dear Willy,

Hartog and I did see [David] Webster last Monday and so far as can ever be with him, the meeting was satisfactory. That is to say that he more or less gives us permission to approach the artist we think we want, or can get ourselves. He is himself excessively dilatory and so everything gets left till too late.

It has been decided to take Pritchard – and I have overcome my misgivings and will try my best to be as co-operative as I can be over that. [Günther] Rennert was refused us – and [Frederick] Ashton offered us. We have accepted – if Ashton accepts. We still hope to get [Elisabeth] Schwarzkopf.

We have heard from inside sources that the feeling of the opera house staff and repetiteurs is all at present pro-Walton and anti-Tippett. This is not surprising – is even perhaps a recommendation! But meanwhile the Walton is ever delayed, so that it is now Dec. 10 not Dec. 3 and a week nearer Tippett (Jan. 27) and making for skimped preparation of the latter. Yet they are scheduled to begin learning Tippett in a week or so; I had this from the head of the repetiteurs in person, a young man called [Frank] Dawes, a Scherchen pupil. And it's clear that they may be in great need to prepare the Tippett now, just because the Walton is delayed. So we are getting a bit anxious about our chorus material. And we would bless you if it could be got to us very soon. Then I propose to do my best to see that all that can be done ahead on preparation is really done now, before an over-due set of Walton material makes work on Tippett impossible.

It's a pity that the way it is is such that Tippett has to take second place to whatever Walton chooses to do or not do. But that is as it were the end of an older story and will all be forgotten in the event. And I am certain we shall be right to hang on to our own date, and not let ourselves be pushed off into a later season. So that if the Walton gets much more postponed I shall begin to make a big fuss.

Anyhow, the scores will be an enormous help to us. We are needing them badly.

Michael

[spring? 1954]

Dear Howard,

a) The relevant sentence in Willy's letter you can see for yourself. (Amusing about Henze and Hindemith.)

b) Now my movements so far fixed are:

BBC concert May 3. So I could be available on that day, or by stay-ing overnight, the next day also. (Webster?)

Then I am probably up to hear John [Minchinton]'s concert on May 6.

Then I go to Switzerland Tues 18th. So I could be available for [Clifford] Curzon as late in May as the Mon before. Perhaps a dinner party? Am back afternoon of June 2nd. But as these next 3 weeks are only working at the little things don't hesitate to fix anything you like, and I'll come up specially.

c) Could you on the quiet pick out for me some few exemplars of Recorder Society's publications? I realise it's apparently partly a matter of printing. I want to see just how many notes go to a page of their print, so to speak, and then maybe to dash the thing off [Four Inventions], mixed up with last minute studying of the music I conduct at Lugano!

d) Could you order me some mass of 24-stave score paper? I think the last lot I had was from Weekes. But Augener's probably have it too. I'm using it for Piano Conc. and am run out.

e) I've fixed with John [Minchinton] that there shall be at least the transcription of the piano part (of Concerto 1st movement) available by June 2nd, when I return. So that that can be vetted for playability.

Then I'll get a date line for the orchestral redaction, correct it all and that will release the full score of the 1st movement to you.

f) I have a heavy feeling in my bones that the Sacher gambit won't come off. So I've been trying to overcome my sense of disappointment after Tuesday, and my sense of a bad omen. I wish I could see what you see, but I don't. I see very good stick work (as in the Seiber) but good old English slap-dashery (as in the Tippett; not even bowings agreed on beforehand; though the composer had taken that trouble in similar circumstances!). The trouble, as I see it then, is that my music needs less of the quick and trick stick work (like the Seiber), and a great deal of *musical* imagination. Of this, so far as I got it in my own piece, I could see nothing. So there we are. I try not to think too much about it, because I get woefully distressed – and things then go out of proportion. And in any case, if it has to be, I shall try emotionally and technically to be as helpful as I can. I'll give up precious time to bowing the whole damned thing, and my John will do the donkey-work into the parts etc. For if this is what we are going to get then I'll try and make it as foolproof as I can. *Spannung* we can't have; but we might be able to trick him into giving the affair something of the sense of an occasion; and the slap-dashery we must try and make as difficult to indulge in as we know how.

herzlichst

M.

[1954]

Dear Howard,

In haste to say – could you put a min. score of Fantasia Concertante into (letter) post for me on Monday – *morning* if possible.

Meanwhile am in a heavy hangover from yesterday in town – such days never now suit me overmuch. But please find means someday somehow to let John P[ritchard] know I really feel a confidence now that we shall really bring it off together. Seeing him was in any case worth the hangover.

Saw 2 acts of *Coq d'or*. [Howell] Glynne is possible I suppose [for King Fisher in *The Midsummer Marriage*]. Dodon is such a dodderer's role it's difficult to know if he can produce a great breezy tub-thumping role out of his hat. I fancy it's best to leave the matter now till John P. has seen the vocal score.

And in first interval ran pat into [Harry] Blech, who said there and then 'What's your best piece for chamber orchestra?'!! So I just said I was writing one and whom for [*Divertimento on 'Sellinger's Round'*]. So he said who had the English première? I said no one to date – and havered a bit. Nevertheless it looked too like the holy hand of God and I hurried away. Maybe he *could* give a very nice glossy sendoff. Could you not just boldly ask him what if anything he means – and if he says he has to see the score and think and dilly dally, then you can be sharp and say – won't do. Thought I'd better let you know.

M.

PS. I mean I didn't commit us, but it was difficult to say no out of hand because he made the approach and asked for the English pre-mière, I think myself it turns really on what he could offer. It's unrea-sonable to expect him to buy without a sight of the score. But it's just what he could do. Because he spoke of looking for repertoire – English small ensemble pieces for general use in concerts of his here and abroad. Could that be so? And if it suited him to make it a repertoire piece, it would begin to make its money back.

[1954]

Dear Walter [Bergmann],

Sorry if these were held up a day or so [*Little Music for String Orchestra*]. But John [Minchinton] is here proofreading them now after me – and finding small things.

The tempo markings have been altered in 2 cases. Is this you or the copyist? If the former, then let them go – if not, have them as I put them.

No 1. ♩ Andante ♩ Comodo (instead of ♩ Andante comodo as copy-ist has).

No 4. ♩ allegro moderato (he has ♩ allegro comodo).

A general question here is that I thought it better to have no capitals on the markings, z.B. [*zum Beispiel*]

♩ andante

statt

♩ Andante.

Because I read the Italian things then as adjectives standing second (!) in a sentence. It isn't important – but if he keeps his capitals, and changes no. 1 back to mine, it must read ♩ A—e ♩ Co—do. Maybe that's better.

I hope the comments are clear, to the corrections.

They are not in order because the corrections were noticed at different times.

I told Max that if they were liked, I'd one day write 4 fantasies to match, and you/he could put them in a little album.

John has just found a copyist has wrong note in the canon fugue! How blind I am.

herzlichst

M.

9 June 1954

Dear Walter,

Herewith [*Little Music for String Orchestra*].

If you preferred the title to be 4 Pieces and with names – then the latter should be:

Canon

Ground

Air

Fugue.

But maybe it's better as it is.

I like the first least. (And I don't know the favoured instruments well enough to see if the little arpeggios and tremolandi are too difficult. You shall say.)

M.

17 July 1954

Dear Willy,

I think you are away, so I shall imagine I am really writing to your nephew [Heinz Schneider-Schott].

The matter is that I spoke last night with the Intendant of Covent Garden, about the delay in casting *The Midsummer Marriage*, especially the important role that may have to be got from outside the House. He retorted that it is no use getting fussed and excited when in any case they have no vocal scores. And this is now becoming serious, because in a very little while the season ends and if there is no decision now, then all is to begin again in the autumn. It would therefore be of the greatest help both musically and certainly even more psychologically if we had enough vocal scores to allow for the casting to be done in agreement and conference and to give out the chief parts.

Now, I can't ring Hartog this morning, as Schott's is closed. So I write direct to you. One score has come by post, and the rest are in a case, which Hartog told me yesterday will be available in about 2 weeks. In my opinion that is exactly too late. I know it costs, according to Hartog, 2/- a copy to post by air. But would it not really be worth £1 to have 10 sent at once? I am willing to pay Schott's the £1 myself!! I write to you in Mainz because I am worried. It not only puts me in a weak position when dealing with the Intendant of Covent Garden, it is also dangerous and somewhat stupid. For example, we have cast the chief tenor role. I have seen him and spoken with him. But I cannot give him any notes! Merely promise them in 2 weeks when he will be on holiday and so it goes on.

Do not let us risk so much for a matter of 10 marks. Maybe Hartog on Monday will think I am being over-anxious. But I am not. No one who has been in the absurd position of discussing singers and roles, without enough copies for even the chief people at the opera house to see what notes have been written for the singers to sing, can understand how difficult and dangerous it is.

Yours
Michael

PS. Will[y] wrote me always in German dictating to a secretary, and I write him in English.

15 November 1954

My dear Willy,

[. . .] As I gather you know already, through [Alfred] Kalmus, the Divertimento for Chamber Orchestra [Divertimento on 'Sellinger's Round'] was a success. And more pleasing for me personally was the fact that Sacher really liked his piece. He was exceedingly generous to me over it – both in commission and in hospitality. I find him and his wife now among my closest friends abroad. And his house is quite like another home to me.

There is news that British Council will record *Child of Our Time* in April 56. This is really good. If Ritual Dances are also recorded, as is likely, then we are well set up.

As to the latter I have indeed worked out cuts for you – but have been dilatory in sending you them. In fact I've lost the list! But I shall find it and send you. Until now life has been very hectic seeing to the opera [*The Midsummer Marriage*]. I think all is as well at present as any new opera production can ever be. I'm very glad you are coming to the première. For I think it will be an occasion. Much criticism, but much attention. I can't help feeling things are all the time going slowly on to our advantage. We are in a very good position already, before the opera happens. So that that ought to make an even wider basis for judgment, criticism and esteem – and for a new set of works. After the Pf. Concerto (which is 1/2 finished now) I shall do a Vl. and Pf. Sonata (of 2 movements) as a change from big pieces – and then I have in my mind a second symphony, which I believe I may at last make really good. Not a long work – rather more condensed. I had the first *Einfall* when I was with the Sachers last May. But the older origin is hearing a tape of a concerto of Vivaldi at Radio Monti Ceneri – conducted by that quite good and coming youngster there named Amaducci (!). A certain pounding C bass, which goes exactly into the new symphony. I am enormously looking forward to writing this – but I shall not start for about a year.

Herzlichst
Michael

[late 1955/early 1956]

Dear Howard,

[. . .] My timetable is the following: I shall either listen in to Tuesday's perf., or come up if I feel like it. Then Wed. morning leave for Lausanne. Come back (by the usual train) the evening of Friday the 18th – either to London or here direct, as seems best. What will be helpful is to know, before I go, the LSO [London Symphony Orchestra] usual rehearsal schedule – and whether they have a special call for strings only. I imagine I ought to be available by the Sat. But might stay a day longer, if it seemed sense.

Then to record a talk for CBC [Canadian Broadcasting Corporation] on the morning of 21st or afternoon of 22nd. But here again if you could find out [Raymond] Leppard's rehearsals you could then talk for me with CBC [. . .] and either confirm or alter to suit. (To some other time on 21st or 22nd)

Then to fit in Divertimento and Act 3 of M.M. [*The Midsummer*

Marriage] for the 22nd evening, and so home 23rd morning to the 3rd movement of the [Piano] Concerto.

As to the latter; CBSO [City of Birmingham Symphony Orchestra] came on the phone yesterday; seeming to say that [Rudolf] Schwarz was a bit hasty in saying all pianists equal. They would much prefer Katchen (the 2nd choice) and wanted to make enquiries as to availability. Was a bit tricky in the event – because point blank questions about my knowledge of and relation to [Paul] Baumgartner did not help. I said honestly and clearly that I knew enough about his background and tastes and abilities to be quite sure of him. Katchen I did not know, and nothing of his style – but imagine him capable. What the next move will be I don't know. Maybe K. won't be available, and that will be that. (CBSO feel him to be a much easier and better draw for their purposes.)

I may have obtained now a possible photo of the production for Willy. And Cov. Gdn will present me gratis with a whole collection of official (posed) photos, which will be taken later at a photocall on 22nd.

I am not yet of the opinion that to end Act 3 after Fire Dance is practicable or right. But I can't think about it at all for the moment. Am finishing concerto slow movement. The whole piece to date is much odder than I had realised. Fiendishly difficult too. Another strange work!

M.

[late summer/autumn 1954]

Dear Howard,

I'd written to Eddy [Sackville-West] (once [Peter] Heyworth had told me he'd phoned him) to give him as accurate account as I could. I've now written to explain that I had not been seeking to present myself to Cov. Gdn as engaged in stirring up trouble for them. But as having withdrawn into purdah, seeing that the decision seemed disturbing, confusing, and bordering on the disproportionate. Maybe therefore if you haven't written yet, you can get it across to David [Webster] that M.M. [*The Midsummer Marriage*] is no longer a question of composer and himself, but of other public figures; and of English musical life per se. But you will in any case write as you think fit. I really do have to get it out of mind. And that happens easily enough – till a letter from Eddy – or Tillett – or whomever comes in.

M.

late (December) 1954

My dear Willy,

[. . .] I've had a confidential letter from someone on the Covent Garden committee which asks me not to play into the hands of the one opponent of the opera, by being intransigent about cutting. Hartog will tell you how I have already 'cut' 35 minutes by merely correcting the timing. (I suspect that it could be that the wrong timing is part of the opponent's game, if he is one of the staff. But maybe not.) But what I am clear about now, is that my intuitions to get vocal scores into the hands of the interested and 'pro' committee members have been sound ones. The time is ripe for people like Bliss and Sackville-West to speak with the authority of knowing the score. So don't let us delay now any more than we must at all. The letter I've received shows the matter is ripe, if not urgent.

Incidentally the writer of the letter wants the Tippett to be got through at all costs 'especially after hearing a play over of Walton's *Troilus*, which is quite effective theatre, but contains nothing we didn't know about long ago. Merely to turn the pages of your opera is to perceive the originality and quite obvious beauty of the music. So I shall be furiously disappointed if anything happens to spoil the project.'

There the letter ends.

Yours
Michael

1 May 1955

Dear Willy,

[. . .] I am very disciplined at the moment, finishing the Pf. Concerto. A warm, romantic work, which I am beginning to like more as I come to the end. Also a much deeper layer of my mind is boiling away over a big-scale choral work, to an apocalyptic theme. It's too confused as yet to talk to you about, at least by letter. The theme is tremendous, but the expression of it will take a lot of meditation and preparation. Text will probably be a compilation, with some original portions. At present I seem to hear the music more clearly – or rather the musical shapes have to form a little bit before all the text is chosen. [. . .]

Herzlichst
Michael

8 June 1955

My dear Willy,

[. . .] I am just finishing the Pf. Concerto. It's a considerable work in my corpus. Not difficult in itself, but has taken a lot of labour to get originality yet warmth. Fresh pf. writing is not easy nowadays!

Then I shall do a little work for a special occasion – a piece for 4 horns [Sonata for Four Horns], to be played on Dec. 20th at Wigmore Hall in a concert containing the Hindemith piece for 4 horns.

Then a 2-movement sonata for violin and piano.

So far as the big choral piece is concerned, that is still in the exploratory and germinative phase.

Herzlichst

Michael

23 February 1956

Dear Werner Pilz,

[. . .] we have had 2 radio performances here of it [*A Child of Our Time*] in English, under Schmidt-Isserstedt, and they have been quite the best performances yet heard in this country. And it has been a great achievement, I think. The work has made a tremendous impression after its 12 years of life. I have had letters showing that people found it more than moving. With such a beautiful presentation, I could not but be pleased myself. It was like a vindication; because it had quite mixed reception when it was first performed. Now we shall get a commercial recording of it on LP discs sometime in this coming year.

One must hope that *The Midsummer Marriage* will also find and receive its vindication in due course. But of course it's a more difficult matter economically. The *Child* has had a great many performances, and that is not going to be so easy for the opera! But it will come in time.

The pianist for the Pf. Concerto is definitely now Louis Kentner. I saw him yesterday in London. I have great confidence that it is a good choice. (Bartók chose him for the première of his 2nd Concerto!) Will you let the RAI [Radio Audizioni Italiane] at Rome know how it is? The première here is Oct. 30th. So Rome could not be before that.

Please tell Herr Petri that I have begun the arrangement of the 5 Spirituals of the *Child* for unaccompanied choir. (I do this work in the evenings – the mornings I give to my new Symphony [No. 2].) I hope the result will be what he wants. But it will probably be a bit more individual than expected. I shall have to treat the choir as a kind of 'orchestra' – and perhaps put the matter clear in a short preface. It really is rather a different singing than we are used to. Not more difficult – just different.

All good wishes

Yours Sincerely

Michael Tippett

16 May 1956

Dear Mr Pilz,

A long overdue letter. The Vienna visit was most worthwhile. I went first to Warsaw (which is too long to tell you about in a letter) and the Poles payed all my travelling expenses back via Vienna. So I was very lucky.

The performance of *A Child of Our Time* was very good. I had excellent relations with Dr Halusa. I got the impression that he might one day, if he could afford it, do a radio version of *The Midsummer Marriage*. But I did not of course suggest any such thing to him. I leave that all to you, or the good folk at U.E. [Universal Edition]. I just found Halusa a very nice person, and we got along together excellently.

I saw [Egon] Seefehlner and had quite a talk with him. He is entirely anti-English except for Britten. But Britten had spoken well of me; so that he seems to be moving nearer the generally expressed Viennese point of view, that modern English music has only two names, Britten and Tippett. I gave a radio interview on these lines, when asked to. I think it won't amount to much music in public concerts, but to an annual piece on the radio maybe.

For next season Halusa had chosen the new Piano Concerto; and hereby begins a tale of trouble.

You remember that Katchen was first chosen for the Birmingham première; and that then he gave it up. After a lot of joint negotiation Birmingham and ourselves chose [Louis] Kentner, who accepted. But he asked on his side for the rights of performance for a year. Hartog was against our giving them to him, but did in the end agree that it probably had to be. Kentner is taking a great deal of trouble. Although the première is not till Oct. 30th, he has obtained a whole day's orchestral rehearsal in Birmingham on June 2nd already; to which of course I shall go. The eventual première will be good I think.

Now unfortunately in Vienna I did not tell Halusa that the piece was tied for a year to Kentner. Halusa told me he was asking [Hans Alexander] Kaul. I was so pleased about all this that without considering the consequences I wrote Kaul a postcard telling him I was very pleased. Then I instantly regretted having done so. Because as you know now it has caused a great deal of misunderstanding.

I have had letters from Kaul, and have by this post written him again. Naturally I am glad he wants to play the piece, and glad perhaps that some of the dates he has made for himself will get postponed until after Oct. 57. He has every right to obtain such postponement if he can. But what I cannot do is to wangle a performance without Kentner's knowledge. Kentner's agents would soon bring that to an end. Nor is it honourable. As I have told Kaul, if we in London have made a mistake, then we must take the consequences. The music is any case a great deal more important than trouble about who plays it in the first year. And Kentner after all was chosen by Bartók to give the première of his Concerto No. 2. And he goes in the autumn for his first American tour. He is quite a card in our hand.

Therefore it is not possible not to inform Hamburg that Kentner has the rights for a year. How that will affect them I do not know. Nor can I judge whether you would prefer to delay the German première so that Kaul would play it, for the sake of his goodwill, rather than to have a more spectacular première with Kentner. But there is no doubt that Kentner will be good. He is learning the piece from full score, is exceedingly musical, has tremendous technique, and is fully aware of the quality of the piece he has got. Kaul on the other hand has many more direct contacts. I do not think that Kaul will throw in those dates where he has already obtained a postponement on his behalf if Kentner obtains the German première. That would make him look too silly. He also knows that Kentner won't be possible for lots of smaller radios etc. He is too expensive. But just as Katchen would almost certainly have obtained the German première, if he had done the English, so it can't be said that any of us were ever thinking of Kaul as the best for it. Or were you? As I read it, Kaul thinks he is on a good thing (he hasn't seen the piece yet!) and is fighting for his livelihood. All power to him! As I have never heard him play I can't gauge his capabilities. So it is rather a shot in the dark. I doubt he is in Kentner's class. And I can't think that he is able to give the piece such a good German send-off. But I may be wrong. Only I would certainly be sorry to upset him.

Because he is at least keen. Only we must keep, as I told him in my letter, a sense of proportion. The piece is only held till Oct. 57, and it won't be performed at all till Oct. 56. Birmingham, by virtue of their commission, hold all English performances till March 57, when they give its London première. All this would not have come up if I hadn't written Kaul an impulsive postcard from Vienna. I must apologise.

Yours very sincerely,
Michael Tippett

29 June 1956

Dear Mr Pilz,

I am still worried that the unfortunate postcard to Kaul from Vienna, and the granting at the same time one year's rights to Kentner, have made you upset with Hartog. Because he is really not to blame. I am myself. Although it is difficult to see what else might have been done at the time. However – I did write many times to Kaul, and in the end we closed the correspondence on a friendly basis. He seemed to be happy enough; especially as he had got Zürich radio, and hoped to get Vienna, postponed in his favour until Kentner's year was over. And, please, I have not myself told Hartog of these dates, because it seems to me that Kaul has every right to try the best for himself, and that so long as Liebermann or Halusa knew, before their decision, that Kentner had rights for a year, all is in order. And I do not want to disturb Hartog any further about Kaul. Nor do I want to disturb Kaul. I have absolutely nothing against him, and I certainly did not agree to Kentner's request for a year's rights in order to take anything from Kaul. I'm afraid that until Halusa told me he was thinking of Kaul, I had not thought of him myself. For I have as yet never heard him play.

It is a pity probably that Germany was not excluded from Kentner, but that is easier to see now later, and afterwards. At the time I was anxious to get the Birmingham and London performances done with as good a pianist resident in England as we could find. After hearing Kentner do a 6-hours rehearsal with orchestra a month ago, I am sure the choice was correct. I have no regrets at all as to that.

I think that if Hartog had handled the negotiations with Kentner, there might have been no rights allowed at all. But Hartog was in Germany. And that is how it is.

If you see or speak with Kaul you must always make it clear that I am just as friendly as my original postcard from Vienna indicated. But that postcard was a very silly and impulsive thing to do, as I realised soon enough afterwards. It has led to a lot of misunderstanding.

I am now deeply engaged on the Symphony [No. 2] commissioned by the BBC. [. . .]

mit herzlieben Grüssen

Michael Tippett

22 May 1957

Dear Willy,

Excuse my bothering you, but I can't remember the name of the gentleman who looks after the *Chorabteilung* at Mainz, or I would have written direct to him.

The matters, for his information, are 2:

1. He asked me, when I was in Mainz, to set Negro spirituals for *a cappella* choir, and I have indeed done so. I set the 5 Spirituals out of *Child*, because that was reasonable to do, and a German translation already existed. Please tell him that the 5 are soon to be printed here in London, and he will have copies at once. *Bearbeitet für verschieden, oft viel, meistens aber sehr leicht 4stimmiger Chor.* I mean, there are often many parts, but all very easy harmonically.

2. The enclosed letter came in a day or so ago, and seems the kind of occasion to do something further on the lines he wanted (he being the *Chorabteilungführer*). I have written to Dr [Fritz] Piersig and said I would like to consider doing 4 for him – English, Scottish, Irish, Welsh. Very simple and direct; as he wants. As these will be rather well known here (I shall choose the quite characteristic and not avoid at all the to us well known) presumably the 'market' is rather in Germany. Is it a good idea if these settings were dealt with directly in Mainz? And can you at Mainz attend to a translation? And can someone arrange the obvious things as to translation (if he uses that) etc, with Dr Piersig for me?

I haven't yet told Hartog of this letter, because he is so worried at present that I shall delay myself with the BBC-commissioned Symphony [No. 2]. But I would very much like to do what Dr Piersig asks. Don't you think so?

All other news is good. But I'll see you sometime in London, I'm sure, to tell you personally of it.

If you think I ought not to do these folk songs, please tell me at once.

Every good wish.

Yours

Michael

1957

Dear Willy,

Enclosed is: 1) Piersig's last letter – in reply to mine of last week. I've just written to him and sent him the first 2 songs. The 4th (Welsh) follows soon – in that my young amanuensis (a very hopeful good young conductor, John Minchinton, one-time pupil of von Karajan) has obtained details of the original melody, clearly out of copyright – and the usual Welsh words are also out of copyright. So I am myself making a new English translation. This will take me a few days to find time to do. (3rd song, in the group of 4, from Scotland, I will do in October.) I think I had better get the few necessary lines about the original of each song typed in London and sent to you later, when we have got translation settled and proofreading read yet to do. *Nicht wahr?*

2) Enclosed also for you the first 2 songs herewith. You will see they are printed from traces. Copied for me by John Minchinton (who wants to do them first in England). I have told Dr Piersig that we can give him these traces, so that he could temporarily make himself the necessary copies for his choirs, while the proper edition is being prepared. The only thing then for him to do would be to write in the German words afterwards. Or direct onto the traces if he liked. May I leave that all with you? (I have not sent any traces to him yet. Just offered them.)

In somewhat haste.

Herzlichst

Michael

28 July 1957

Dear Willy,

Could you give the following information to the necessary good folk of the Weihergarten? I have today written to Dr Piersig, Sängerbund NWD [Nordwestdeutschland], to say that I have already completed his 4 *Chorsätze* on tunes from the British Isles and that it now transpires that:

1) My 2 first, English and Irish, are quite free of copyright altogether.

2) My 3rd, Scottish, is too strictly held by a publisher here, and so I will do another, better (!) chosen.

3) My 4th, Welsh, will be free, when I have traced the original tune, and found fresh words.

Therefore – I propose to send a copy, both to Piersig and to Mainz, of the first 2, and if possible the 4th also, this coming week.

The new Scottish *Chorsatz* I shall not now dare to do until I have finished the BBC Symphony [No. 2] commission, probably in October. I have told Piersig therefore, that he is free either to perform only 3 of eventual 4, or (*hoffentlich!*) to begin with the 3, and add the others later, if he has time. That I in any case, will complete the set – for I cannot afford to insult the Scotch by leaving them out!

I am not too disturbed by this, because the settings only took me 3 days or less each; and also, in the event, I didn't much like the Scottish tune when I came to work upon it. I can therefore do better.

I asked Piersig to let me know date of the performance, as someone already wants a first performance of them here in London, immediately after, in a rather nice concert of folk song settings by Stravinsky, Schoenberg, as well as Holst and Vaughan Williams.

So far as publication matters arise, I should very much like to see the German translation; particularly as to how the words are underlaid. Thus:

1) England – 'Early One Morning'. The words are simple language about on the date and level of *Des Knaben Wunderhorn* collection. But – I use the 3 first words as a constant refrain – as though (but I am not translating) the German went 'Frühe-e(s) ein Morgen'; *Hauptsache* is therefore that the eventual German words have this rhythm and are nice. *Nicht?*

2) Ireland – 'Lilliburlero'. These words are burlesque, Irish dialect of 17th century. 'Ho! Broder Teague – dost hear de decree', etc.

The curious thing is that this dialect is nearer German than English – 'broder' and 'de' (for 'the'). The number of words is very small, as practically everything sung is the tag: 'Lilliburlero bullen a la', pronounced indeed as German!

3) Scotland: as yet unknown.

4) Wales: words also unsettled.

I am writing this now to you, because I don't know to whom else I write. Can you be sure and explain these points to the eventual translator? You see, it can only be explained by someone who knows both languages as you do.

I shall in any case endeavour to send with the typescript copy of the words, a short note concerning the tune etc, for prefacing to the appropriate number.

I have called the set: *Four Songs from the British Isles.* 1. England. 2. Ireland et al. So that I expect you will decide to issue them singly, rather than together? But that is a matter for the *Verlag*.

I am quite pleased with the songs. They have turned out very simple and easy, and yet reasonably characteristic of my own ear.

For the rest, you will be pleased to hear that the day before yesterday I had a letter from Library of Congress, Washington, with an offer of a commission from the Koussevitzky Foundation [eventually resulting in *King Priam*] for a choral–orchestral work of 20–30 min. duration. Honoraria $1500. This suits me very well, as there seems to be no time limit. I have no idea why they should pick on me, but I consider it quite a feather in the cap. Other commissioned works of this kind have been, I think, *Symphony of Psalms* and Britten's *Spring Symphony*.

Meanwhile I am on the last lap of the Symphony [No. 2] – and it still seems to me one of the best works I have done.

All good wishes
Michael

14 November 1957

My dear Willy,

I have finished the Symphony [No. 2] for BBC. Last Saturday. It's been an arduous labour, but extraordinarily exciting. It's one of the best things I've done. A new (for me) marriage of terseness and orchestral imagination. I have never before (except perhaps in a different manner in Qt 2.) come so close to the classical ideal of variety in unity. When I come to Germany in March I shall bring a tape or disc, from the *Uraufführung* on Feb. 5th.

I wrote to Prof. [Martin] Stephani about the *Child* in Wuppertal – and had a very moving letter in reply. Then I even saw him for 2 hours in London. He is going to see if I can't be invited officially for March 7th. But in any case I shall be there.

Now – I do want a long leisurely talk with you, if I could have it. I haven't seen you really properly because I have been so wrapped up by the Second Symphony, so what I would have liked would be to come to Mainz after the Wuppertal performance, and to stay a night with you. Then on one day or the other to have a few more words with some of the good folk at Schott's. I shall be in the middle of the (commissioned) piece for a girls' school [*Crown of the Year*]. And want to speak about this, and my hope to do now some string pieces for the Mainz school series – as I promised, I'm afraid, 2 years ago. I want to do these smaller things while I am slowly preparing the scenario for the new theatre venture [*King Priam*]. So would it be possible to be with you thus?

[. . .] For myself (and for your information) I am going in 10 days to consult T. S. Eliot. I did this before the *Child* – but alas, not before *The Midsummer Marriage*.

[. . .] We have now put Ritual Dances (in cut form) onto the 4th side of the discs of *A Child of Our Time*. The music comes over this time with great power – like an unending stream of fine sound. These discs will do a lot of good. I shall certainly bring either a commercial copy, or a repressing for you, in March.

Hope you (and Ludwig [Strecker] and Heinz [Schneider-Schott]) are fit and well.

Herzlichst

M.

21 November 1957

Dear Willy,

Thanks very much for your letter. I have just phoned Schott's to confirm that the 3rd chorus (*Chor-Satz*), the Welsh one, did go off to Mainz, before [Walter] Bergmann went ill. So that was in Aug.–Sept. already. Two copies of the music went – one with English and German translations; one with original Welsh. For use here, the Welsh original is *mehr als wichtig*. It might well get the piece into a Welsh Eisteddfod – which means in numbers a tremendous thing.

I have already begun the 4th chorus – the Scottish. I shall send it, both to Bremen and Mainz already next week.

I have called it here in this letter the 4th – but in the order of the performance it is the 3rd. They go English, Irish, Scots, Welsh. And you at Mainz have already everything but the Scots. (Will you confirm with Petri that is so? We have had no acknowledgment here yet.)

I think you can set your mind at rest that the new libretto [*King*

Priam] will have *keine allgelangere philosophische Abhandlung* – perhaps *keine philosophischen Abhandlungen überhaupt* [no long philosophical plot, as a matter of fact no philosophical plot at all]. The Homeric stuff doesn't lend itself to anything but powerful tragic drama – and for myself I naturally could never go back over old ground. *The Midsummer Marriage* is an unrepeatable experience – per se. It may yet prove that this work will be *ausnahmefallig*, when the air clears a bit. But I am not interested in defending it. Though I want to talk to you all the same about some matters of policy with regard to its music.

I shall write Rennert soon. I must get the Scots song finished, and one or two of the smaller pieces that have got delayed. A little folksong arrangement for children's voices in unison, with 3 recorder parts above. I write it in a hurry for the Pestalozzi Children's Village, and want now to see it through the press.

I spent a day last week with Christopher Fry, whose verses I use for the little school piece I must now write for Badminton Girls' School [*Crown of the Year*]. The voices present no problem. The instrumentation for the children does rather. But after just doing 2 days hearing all the music at my old grammar school – from 8 to 18 – I have a clearer idea of how to do it. Though it's no use deceiving ourselves that English schools are very ready yet to move towards the newer writers. Vaughan Williams of course – and already some Britten. However it will come. (I like doing this side of things too.)

On Tuesday I go to see T. S. Eliot, to talk to him about the new opera libretto. He is an old friend. He helped me on *A Child of Our Time* – but I'm sorry I didn't see him over the first opera.

It is possible that I shall go to have a week's holiday somewhere on the Continent before March 7th – and come to you perhaps on the way to Wuppertal. Then we could go on together – unless Stephani wants me earlier for rehearsals.

Yours ever

Michael

28 November 1957

Dear Mr Petri,

I have just finished the No. 3 of the *Four (!) Songs from (!) the British Isles*. (Your letter writes 'Five' and 'of'. Four is the correct number. And I think 'from' is better than 'of' in this case.) We shall transcribe this No. 3 onto traces this weekend. I will then send you

(Tuesday probably) a copy of the music and the English text – and Dr Bergmann will send you a further copy of the music with his German text, I hope during the week.

We will send *die Matrizen* direct to Piersig at Bremen (Tuesday, I expect also).

As to the Welsh – the No. 4 – it is very mysterious. There is little doubt (I confirmed this by telephone yesterday) that Schott's, London, sent you the German text on one of the two copies of the music. (One had English and German – the other English and Welsh.) But it's clearly useless to discuss by letter where this copy is now – as it is 2 months since it went from me by hand to Schott's, London. So I have already sent (by post) my last copy of the music to Dr Bergmann; and he will make you another underlaid copy of the German text, and send direct to Mainz. Let us hope this one will be visible.

Now – the question of the *Volksgut*.

Yes – all 4 are *Volksgut*. I shall put on a separate sheet of paper the necessary information. I have not changed the melodies from the usual version. [. . .]

Michael Tippett

4 December 1957

My dear Willy,

[. . .] I saw Eliot and had a most useful and practical talk with him about my proposed new work for the theatre [*King Priam*]. All the advice I have now had, from Peter Brook, from David Webster and from Eliot, seems to be consonant and I think I see the next small steps clearly. But I do not want to hurry anything at this stage. And each of the 3 quite different people 'advise' me to clarify endlessly what it is I really want to express; so that when a scenario does at last get set down, it will be reasonably close to the real form of the eventual work. I shall certainly send you a copy to see.

[. . .] Good wishes to you all

Yours

Michael

8 February 1958

Dear Willy,

[. . .] John Minchinton, the excellent up and coming young conductor of the enclosed concert (Berkeley *Four Poems of St Teresa*, [Adrian] Cruft *A Passiontide Carol*, Rainier *Sinfonia da Camera*, V.W. [Vaughan Williams] *Flos* [*Campi*]), has just been speaking on the BBC Home Service about my new Symphony [No. 2] for Wednesday. Very dignified and objective and good.

For your interest I have myself put down some money to make possible the concert, for the sake of Priaulx Rainier's piece. It's her very best – and Minchinton will give it a fine and *well*-rehearsed performance, with advocacy and passion. I think it's a piece which he can well have in his repertoire for Continental radios. He believes in Tippett, Britten and Berkeley (Rainier is only an exception, in this one work) for England; Messiaen and perhaps now Boulez for France; Dallapiccola for Italy, and Fortner, Henze and Hartmann (in that order) for Germany. Quite interesting. He has been given by Boosey & Hawkes the first performance of Stravinsky's *Agon* in England; which he'll do in a late-night special concert at Festival Hall in May.

He's *pour le reste* a pupil of von Karajan and I think, apart from my personal affection, is the best of the young English we've got. A conductor who is really interested in new music as well as the classics and the pre-classics. It means a great deal to me if he comes through successfully because so far there is no conductor in England who does what I need, except to a certain extent Pritchard. So a young one is of prime value. However, I didn't mean to write all that. Let me know sometime if my plan to come by plane on March 3rd is alright.

Yours
Michael

18 February 1959

Dear Heinz [Schneider-Schott],

Could you answer some questions for me please? [. . .]

1. Max Steffens phoned me yesterday to say that there had been a telegram from Preusser Summer Academy, Mozarteum, Salzburg, asking me if I can give a composition course there in the period of the Festival this year.

I have written in answer that I need more details etc. I am unsure that I could do it *überhaupt*. For example, I do not teach or criticise *Zwölfton-Musik*. Nor do I know if I really want to do it, because it is exactly my holiday period as fixed. The question to you is: can you give me any idea of whether *das meines Komponistenberufes wegen lohnt* [whether that is profitable to my profession of composer]. I am not a teacher, as Hindemith or Fortner are. I compose, I conduct, I lecture; but I have never given a composition course. The trouble is I can't evaluate such a request as this from Salzburg. Nor can Max, and Hartog is away. Can you help me at all? I am only really interested in the furthering of my reputation as a composer. *Für mich, Komposition bleibt die Einzige und Hauptsache.* To give up time to Salzburg will delay the new opera. Will it do anything good in compensation?

[. . .] Sorry to be a nuisance. The composition of the new opera [*King Priam*] goes well.

Herzlichst –
Michael

5 February 1962

Dear Ken [Bartlett],

[. . .] I am composing faster and better than ever! And I think *King Priam* is tops – as we say. However, I wonder whether you can turn your attention sometime to considering who ought to be invited to Coventry or London (the latter is easier, dates June 5, 8, 11, 18) from German opera houses. I think it possible we could fix things somehow to help (financially) either from Covent Garden or Schott's or the German house involved etc. But I'm certain that it's much better to see the piece on the stage – unless Düsseldorf has already decided to play. We need your advice because Ian Kemp here (and I) are really ignorant of the German situation, yet we feel *King Priam* is a top knotcher.

I know you yourself felt the world of Greek heroes to be perhaps stale. But I doubt if you would feel that in the event – it will come out as very fresh and very contemporary.

Greetings and to Alex.
Herzlichst
Michael

11 November 1962

Dear Ken,

Two matters:–

1. I hope Karlsruhe people have read the notes about orchestra for *King Priam* inside the full score. Because this was where Covent Garden

muddled themselves – in that it is made clear that the number of violins is not proportionate to the wind players at all (since they never have to balance the sound of heavy brass wind) and so the violin part was conceived as for a relatively small number of good players. Anyone examining the score would see that at once. In England, Pritchard did not exercise proper control, did not really understand the matter, and in consequence put a great deal of the violin part onto the piano! For the revival in January, with another conductor, I am having this put right.

2. I have agreed on your advice to accept an invitation to this Berlin affair next April. I have told the British Council to say that, with regard to possible concert works of my own I might conduct, the pieces seem to be the following:–

a) Second Symphony –very difficult

b) Ritual Dances from *The Midsummer Marriage* –very appropriate to their overall conference title 'Symbol und Mythos im Spiegel der zeitgenössischen Kunst', but again needing rehearsal time. It's an orchestral display piece (with a kind of symbolical 'story') about on the level of Ravel *Daphnis et Chloé*.

c) Handel Fantasia for Pf. and Orch. This is only a 12–13-minute piece, which I would do with Margaret Kitchin as she is playing it at that time already in Germany (radio not concert). The advantage of this piece is simply that it is short. That means it can be rehearsed. From my experience of these sorts of gatherings, where most of the invited composers expect to conduct one of their pieces, the real problem is proper rehearsal.

I am writing you all this at length in case you felt you could or should intervene with Senatsrat Dr Kuhnert, or some other more musical personage, to help settle what, if anything, I should conduct. Because you may yourself, as neither I nor Ian Kemp can, have a much better idea of the sort of thing it will all be, and the sort of musical piece suitable in the context.

Meanwhile I expect to see you soon, in Mainz and then Karlsruhe.

Herzlichst

Michael

18 February 1963

Dear Ken,

[. . .] I am fairly well looking forward to doing the concerto with the orchestra, but don't want to get involved in too much public lecturing. The real reason being, that owing to all the performances lately, and having had to be ten days in Brussels, I have got behind hand with the Edinburgh piece [Concerto for Orchestra]* and need to keep all outside engagements to the minimum. There will be quite a lot of preparation on my part needed in order to conduct the Second Symphony [in Berlin]! To have to prepare a serious lecture to an important public would mean valuable time taken away from my regular job.

Yours ever
Michael

8 May 1970

Dear Ken

[. . .] Since getting back from Karlsruhe I've been 'under the weather', *wenn nicht fortsachlich krank* [if not actually ill]. I ought really to have had a holiday then instead of conducting. And it's pretty clear I've taken on too much conducting this year, and must learn again to find my limits. But I enjoy (so far) helping to run the Bath Festival and also, of course, the occasional conducting trips to America and the consequent holiday there.

I'm doing 2 further songs (for tenor and small orch. ensemble) which will be added to that which ends Act 2 of *The Knot Garden*, for the character Dov. The one already written (in the opera) is a kind of envoi. The 2nd will be a kind of *Wanderjahre*. The 3rd will be a Return (to the town) ending with a very moving quote from a poem of Pasternak. The words are mine (to the 'poems') and will interest you when you see them (I mean you personally, I guess). If I can I hope to finish this small piece (a parergon to the opera) by end of the summer and so, at long last, set down to the new Symphony [No. 3] which I've had in my head for many years and which might be a stunner. I'll tell you more about it when we see you in Dortmund.

[. . .] Tomorrow I go to spend a day with Peter Hall to discuss how *The Knot Garden* will look, at Cov. Gdn. Exciting!

Herzlichst
Michael

* Pressed for time, Tippett resorted to using material from *King Priam* for the third movement.

31 July 1970

Dear Heinz [Schneider-Schott],

I am afraid that moving into this new house [Nocketts] has meant that lots of papers got mislaid. This morning I found the invitation to the Schott 200th anniversary celebrations in Mainz. Did I ever reply to this? It fell in the Bath Festival period, so I could not have come. But I had certainly meant to send you congratulations and greetings.

As your uncle [Willy Strecker] knew already I have always had a continuing affection and loyalty to the 200-year-old house. And am proud to be one of the house composers.

Probably I grow old and forgetful. Please accept my apologies. Composition alone seems to go on undiminished.

With all good wishes.

Yours

Michael

2 September 1971

Dear Mr [Lawrence] Kelly,

I will certainly be guided by you as to the better sense to do *The Midsummer Marriage* in 1972 [in Dallas]. It seems good to have approached the National Opera Institute.

I am disturbed by your deciding to cut the opera. I am not dead against cutting, and indeed the version on the records is cut. Beyond this there were at one time some more minor cuts in one of the Covent Garden revivals, but the number of minutes gained was not very great. It was then seen clearly at Covent Garden that further cutting would only make the music and action incomprehensible and by so doing make the opera seem longer. The point really is that I cannot see what would be served by a première in America of *The Midsummer Marriage* in a mutilated form. I could not as a responsible living composer agree. I would just have to wait till the American 'theatrical habits and mores' were more courageous!

I am wondering indeed whether I answered your initial query, as to whether I thought *The Midsummer Marriage* was the best of my operas to present, correctly. Would it be better to go for *The Knot Garden* which is so condensed and fast an opera that it plays at 1 1/2 hours at most, and yet seems a big piece? If you have not seen a libretto and score, I am sure John Ardoin has both, and he has also a radio tape of the Covent Garden production.

If you still decide to risk *The Midsummer Marriage* the possible Jenifers over this side are Elizabeth Harwood and Rae Woodland, i.e. with voices big enough for your large theatre. The second name is most likely to be free.

I have been thinking about conductors, because it means the most of all to have someone who knows my idiom and style. The possibilities here, for the fall of 1972, would be Charles Groves, of the Royal Liverpool Philharmonic, and the young David Atherton, of Covent Garden.

Who had you in mind as a producer?

With all good wishes.

Yours sincerely,

Michael Tippett

6 August 1981

Dear Ken,

I'm just sending Clifford Caesar, in Schott's London, the first 2 sections back of your German vocal score [*The Mask of Time*] – with some minor comments. All works out very well it seems to me; ignorant that I am as to real German.

Remains the question of the first section title: Presence. This was never ideal, in English already. There is no good English word for simple, ontological reality. The acceptance or postulation of the universe as 'just there', rather than matters of how or why a creator or a big bang. The words Being and Existence tend to be thought of as concerning living things only. The Given has no poetic resonance at all. Presence does work to some extent.

Gegenwart is surely only temporal – the Present (in time). It must be both temporal and spatial. Someone has suggested that *Presenz* has this double meaning, like the English.

Love to you both

Michael

Francesca Allinson

Tippett met Francesca (Fresca) Allinson (1902–45) through his cousin,
Phyl Kemp, in 1925. Allinson shared Tippett's political sympathies –
she was the conductor of the Clarion Glee Club, a choir affiliated to
the London Labour Choral Union – and their discussions ranged
widely over such subjects as pacifism, homosexuality, music, literature
and theatre. As well as introducing him to Purcell's music, Allinson
enlisted Tippett's help with her research on the influence of Irish folk
music on English folk song, and the two worked briefly on a joint
project, The Irish Contribution to English Traditional Tunes. *(It was*
never completed, and Tippett eventually presented it to the Vaughan
Williams Memorial Library in London.) Their personal connection
was a close one and their relationship of extreme importance to
Tippett, according to whom they even contemplated marriage at one
stage. (Though Allinson was a lesbian, both of them wanted children.)
Besides offering each other emotional support and commiserating
over their health problems, it is clear from the letters that Allinson
helped Tippett both financially and with his domestic needs, especial-
ly in the wartime deprivations. In 1945, in despair over the war and
her state of health, she drowned herself in the river Stour at Clare,
Suffolk. Tippett dedicated the Fantasy Sonata (later renamed Piano
Sonata No. 1) to her, and the song cycle The Heart's Assurance *to her*
memory.

[winter 1938]

Fresca dear,

[. . .] I'm all frozen up here, but when I am engrossed in the work, I
am very happy. Wilf [Franks] is off on the razzle for another period it
seems, and that gives me odd twinges when I feel very ready for some
sort of love that is much more clearly reciprocal. However, perhaps
such dreams are just idealisms and illusions. Meanwhile the music
seems to be very productive. I've been reading Dent's book on 17th-

century English opera.* Most interesting. The great hope soon now is to get rid of my depressing classes and write and brood and study more consistently on end. I must see if I can save enough to do without the classes during next July and so get a month to myself on a clear run. The great difference since the (your!) piano work [Fantasy Sonata] is the greater consciousness of what I'm doing and less 'inflation' to borrow Jung's term. Consequently the great art in its proper sense. Whether the piano work is really going to prove the turning point between the compulsive writing of adolescent experiments and tormentings and the more assured writing of maturity, is yet to be seen. It's possible. I'm getting less ashamed of the simplicity which is returning into the work – e.g. less 'afraid', because it isn't following the stream of European atonalism. Consequently the style is becoming more uniform, though there are still jagged edges and crudities not completely assimilated. The new work [Concerto for Double String Orchestra] is like the piano work in that it is direct and doesn't beat about the bush and is clear in form – I know what I'm doing at each point. The slow, middle movement is being written now and it's entirely diatonic and simple and we shall see if it succeeds.

The snow and the cold makes London seem miles and miles away. It's a lovely feeling and the work proceeds.

All my love to you both and to my own Cornwall. A Merry and Happy Christmas [. . .].

Michael

[1940]

Fresca dear,

It's certainly a trifle uncanny – after writing you, in the aft[ernoon] I went to Oxted to shop, to the accompaniment of an air warning – after tea at home I got down to work feeling as I thought a little oppressed by the heat and by an urge to get some music done and eventually sat down at the table to sketch out the first 4 fugal entries of the pogrom [in *A Child of Our Time*] – as I did this I heard the sound of German planes and firing – I had the oddest of feelings as I deliberately completed the 24 bars and then the restlessness was too much and I went to chat to Ben [Lewis] – the warning then went and

* Edward J. Dent, *Foundations of English Opera: A Study of Musical Drama in England in the Seventeenth Century* (1928).

Bron [Wilson] next suddenly cried 'look at those things dropping from a plane over there' and to the sound of gun-firing a fight began over Oxted and over our heads, as it seemed.

Mercifully I have a feeling that this of last night has slightly broken the charm and that I can (and must) go ahead as fast as I am able.

I have written off to order Grove[*'s Dictionary of Music and Musicians*, 4th edition] today and paid £7 10s down for the most of it. I feel it will give me plenty of reading matter on my own art – a thing I'm much in need of every now and then – and at the moment especially.

In case of accident I might say, that all the 4 [*sic*] early scores that matter (Symphony [in B flat], Quartet [String Quartet No. 1], Blake [*A Song of Liberty*], Piano Sonata [Fantasy Sonata], Str. Concerto [Concerto for Double String Orchestra]) are also to be found in the vaults of [Schott] Mainz. The only new score is the oratorio [*A Child of Our Time*] – Freddy May's father has the clean score up to No. 16. (I have a pencil score here, pretty accurate, and a piano reduction to No. 8.) The numbers I am writing from 16 onwards now are of course only in pencil on my desk. If anything horrid should happen, I think the first 16 numbers are still worth preserving AMDG – and as far as English music is concerned, for the hint of modern English recitative. But I am not anticipating such trouble, nor have any premonitions forced themselves to my notice.

I shall come over again sometime when I get too restless and life too ominous. Ben is on holiday here for a week – which is friendly, though a little war-minded. The main job is to get the pogrom done and the 'Go Down Moses' – by then of course, London classes will begin again.

Love –

M.

[1940]

Fresca dear,

[. . .] There were two big bonks here last night which turn out to be bombs beside the Hurst Green factory – unloading, I fancy. Sooner or later I feel we shall least be shot out of our beds! And I want by the way to farm out various copies of the oratorio [*Child of Our Time*] music – I should think that perhaps your cellar is the best place for the ink full-score if I keep the pencil one here. The pencil one is accurate except for some details of bowing etc and some notes – I shall have to show someone how it could be copied from – there are one or two shorthand devices. Not that these bonks affect me very much having got very fatalistic and re-believing in my star and that of my nearest and dearest. They woke me up, but I was too sleepy to consider their implication – and they were not so near as the [Madame] Tussaud bang was to [Hugo] Strecker.

I think I've got the better method for redoing the 'Go Down Moses' – so that'll be done today and tomorrow – and then I'm putting the 4 new numbers thus completed on to the ink score – partly not to have all the ink copying at the end and partly to have a double copy – there may have to be minor, or even major alterations afterwards. As soon as I've copied in ink these new numbers I shall move on to the final 4 of Part II.

I may come over to see you in the week if I don't go to town – I am not going to town if the stations are being bombed because it'll be such a nuisance getting back, and also soon I suppose I shall have to go to town for and with Edric [Maynard] – and Denis's first Tribunal can't be long delayed at Fulham. I'll send a message through Joe if I'm coming over.

[. . .] Please will you keep this week's *Times Lit. Sup.* which I left on the piano – it has a devastating review of [T. S.] Eliot's 'East Coker' which I brought for Den [Newton] to see, but I haven't read the other contents, so please don't throw away if you can find it still.

Much love
Michael

[1940]

Fresca dear,

[. . .] I'm off down to Oxted this afternoon to get one or two necessary stores for the season (before too much tax) – e.g. type-paper, envelopes etc – (I've asked Freddie May in town to get me some score paper also) – also going to replace the breakages of my blue china set – and the knives and spoons etc which are needed – all this preparatory to sitting down and paying off the bills at leisure – not that I am going to buy very much really – I am going to get a reasonable porridge-saucepan – the double ones – proper porridge is not the quick Quaker rubbish, but true oatmeal! That means soaking the meal in cold water during the day in the inner saucepan and cooking in the bain-marie in the evening for heating in the morning – I commend the system to you for the lads – one makes plenty at a time and the first breakfaster leaves the bain-marie just on a faint gas for the next comer and so on.

I'm annoyed at the purchase tax because it will automatically take so much per cent of one's money into the war game [. . .].

I see my way clear musically now to the end of Part VI [of *A Child of Our Time*] – this ought to mean a fairly continuous flow. I got underway with experimenting over the 'Go Down Moses' spiritual, hit on the right, and very moving, manner of setting, only to find eventually that I'd left milk on the stove which had boiled to a disgusting smell – such is the way of creation!! It does look rather as though the next phase of the war is blowing up, so that the pogrom is in time. I see that USA seems to imagine an attempt at invasion as possible – or at least is not prepared to believe that we are all that stronger in the air battle now raging – sometimes I can believe an invasion as part of this last phase in Europe, though I find it terribly difficult to make sense of militarily. It appears to me too risky and difficult to be worth it – but there again one may not have the real facts as to the relative armed strength etc-and some diversional attempt at trouble here may be a necessary part of the whole military movement against the British power in Europe [. . .].

I shall be a week or two on the pogrom and the 'Egypt Land' spiritual – then I come to the boy's singing in his prison – the mother's desolatory solo – the alto's observations on the general break-through of the demonic elements and the 'cry for peace' of 'By and By' – this will be reached end of Oct., early November or a bit later – (the Part II and the meditation on meanings will be in the late autumn). It is very possible that these last numbers of Part II will take place during the general Battle of Britain – and that possibly 'By and By' will correspond to an armistice! But I wouldn't like to predict so exactly.

All love –
Michael

[1940]

Fresca dear,

[. . .] There are one or two unforeseen expenses which I am incurring – apart from the records and some more ones if I can find what I

73

am looking for, there is the extra score of the oratorio, and two books which I feel I need very badly for the slowly maturing conception of the 'masque' [early drafts for *The Midsummer Marriage*]. If you can manage to spare a £10 that would be wonderful – or half that if you can't. I am going to finish the clothes problem on Friday when I go to town – and 2 towels I need.

[. . .] I'm deep in the technical problems of the music to these 4 numbers, and so it's much better with me. And I know quite well that the experiences dealt with in Part III are not particularised of the war at all and that it will be wrong if I get them tied up. Part II finishes the 'journalistic' music, even if the journalistic events continue.

I've written David [Ayerst] to see if I can go there for a break after completion of Part II and whether it's quiet!

Love –

M.

[1941]

Fresca darling –

Your letter and enclosure came this morning and all is very well. Rimingtons are doing fine with the records [Fantasy Sonata, played by Phyllis Sellick] and I shall send you a set from myself next week. I shall perhaps bring it on Mon. week – for the Mon. is the day – I thank Veronica [Allinson] for offering hospitality for the night – that would be lovely – and I'll pop home by the early Tues. train – also I may bring you a very early Christmas gift in case I don't see you later – I think I *must* give you *The Waves* [novel by Virginia Woolf, 1931] because it's so much our own book in some curious intimate way. I'll try and get it in London on Thurs.

Another nice story: I was getting on a bus to Morley at W'minster [Westminster] on Thurs., and a man, a commercial traveller I am pretty certain by his manner and case, hovered round then said: You are Mr T. – I've just come down on my job from Birmingham and have just bought a set of your records. He'd recognised me from the photo! He was so excited at the meeting he couldn't take his eyes off me and I was very gauche. He'd had it recommended by a pianist friend in Brhm [Birmingham]. He was so exactly Eliot's new lower-middle-class culture! and a very nice chap into the bargain. This makes the publication ever more hopeful on the sales side – but there is no paper for it – Hugo [Strecker] rang up yesterday – his call-up papers had arrived and he told me the news of the sonata, when settling the various things at issue, before he went. (He's gone into the Pioneers of necessity.) I want to talk to you about the possibility of engraving via America. I'm going to explore the price of photographing a few copies here. As I am putting up the dibs, I may as well go ahead if sensible; Hugo won't mind.

[. . .] The man [Walter] Bergmann who played the thorough-bass at Morley for the Purcell is quite a find to me. He knows that period in and out. He's also one of those careful Germans who spot any missing dot a mile off. He's doing the piano reduction of the new work [*A Child of Our Time*] for Hugo and me. He's so good, that I am going to give all the oratorio parts and scores to him to collate etc, as a private job. (He's an out-of-work refugee and an unusually nice one.) I'll post you the *Times* stuff on Mon. We appeared again [in concert reviews] ([H. C.] Colles it is) yesterday, drawing the moral. But I want to show them both to [Walter] Goehr tomorrow, when I see him again in the middle of BBC broadcasts from Maida Vale. [. . .]

Love,
M.

[1941]

Fresca darling –

[. . .] The fellow Walter Bergmann who plays the thorough-bass at Morley for me is now [working] in Schott's shop. He is an enthusiast for such music and also deep in all the publications and editions – (he's finding the most fascinating German stuff in the back of the shop – heaps of material – the equivalent of the stuff we like in English – all brought out in the last 50 years in Germany – Schott's have specimen copies etc) if you wrote to him at Schott & Co., 48 Gt Marlboro St, W.1, he'd love to hunt around for you and knows so many of the likely folk personally. If you write direct it will save me being an intermediary, which is difficult now because I have so much to get on with for Morley and my own affairs.

[. . .] I saw somewhere in a note on Frank Howes of *The Times*, that he was a specialist in English song in his young days, being editor of the *Journal of the EFDS* [*English Folk Dance Society*] from 1927. If you think any good his address is Newbridge Mill, Standlake, Oxon. He would have a pretty good bibliography at his fingertips.

The early mediaeval stuff I told you I was looking at, discusses the origin of musical counterpoint as arising out of the necessity of uniting differing metrical poems – trochees with anapests etc. I can't help thinking that one, perhaps secondary influence, will be in the nature of English verse rhythms before and then after the classical (Latin) influence of the renaissance. Anyhow it's an intriguing business and brings forward a further line between verse and music. But I can't get the verse rhythms into my head – so I can't keep consciousness of what I am doing when setting verse myself – especially [Gerard Manley] Hopkins, whose rhythms are beyond me. Not that I think that is the true *musical* way of proceeding – declamation is really a dramatic art – song is something else, I can't quite get straight – a capella singing is a branch of musical art and thoroughly destroys the verse rhythms. I shall return to the Eliot songs in the end.

The [*Man with the*] *Seven Daughters* is going by the board I fear. The masque gradually accumulates. I feel I might do a tiny one-act 'classic' opera as a tour de force, but a full scale opera buffa is not really me I think, because not essentially about the things I am deeply interested in *socially* and spiritually etc. Add those reasons to the hopelessness of full-scale opera, sung drama, in England, even if I really did cast away from the pseudo-Wagner stuff and get back to the true line. That seems to me best done in a little work – perhaps even something which might curtain-raise or fall to a *Dido* performance.

I am living a very full life at present. *Eine Blütezeit*, without the romance! [. . .]

Love

Michael

You come in on my complimentary tickets – unless we find them too close. Will phone Joe. Edric [Maynard] is to go to Layard if job found near Oxford – and some of us will guarantee a limited no. of sessions with Layard. I think he is vegetating in peasant form and perhaps for the best.

[1941]

Fresca darling,

I'm too excited generally this morning to be coherent – things seem to be panning out so ridiculously. I've written Edward [Lockspeiser?] and sent a 'blurb' and a *Child* – because he must be in with Bliss and the British Council and the *Child* is exactly the goods for broadcast to America – or one of the 'parts' – meanwhile we're feeling round towards the Hallé and a Manchester performance.

Next a set [the Fantasy Sonata recording] is to go by plane to H.M. Press Attaché in Stockholm – this comes from [Marcus?] Dods – who also says that Eddie Sackville-West is all over the records last week, saying he'd like to meet me. At Stockholm they may be played at a diplomatic party – think of it! I hoot with amusement.

Finally I've been ever so much touched by the enclosed letter from an engineer and the appreciation of his girl, whom I don't know. It moves me more than Stockholm. I've got a very nice review to send you of Scott Goddard [see p. 24], when I get hold of it again. [. . .]

[. . .] I can't get to see you yet because I must finish the new work [*A Child of Our Time*] – (another 3 weeks hard) – and then take a spell of moving around again.

Give all love to Jude [Wogan] and thank her more and again for the apples.

I am going to renew the offer to Schott's to capitalise on the engraving of our sonata – I made it originally to Strecker *père* in Mainz. It seems the way out.

Love and love –

Michael

[1941]

[. . .] Am despondent today both about life, the war and my own music. I'm even inclined to doubt the wisdom of being with Schott's since this struggle to get into the clique of BBC etc is so hopeless for the composer himself to undertake. My only hope is that it will be better after the war when Hugo gets back and the father [Willy Strecker] comes over from Germany. Bergmann anyhow has seen the light and is trying to save me what he can so that I can write and not have to chase around trying to place the stuff. Steffens promises me copies of the [Fantasy] Sonata if he can get cover-paper, and quite soon. If that actually happens I want to hand over the publicity to you and others – e.g. send Clifford Curzon for instance copy and records. So much could go on while I was in quod.

However presumably I shall recover my serenity in a day or two and believe that if I go on writing it won't matter if the acknowledgment is incessantly delayed.

One day the oratorio will get done and come into its own. There's so much I want to get down on paper. Why did I get so entangled at Morley?!

Much love
M.

[1941]

Fresca darling,

It's when you are away like this that I miss you most. I suppose by now we belong to each other in some particular way, though whether our manner of living corresponds, I don't know. I think I'd like it if you lived and worked here at times for more than the snatch[ed] day. [. . .]

I fancy these notions are due to the more particular quietness of the cottage now – with everyone away, the war, and the wintry weather. Since the war there's been precious little opportunities for congregation of the 'boys' and various sorts of parties – I suppose that will come back again when London returns to its magnificence. I mean by all that, that there's a side of me which is in tune too with your gaiety – though I tend naturally to withdraw more to browse. Perhaps the main trouble is just that you aren't in London, or E.G. [East Grinstead], so that I can't go to the cottage as from seeing you in some typically London-you house. It's good having David [Ayerst] in London – but he is not you! There now – that['s] enough. Don't worry at such a mood. You know how I go from colour to colour – like the Yorkshire fells. And so of course do you. Actually in my inside I'm still on the gay, light side, and working awfully well. Evelyn [Maude] comes back today – classes begin next week. With God's good luck this firefighting nonsense will clear itself up or misfire – that is, appear as only a subjective fear. And this monstrous war at least cross the half-way line. Oh, what won't peace be like – a spree? sure – somewhere and all together.

Love
Michael

[1941]

Fresca dear,

Don't trouble about writing – it will all be easier by talk when we meet. I miss you rather, and hope you'll come and stay for a bit later on. David incidentally thinks I'm suffering a bit from loneliness, but at the moment (that may be) I am living at my creative best and up early.

[. . .] Also the national registration for fire-watching in Sept. seems to bring me in head-on conflict with the authorities. I think I can register but only more or less to refuse to watch – I fancy I am too much wound up in my artistic life and hence feel these other things as desperately disruptive – am raked to them. [. . .]

If work goes frightfully well, as it is, I'll come and see you soon – will it be OK? Also, will you ask Den [Newton] if he could see to a new (cheaper paper) printing of the *Child* for me? if I sent a corrected copy.

Love, and love –

M.

[Frank] Howes of *The Times* 'definitely' likes the [Fantasy] Sonata and will review there.

[July 1941]

Fresca dear,

[. . .] I'm becoming exceedingly tired through too much class work – I've refused to do any in August – so have 2 weeks more to go. I was up in town yesterday Sunday to play oratorio to a man Goehr, who's a friend of Hugo's, works for BBC, conducting and arranging – a first-class musician – it was a great delight, though *very* tiring, playing to him – and he was much taken with the oratorio, including the spirituals – and absurdly complimentary – says there isn't a note of English music in it! – but stems straight from a tradition of Bach, Handel and late Brahms!!! *Vier ernste Gesänge* – which I don't know very well. He thinks that good and suitable to the general theme. Anyhow it cheered me and reassured Hugo and is another door through into the professional music world. I'm loaning him the full score so that he can amuse himself examining the patterned ariosos. I hope to interest him in the Double Concerto [Concerto for Double String Orchestra]. [. . .]

The little Karl [Hawker] seems intending to go to London on the run for a bit – to have a room at Billy's – who is very lonely there. As far as I am concerned, in Papageno's words: *Ich bleibe ledig!* A gentle and occasional liaison shall we say.

Much love and to Jude [Wogan].

Michael

[1941]

Fresca darling,

I too have conked-out, though not so completely. I played [Edward] Lockspeiser the *Child* under a growing 'flu and went to bed at Layard's and then home here instead of Wed.'s classes – I went to town Thursday – Friday was OK – but today have been in bed till now, am up and sitting in complete lethargy by the fire. And the new pf.–orch. work [Fantasia on a Theme of Handel] is still not ink-copied – however I ought to be able to begin again tomorrow – otherwise Oxford was a success and the children nice ones – especially Harvey and Angela, Aubrey [Russ] and John [Amis]'s pair of friends. Edward is very much under the weather and the analysis is sucking him to perdition. His woman on the contrary went to John Layard for her curious tricks of missing bars and beats in singing, and John helped her in 12 sittings to a most lovely set of Jungian, religious dreams – the last one a real miracle – John showed me the analysis and has the permission to publish. As Jung said somewhere, whatever the dream meant to the dreamer *es sagte mir unendlich viel* [it told me an endless amount]. I'll tell it you when I see you.

I think the broadcast date to USA is Dec. 11; but so far I'm too lethargic to write to New York to anyone – I shall write eventually to Sari Dienes. I've refound Paul [Dienes] and will tell you about him when we meet.

[. . .] I've just finished *To the Lighthouse* [novel by Virginia Woolf, 1927] – such exquisite and mature art – I am not surprised the price was what it was for her. Will write again more fully later.

Love –

Michael

[. . .]

[November 1941]

Fresca darling –

I hope at last you're better. I've begun to pull out of 'flu and colds and feel more normal. There's some idea of my going down to Cambridge to see all the boys on Dec. 6–7 – staying with Karl [Hawker]. But principally I'd like to see you. There's so much accumulation of news.

I'm now more vegetable-like again and am trying to finish off the letters due over the [Fantasy Sonata] records. I'm writing to Solomon, and Harriet Cohen – who was the pianist you thought to send to? Was it Clifford Curzon? he seems to me very close to our humanitarian views as he has signed a national petition about night bombing. Are you in a state to deal with it later – also can you get hold of an address for me which would reach Arthur Waley, whom I met through Phyl [Kemp] and who is very keen on new music. I had a card from N.Y. from Peggy, and it seems as though the score [Concerto for Double String Orchestra] is at last reaching N.Y. But I don't hold much hope for it. I'm thinking that the polyphonic attitude from which it was written is not an easy matter to get from a score when looked at with our usual eyes. The rhythms look innocent and even ineffective – the play and tension between them is not felt from the score without an instinct for it. I'm reluctantly being driven to realise this.

The new pf. and orch. work [Fantasia on a Theme of Handel] is completed and is quite 'tough' – that may make a break-through, and I sincerely hope it does. There is not any overdose of polyrhythm in it, but some very nice bits which will perhaps whet the appetite or stimulate the curiosity. I've felt rather isolated lately, and see that that's a usual effect of having an individual point of view. As you remark – or imply – I need good friends very badly.

Meanwhile I am trying to temper myself to face the showdown with the authorities soon. If I am so wound up in music that the struggle on the social plane gets me a-feared, then I shan't fight it well and be much more hurt if it comes to real sacrifice. There's the threat now of a total conscription into the Home Guard because the firewatching has proved ineffective. Willy nilly – that means a collision, because the H.G. has to shoot etc. It has this advantage, that the fight is absolutely clear cut – but I suspect that the penalties for refusal will be clear cut too – so I'm trying to face up to it and to make the best of it. For instance – if I had to go away for a bit to be entertained by H[is] Maj[esty] in a quod – would you officially reside in the cottage and keep it warm for my return and out of the billeting hands etc? It'll be most likely a matter of time and/or so many months. On the other hand so many of the lads on the land will be up against it too that the nonsense may be too general to pursue too far. I haven't found out the facts of all this yet – so far it's press rumour, but pretty correct.

Write me a card saying how you are and what your plans are. You seem far too far away.

Love
M.

[1941/2]

Fresca dear,

[. . .] I've long wanted to try an experimental hand at an opera with recitative and all and have just spent the morning on a fantastic plot to be called: *The Man with the Seven Daughters*. He's a widower, the daughters are called Gert, and Daisy and Doris, and various names and all go to work of sorts except the littlest – who goes to the secondary school. The first scene is breakfast during which all the daughters get ready to go to work and eventually the littlest goes to school and the man is left to wash up – but he's more likely to read the morning paper till the pub opens – (of course you realise at once that having seven daughters he is the most unconscious man in creation). The next scene is probably in the pub, because the man's only crony is the barman and the barman's wife – a deep bass I expect and a shrill mezzo – and here the man relates his woes and plays darts possibly with members of the chorus, one of whom is probably Jeffrey [Mark] – but the scene comes to an inglorious end when he is fetched away by the littlest daughter who wants her dinner and he leaves amid the scandalised exclamations of the bar in general – one realises he is a wastrel and refuses to carry out his duties. It is probably Saturday and all the daughters have their half day – and in any case the real event is the arrival of the handsome cousin from the North – he is a lyrical tenor and is very attractive of course. There ensues the most terrible complications among all the daughters as you can perceive, and I haven't thought them out yet, but in the end to all their chagrin he takes the littlest daughter to the cinema! At this the other six daughters turn and rend the father and to such a degree that they do him in – (he becomes completely unconscious, sinking into the great mother) – naturally, though none had suspected it, the man is really the only centre of the household and once dead, all the daughters 'fly apart' – they may fetch a doctor and the news flies round, and the barman comes to grieve and various strangers from the bar and when the chorus is assembled they are very shocked at the heartless ways the daughters are going on, who are preparing to leave in their various ways – but beer and chips fetched from the fish shop lead to an out-size Mozartian or perhaps Verdian finale, on which they all go out and leaving the sozzled barman sentimentalising over his dead friend.

I feel this is a suitable offset to the *Child of Our Time* and ought to go a long way to restoring the balance. 'Take a boozy short leave of your girls on the shore' as the chorus says in *Dido*. All in that spirit – and think of seven-voice female recitative!!!!!!!

Much love to you both,
Michael

[1941/2]

Fresca darling –

Life's quite mad. On Mon. these people (ENSA) [Entertainments National Services Association] offered me the Musical Organiser of Northern Ireland Command at £500 p.a. I refused!! – It meant no composition and whole time organising of pretty retrograde music – so I chose to be poor and free. David [Ayerst] agreed with me. I fished him out of the W.O. [War Office] to advise. He thought it not me at all and inconsistent with my sort of quality.

It would have been an easier decision if I weren't financially a little strained – you see – this constant seeing people who all live on big salaries (Goehr etc) and the train fares etc, etc, and I counting the pennies. So if you are flush it would help a bit. I haven't dared find out what the bank thinketh! But I'm very careful. I need to get some new clothes – pyjamas and pants – and I've got to have a crown on a tooth that disappeared into my throat. Meanwhile it's nice to feel that one's 'market' worth is as high as that even in the 'second' profession – and the turn has come in the first. D[avid] thought it stupid to go away from London for the next 5 or 6 years. The Reservation business is one of my usual scares. D. and Evelyn [Maude] both think that the H.G. [Home Guard] nonsense will have to be under Military Service Act and the conchies left as before. But I have to get myself used to the idea of trouble if it is to come. And I don't really fear it. I don't really think I'm for it either. So don't worry. [. . .]

Love and lots and lots

M.

Is it very wrong to refuse ENSA and depend on good friends? Evelyn said 'not wrong'.

6 February 1942

Fresca darling –

Hope you do come up Monday – I want to see you badly and I am up Tuesday, Wed., Thurs., sleeping in town Tues.–Wed. – the first with Mrs [Eva] Hubback, the second at David [Ayerst]'s – or *anderswo*. The Hubback date is due to Tribunal matters – I went last Tuesday and to everyone's surprise lost! Non-combatant military duties. There was the initial shock that a person of my quality can't get by while the Wilfs [Franks] etc can – but subsequently when I got home and began to realise in my body that the music must go whichever way I travel, I cried like a child. Now I feel better, but lost. David and everyone almost else, is trying to get me to compromise – but I am realising that mere social work won't replace the music – only pacifist witness against the whole madness can do so. I am going through a considerable moral crisis and on the issue will depend whether I can witness outside or inside quod. I am not frightened by quod any more – but my friends are for me. I intend to do that thing which will most clearly show the measure of the world débâcle, now that my own island has been shattered. It will only be for a time, whatever I decide to do. Mercifully, as Evelyn says, a portion of my musical self has got out into the big world and Goehr and others are willing to hold its baby hand while poppa is away from home. I want very much to have the knowledge that things will go on for that side of me by my friends while I am doing my other, enforced job of witness – that will make everything ever so much easier. Goehr has already assured me – and he is very grateful for all I have done for him – he intends to play my music wherever he can, especially if I am not there. So I shan't feel so desperately lost and lonely. Look – ring me when you can and we'll meet Tuesday or Wed. or Thurs.

love

M.

[1942]

Fresca dear,

[. . .] Work has gone very well and the 4tet moves [revisions to String Quartet No. 2] But the prison walls worry me and sometimes dry everything up. I am frightened in my body, though unafraid in my mind. Evelyn seems to think it may finally come to grips with all the long traditions of fear, from childhood up.

I saw Nancy Browne. You can't 'offer' anything, and you can't expect a headmaster to give you a job for to evade the Tribunal decisions! So it's a matter of pleading 'reasonable excuse' in the work I do, and a very slender chance of its being accepted.

Was glad to hear Jude [Wogan]'s voice on the phone and what she said. Hope it all comes out alright and a love based on the great quiet after the storm, and not with admixture of hysteria any more.

Yesterday and today am hampered by an inner chill – very horrid. Blake always got such whenever he went to N. London – Hampstead countryside etc. He didn't believe in 'discipline' for this ailment because he didn't think the Lily should learn of the Rose.

Much love –
Michael

1942

Fresca darling,

I've been ever so much better since seeing you. And I think I got a lot of kick out of hearing the 4tet [String Quartet No. 2] played well. Anyhow I seem to have got back some poise, and hope I shan't be so stupid and querulous when such a thing happens next time. One ought to be able to keep one's affections to oneself – at any rate in a time when such grim horrors are elsewhere.

I've finished the Hillary* – and I didn't like it as a book, or its sentiments – but it satisfied my curiosity. As David suggests, he probably exaggerates his own unregenerateness, like all 'conversion' accounts. But he certainly was a shit. I could hardly believe the hospital account. Is that what being an officer comes to? It ought to be sobering to the RAF worshippers, both as to the sort of men and the terrible price paid. It made me feel quite thankful for the little Den

* *The Last Enemy* (1942), autobiography of the fighter pilot Richard Hillary.

[Newton] – the unheroic, pacifist, escapist, anything you like – but with gentleness. Did I say to you before? I found myself writing someone that 'it is odd to feel oneself tough *because* one is gentle'. I have got round to feeling things like that. I mean of course an inner toughness and outer gentleness. And that hitches on to the notion of the beautiful things managing to get fashioned and preserved in a world of destructiveness. So that it all clicks together in a certain whole – in face of this, that. That I take to be step 1. Step 2 is some form of awareness that there is a different sort of whole combining this and that, which one esteems and accepts and reaches after while knowing and accepting that outwardly one has to live that and not this. Parts of all this high-fallutin' are admirably discussed in *Grey Eminence*,* and helped me to get clear. Anyhow I know that the source from which the beauty springs is where the gentleness springs and that the source is not completely of this world in the ordinary sense and that to be in constant contact with that source is life, despite any outward death, or prison. And it's because of all this awareness in my better moments that I won't seek to escape or fight a way out of anything that ought to come. I had a moment's jealousy I think on learning that Britten had Stuart Morris, head of the PPU [Peace Pledge Union], to speak for him at appeal, Willy Walton to vouch for his musical quality, and that, before the same Tribunals as myself, he got unconditional. I am pretty certain now that it is just, somehow or other. Neither here nor there. It does not matter who is taken and who remains. Nor is the retreat into any spiritual pride at being 'fake', permissible. But it's a considerable danger. I have felt, for some time, very warm to Britten and would like to meet him. I shall try to do so.

Eliot, at my request, has sent me *Midnight Hour*† by Nicodemus – a book that you will want to read eventually. Eliot grieves at my pacifism but rejoices at its uncompromising quality.

Goehr has gone back to his original idea; Bach, *Kunst der Fuge*, Mozart, Serenade, Seiber, work for ob. and strings and some other modern. He wanted to do the slow movement of the Double Concerto, but I feel, despite the temptation, I ought not to appear on the bills again. He also wanted a Turina work, which I have turned

* Aldous Huxley's biography (1941) of the French monk Père Joseph.
† Neville Channing-Pierce's journal for 1 May – 30 September 1941 (published pseudonymously in 1942).

down. I've sent him instead the score of the Stravinsky *Dumbarton Oaks*, which would be ideal.

Wish very much you were going to hear the 4tet [String Quartet No. 2] because I'd like your judgment on it. But I dare say we'll get it done somehow else: BBC or Nat. Gallery. The BBC are nibbling at the [Orlando] Gibbons recital. That would be grand.

Morley are a bit anxious about the initial payment of the Stratton, so I'm trying to turn in my guarantee ahead. If you can do same they would be grateful. The concerts won't pay their way but I believe they'll do their job, and are good publicity.

Mrs Hubback is now quite convinced I shall be let free – the eternal optimist. I am more sober! I've had an income tax which is staggering – £24 on an earning of £176 (including sales to Schott's). [. . .]

M.

[1942]

Fresca darling,

I thought of ringing you last night, but I realise I don't know the geography of Cyril [Allinson]'s phone and whether a call would get you. I came back from town yesterday, and after all this constant palaver of seeing people and strange beds and winter and the need to get Goehr's new score finished for him so that I can start my *a cappella* motets [Two Madrigals: *The Source*, *The Windhover*], I couldn't face any more travelling, nor Karl [Hawker] and the boys – I'm growing middle-aged! So I sent him a wire – then had a telephone call to go today, Sat., to take the Goldsmiths' Choral Union rehearsal of the Beethoven Mass, for 2 guineas. Reluctantly, thinking of the oratorio, I accepted – it will be odd to handle 100 voices – which they get on average at rehearsal. I think I shall prefer Morley and its 30.

Hugo [Strecker] is gone and so I came right up to old Steffens, the head of the firm in England. He says that Hugo has left an inextricable mess almost. For months I could never get any word about music, but only troubles about his latest girl. I had an idea that Steffens was OK really – so talked to him frankly and he on his side was in the same mood and there and then made out terms of contracts for the 3 MSS [Fantasy Sonata (Piano Sonata No. 1), String Quartet No. 2, Concerto for Double String Orchestra] other than the oratorio. I get £10 10s on account I believe. Any how it's very satisfactory. Steffens also is sending me with his recommendation to Stainer & Bell when the *a cappella* work is finished – which is generous – because they will be the only possible money-making sort of things in England at first.

I seem to have become Goehr's adviser at times. Also I have for the moment persuaded him to open 'my' concert with Gibbons string fantasies – 4 of them. He also does one Purcell 3-part sonata in another programme. He hopes to get BBC interested in recitals of unusual 17th- and 18th-cent. stuff that refugees have brought over and through me (and so you) to include English stuff – which is the right way to do it. He wants the English stuff in order to temper the German with the specific English quality – and that's I think where I come in myself and my own music with him – he does sincerely like it – so after the new work I shall show him the String Concerto [Concerto for Double String Orchestra] and try and help him to a concert with enough strings – because he hopes to go on concert-giving of an adventurous order, but without the colossal fees to 'draws' which he has had to do for the first lot in order to get away with it. To stand behind a conductor like this, is what I always hoped for and is like the Vienna of the old days – the composers and conductors and players approximating to a unified professional society. I expect it happens here each generation, but also there is something a bit more to it this time, because the whole standard of taste is wider and based on better scholarship and the BBC and others have taken the burden of the endless production of the hackneyed off our shoulders and left us free to collect up the audiences for the more discriminated stuff, without which no real high level of taste can obtain, and no good native music either.

[. . .] I see I shall be de-reserved in Jan. or Feb. and so will come naturally to Tribunal in the end. That doesn't worry me. Counting on an Appeal should I get into difficulties, I shall still be at large on Mar. 21. Also it is really fairly well on the cards that I shall get the exemption I want and all serene.

I shall order your records – for the moment to your account because they've got mine in a mess and tell me I owe £22, when I've paid everything on the nail. It's I think Aubrey [Russ]'s share in the recording fees and a muddle of my £15 cheque for my share.

Love
M.

[early 1942]

Fresca darling –

I was going to write you in any case even had I not got your letter and MS* this morning (I haven't looked at the latter yet) because I was thinking last night before I went to sleep and with a pang how much I have missed you all these long months – and the idea of seeing you soon is really exciting. If you were to be here in April that would be perfect – because I shall have finished the two *a cappella* pieces [Two Madrigals: *The Source*, *The Windhover*], will have been to Mother the weekend after the concert, will have the week's Easter break from classes during early April, and be so naturally ready to have company and of the one whom I most want to see. The appeal will probably happen at that time and it's quite possibly a success. I am quite decided and no further *arrière-pensées*. Evelyn [Maude] now tells me she never had any doubts but forbore to influence – yesterday I got a letter from Aubrey coming right out on the same side in no equivocal terms. I saw Eliot yesterday to announce the decision and he seemed both to expect it and to agree. Mrs Hubback has also come round. David [Ayerst] alone still demurs. Stephen Spender is in the Fire Service and is now on a scheme of adult education at the depôts. David would have me start choirs there, after enrolling myself in the NFS [National Fire Service]. But I just haven't the mind that can give up chorus in the Corps and Morley to do others in the NFS depôts to please the conscription laws. It strikes me as a lot of fake idealism (David's: 'doing something positive for the community and showing one's willingness to sacrifice' etc etc). Paul [Dienes] took a hand in a long letter saying how close he felt to me personally but how much he inclines to think Alan [Bush]'s organising of concerts of Russian music in the RAMC [Royal Army Medical Corps] for the sake of the 'new world' is the way out – because to sit in prison is negative. The nonsense of all this is that they all sink through the floor at the word prison and forget that the great merit of the institution seen even for my music, is that the period of sojourn there is *limited*, while the mucking about in the NFS etc is as long as the war lasts and probably after. I have since found out that the average sentence is 6 months or even 3 – meaning in fact 21/2 to 41/2, or something like that (good behaviour). So what the palaver is about I don't get – even

* Allinson's book on the origin of folk song.

if I wasn't sure that as a man and myself I must go this way. I have come to the conclusion that for certain people the whole idea of sticking to one's guns and gladly accepting the limited consequences – the punishment and then coming out again free and one's own master – is something which almost frightens them – because it reflects so easily on their own position. For David gives up his headmastership to go into the 'thick of the war', gets snowed into a cushy job at the W.O. [War Office], comes then to feel the whole war as useless and a lunacy, and there he may be for the best years of his life. The more efficient and responsible he becomes (as he must from his own quality) the less he will get himself out even afterwards. So oddly enough the way I intend to go is both proper to my character and certainly more sensible than to enter the network of conscription laws. So that is over.

I stayed the night with Eva Hubback – and we soon got boxed with the above subject and she came to my view. Then we talked of my personal life – including Wilf [Franks] and you. Wilf only by implication. She has also had the dual pull like Evelyn and us. She also told me of a happy marriage between people whose closeness was not primarily biological, and it was rather fun talking to her. Did you know (she told me) that she is a pure Jewess? She says she has never fallen for one of her own race though she likes them.

The Gibbons: I went to rehearsal and Goehr and I learnt a lot and sat for 2 hours afterwards re-scoring – this wasn't put into practice for the broadcast, but will be for the concert. It's the ineffectiveness to the naked ear of cellos without basses – and I hadn't realised how little the basses effect the counterpoint and how indeed they improve it. Finally we have a few bars coda of the 4th piece in which all 3 parts are doubled lines (like on the organs of the day) and incidentally my own Concerto [for Double String Orchestra]. I expect the broadcast remedied what Goehr needed by microphone placing – at the concert it will appose by scoring – though even in the broadcast I had scored some passages in 8ves and one in 3 8ves!! Violas, cellos, basses as in Mozart. I'm learning a lot about arrangement. Will write later about the MS when I've read it. I think that dress is OK. I like you to be *auffallend*, especially first public appearance after a long illness.

Love,
M.

[March 1942]

Fresca darling,

[. . .] The criticisms of the Fantasia [on a Theme of Handel] centre round the two first variations (you and Jeff Mark) and the bit in the middle which worried Edwin Evans and Sackville-West. I think their point is only really a matter of orchestration and due also to Goehr's sudden stoppage of the movement at a wrong point, which he felt he had to do to keep the orchestra clear. What you and Jeff felt about the start is more difficult, because in fact the first variation was acoustically not there, owing to some trick at performance – though Jeff gives other factual criticisms from the copy itself. But I can't decide till I hear it again. We are angling for a broadcast. I've also an idea to try Goehr at a concert in Cambridge and/or Oxford. Your feeling that the work was Continental is really my feeling too. And I think it's come for good. It's a sort of growing up inside. And it goes hand in hand with my increasing knowledge of the English tradition! I think the oratorio [*A Child of Our Time*] will sound even more Continental too – the point is that the temper is of that order, irrespective of myself. I am quite happy about this, and indeed welcome it. Not but what the English ancestry is really there all the time – it's the technical equipment that is growing intellectually maturer and consequently then English, as per Bax, V.W. [Vaughan Williams] and Ireland etc. See you Friday.

   Love
   Michael

[April/May 1942]
Grand Hotel, Plymouth

Fresca darling,

[. . .] Cambridge was an odd change. Karl [Hawker]'s brother is a very different kettle of fish. Dark and handsome – like a Brittany sailor – very serious and uncommunicative. Paints after [Walter] Sickert – Karl paints after Henry Moore. They share a little room and what with the girls Anne, Joan and Edwina, it's very much *La Bohème* atmosphere, on a simple scale. Karl and Den [Newton] were good friends till they got a trifle drunk. [. . .]

Saw Paul [Dienes], who is reconciled to prison and offers to get me books if I need them – also gave me a set of records of a Prokofiev Violin Concerto.

Phyllis [Sellick] can't broadcast the Sonata on the Continental [Service] till May 19 – will warn you time and wavelength when I know and nearer the event – like you to judge the excision from the first movement.

By the way – Aubrey [Russ] is now unable to pay his share of the original Decca bill for recording – so I must find another £12 10s. Can you help me thereto? I'd like to settle the whole matter up – especially as I should like to get the madrigals [*The Source, The Windhover*] on to a record. Otherwise I'm managing for money pretty well. I bought a pair of long corduroy trousers in Cambridge, to use at home, the winter. Got a single coupon from Karl to make it possible.

I've had the preliminary notice of the Appeal – so it will be in 3 to 4 weeks' time now. If I can't have both witnesses, I shall keep Aubrey and present a letter from Evelyn [Maude] about one specific point.

You'll be ever so welcome when the time comes due – and I'll be in a lovely mood, starting on the new 4tet [String Quartet No. 2]. I feel the stirrings of it already – and will be champing to begin by Saturday, when I'm home.

Love,

Michael

PS. I've decided to print Den's setting up of the oratorio text – 500 copies. It's a lot of copies, indeed, but I've run out, and only a large number is economic. We shall probably be able to get rid of most of them at the first performance.

Don't forget to send a copy of the Fantasia [on a Theme of Handel] to Peggy.

Anything you get typed out further of the monograph – please post and let me read.

[1942]

Have been meaning to write you these last days but have had terrific correspondence trying to get publicity for these wretched concerts. I definitely need a private secretary! Now, am beginning to see the way through the wood. In any case, this sort of life, with occasional town visits to see Goehr, rehearse with [George] Stratton, etc, etc and go home to composition is my proper life and somehow or other after the war it's got to be a permanent one and the classes put finally aside. I am clear definitely on that. I think it means somehow living a little closer, with less money to spare – and it's a matter of persuading Hugo [Strecker] to take over some sort of collected financial guarantee, partly perhaps from Schott's. Otherwise it seems I shall never get out of the traditional English teaching rut, which engulfs so many, and just prevents your accumulating all your energies for a particular work and then coming out to look around after and turning to performances again. However it's no use thinking this in the war, but it's a lot of use trying to compass it for when the peace comes. It means that I am ready at last inside and have won the right to the freedom by an inner discipline.

Meanwhile the 2nd movement of the new 4tet is nearly done – and it's made of harmonies which any German romantic would have used 100 years ago! Sevenths and ninths and all the things that are not in the Sonata. Isn't that odd? Yet it seems tolerable – except a few bars which are bad Wagner, but I can't alter as yet. I've got ideas for the Chamber Orch. Concerto I want to write for Goehr: which is just the other way again. Stravinskyish in technique, if not in material. [. . .]

December 1942

Fresca darling,

I shan't come to you at Christmas but soon after. I've fixed now to stay here as I only get that one week off – I'm myself again now because I'm at composition – the 2 *a cappella* madrigals. When they are done (and they won't take long) I shall come to Mill House and do various other tootlings around. The *a cappella* things are great fun – a most absurd mixture of vocalisation and romantic word declamation – romantic in the technique that is (*à la* Moussorgsky). So that both sorts of technique are used at once!! A conductor will also be an impossibility – it's 8/8 alright, but with constant irregular 3s or 2s. This is for *The Windhover* of Hopkins and does exactly suit the falcon's flight. The complementary one [*The Source*] is to be low and sullen (a river breaking into spate). They will be a grand pair.

I want to talk to you more about the songs on the lines you have written. Could you explain, or rather exemplify your ideas from the lutenists? I suppose they are dialogues between the lover and his lass. It certainly knocks out the Eliot I have in mind. I'm not sure it's my job to attempt it at all – except in opera and *Singspiel* etc. What I've got in my head is the radio. Songs have come back, like all chamber music, because the radio can more easily produce intimacy than publicity. The string 4tet is its best medium, received into the parlour-fireside. How does that (the non-visual element) affect your *diseuse* notions? I don't think I can write for the lieder recital – it's a most unsympathetic concert to me. But I compromise by liking song groups (if reasonably of one piece) in mixed programmes like I do at Morley. Is it possible to treat it semi-dramatically as an atmosphere? So that the singer unlocks a door into a certain romantic (or even more purely aesthetic) world into which garden the audience are led. This would make my Eliot possible again – but in those particular poems it would be a terrific tour de force. Surely the *Chansons de Bilitis* are of this order? It's not what I really want. I want a revival of the more classic outlook and the more vocalised line – where the singer (and the *voice*) all the time leads. This is to reverse the Schubert–Wolf movement, where the accompaniment increased in weight. My desires, in the past, were only possible given a great general interest in singing as a virtuosity. When the coloratura went from the voice to the violin that killed the very artificial but fascinating chamber cantata which were little bits of opera. A portion of story explained the *raison d'être* of a singer's platform appearance, and within that convention they all got down to the real musical business. *Shadrach* is the chamber cantata in a debased form (a portion of negro oratorio). I have thought of taking folk-song situations. But I think there is somewhere a proper modern solution, perhaps even on the lines of *Lindberghflug* [cantata by Weill]. Actually I've resolved the thing generally in the oratorio: by showing the mythological in the contemporary event. So much for modern tragedy to replace classical. It's modern comedy which is more difficult – hence my preoccupation with opera. I know that the masque [early drafts for *The Midsummer Marriage*] I have growing inside and out, is the solution on the grand scale – the *divina commedia* – I can't quite decide whether I interpose a continuity of manners on the way towards the masque (which is *Singspiel* not pure opera).

Please let all these speculations stimulate you soon or late to some sort of response. It helps me to find my feet and make decisions.

A piano tuner comes tomorrow, so I better let him tune yours too.

Get better quickly.

Love,

Michael

[1942]

Fresca darling –

I'm sure you're wise not to come to London in this weather – but I shall be thankful when you're properly well and I want to see you about it all badly.

For myself I have felt gayer again because some minutes before you rang through I had managed to get going again on sketches for the 2nd madrigal [*The Windhover*] – appropriately enough the first one, the light one, was finished 2 days before Tribunal and the dark one comes now. I feel inside much like I used to do in the Wilf [Franks] period – something at the pit of the stomach – but it's easier to sustain and many of the soldiers must have it about leaving wife and kiddies. What has principally happened is that the shock, aided by a long cross-examination at David [Ayerst]'s, produced the most unequivocal series of visions and dreams I have had – I realised that the old shame and fear was hiding behind the pacifism, just as it has hid behind physical cowardice of adolescence and homosexuality, of later years – and this time I seem to have accepted it more fully – so that I feel I have the strength to walk forwards or backwards, to live in the light or the shadow, to be the respectable member of society or the conchie–scapegoat. If the division is forced because of the general situation then I sit down among my own, while knowing – to myself – that the others are my 'own' too. I have run with the hare and the hounds all along – but if covered it appears a cowardice within before the *facts* of division in the great world. What David wants me to do: to compromise is somehow an attempt to bridge over the gap again. I seem to be driven towards a cutting through – tolerance is a great virtue, but not of all kinds. Germany went down before the *furor teutonicus* partly because all the middle people hid for safety in compromise. In England we're a bit tougher. Also, whatever serenity, even gaiety I possess is not an escape just because I have always been linked to the outcast and the scapegoats. However morbid it may appear it is for me a vital link – if I don't accept it when it comes I would cease to be what I am. Thirdly there is a feeling that I might really be able to do something to break the anonymity of the 700 or so young ones who [are] in gaol already – for they are the future too. At least in my choral circles and my own profession the issue will be inescapable because I shall publicly explain what I am doing. It was hinted that if I went to O'Donnell I could don

95

the blue uniform and be librarian or some such for the RAF orchestra. That is the usual way out for my colleagues. David does not want me to take that but to go back into London social work, thinking I would have some spare time to write in, and might find myself conducting choirs in shelters and clubs. Do you see the unreality of all this? I can't help feeling I have done my whack of social nursing and that if there is to be a new life it will be a different experience altogether. For pacifism really is something to me – not for what it is now, but for its future, in an England becoming more insidiously *Führer*-ridden every week. Heroism at all costs, as [Eric] Kennington paints – and what is to prevent the political powers fighting over the body of the heroicised RAF to make it their SS, their Communist Party? If Kennington could but once paint the young C.O. [conscientious objector] sitting in the 'glasshouse' (the military prison and pretty grim) among his blue boys, I should feel England were safer – because of the generosity and the recognition of the double necessity, the healthy tension. Everyone hopes I will compromise, because the other thought is troublesome and horrid – David even accused me of wanting to go to prison merely to spite the state or myself. That is partly his defence against the intolerable nature of this monstrous world-conscription. Naturally the authorities hope I will compromise too, for there will be a certain moral difficulty in committing me to quod – while there is hardly any difficulty in sentencing the anonymous youngsters – poor kids. I only wish I had a name like Walton to play around with! [. . .]

all my love,
Michael

[early 1943]

Fresca darling,

I had David [Ayerst] over 3 days at Xmas – and Karl [Hawker] made a visit and Bryan [Fisher] – D. enjoyed himself and was much refreshed – at the end of the 3 days. I was a trifle overcome and more so when the C.O. [conscientious objector] out of the army Christopher Lake appeared and Billy as a makeweight – so this weekend I put off the Oxford young couple Angela and Harvey and even held Sackville-West at bay when he asked to come the weekend – which means that I am working at last at the 2 madrigals and more or less in peace for a bit. Curious, experimental stuff it is – interweaving rhythms which I can't theoretise but only pattern out by instinct. Not altogether my cup of tea really, because the scale is too small – I prefer a canvas where one has room to use a greater degree of variety. However – meanwhile the masque [early drafts for *The Midsummer Marriage*] comes up again – it does look as if the *Seven Daughters* will be still-born poor dears, though they may return and claim a proper birth. The masque is straightening itself out, though it's very difficult to make neat transitions to the mythological material – but it retains its gaiety. It's in the true *Zauberflöte* tradition, something I've always known would take place. I saw some of Sheila [Busch]'s students dancing yesterday – at Oxted. Frightfully good, especially the dances to Gershwin *et simile*. She seems to be reaching out to the same sort of fusion between classical and romantic (ballet and central European) which all of us are engaged with – you must see it sometime – I was quite surprised. I wore my spectacles and really saw for the first time.

You haven't scotched the Eliot songs really – I don't want to do them just now anyhow – but put these madrigals aside and finished and proceed to something very near my heart – the new string 4tet [No. 2]. It will be a deeper-seated work than the [Fantasy] Sonata [Piano Sonata No. 1], and I shall aim at getting it on records in the same way, so as to have a good representative pair on discs. [. . .]

Heaps of love
Michael

[early 1943]

To talk practical politics: the hope that returns so easily is probably necessary for me to write, but it's deceptive. Until the decision I have to be able at any moment to put the music voluntarily aside. Also I might very much rather have the matter decided at once now, but the weeks' grace are probably essential. First of all I have to finish the 2nd madrigal [*The Windhover*], sell the copyright to Stainer & Bell, and perform them at Morley if possible and launch them thus. Secondly the concert Mar. 7th must be got through and the new work with Goehr's help sent on its travels – this means printing a leaflet of criticism etc and hawking it around. If I am taken away before this is completed, I think it's something you could manage for me. It may mean visiting Manchester and such places to interview the Hallé and so on. It can only be done successfully at the start in person. Next I must prepare the String Concerto [Concerto for Double String Orchestra] for Goehr to produce – either by helping his losses on the expenses of a big string band and/or rescoring the work so that it can be played temporarily with few strings and double woodwind.

Goehr thinks to offer Boosey & Hawkes our 'arrangement' of the 4 Gibbons fantasies. The editing might even be done in gaol, on my side. What I have got Goehr to see in the Gibbons is the modernity of the music and the need for a different notation from [Edmund H.] Fellowes. You will hear on Nov. 7th. Goehr is broadcasting this, as a try-out, to the Continent next Wed. morning after the 9 a.m. news on the *Continental* wave (as George Walter and the Orchestre Raymonde). I think his times are always 9.20–10 a.m. every Wed. And the programmes are very great fun. I go up Tuesday to BBC to the rehearsal.

Finally I want to see you about the songs etc, because that can be meditated on if necessary in quod – and I believe that through V.W. [Vaughan Williams] and Eliot you could even get material in to me, and stuff which I can hear without piano. So get well as soon as you can. There's further the problem of Morley. A lively little choir, dead nuts on the English stuff – and Bergmann to fall back on for donkey-work and rehearsal if you were unable – might well be your cup of tea – and you would be the nearest to myself I could find for them!

Mar. 7th is only settled to the extent that after the concert we [have] tea at David [Ayerst]'s – when the party clears away – you, I, David, Layard and John Campbell probably go to dinner together at leisure – we've decided to send the boys off to flicks, because it's difficult to take Den [Newton] and not Bryan [Fisher] etc, and the dinner will be rather older. OK? Den tells me you think to come in trousers – I'd rather you didn't. I want to be able to take you to meet Goehr in the artists' room, and his wife, and Phyllis [Sellick] and the orchestra etc, and it'll look a touch of masquerade, and in your proper dress you always look essentially feminine and good. Change at David's if you like after. On this occasion it is for the boys to wear their corduroys, and Wilf [Franks] to wear his beard and his green trousers, and [his girlfriend] Meg [Masters] her peculiar make-up – but I shall be in a suit and you will be virtually my wife – that is to say something besides our joint selves, something public and professional. I've got Goehr to give me two seats not too close, but just nice. Row M!

Adrian [Allinson] was at the Solomon concert and rushed up to me most friendly – he is coming to Mar. 7th – perhaps I'd better ask him to the party – in fact I will. I've asked Alan [Bush] and Nancy – but Alan is in army, though Nancy will come.

Uncle Tom Eliot might conceivably be there – and if so, I want to introduce you to him.

I've taken the burden of expense of the tea-party off D.'s hands – because he's been so good to me, putting me up each week at his expense (wish you had a room in town again) – It'll be £3–£4 – so probably we can share it. I've given all the boys tickets, and even, by a wangle, Ruth [Pennyman]. John Campbell, at David's, the dearest person, will do the catering and I shall give him money enough ahead.

M.

[early 1943]

Fresca darling –

Your note reached me in bed with mild 'flu, instead of classes etc – but tomorrow I hope to [get] up for rehearsal, though I must put off the afternoon choir for further rehearsing. So it's a thin week as far as earnings go, but I just don't care very much. Hope to feel myself again tomorrow. It's just as well to get this over before Sat. I finished the 2 madrigals [*The Source, The Windhover*] yesterday, and that's always a dangerous moment. The thing to do Sat. is to hear the Gibbons, then lie out the Brahms. Hear the tiny Berlioz and the Tippett, and lie out the Strauss! There's a couch I think in the foyer itself.

[. . .] The *Scrutiny* chap, [Wilfrid] Mellers, and his wife are coming from their farm in Warwickshire – if you see two unknown young 'uns arriving at David's – go ahead – introduce them to Den etc. You'd better lie in state on David's bed!

Till Sat.

Love –

M.

[early spring 1943]

Fresca darling,

[. . .] I've written to Den to say that if he hasn't yet ordered the printing of the 500 texts [for *A Child Of Our Time*] then I want to reconsider the whole matter. Should a text without music be put on sale? Pro: that it arouses interest and expectation – con: that it puts emphasis on words and ideas. Shall I rather make do with what few remaining originals I have and delay a reprint till a performance? Shall I get 500 nice prints in stock while the going's good? What do you think on all this? [. . .]

[. . .] I fear the spring has moved me too – but the music is flowing fast, I imagine that all that will come of it. This flowing of new music makes me 'frightened' of prison – but I don't see how it is to be shelved unless the appeal is granted. I don't think a person like myself is any good 'on the run' – do you?

Let me know when you decide to come. I am here in considerable settlement now and for some time to come. So make your own date.

Love –

M.

9 March 1943

Life is fearful – composition hopeless. Morley concert on Sat. Bedford Wed. evening next week – interval talk with Peter Pears on *Fidelio* – 8 p.m. – Nat. Gallery with Morley on the Thursday, day after!! Two local choir concerts Sat.–Sun., 20–21. Still thank god it's all at one go. Don't forget the new 4tet [String Quartet No. 2] is Sat. fortnight – Mar. 27 – but will be broadcast Ap. 8.

My father hit in the raid of Exmouth – slowly getting better – head and knee wounds healing – but blast has shaken him badly – and the whole business upset my poor mother – if you feel to write – it's 12 Louisa Terrace, Exmouth. (24 killed) horrible business. 170 suffocated themselves in a shelter in London last week through panic – actually no planes over London itself at all. Shows the danger of crowds.

Am *very* tired – but gay. Have done first section of new piece [*Boyhood's End*] – Peter finds it a bit wild I think. Shall *have* to take fortnight off from writing to do all the shows. Main news, that is.

Love –

M.

March 1943

Fresca darling –

[. . .] Father is really not in danger I think, after seeing him – very weak, but lucid and due for a very slow recovery. Mother not suffering from shock at all.

[. . .] The 4tet [String Quartet No. 2], as music, is the goods alright
– but the Zorians [the Zorian Quartet, founded by Olive Zorian] are
as Norbert Brainin described them – 'silly girls'. I'm going to try the
parts out with the boys and girls I generally use who are much more
like the 'cat's whiskers' – and give them at least a try-out at Morley –
I have a whim they may be smashing, and would make a good ensemble for an eventual record.

The Monteverdi madrigals are just super – oh, but most lovely – and
sensual! Meanwhile in this lovely springtime I dreamed of kissing the
angelic Tony [Hopkins] – you and I always had good taste together!
Den, I fancy, is just on the turn of the tide and will fall for a girl any
day. It's just at that turn and springtime that I lose my heart to them
all without exception – I nearly kiss Tony in fact and on the tube – but
I don't. But nearly tell John Amis (who may be in the Studio on the 8th
[April]) that I would like to, without his really seeing that I am nearly
for kissing him. Well, well. Lovely to see you again – let me know
when you think of reaching the cottage.

herzlich
Michael

I went to play the [Fantasy] Sonata [Piano Sonata No. 1] and
Fantasia [on a Theme of Handel] to Clifford Curzon who hopes to
play them both – most successful meeting.

April 1943

Fresca darling –

[. . .] A fearful rushed note: so much writing to do now – 2 enquiries
for works possible to perform in this morning – begin to pay the price
for having come over the top. 4tet [No. 2] has been a mild wow in its
way. Goehr hopes to follow up with Str[ing] Concerto, Wigmore, in
July. 4tet is at Nat. Gall[ery] May 17, at LPO [London Philharmonic
Orchestra] Music Club (through the very nice John Amis – new family member) week later. Leicester July 1. *Autrement* – will I write a
mass for Canterbury Cathedral? – NO . . . *Und so weiter.*

[Ernest] Bevin has written that he sees no valid reason for my not
going either on the land or to prison. Letters from Bax and Boult . . .
but won't move Bevin I'm sure. Evelyn [Maude] thinks a short sentence
the only way of settling the Min[istry] and a bit of encouragement to
those who have to go in. Billy is in now; 6 months or a year – have not

heard yet. Will take up his case at Appeal and try and get him out.

So am ready to go in now if it can be, while I've not started on a big work. Am not in the least degree worried by it. I've decided it won't hurt my public position and that's all I worry about. It'll probably do it good, if anything. But in general it won't count one way or another. I think things have been unduly merciful, and I've had time to get in a good position. So am ready and almost anxious to pay the proper price. I've been troubled by bread, too. I decided at supper last night to open a bottle of plums from the cupboard because we can always refill the bottles. I've also broken into some of the 1941 plum jam. As Den has brought 5 or 6 pounds of sugar, it's OK – that too. I have no jam left otherwise. Have been needing a bit of feeding up – getting and looking very thin. This wretched war food.

Thanks for all the books and the paper. I have an inkling of what goes on inside you during this sort of period and don't ever feel in any way separated from you whether you write or not. It's much better you should be quite open about yourself, while being sensitive to others' possible feelings. It has to be done gently: when the time comes. I've just been getting this sort of thing straightened with the little Tony [Hopkins]. I don't like being in a misunderstanding – but it always comes down to the matter of making them see that love between good and real people is good and not a perversion. And when they accept that they are themselves further widened thereby. [. . .]

Grüss Gott,
M.

1943

Fresca darling –

Have now myself a hopeless fluid tummy and colly-wobbles – the last 3 days – doesn't seem to go – very horrid. But it's a lovely spring lassitude and I sleep 10 hours. Today Bergmann comes from town to decide on the last details of the oratorio [*A Child of Our Time*] which is to be engraved immediately! Also Schott's (Hugo [correctly Max] Steffens) have decided to give me £100 for last year, and d[itt]o for this, later. Isn't that exciting? So I'm dreaming of getting rid of one day's classes – whereby I shall become I'm afraid no richer – because with tax £100 isn't that amount at all. In fact I shall be a bit poorer but with much more leisure again – and that matters.

Morley is bursting with ideas and offshoots – and there's tons and tons to do.

All you said about 4tet [String Quartet No. 2] I agree with. That's just how I see it. I think incidentally the slow movement is alright, when you hear it naked. It's to be done soon at Nat. Gall[ery] and at Leicester on July 1st. Hope to wangle Cambridge later. I'll write when I feel a bit better again.

M.

15 May 1943

Fresca darling –

In case anything does happen and I'm away a week or two – Evelyn [Maude] is me personally in the prison – but you would visit if it were long enough to get one. John Amis, LPO, 295 Regent St, W1, is my official person.

Evelyn will write you after 21st as to collective efforts to pay the lawyer and/or fine. I intend to go in, in lieu of fine, until the professional date needs me out – just to show my willingness. And have a short holiday. I leave E. £20 – but have told her to use £10 at once on lawyer and to do more if necessary – let Amis have £5. And so on – I shall pay my own way in so far as B.B. [Benjamin Britten] and you and Oxted PPU [Peace Pledge Union] and whatever can't manage. I am ready to take responsibility for myself, but it's also a public do too. Here's the other bill for July 17 – but you'll probably be whacked by the afternoon one.

And now – July 4th is BBC broadcast of Fantasia (Handel theme) Sellick playing – Sun. at 2.30. Cantata [*Boyhood's End*] is down for Wigmore Hall Aug. 7th – 4tet [String Quartet No. 2] from Wigmore Aug. 21.

I'm so unworried by June 21st that you can be unmoved too. I'm pretty certain it won't be for long and will be exciting in its own way – and a test. [. . .]

M.

18 May 1943

Fresca darling,

[. . .] The enclosed gives you a 4tet [String Quartet No. 2] broadcast. It's also going to be done in Wigmore again in August (Gerald Cooper concerts). All in all it's getting 6 performances now. Not bad! Goehr will do the Double Concerto at Wigmore on July 17 – which I suppose I shall miss – *Schade*. And he's busy trying to raise a committee to raise funds to do the oratorio [*Child of Our Time*]. He might ask you on his committee! But one of his wild ideas is Paul Robeson by telegraph from USA. I'm leaving it all to him – it's more or less in connection with campaigns against anti-semitism. Actually Goehr knows more than others that the work is going to be a big thing and is already proud of his protégé. Let him be – *ist mir egal*.

I'm leaving all the professional stuff in the LPO hands – i.e. in Johnny Amis, by arrangement with LPO (Musical Culture Ltd) – This works ideally. Schott's are getting out a brochure with photo, to pass around – and but for the war we'd sail over the top with publications. But as it is, it has to go slow – and that may be better.

Oratorio is engraving now.

One of the things making for happiness is the real friendship of Britten. There's a spontaneity about our association which has a good flavour. And with my easy tolerance, there's a sort of artistic group forming which has candour and comradeship, not dominance, as its basis – and can include Bergmann (and Ben's B., a one called [Erwin] Stein at Boosey's) at one end and the baby Tony Hopkins at the other. And a much more direct contact with the actual musical amateur that likes our stuff. That is 'secular' – renaissance and gay – turning for the moment from the war – and from *Wozzeck* – (and the oratorio, quite rightly) – religious, is the necessary cultural form of 'fear' – awe and reverence in its better forms – for the moment we want music not of fear, but of agreement and gaiety. Our real danger will be too ready acceptance. This is already Ben's problem. It won't ever be mine in the same way, as Johnny candidly tells me – 'I'm not handling your music for anything. I'm going to get out of it – it'll never be a popular success anyhow'! But that's just the measure of the spontaneity and quality of association. Tony, trying to let me down gently, said last week: 'Sorry to disappoint you, mate, but I'm going to learn the Howard Ferguson Sonata.' I doubt if a composer has ever been so refreshingly set aside – I was enchanted.

Now I'll stop – and come and talk to you – have a very gentle and odd story to tell you about Tony and myself. Feel gay again today – and the feeling in the tummy is less.

herzlich,

M.

104

See – I've got through and am trying to feed myself – am eating up the bottled fruit for suppers, as it's not all keeping now – and cooking endless potfulls of spinach-beet. Probably, though, the irresponsibility of prison will fatten me.

See a lawyer on Thursday – and will have news thereon by the time I see you.

[May/June 1943]

Darling –

Your letter does not seem to me strange at any point – in fact it seems to me just natural sense. I have an idea even that the whole tummy trouble is part of the 'way' – and besides being apparently the weakness is also the toughness – or will be. It won't add up ever in purely physical terms of health, because that path never has done – and those who had such generally mortified the flesh for deep-seated reasons.

[. . .] Once in the lawyers' hands it is very difficult to remain a human personality. The 'counsel' by the way costs 25 gns for Oxted – and I've just said yes because I can't very well say no. I expect between the lot of us we'll manage it. I definitely want a small sentence (to appease the Ministry's legal claim) and keep one contact with the 'boys' (Billy is in now) – and a moral win or approval for the cultural-v-total war stand. The lawyers want a head-line case and V.W. [Vaughan Williams] in court and what not.

There – will tell you how it goes when I see you.

Love –

M

June 1943

Sweetheart –

[. . .] I go on Monday to have a sort of special appeal interview at the Lambeth Labour Exchange. This I guess is the last act of the comedy before the prosecution.

One or two good things. Dr [Alfred] Kalmus of Universal Edn who runs the Boosey & Hawkes concerts is hoping for the new 4tet [revised String Quartet No. 1] for a concert in Feb. But the selection is in Dec. So whether there is any real hope of finishing it by then is rather doubtful. Anyhow the request is something in itself.

T. B. Lawrence of Fleet St seems to promise a performance of the 2 madrigals [*The Source, The Windhover*], but nothing to be done till after Xmas – choir has too much on hand in the meantime. And both these two gentlemen think I am right to stand out. So I don't think it will be taken too hardly by colleagues, though it will by institutions, like BBC – luckily there are sympathetic individuals within the corporation.

[. . .] So life is tolerable while waiting for the blow to fall. Will see you soon.

Love

M.

[7 June 1943]

[. . .] The cantata [*Boyhood's End*] was a great success at Morley on Sat. – in fact everyone seems to feel it's the best thing I've done except Den [Newton] – who thinks it unvocal and a too impossible text! but he's quite in the minority. Actually the whole thing as Peter [Pears] sings it is very moving – so they, the 2 [Britten and Pears], are much pleased with it and will do it in public-k-er place as soon as maybe. I think myself it is good and am not surprised now that it has taken since Xmas. By request we may in any case repeat it at Morley on July 17, when there is a purely choral concert on with B.B. conducting *St Cecilia*. Peter singing in the show – and the first performance of the madrigals. I'll show you or send you bills of that – and of the Goehr Wigmore concert of the afternoon of the same day at which Double Concerto [Concerto for Double String Orchestra] is for – herewith a bill of that enclosed. [. . .]

M.

[June 1943]

Fresca darling,

[. . .] I can't take June 21 [the date when Tippett was to be sentenced] seriously, but only because I have thought about it so much for a year – I'm afraid it's really more serious than we think – though I mean by that only that there will be sentence – but perhaps only a short one.

Meanwhile I've actually started doing the new movement for the first 4tet. Haven't heard Britten's yet, but expect I shall feel as you do about it. He's been talking to me a lot about himself and his music. They both seem to like the cantata – and so does Goehr – it's quite a serious work, and in one place very moving. I've been down to see Goehr and got the Double Concerto in train for July 17. Thank you so much for the book, comb, oatmeal etc.

I did enjoy the lovely sunshine in the Mill House garden. It's a dope I'm given now to play for me tomorrow on the radio – you'll hear if you listen.

Hope to see you soon again.

love

Michael

27 August 1943 [after release from Wormwood Scrubs]
Mevagissey

Fresca darling –

The wire that Tony [Hopkins] had not opened all Sat. we opened in the train – found that the Portloe lodgings were cancelled for RAF billeting – so we risked it and by great good luck got in here at Mevagissey, which is perhaps better. Meanwhile I'm very slowly thawing out – the young uns find me rather subdued and remote. It seems to act like that – but am not quite so hungry as I was. [. . .]

Come as soon as you can to the cottage: I think I shall begin to assimilate a bit when I get home there and back into the rhythm of music and work. At present it's been too sharp a break – and as though one had seen the inside of a pot or drain, that it's not right to do. And I'm still unsure of not going back.

How good it will be to have one's own breakfast coffee anew, and porridge and jam at tea – and to re-enter the atmosphere of the music and the cottage – let me know when you are likely to be there.

Love –

Michael

Am at Mother's the 1st half of next week. 12 Louisa Terrace, Exmouth – and home at Oxted by the Thursday.

Apparently British Council sent to Schott's for parts and score of the 4tet [String Quartet No. 2] for Sweden while I was locked up! Pretty ironical.

6 September 1943

Fresca darling,

[. . .] on the 21st there is this 50th ann[iversary] Festival in

Northampton at St Matthew's church which Ben [Britten] has written an anthem for [*Rejoice in the Lamb*] (just printed) and I am writing (after Ben's extraordinary kind and persistent effort on my behalf when I was in) a Fanfare for Brass [Fanfare No. 1] – which is gay and serious – and rather good. So I suppose I shall have to go to Northampton and will take Den of course – there's also a commissioned Madonna from Henry Moore. Then on the 21st and 22nd 2 of the nicest chaps come out of the Scrubs – both of whom we shall all get to know – one a serious, gentle sculptor called Arnold Machen (my age or approaching) – the other a young 'anarchist' of the John [Amis], Den age and ideas – a natural member of the young family. And on the 24th the sonata is done by Sellick at the [National] Gallery. So all in all Den's visiting week coincides nicely with a rush around.

October is less wild. The 16th is a Morley do – Weelkes, Kodály, Hindemith, and on the weekend after, 23rd, Peter and Ben hope for a stay here at the cottage, with a concert to do at Haywards Heath on the Sat! It's the first free weekend for them. After that I had hoped to have cleared off: oratorio proofs [*Child of Our Time*] – fanfare – possibly song for Peter – new 1st movement to 4tet I – and so to be able to take another short holiday – probably Exmouth (or with you by the sea somewhere?) – and come back for the Britten–Tippett do at Friends' House Nov. 6 – where Clifford [Curzon] is to play the Sonata – and then to shut myself up, mentally at any rate, to begin and carry through the new Symphony [No. 1]. I tell you all this so you can have an idea of my plans and do what you like when you think good.

I've decided the time is ripe to float the oratorio willy nilly. The first idea was a Britten–Tippett do again – to have his *Sinfonia da Requiem* (20 mins) as 1st half. To get a special choir, hire the New London Orchestra etc etc. A guarantee fund of £300! – and the little Alison [Purves], Tony [Hopkins]'s girl, offered us £50 on the spot – which Tony agreed to! Ben would fork out– and I think I could throw away one of Schott's £100 – or rather the whole lot nearly after this goddam income tax nonsense. Then Johnny [Amis] put the proposal up to LPO – who are discussing it – but refuse Britten in the same programme – something classical – and Boult to conduct – to be in their London series at one of the theatres. Ben thinks this a bit unfriendly – but if they will place it and don't need a lot of guarantee I think it probably better.

Meanwhile I have driven Morley to agree to a flat rate – only £125 p.a., an average of 2 classes a week and my director's work – but it means nicer type of work, all under one roof – and that, with occasional outside jobs (deputising for Tony!), and the £60 that comes into the bank from your bank. I shall live. It's OK at present because of the money from Schott's and because I'm fairly decided to use up any savings in what is really a capitalisation: concert performances to establish one's name and reputation. Sound?

I have agreed to do up the other cottage at £20 for Miriam [Lewis] etc: and I have the money. This is again just informative.

[. . .] Mother and Father well – though ageing – and very nice time there – nice time with David and La[rema] and children at Mother Ayerst's – lovely kids and D. is quite sweet with them – another on the way – to be called 'Scrubs'!! They loved being in the cottage and La spring-cleaned it – but the problem of sheets is becoming acute. D. wanted to repay by buying a pair – the shop man said: 'You'd better have a couple of aspirins before I tell you the price' . . . 14 guineas the cheapest pair! Have you any getatable anywhere? for when you come.

That seems all the news . . . it was just heaven to be in the home again. It *is* a lovely place really and one is damned lucky.

all my love
Michael

10 September 1943

Fresca darling –

What do you feel now about counsel's fees – or is it too old a story? I see that the whole thing came to 18 guineas – quite moderate – i.e. less than expected – so far I have paid the lot. Do you think it a matter for Harry? I hesitate to ask B.B. [Britten], who did offer – it would have been easier if Evelyn [Maude] had done so at the time! The trouble is that it's such a chunk out of my economy. However don't worry – let me know what you think.

[. . .] I've been so horribly stuck with proofreading. [. . .] I've had to do all the oratorio stuff for printing at once. And the Brit[ish] Council have been badgering Schott's (while I was in) for a score and parts of the 4tet [String Quartet No. 2], for Sweden. And copyists are so inaccurate. But isn't it ironical wanting one's stuff, and that actually written while disobeying the law? [. . .]

dein –
Michael

16 September 1943

Fresca darling –

It *was* good to see you. Soon I feel you'll be about in town and that will be grand. I need to talk to you ever such a lot – get a bit musically frightened; being now as it were 'launched'. I am afeared of getting out of my proper balance by a lack of true humility – which up to date I think I've had – at any rate patience! And also these seem queer dream-like days within this war – 'gay and grim' – that *Spruch* of Yeats, that's kept by me.

And the dream – I can't help feeling that there's a somewhat special psychological balance for people like ourselves – perhaps it says that we can't force a union of our 2 sides – masculine and feminine – that they may have contrary, if complementary, functions. I'm beginning to doubt the absolute claims of what is called normal psychology. Life is just a bit more mysterious – and can't be contained in formulas.

I've finished my blessed Fanfare [No. 1, for brass] for Northampton (Mon. and Tues. next) – and feel terribly, terribly tired. I'm a silly Billy – and must quieten down to a sedater and more regular life – music to order is just *not* my meat, even for a Continental Marie Rambert! However it means now finishing one song for Peter (he's going to sing a 10-year-old baby song of mine already) – and then to proper work – the new 1st movement to [String] 4tet No. 1.

Eric Blom fell for 4tet 2 with a crash (Leamington on Sat.) – I'll show you the *Brhm* [*Birmingham*] *Post* cutting. Goes a little too far – something like 'breathtakingly beautiful' – but other than that, just the right crit. Schott's are doing a min. score and parts alright.

I live in *such* a dream world, half the time. I hope it won't mean a fearful crash when peace comes – because in some ways it's a defence against the horror. So that perhaps prison was a good thing – to come closer to something.

D[en] will be here for a week's holiday as from Sat. I'll find out if his prison is really likely or imminent – and get him to phone you at Mill House. But see him in Cambridge on his own ground – not with C. and V. [Cyril and Veronica Allinson].

My love to them – and to you
Michael

[September 1943]

Fresca darling –

To answer your letter round about; just before it came I was pacing the cottage undergoing the ever recurring 're-conversion'. It's come about just because of the impact of notoriety – and particularly, or more personally, from Northampton, where I was B.B. [Britten]'s 'younger brother', asked to show 'his' talent and promise – all out of B.B.'s unconscious and sincere desire to help me to win recognition. And because his, Ben's, enormous popularity and success has been making me try to force myself along at the same pace and towards the same ends. And I come up with a shock against the refusal of my creative activity to function except for its own values, and they are just hopelessly at variance with the complete industrial, mass-entertainment set-up: nearly as violently as Blake's, or [Eric] Gill's (or perhaps also Stravinsky's). It's not that I can't write a fanfare on demand – but certainly that I can't write a second! nor, seeing the 2000 pre-sales of B.'s Northampton church anthem, can I do the like, as he would hope to reach, say, at least the 1500 mark. It's almost no accident that Schott's are in no position to handle such orders, or engrave for an immediate market. Very well – I renounce once more – and that is why the notoriety won't in the end hurt me. I have just no sense of 'limelight', though a great deal of public responsibility – and all the time I am aware that everywhere the real division is active: that I speak from a set of values which are not those of even the majority of my colleagues. My instinct, say, to avoid the LPO despite possible financial advantage, for the first performance of the *Child* is of this order, because the LPO stands completely within the new doctrine of state-financed entertainment – and I don't. The senses, as Blake taught, are the only gates of the soul in this bodily life. Art is one of the means by which these gates are polished, these windows cleansed, that we may enter the world of imagination in which the soul delights with propriety and even exuberance. What in heaven's name has all that to do with the argument as to the necessity for entertaining the proletariat, where before we entertained the bourgeoisie? It's true I don't want to go into even a Blakeian wilderness; and I therefore keep before me the Elizabethan ideal of various planes of acceptance: dramatic entertainment, spiritual drama, poetry etc, all in one. As has been for the *Child* and will be again for the masque. But it got to such a point some days back, that I couldn't finish another note of the dopey song for P.P. [Peter Pears] and snatched up the 4tet [String Quartet No. 1] movement (which is good tough serious music) wherein I am sunk in a sort of joyful oblivion. Deep, deep down I realise that the struggle is quite eternal, and that to evade the consequences of the struggle is to sell the soul. And one of the first consequences of the struggle is the fundamental aloneness of one's most important acts despite the gay warmth of other acts. I think this has always been the mystic's experience. Contact with the spiritual world is single, even though the desire is for the unitary life of unity with all creation. The stigmata appear in the solitary cave, but the eating and drinking is with the bretheren. [. . .]

All the above is singularly inappropriate to your letter, which I found very moving and tender – but it's probably an answer in a more masculine manner. I bless our relationship, which I take to be a reasonably rare one – a slow deepening without the horrors of possessiveness and jealousies. It's a pity you can't get to C[ambridge], Johnny will miss not seeing you. Den [Newton] has a girl, I think, or at least someone of that sex of his own partiality, which sounds good. I'm not answering your letter specifically for the reasons you said – but I took it all in and feel with – besides being fascinated by what you tell me of yourself *et autres*.

Love,
M.

24 April 1944

Fresca darling,

[. . .] I've had a lovely weekend, both in the June-like weather and writing – which as usual meanders along. I never seem to be able to take advantage of such times to write quickly – I just waste hours of time looking around. It's an odd sound that's happening – warmer in some ways, and tougher – but perhaps less adaptable material, at times very impure. It's what I would call typical 'middle-period music' when one seems to reach out in all directions under the impulse of new-found strength and so you get exuberance rather than refinement. But I dare say you can't reach a better music of a 3rd period till you've gone through this mill. Nevertheless this Symphony [No. 1] will be a step forward as far as non-existent good English symphonic works go; it's got drive and it's highly wrought and never gets bogged in vacuity or hitched up into an orgasmic emotional discharge which is the weakness of the Walton Symphony.

See you again soon.

Love –

Michael

[late April 1944]

Fresca darling

I've got home from dashing around and am now deep in work and happy. I enjoyed the trip to Stamford and Leicester, and came back refreshed – but with a voracious appetite for long days in the cottage and the gradually lengthening Symphony [No. 1] score. [. . .]

We've given up a second London perf. of *Child* because it's difficult to see how we can cover expenses, and the first has done its work in that Liverpool has an autumn performance in mind already, and Leicester one in December. We can reconsider London again for the next spring, better perhaps. [. . .]

Love to you all

Michael

4 May 1944

Fresca dear –

[. . .] Have had to take my eyes seriously all of a sudden and to begin some sort of re-education. I've not quite yet got it systematic – and I think I'd better see a good Bates method* chap if one exists. [. . .]

Den was here (and John [Amis]) after a Morley concert. He's such a nice lad – and growing now at such a pace. I fancy that he's taken a sudden jerk on again and that the need for physical warmth which he had of me is passing: he's probably begun to feel surer of himself as he gets on so much easier now with new folk he happens to meet. Luckily for me I haven't become seriously entangled in this manner. I have always known that the pace of the friendship has to be set by the younger person, and that in his case in the long run it's the intellectual stimulus he really wants. All this brings up the old question of the impermanence of some particular form of relationship, and that the matter seems to have to be resolved into music in the good old fash-

---

* An exercise system for improving the eyesight.

ioned way. But now, at this age, the music of course has the real pull over all, and the matter resolves itself very quickly.

William Glock is getting married to his Clement [Davenport] in a week or so. I think they are folk we shall like very much when we can remake our circle more permanently after the war – and that always seems to turn out in my mind as after your weakness passes. There's also Peter Watson of *Horizon* who is a sweet gentle chap of our own age – and with an encyclopedic knowledge of art in the widest and best sense.

I guess it may be the coming storm, but following on some considerable nausea as to the war and all things of it, I have got emotionally fast-centred in the cottage here, and the Symphony [No. 1], and am abstracted from London and Morley. It's also partly the spring which I've wanted so much. I hope to have managed a 6-week stretch in July–August. But it seems too good to hope for in the world as it now is.

I've agreed to write a 3000-word pamphlet* for PPU [Peace Pledge Union] – 1d price, and 10,000 sale. I'll probably send you the MS to vet before it goes to press. It's a very forthright and clear-stated exposé of what I think to be something of the underlying processes in the relationship now of artistic creation and the mass society. That's why I've agreed to do it for PPU – because I want to talk to the youngsters who, however unconsciously, have contracted out of something, and who must build from the new position consequent on that shift. Also I want to make public again my stand against the mass state at a time when they would like to gloss over the past indiscretions and 'try out' the new name.

Don't fear as to the masque [early draft for *The Midsummer Marriage*] – I shall come to it instinctively at the right time I'm pretty sure. It has the same accumulation and inevitability as *The Child* had. I expect I shall get a whole mass of stuff 'digested' out by the Symphony.

Love –

Michael

11 May 1944

Fresca darling,

[. . .] I've been exercising my eyes on my own, seriously, and there's already an improvement. It really is rather miraculous at the time – the

---

* 'Abundance of Creation: An Artist's Vision of Creative Peace' (1944).

trouble as yet is that the better condition doesn't remain. However if I persevere when I'm here all the summer, I ought to get somewhere. I'll tell you all about it when I see you – it's too much to write about just when I am short of time. I may go later on to see the woman whose name and address you sent.

[. . .] I'll write again sometime. The Symphony begins to gather speed and take substance and I like it better. It's got a lot of power and guts.

Much love –
Michael

12 June 1944

Fresca darling –

[. . .] We have had very little aeroplane armada effects over us. Little to remind one of the battle. I came down in the train with 4 soldiers due off the next day. It was not pleasant. One was shattered and clearly felt he was going to his death. Though Evelyn [Maude] tells me that the losses are much much less than expected. I hope with one half that Germany collapses and that it stops – and with the other half that we reach stalemate and so force a much deeper adjustment on us all. I imagine it's going to be the former and it's a tragedy. Germany will be the scapegoat and will be dismembered and reduced to a colony of big business, with labour gangs snatched into Russia.

The Symphony [No. 1] goes along slowly, but good. I must send you the Canterbury anthem [*Plebs Angelica*] – classicising though it probably is.

herzlichst
Michael

June 1944

Fresca darling –

[. . .] The Symphony progresses slowly. It's a 'big' work, for me – rather on the oratorio [*A Child of Our Time*] scale – so will take the rest of the year anyhow, and will be followed by smaller things for a year at least, I suppose before the masque [early draft for *The Midsummer Marriage*]. But I am probably happiest in these productive periods – it feels to be like a good year of one's life – last year, with prison and what not, being not so good a year. But in these productive periods one seems to withdraw from the outside matters of one's *renommée*, performances and so forth – not caring so much – while the new works are written. But last year, when so little was done in that line, was a very good year from the outer success point of view: all of which seems to work out very well. [. . .]

Love –
M.

9 July 1944

Fresca darling,

Father died on Thursday, as peacefully as can be imagined. I go to Plymouth on Monday to see to the cremation. Mother is wonderfully well, considering, and I think will come through quite alright. Peter [Kemp, Tippett's brother] comes today for family chit-chat. Mother won't expect a letter from you, and in any case will hope not to have to write one back. She is snowed under with them.

I am now beginning to be less tired. I shall travel back home Wed., and then off Friday, all being well, to St David's, Wales, for a week with Den [Newton] and John [Amis]. Looking forward to it no end. I shall then see when I get home again how the bombing goes and the music in consequence. Also Bron [Wilson] will have had her baby, and Miriam [Lewis] may be still incapacitated by her stroke and fall, so that it may be policy to move to a room with a piano in Cambridge or wherever. However I'll settle that all later. [. . .]

I worry a bit about all these delays to the Symphony: but it's no use. Wars are not ideal times for composition, not modern wars, and it's no use crying for the moon. I still hope to get 5 weeks clear writing, and shall do that at the cottage as long as it's tolerably possible. I may take to sleeping under the piano! I gather Miriam's roof now leaks from shrapnel, but I'm more interested to hear how many bombs are brought down round about while I've been away, and what Evelyn thinks to it – who has considerable common sense on such matters.

Much love
Michael

20 July 1944

Fresca darling

This letter is on the new supply of paper, for which many thanks.

I got to Waterloo yesterday as the siren went and 2 bombs whined over the building – so I went straight down here, waiting for the connection in Croydon which was delayed because they'd hit the line and while the woman at the speaker announces: 'Your attention please! Your attention please! Hostile aircraft approaching . . .' I'm amused at their being called aircraft. It seemed lovely to reach the Halt, although it is in fact rather worse here than when I went. The A.A. [anti-aircraft] are getting better shots. 5 have come down in Broadham Green, just behind Hurst Green Church, but only damaging houses everywhere and people cut by glass. Bron has her ceiling down in the front room and lies upstairs in much mental distress clutching the new babe, born on Sunday – a girl. It's a bit difficult to adjust to. Yesterday I just sat staring out of the window when one stopped, until brought to earth by the bang. Evelyn at the other end of the phone had rapidly left her window for a better spot. However – I expect I shall continue here after all. I write better – and I don't quite like leaving Bron and Ian and Sheila and Miriam in the thick of it. [. . .]

There's one just gone over now. The musical difficulty is to keep our ear open for them while using one's ears for other more subtle purposes. Perhaps the whole war won't be much longer now.

10 August 1944

On Tuesday at 5.55 a.m. the thing decided itself. The other cottages destroyed – both children and Miriam and Ben unhurt. Jack in hospital and will recover. Bronwen dead. We are all pretty tearful – a real tragedy. I felt it like my own.

My cottage is not to be lived in at present. Present address will be c/o Shaxson, Elsted Manor, nr Midhurst, Sussex. (Tel. Harting 92.) Will be there from Friday midday. Shan't stay for Bron's funeral which is Sat. Will send a wreath from you or us both.

Love
M.

2 January 1945

Best beloved –

Everything has come safely – many many thanks. The cottage is still a muddle mostly because the spare room hasn't been put back, so that there's an accumulation everywhere else. The good Mrs Brown is busy now scrubbing my bed-room, and every fresh scrub brings the floors back to a bit nearer their proper colour. But it'll be a wonder if the white mortar ever really comes off entirely. The walls go successfully whiter and have nearly dried out. The next job I think is to try and get curtain-rodding put up by a carpenter. I hitch up that dark red materi-al you left, it's lovely in colour.

The pipes did not freeze, to my surprise, and though the cottage still strikes colder than it ought, we shall gradually overcome that as it's lived in continuously and the weather slowly warms.

Our Bach–Purcell concert at Friends' House on Sunday last sold out! Despite rather a 'crab' from *The Times* it was really a great suc-cess, and I enjoyed every moment of doing it. I do not enjoy trying to get a tolerable performance of the *Child*. I shall have to go through the ordeal again, end of February at Albert Hall.

Hope now to get back on to the Symphony [No. 1] and get at least another movement done.

Your piano is a problem I must tackle too. The blast has in reality lifted all the 'ivory' off the pegs, which gradually comes off key by key, till one will play on wood only soon. Also I hadn't realised there's glass inside too. So I'll consult Chappell's about it first, and then, if no go, my own local people. Will write more later. Am 40 today!

Love to you all –
Michael

January 1945

Fresca dear –

I wish I had realised it was your birthday and I would have greeted you properly and according – but the lord sent you a good present, if the work went well for a morning.

I shouldn't worry, dear, as to whether you are destructive or not, because it isn't at all like that. Spontaneous, irrational, irruptive living is a value of its own which can be oneself. It is not destructive at all of itself – but to people in whom this is the shadow side, it may exercise a remarkable fascination – a desire and need to come to closer contact with this polar opposite – and in that person the object of the fascina-tion may appear to be the cause of drawing the underside of the 'con-trolled' person into destructive operations – but the first point is that the irrational, irruptive pole of a 'controlled' person would be quite harmless, indeed would be exceedingly beneficial, if they would live it out and come to terms with it and see it with clear eyes instead of with fascination and all the attendant unconsciousness. If the two Js aren't quite whole persons in this technically psychological sense, then either you run away or you take the relationship with all its *Unzuläng[lich]keiten* – its fascination and its polar danger. The idea that *you* are the activity of destructiveness is I'm afraid rubbish – that is the misunderstanding of J.2, despite the numerology. If you are fascinated yourself to such a degree, or in such a manner, that you project the word of the father–lawgiver onto J., so that his projections in you become laws of *your* being – then 'go to it' and the lord be with you – as he will. There's everything to be said for living as opposed to understanding – a statement of values which betrays my own shadow. I think however probably the way along, or out, lies on the path of a subtler relationship of feeling – a deeper union springing from sources wider than the chaotic and impulsive. If you remember for a moment how the impulsive in the art creation, or even art reception, is refined by judgments of feeling, which you can do very well, you can imagine what such a combination is in relationship – it lies, my cherub, in you, to that extent. Love is not at all only the chaotic – there is a reaching out towards something deeper, or wider, or lighter – perhaps it's a something which takes a Jessie, or the two in the phone-box, and can hold many more strands of feeling within the one woof.

    Grove came this morning. Schott's have given me one of the 30/- volumes free! The one, oddly enough, in which I appear.

    Much love

    Michael

Tell Den I got his letter and will write – or anyhow will bring the Essays on Sat.

Alan Bush

Tippett became acquainted with the composer Alan Bush (1900–95) through Francesca Allinson in the late 1920s. At the time Bush was teaching composition at the Royal Academy of Music and starting a two-year period of study in Berlin, in addition to acting as music adviser and conductor to the London Labour Choral Union. In 1935 he joined the Communist Party and a year later formed the Workers' Music Association (of whose executive committee Tippett became a member). Bush's political credo found expression above all in his choral music and his four full-length operas. Tippett's letters to him evince a vigorous and sometimes heated debate on the distinctions between Trotskyism and communism, but their differences never stood in the way of their firm friendship and they remained mutually supportive colleagues.

28 February 1934

Dear Alan,

[. . .] You are lucky to be writing – I haven't had a moment since I finished the Symphony [in B flat] in Nov. I don't think you'll like it. The first movement anyhow is badly written. And the orchestral idiom was too new to me to be quite free of the scores I have looked at – you'll have to make allowances for that. But I think I'm prepared to stick by it. It'll have to stand now, with a few tinkerings in the first allegro. [. . .]

Yours
Michael

23 May 1934

My dear Alan,

I am going to appeal to you on a delicate matter and I can't help it because it seems to me necessary. As you may know I've been very much bound up with Wilf [Franks] for the last year or two. You have been very near to him at one time and that is the present bond of union, even if there were no other – and there is. But leaving that aside, my trouble is a growing dissatisfaction with the manner of Wilf's living – feeding and clothing himself on charity – he hates it even he is good about it, and I hate its method also, and so much so that I want to make an appeal for him to end it. There is a so much nicer way of doing it. Therefore David Ayerst – *Manchester Guardian* friend of myself and Wilf, and you may have met him at my Morley concert – have agreed to put up yearly £10 for him, to be paid by me half-yearly to him. And we want to raise £50 in this way, to assure Wilf a safe pound a week. There is to be absolutely no moral obliga-tion behind it. It is to be given out of straightforward love for him, for his own unwarranted self, and to work out his own destiny as best it seems to him. Actually he wants to paint if it really comes his way (I've talked to him about it), and I with a tiny amount of savings I no longer care to keep, will give him a lump sum down, up to £50 if I can, to set himself up with.

Will you join us in this – £10 a year? You see, Alan, I can't take £10 p.a. as a more serious item than tobacco or any luxury, and goodness knows Wilf is a pardonable enough luxury to those of us who really care about him, and I think inside yourself you do, as I do. Maybe £50 a year is too small for him to do anything on, and I shall make efforts to get more, but I don't think everyone can be trusted to contribute to his 'fund' without *arrière-pensées* as to his worth, gratitude to use etc etc. And Wilf sees this small sum as something like real freedom from distressing personal charity as well as from a labour market already overstocked and disgusting.

I have written therefore to Rolf [Gardiner] because they did care for one another very much for many years and Rolf ought to be able to see it with kindly and generous eyes – also to another nearer friend of Wilf's, a Miss Judy Wogan who runs a theatre – actually where they performed that unfortunate out-of-work play that you and I, I think, financed somewhat drastically. But this is not such an appeal – this is Wilf himself and is going to mean a very great deal if it comes off. Now, if you don't want to, curse me and say 'no' bluntly – and any-how it's all in confidence – and forgive the suggestion if it seems unwarrantable – but I'm too much in sympathy with you to be afraid of your wrath and so I've just written badly and boldly.

[. . .] I am growing more revolutionary now again – my revolution-ary cousin [Phyllis Kemp], who you met with me at B.M. [British

Museum], is living with me, because she is out of a job for the moment and is teaching me a great deal of 'technique' on the subject – and anyhow I'm going to set some lovely Blake words against Tyranny and Slavery [*A Song of Liberty*, from 'The Marriage of Heaven and Hell']. But it'll be a long time before it gets done.

Have you finished the piano concerto?

Remember me to your wife.

Ever yours

Michael Tippett

24 July 1934

Dear Alan,

[. . .] I should like to see your *Songs of the Doomed* – have you a spare copy? Somehow or other I'll have to get to see you and borrow a score for a bit. I haven't written any songs – but I want to write a revolutionary choral work on some Blake words and would like to see how you deal with the problems involved first. I'm away all August with Wilf – first of all doing a musical and comfortably romantic hotchpotch operetta [*Robin Hood*] with the Cleveland mining villages and then hiking to Pennines with tent – Wilf carrying most of the gear I'm quite certain – though I am stronger than I look.

The BBC tried over my Symphony [in B flat] and I had eventually to conduct – and they were not a little amused! What's to come of it I don't know – I'm very happy at work on a quartet [String Quartet No. 1] – my really pet medium.

I want to see you a lot to talk Communism with you seriously. I've got it badly for the moment – when you are not away in Sept. I'll come to you and bring Wilf – unless by any happy chance you could be persuaded to visit us both here – it would be a great honour – perhaps for instance you could come home with me on Sept. 13 and we'll take Wilf as well – think about it and accept. But if reluctant we'll come to you.

Yours

Micky

July 1936

Mein treurster Alan,

I don't know what you want to do about Wilf this year. For myself

I am quite willing to go on letting him have the means to keep himself out of unhappiness etc because I said I would and meant it and mean it, which is more important. Because I don't think there is any sanctity about things of this sort. They are valid just so long as they are and no more. Wilf is now at the school but heaven alone knows what he will do with himself and how he is to get away with it eventually. I am no longer in the same emotional dependence to him, and that is a great essential, but as I knew from the first I have a natural loyalty and also a sense of (probably false and sentimental) humanity in this instance. I therefore without great sacrifices, which would cripple me, at all am bound to go on supporting him as I have undertaken to do. I let him have £5 a month, £60 p.a. that is. For you, best of friends it is absolutely not I think a serious matter, that of loyalty, I mean it need not be morally. So let me know sometime at your leisure what you want to do about it. Or just leave it.

On the other matter. I think sometime or other you will have to read the opposition case with even greater objectivity than I have probably read the orthodox. There is a book just out which I think goes very reasonably into the whole polemic, by that I mean it puts the case at the time it really first came to blows in 1928. That is to say that it is as it were the basic document of the opposition from which their whole criticism and antics has followed. [. . .] It is by Tr[otsky], *The Third International after Lenin*, and is the criticism of 1928 of the Comintern programme, so quite fundamental.* In fact he got kicked out for it. Because it makes the break so clear as to be unavoidable. I don't know whether it really is an effort to convert you thus, but as well it is a more friendly wish to hear your reply to the fundamental question of 'Socialism in a single country' from which the whole divergence springs. And the forecasts as to the C.I. turns, which T. was able to make from his analysis even in 28. That is truly remarkable and very difficult to get over for me. If he predicted so accurately what is the secret. I might point out *en passant* that your remark as to the ineffectiveness of T.'s efforts to bring off a rev[olution] after so many years is two-edged. What about the C.I. and the whole of the S.U. [Soviet

---

* The International movements (First founded 1864, Second in 1889, Third in 1919) were an organization of socialists, anarchists and nationalists whose initial goal was to reform and improve the conditions of labour for the working man, and to unify the socialist parties and trade unions. The Third International of the European socialist movement, formed by the Soviet Communists under Lenin, was better known as the Comintern.

Union] behind it, in the same period. Much more damning I'm afraid. It is part of our case. The existence of continual good situations for the rev. class struggle turned into a series of defeats. A party and International that sets out to win the masses from reformism and 13 years afterwards with a mass party, or something near it, can only blame the Social Democracy for not bringing off what reformism never set out to do. And so on . . . I won't bore you further.

    Much love to you all

    Michael

July 1936

Dear Alan,

    Don't be worried by these rows of letters. I get into the habit of writing a whole batch to someone and then stop for a bit. I am beginning to see the way things are going on the Continent and it seems to me to be as serious as it could be. Partly because I am in the middle of reading a fully documented account of the socialist movement just before the war and during it. It is pretty melancholy. I have before me the joint manifestos in German and French of the two S[ocialist] parties just before the war. The international appeal to a general strike. The international demonstrations, the telegrams and visits between the G[erman] and F[rench] socialists the last week before it happened. And then the sudden change. The Kaiser becomes the bogey, not capitalism, the Tsar likewise. Then one turns to the present situation. Germany is off the map. The Allies, centred in the L[eague] of Nations, are feverishly arming. They proclaim peace, because they are not ready. What is the international Labour doing. Stating in print and in conference, in parliament, that it will fight for the L. of Nations. The Dardanelles Conference is the last act of the encirclement of Germany. It happened before the last war. This time it is the answer to [Hjalmar Horace Greeley] Schacht's visits in the Balkans. Germany's answer is the pact with Austria and the understanding with Italy. Frightened by this Br[itain] gives in to the Arabs (very significant) and tries to win Italy back by withdrawing ships from the Mediterranean. Hitler tries out his powers in the Danzig affair. [Arthur] Greiser cocks a snook at the L. of Nations while the Czech Jew shoots himself there and leaves letters to [Maxim] Litvinov. *The Times*, the *Manchester Guardian*, King Edward. Symbolic names. And the effect on me is deplorable, because my one hope is that the Br. Empire will go under and Hitler win, rather than the reverse and the whole business begin over again. I hate the Empire as I hate nothing else. It is the key pin of world capitalism and it's our job to bring it to the ground. Actually a defeat of England means the freedom of India. I am afraid the S.U. to me cannot alter the fundamentals of this situation. It is the S.U. not the L. of N. that is looking for allies in the war. The imperialists have the whip hand and will dictate the terms. This was shown over Abyssinia, the Cap. powers went their way, public opinion of Litvinov did not matter to them. All they want L. to do for their promised support is to get the workers behind the armies. How? by the slogans, collective security for the Liberals, peace-loving states for the pacifists, democracy versus fascism from the S.U., defence of the S.U. for Alan Bush. And so it goes on I'm afraid. Well you won't catch the internationalists. Our minds are on the concrete problem now. How to survive in the opening phases of the coming war and how to organise illegal literature etc for the eventual turn against them while shoot who led them into it.

Conscription is coming in this country. Our chance to get an international in existence in the army itself. L. of N. peace front is worse than useless, because it takes your mind off the real problem. The preparation for a seizure of power as the result of a war. So Stalinised do you all become that a pacifist is worth more to you than a 'leftist' revolutionary. [Fred] Zeller has been sent to prison in France for work among the Fr. army. But he was also set upon and beaten up by the YCL [Young Communist League] at the wall of the communards. Very significant. In exactly the same way Mr [Emil] Burns, official of the party here, attacks Ben [Britten] as counterrevolutionary because he hasn't joined the L. of N. Union. But gets away with Ashworth, the fellow who was such a nuisance when you and Nancy were here. Of course I know that isn't the whole story of the party by any means, but it is significant. A revolutionary attitude to war is suspect. We must wait till the war breaks out etc. Futility. Not even the widest international promises and peace fronts were any use in the last war. Why should they be in this? The lesson of the last war, the basis of the 3rd I[nternational], was that nothing could stand through the war but an intransigent revolutionary internationalism. The L. of N. is neither one nor the other. Nor the R.C. church, nor the pacifists. Nor the 2nd I. What of the 3rd I. and its flirtation with all the latter? I'm afraid I no longer trust its leadership though I like its rank and file in this country.

This 7th Congress states that the fight is now between democracy and fascism. Balls. It is as ever the fight of the proletariat for an international socialist society. The fight for democracy belongs to the old Fr. and 48 revolutions. It is purely retrogressive to answer the retrogression of capitalism to fascism by a retrogression ourselves. We have got to go on ahead and strike out for a line which cuts right across the coming imperialist war. This the slogan defence of democracy can never do. It is the slogan of the enemy. It can not be used to our advantage. This is the whole lesson of the last war. Do not throw it away so lightly because the S.U. is also involved in the next war. Wait till the 300 m.p.h. Br. bombers go for Moscow as Churchill will manage somehow. It will be too late then to stem the patriotic fervour you will have stirred up round the L. of N. and peace. Sorry but I'm not an optimist.

Much love anyhow and will see you soon.

Michael

8 July 1936

Alan mine,

[. . .] Do you realise the significance of Danzig? Do you see how it is the test of internal socialism? Just as the sun showed so soon after the Hitler *empiètement* how low was the feeling for internal, w.cl. [working-class] solidarity, so that Hitlerism polled 90% of the votes against a United Front of the 2nd, 3rd Internationals and the R.C. Church – so in Danzig again we shall have a new Marxist or realist test – will the internationalism of the Soc. movement be stronger than the Nazi nationalism? It's no good deluding ourselves – these tests of history must be read or Marxism is not a science at all. We shall be able to tell how much the U.F. has healed the German wounds of the '3rd period' and how much the old internationals can bring back a sense of w. class internal solidarity – You see, on that turns the whole problem of a new International. The demand for a 4th I[international] came actually from the German group after Hitler. They believed, from within, that both the old Internationals had falsified their positions in face of the enemy, and that to build them again was hopeless – the Saar only confirmed this view. Danzig will test it again – will the U.F. and the League of Nations be able to stand against Hitlerism? It certainly has more chance this time – but it will fail just exactly where the U.F. turns to make a pact with L. of Nat. – just there, the Nazis pounce on it, and raise the slogan 'Free Danzig', 'Against the L. of Nations [Maude] Royden' – in other words the 'war of liberation' political force is all on the side of the Nazis – it is important to remember that in 1919 the Danzig German dockers refused to handle Polish stuff, in the war against Sov. Russia. Where are we now, 1936. Isn't it true that despite the enormous soc[ialist] construction in Russia etc the German dockers now would refuse to handle stuff in a war of Poland and Germany? Why? We need a Marxist evaluation of this – why has the 3rd I. founded in 1919, on the wave of internal rev., gone lower in power, despite 10 years of revolutionary movement up and down, and an increasing strength of soc. construction in the S.U. [Soviet Union]. These are the questions which are bound up with the struggle over the 4th I. My chief criticism of all the C.P. [Communist Party] lot here is that these questions cannot be discussed openly. That is 'counter rev[olution]ism' and means immediate expulsion, and the YCL [Young Communist League] are being told from above to bring about the expulsion of the S. Militant group even when a baby one of 25 to 30 young people. Evidently they are afraid up 'top'. Now why? Perhaps the YCL have got it all wrong – I should like to know.

dein
Michael

6 October 1939

Dear Alan,

[. . .] I should also like to see you one day, perhaps a visit on a Sat. – I have a choir to do for the RACS [Royal Arsenal Co-operative Society] on Sunday afternoons now. I would like to know what you think of things and about music. I am contemplating an oratorio on the Grynspan story [A Child of Our Time] and it seems probably that T. S. Eliot will write the words for me. But it won't be political – in the strict sense of the term – I seem to have drifted out of serious politics some time ago – the music demanded too much and the politics ceased to excite me. I lost touch with my one-time associates, who appear to be under lock and key anyhow. I like predicting the facts and events, but it stops there.

Love to Nancy and the children.
Michael
Send me a p.c. if you will about 'Prison Cycle' rehearsal. Thanks.

6 February 1940

Dear Alan,

[. . .] I fully understand about the String Concerto [Concerto for Double String Orchestra] and your orchestra – I only asked because of my impatience. I have faith in this particular work, and am besides longing to hear it. It's gone now to America on one side, and yesterday I took a score into the BBC. Whether I can control myself from trying it out at Morley is another matter!

My Piano Sonata [No. 1] is going to be done after all at next Morley concert – Mar. 17. Come if you can. It's a reasonable hour – 6–8 p.m.

Don't take my strictness on your article, or anything else, too seriously. I have a different temperament-ed sort of mind from yours, in that I perceive things more quickly than I can systematise them. I perceive all sorts of things just now which I can't fit into Marxism (or perhaps my Marxism is permanently narrowed by my mind). I have no final guarantee that these perceptions are objective until they accord with someone else's system. But to people of my temperament these perceptions are the direct, immediate method of objective experience and are trusted as another person trusts logic. As far as I understand my job at all, it is to give expression to these perceptions, clarified and enticised to the limit of my ability. I might perceive too romantically, or entice too classically – I am hoping to attain to some durable balance. The question of assimilation of the 'classical' tradition is the point I've just got to, having lived out the jejune romanticism of my adolescence. And this fascination with traditional artistic values looks, I should imagine, somewhat reactionary – because the two often go together – as in T. S. Eliot. But what I get from, say, Eliot's literary criticism is the classical attitude of mind, which somewhat suddenly begins to flower in my own mind. And it does not worry me where I get it from. I am reaching out towards opera – some years ahead. But you will see the same process in the oratorio I am doing now [*A Child of Our Time*]. Almost a resuscitation of a traditional form. There are choruses, arias, recitative (!) and chorale. It is only the content and one or two more subtle means of expression which are modern. The recitative in principle goes back to Lawes and Purcell – the arias to Handel – but the chorales to Negro 'hot' singing. (I admit that tradition may be somewhat abrupt!) The content of this oratorio I have had to accept almost like revelation – I concentrate all my attention and critical faculties on the technique of the presentation. If I don't do that the 'content' gives me nightmares – it's very near the edge.

Best wishes
Micky

19 March 1944

Dear Alan,

Thank you for the lecture last night – on behalf of Morley College. If we manage to do our autumn series, I'll write you again. These series are tricky things. A good one draws a full house, 200 or more. But it needs star names, and at present of the older generation rather. (Herbert Read *par exemple* and Vaughan Williams.) But a lot depends too on careful preliminary lay out and good publicity. We'll do better in a next venture.

I found your argument (which I've heard you argue before of course) more satisfactory than your examples. They rather worried me as being too unscholarly. I could make out a better case by such means for the 'other side' – but it would be pointless to do so, and would 'prove' nothing. For however much attention to details may show that the art rhythms in history are not perhaps so immediate to the movements of social demand in all cases as we think, yet the interaction of social life and music, one part of it, is obvious just because music is a part of social life. I remember way back at the conference in the Queen Mary Hall thinking that the title 'Music and Life' does more harm than good – because it seems to postulate exactly the nonsense it sets out to disprove. And I'm quite sure that for the audience last night the problem of 'music' as antithetical to 'life' does not obtain. Also [Ernest] Newman is already *vieux jeu* to boys like Amis and [Antony] Hopkins and their age. Their gods are you and me and our generation – and in most cases that I know our generation live in pretty close contact with the musical social life of the time. I know it's beginning to weigh quite heavily upon me, when I begin to realise how much we are looked up to as to set the tone for so much common music-making. (I leave out of account for the moment the orchestral concert racket.) I feel more clearly now than I did that in my opinion your best service to our time is your musical gifts. I remember your performance of the 3 pieces from Berg's *Lyric Suite* as a drinking in a thirsty land. Now that for a precious moment new music is almost an economic proposition, I wish you were there and about to help widen the breach. But

I realise only too well how you are caged up in the RAMC [Royal Army Medical Corps]. I wish you were not. Also I wish we could float more of your works out on to the flood waters – or the tiny stream rather – of the slowly rising interest in English music of the day, that is not Bax – or even Ireland – but on cleaner, tougher lines. I find there's a real young audience growing up, some all but hopeful, which seems in sympathy with what we are trying to do; meaning 'we' in a wide sense. There are even young ensembles like the Zorian 4tet [founded by Olive Zorian] who want (!) to play the new music to the new audience. Odd places like Leamington, the Gallery at Leicester, Morley College etc which are offering tiny platforms for these ventures. It's a healthy sign. I must see if we can't take *Dialectic* [string quartet by Bush] out of the box again. I personally would like to revive the *Songs of the Doomed*, but I gather you told Amis you thought them inappropriate at this time. Is that final, or would you let me have the score and material? I thought the vocal line damned good, I remember – and something which the very young might well emulate. I like too the cello and piano piece [Concert Piece, Op. 17] and nearly managed to get a Morley do of it, but [Norina] Semino fell through. Boosey & Hawkes now, who are good publishers, and have as much EPT as they need, can't they do *Dialectic* at one of their concerts? I hate to seem interfering, or I'd go and ginger up old [Alfred] Kalmus thereabout. B. & H. incidentally, seeing how new 'music' is beginning to rise in stock prices, have decided to turn their newsletter *Tempo* into a magazine for and about such music. That's really a very good sign too.

Have you enough free time do you think to take over one of the concerts at Morley? (monthly Saturdays at 6 p.m.) But I'd have to talk that out with you. I think it a good idea. We're always a long way ahead. I'm now planning the autumn.

All good wishes

Yours

Michael

If these vague amorphous wishes all break on the rock of RAMC duty don't bother to answer.

20 September 1944

My dear Alan,

Glad to get your letter. I only got back into a sort of residence here on Tuesday. We had a flying bomb 6 weeks ago that destroyed the other cottages, killing Bronwen Wilson, Ben Lewis's married daughter, and though the grand-parents, son-in-law and babies came out (of the Morrison shelters*) it was a considerable shock – and it knocked my new bungalow sadly, to the extent of eventual partial rebuilding, and present discomforts. I have been glazing and trying to make some rooms bearable for the coming winter. However I'm thankful to be back. [. . .]

About the spirituality in the *Child*. Did you ever see the [Paul] Robeson film, *The Proud Valley* [1939]? There, in the mining valleys, when the community wants to express its grief at the death of a work-er by pit accident – the Negro, the comrade who has been gradually accepted into the community leads the singing; and it is 'Deep River'. I did not know about this precedent before I had chosen my own spir-ituals, but I saw that it was simply the same function at work. I mean, that spirituals used thus, are functional; to express common emotions at a common level. They won't bear examination as a function of social teaching, for the reasons you state. But just as in the Robeson film one finds even Welsh folk humming to the Negro spiritual at the emotional climax, so it can become a common emotional experience within a certain sort of setting. I dare say if you sing it at a church parade or whatever, it might be shifted over towards the 'Jesus' ele-ment. But that does not happen very sharply with the film, nor with the *Child*; because there the preceding solos set an atmosphere of a dif-ferent sort, so that the associations are more toward the Negro ele-ment for its two other characteristics; its cry of an oppressed race; its connection with jazz and that popular musical idiom. In fact, the spir-ituals did enable one to have 5 solid chunks of tonal mass in the mid-dle of the tonally fluid music in the solos and choruses and recitatives; and to draw material musically from them, so that one of the solos could become a Kurt Weill tango without too violent an artistic shock. I don't think in fact that the listener experiences the spirituals in any 'Christian' way, but at some other level. I am quite sure, of course, that he does not experience them at the level you probably would wish; i.e. more conscious political affirmation. I am afraid I got caught up in the drama of the whole thing beyond my political powers, so to speak. I chose the spirituals by instinct, because I knew indeed of no positive

* Portable steel air-raid shelters used indoors.

social songs with just those terrific common emotional powers. And I believe I was correct, for the work I was doing. Something you said made it clear to me. I realised afterwards that I had intuitively taken [Herschel] Grynspan as hero (rather than Dimitrov) because it is the portrayal of men and women who endure without 'the key', and yet endure; whose heroism is of an almost unconscious toughness. In the same way, though my hero is anything but non-violent, and stands for all the men and women drawn into the war (that is the symbol of his shot) he has all my artistic sympathy; much as Shakespeare may have felt for Othello, without thereby preaching wife-strangling. (Incidentally one critic accused me of advocating political assassination!) Further, despite Dyneley Hussey's misgivings, the soldiers in the audience were not defeatist, nor does it have that effect. I had innumerable letters telling me of the courage and strength it gave people unknown to me; especially mothers of men overseas. I was not unduly surprised, because the real hero is the 'Little Man' in all his extraordinary passion of endurance, within a world of, to his eyes, vast uncontrollable catastrophes. And it also sees that Hitler (and in some degree every modern national dictator) is the Little Man deified, filled out with all the powers that the millions of little men have delegated. And then it showed the still typical Little Man brought up, beyond his conscious powers, by the forces of history into an equal and opposite action to the dictator; the Man of Destiny – and the tragedy that results from the dramatic clash. (Tragedy in an artistic sense, not moral.) I am of the opinion myself that not a great deal of conscious positive activist politics could enter successfully into this type of artistic work. If it is nevertheless to be judged reactionary, then I imagine it means that it is a barometer of its time even in that. The whole work is that of an impression, of something suffered. Hence on one side the power with which it describes the passion of endurance of our time, and the other the lack within it of political directives. As it is consciously of man's shadow side I am personally not distressed that man in it appears in the shadow; and I myself lived very close up to the shadowy depths at that time, to the extent that Evil seemed to haunt this cottage like a presence. I had no more power to exorcise it than to stop the blitz with which it coincided. All I could do was to keep my courage as best I could and I twice ran away; not from the blitz, but from the moral horror. I am not able to deny these experiences and I am also aware how common they are and just what they have to do with the depths and the pity that sound in the *Child*. And that's all I know about it.

It's to be broadcast Wed. evening Oct. 25th. Sargent will do it at Liverpool on Nov. 11th, preceded by the Mozart Requiem. And I have to do it at Leicester in December. There's also enquiries from abroad. I expect it'll have its day for a time; but the general mood will change of course, until the next war begins to rear its head. Perhaps it won't, in our time.

Morley is full up till after Xmas and a lot of it for the spring. It depends just on the answer of some other folk. I'll let you know quite soon. If I can fit you in, I will.

I shall certainly come to the programme of your own compositions and publicise it too as much as I may. I've got a Friends' House concert for Morley's benefit on Dec. 31st, and perhaps our programmes might carry an advert of your Jan. 6 do?

I gather that you've realised how much of your piano works has got into my Sonata [Piano Sonata No. 1]! I didn't realise it till afterwards, or it might have been more. I'm afraid it's a naive way of saying how much I learnt from the study of your music. It came just at the right moment. Latterly the influences have been all from the past. The Elizabethans and Purcell and Monteverdi, and in the new Symphony [No. 1] even Pérotin!

Like to see you sometime.

Yours
Michael

[autumn 1944]

My dear Alan,

Excuse my writing again. As you may have observed, and may remember, I seem to help clear myself (as far as I ever get clear) of the dead weight of *Weltschmerz* and other allied emotions, by writing people of intelligence. This is not so much to bother them, as to give myself the illusion of corresponding, and of discussion, which I miss very much. Since writing you last it has been dawning upon me that the *Child of Our Time* is only too continuously a document of our day. Its deepest sympathy, in fact its hero, is the modern scapegoat – who are often whole classes of people, such as Jews, Negroes – and in my opinion political groups like anarchists, Trotskyists. I am of the opinion also, as far as my psychological insight goes, that this is true scape-goatism: that is to say that the ordinary man, and the demagogic ruler in face of the masses of ordinary men, are catastrophically unable to accept responsibility of social errors etc, etc – which, nowadays, we have little means of diverting upon God, or any transcendent princi-ple. Actually this moral problem is also in Marx of course. On one hand you have the capitalist class depicted as the individual responsi-ble agents of an immoral society; on the other hand you have the whole process given an aura of transcendence through the Dialectic. (It was also in Christianity. Is Judas a bad man, or the involuntary agent of the divine drama of atonement?) I am not meaning to ques-tion the moral truth of Marx's judgment in this – only to disclose, what is not always realised, that there are mental conditions within which man has thought, for centuries past, always coming up against the same type of dichotomies and paradoxes that lie in the nature of our intellectual apprehension.

To return to present day: I feel that the war is felt by people deep down to be a confusion and an error: a disillusion. The process is well described by *Mass Observation: The Journey Home.** People speak of another inevitable slump – another way (usually thought of with Russia). A desperate effort is bound to be made to put over the idea that all modern wars spring from the aggressiveness of certain coun-tries, and one in particular. If it won't matter whether this idea is fed by Left or Right (as it will be, by both) – the psychological conse-quences and processes are the same for both these viewpoints. Germany will be the next great example of the mass scapegoat. And there the oratorio will speak to this condition, though it will do so by the symbols of Jew and Negro! Actually the whole political set-up can't last. Morally, for the above reasons, everyone will be forced to 'punish' Germany, and to disarm and de-industrialise her etc, etc. Because such is the thesis that alone seems to make sense of the destruction of the war. And the victors are to remain armed against a possibly resurgent Germany. But also in point of fact a new modern nation has been produced by this war – Russia. She will have a vast military machine to watch the German E. frontier, and USA–Britain will have such, to watch the W. frontier. But in the no-man's-land will

---

* Mass observation: study of the details of people's daily lives. A society of the name, founded in 1937 in London, used observers and interviewers to discover the habits and opinions of communities.

be nothing serious to watch: until of course one or the other decides to make of this vacuum an attempted bastion. So that, as I see it, very quickly the military or power-politics forces will be moving exactly contrary to the moralist psychology. The latter will change, because it is only the present symbol of an inner *Einstellung*. A new symbol will be found for the projection of the attitude: a new scapegoat. 'All would be at peace, like in England, if only — were to play the game.' And so on. (The 'Polish Crisis' has all the necessary psychological material ready.)

It is very easy to deceive oneself in these matters. One is apt to believe that a national sympathy with Russia indicates a realist sympathy with its economics, its realities. It isn't always clear to us to what extent it is possible to have a mental Russia – an image expressly designed to satisfy our present need. If we do not realise this, we get shocked and surprised when the image shifts. This came home to me first with tremendous force when the Germans attacked Russia. The mechanism of this scapegoat business is so emotional that the 'workers' fatherland' can be made a reacting Jewish plutocracy – or anything you like – within a decade. On the other side, you can get [Joachim von] Ribbentrop and [V. M.] Molotov drinking together in Moscow, or whatever it is, and the reverse in so many hours, almost. There is nothing whatever objective and factual to prevent it, I fancy – because mass man is completely the slave of his own inferiority. His chief desire . . . at the moment is to be let alone and to be allowed to go home and enjoy his wife – but he has no moral resistance against mass conscription whether for war or labour – and that is the case over the whole Western world, including, to my seeing, the Soviets. In conditions like these the largest propaganda apparatus probably wins. This goes for all minority opinions, like Trotskyism, anarchism, pacifism. They are still-born in a mass sense. I don't look to any of them to save the political world, whatever they themselves may imagine. But I also feel that Marxism in any traditional sense is also 'still-born' on these decadent dogs as against the propaganda power of the state machine. The CPGB [Communist Party of Great Britain] will always tend to act, by the force of circumstances, as though it were the foreign policy of USSR. And it will be so treated. In a head-on collision with that state it would be suppressed, without affecting the conscription issue: for Russia would by then be the mass psychological scapegoat and would appear to all as Germany does now: and Russia probably does now to

Germany. The Churches are equally powerless in these circumstances. They can be suppressed also without unduly shaking society.

I hadn't meant to write at this length, and what will I know seem horribly muddled, blasphemous and defeatist. It is only all these if looked at from the security of any point of view where you believe that you are on the stream of the control of events. You believe, I fancy, that you are thus, through your political life. I have the tendency to believe that I am only thus in my activity as an artist. Politics, at present, seems to me to become catastrophic consequences of power clashes, and, for some odd reason I cannot explain, I am emotionally outside and tolerable uninfluenced by these power combinations. My pacifism springs from this psychological fact, much more than from any sense of moral value. Hence I never preach it, morally. I often discuss it with soldiers and RAF, because I'm interested in the extent to which it has moral value for them. So often it is regarded by them as the way of the Saint, and hence not feasible, for them, poor mortals not being a saint. I like to try and see to what extent they can accept it when it comes out in an ordinary mere man. If I do have sympathy it goes at once to the underdog: the little chap: the ordinary soldier; the workman; the dopey; the child; the scapegoat. For some unexplained sentimentality, which is too deep for eradication it appears, these sympathies are immediate and not conditioned by the names. I remember when the chaining of prisoners racket began: my relation was simply: I am on the side of the prisoners. In the war: I am on the side of the soldiers and the sufferers without undue distraction; be they Russian or German. It's a very feminine attitude and has probably too little of the male. But I dare say it's also partly conditioned by the catastrophic consequences of male political pride – which has yet to bring further catastrophes on our own conceited heads. I feel the message of the oratorio is fundamental. I would know my shadow and my light, so shall I at last be whole. That goes for nations and individuals, and even classes. The modern state is so Calvinist that it is truly frightening. Before our eyes justification by works, which is an arduous discipline, becomes justification by faith, and the chopping off of heretical heads. No wonder there is a Catholic Revival. It's in the nature of a reflex action, and could be predicted.

All good wishes and forgive this scribble.

Herzlichst

Michael

PS. You'd better read the letter first. I hadn't meant to send you this, because I didn't want to upset you further. You will loathe it. It will seem so hopelessly muddled and sentimental. It is and it isn't! It is also, in another phase, Lenin's *What is to be done?* of 1893 or whatever the date is [1902]. It summons certain small numbers of people towards the formation of an elite, if you like. Hence its accent on personism. It makes clear to these youngsters who have gone, often, inarticulately to prison, that there are other social problems – e.g. usury – which have to be reckoned with; let alone the way we are going to react to the deep-seated change in the climate of opinion towards technical and materialist self-destruction. I am doubtful whether what I have in mind can be done by the organisation of a Party. I am not sure yet how the association I envisage is to work; nor its application in any way to overt politics. The new thing I want must be born in the full daylight – and it demands a justification by works. First of all it must stand you on your feet upright – even to the tune of going to prison. The heroic virtues must, unfortunately, be the initial self-dedication, the call. But, not Calvinist, or merely moralist. Hence the best of gaiety. 'Grim and gay' as Yeats said. Because Calvinism is the old split; the unorthodox is the scapegoat. Hence the real and much more difficult dedication is the problem of the 'whole man'. I am preparing an opera on these lines! My 'whole man' looks very much like Lenin's dedicated revolutionary – and the impact such men might make on the change in the climate of opinion. The added and new technique of that of deep psychology. It's too long for explanation by letter.

9 September 1962

Dear Alan,

I am curious to know what you thought of *King Priam*. I deplore our 'distance' (as composers) from colleagues; but can see no other way here in England. We're just preoccupied with our own sphere of work.

As to your request, I'd rather meet and talk with you and Nancy for our own sakes than debate in a meeting. But you no doubt could well answer that we should do both. The trouble, as always for me, is time and energy – not made any easier (perhaps deliberately!) by being 100 miles from London. I have a fantastic series of commissions to carry out this winter.

However, as it's you, I certainly ought to say yes, much as it misgive me. So let us take a risk (of my being too hopelessly involved to manage suddenly) and plonk for the 22nd January.

I doubt if I can accept your nice invitation to stay the night – I'd be more inclined to drive home late, so as to begin work again the next morning. Or alternatively do a London morning – which for my sins I sometimes have to. Anyhow, that can all wait till nearer the time.

About the war-cry in *King Priam* – no, not a Red Indian cry that I knew of. That is, I invented it out of my general store of memories. I thought indeed of varying it, but I got a bit fatigued; and I don't suppose Achilles would have varied it much.

I was excited by doing *King Priam*. It had some tremendous directness of utterance that pleased me, and that I worked hard for. Also, I was bucked by its manifest success. Over-sold-out on the last performance! I think it may go to W. Germany in the spring.

I hope of course to do another opera in some years' time. As different again. I find it a vastly stimulating form. I imagine you do too.

Till January – unless you are near Bath in the meantime. We have plenty of spare bedrooms.

Love to you both

Michael

PS. Phyllis Aschraf-Kemp lost her husband recently; died in E. Berlin.

June 1977

Dear Alan,

Thanks for everything. I didn't like the Henze opera [*We Come to the River*] much. I found the libretto un-focused with the 3 stages – and the music un-focused in another sense and without much depth. The politics, if that is the right word, I found (forgive me!) naive.

As to the other matter: I think we got a little at cross-purposes: at least I did. For I have certainly no principled view that music now should be international in character. The trouble is really that I find 'national' a term which is irrelevant to what I am doing: though clearly relevant to what you are doing. My comments are flawed with subjectivity! I always took those remarks of Stravinsky's with a grain of salt. I find much of his music magnificent in the sense I find other great composers' music magnificent – right across the 'political' or historical board, shall we say.

My big public, as of now, is the younger music lovers of America. So far as I can see they esteem my music in very little sense as English – but as Tippett. And I guess this somewhat to do with the fact that all my major works with words, since *A Child of Our Time* onwards, deal with material that is not national at all, but crosses all frontiers, or is at least relevant everywhere. So the whole non-vocal musical oeuvre gets tinged with this connection. The enclosed 'throw away' which came through the post today – and which I have had no hand in – seems to imply the same 'connection' in my 'native' country.

As you well know, that is how I would wish it to be.

Glad you have tickets for July 7 [for *The Ice Break*]. I'll get a libretto to you – though you won't dig it much, I fancy: either in language, which is American English, or in matter, which is not your line. Maybe Nancy's more – to whom all my love as well as to you, dear Alan,

Michael

Douglas Newton

Known to Tippett as a writer and poet, Douglas (Den) Newton (1920–2000) assisted the composer in preparing the text of A Child of Our Time *and the early drafts for the libretto of* The Midsummer Marriage. *The two were personal friends as well as collaborators, and the letters leave no room for doubt that they were also lovers. During the Second World War Newton, like Tippett, was a conscientious objector, and worked on Francesca Allinson's Doolittle Farm. After the war he was an editor, journalist and scriptwriter for the BBC before moving to New York in 1956. There he became an assistant, and later full, curator at the now defunct Museum of Primitive Art. A specialist in the arts of Oceania, on which he wrote and edited many books, he oversaw the transfer of the museum's holdings to the Metropolitan Museum, where he had been appointed chairman of the Department of Primitive Art.*

23 November 1939*

Den my boy,

[. . .] Many thanks for the copies – 'telescope' has already had to go because it has proved unsingable. I've had to come down to 'measure heav'n with a lens' – I guess that 'I have no money for my dinner' will also be unsingable in this connection, because it's too matter-of-fact in the rest of the imagery – I don't think you are really right about 'sweetheart', which has a long ancestry, but I will take more advice and cogitate. Actually I have to decide things now willy nilly because the music is pouring out – the soprano song after that one is already sketched out – 'How can I cherish my man'.

[. . .] I've thought of the most surrealist plot for a play or our opera [originally conceived as *The Man with Seven Daughters*] – beats 'music at night' into a cocked hat!

Yours ever
Michael

* Referring to an early printing and refinement of the text for *A Child of Our Time*.

24 June 1940

Dear Den,

[. . .] When the bombing comes to Oxted I shall go down the road to help – I don't feel equal to going ahead of myself into something that I don't believe in on the manner I believe in my job as a musician – the war is for me an earthquake – though an avalanche will do for that matter – when the earth quakes I quake too – and my house quakes and the roof falls on my head and there is salvage work to do – but it's still an act of god as according to the fire insurance. I can't for some reason give up time to learn fire drill and first aid ahead – and so I behave like a neutral country – I don't agree to a defensive alliance in time – and so on and so forth. Perhaps what you'd better do temporarily is (to learn to bicycle) to stay here for a bit and go over daily or at 3-day stretches to E.G. [East Grinstead] and give them good assistance – if you draw the dole from here you could pay your food value and have a bit over to feed yourself in E.G. middays, because you could come to some arrangement with some of them there. It takes about 1 hour to bike there and it's a lovely run – and as I say, they're making a brick-house where you could be in the mid-week and not have to come home and give me also 3 days alone. As long as you were away playing the husband and I am at home as the wife I don't see why it shouldn't work at least for a bit – and if you have the spare room you can be in there to your heart's content as no firing is necessary now – if I find it hurting my work I could tell you. You might also put your name down on the exchange here (Westerham) as wanting to do land work in the neighbourhood and there are farmers we know nearby. If this can't be done about the dole, you must get dole in London from 23, say, and bike up to get it once a week. [. . .]

Love,
Mike

11 November 1941

Dear Den,

I'm glad you're at the oratorio [*A Child of Our Time*] as I'm quite ready for the new copies. The [T. S.] Eliot quotation comes from *Murder in the Cathedral* – one of the choruses in the second act I think. I can't quite tell if I object to all the words you suggest till I saw it sketched out. On the whole they seem fairly sensible because they do make the matter of the music quite clear. I'll ask Schott's about the copyright and write you on a card – all that happens is 'Copyright by Schott & Co.' – but I'll ask about that too. I expect Hugo [Strecker] would like it on.

I'm such an innocent that until I spoke with Aubrey [Russ] I had no idea Sackville-West was a pansy – and it's always the same – if we meet, it would never arise. Especially where my professional work enters I never give the impression that that matter is a discussable one – and I suspect too that's why I never get away with it except with someone who insists like Karl [Hawker] – and then that doesn't last, because art and seriousness and inferiority feelings and what not enter the relationship and seem to go in a muddle with anything more intimate. And the probably more final truth as Evelyn [Maude] and I were talking of, is that intimacy is not really dependent on certain climaxes of sensuality and very often they shatter the more sensitive thing – unless they are themselves the desired expression of the intimacy. But it seems to result in an even more ascetic life.

I suppose for you and me there's a slight adjustment to be made because I am sensually more indulgent, or rather potentially so – and more extroverted if you like – and also I have lived longer thus. But it's an adjustment which isn't a problem to me at all really, having too much instinctive sympathy with your naturally reticent affection. In any case, oddly enough, it's not my own sensual expression that I want or miss, but I wouldn't have you miss some experience for unreal inhibitory reasons. And this is only to a very gentle degree – because the sort of Freudian un-reticence I regard as the devil and pernicious nonsense. If one's fate is to explore the ways of affection and love as people who have 'put our groping hands away' to quote Rupert Brooke – then it's a very reputable and responsible one. In your nature you are more like Evelyn, to whom the specific acts of love are charged with all the significances of love, and love only – scarcely at all of sensuality or pleasure. For myself, as usual, I'm one of those hopelessly mixed people who suffer both sides without holding firm to the one or the other reality – the circumstances, and my own fate, throw me constantly on to Evelyn's side – and there I properly belong. So you need have no fear.

[. . .]
Love
Michael

17 November 1941

Dear Den,

As you say, Den is Den and K[arl Hawker] is K. and that's very satis-factory. I am not one of the people much gone on the usual Freudian theories of repression and see little value in sex as sex, even if a refined pleasure *à la française* – but that may be because I am more like you than appears and have got to know about other types of living for liter-ary reasons, rather than lived them as parts of myself. I am also struck with the fact that it is the extroverts who talk most and set the tone and are the supposed norm. It's a lot of rubbish, in point of fact. But it's more difficult sometimes to hold to the introverted instincts in an extroverted world, and one which has been going gay after Victorian prudery.

So there's not much to worry about, and for more people than appears at first sight, sex is only a deluding cover for deeper and more spiritual things – and clearly, where one admires and values another, sex may well be an irrelevance, and an impertinence. It appears, if at all, outside the other values. That is always happening. It's the awak-ening of the other values between Karl and myself that kills the sex stone dead. As soon as he wants my view on his pictures, and knows instinctively that I must be true to my real self, he knows that no pay-ment in sexual coin is necessary etc, etc. So that it enters even into the Karls as well as the Mikes, and Dens.

The above is expressed in a guess work of Karl's unconscious psy-chology. Seen from my own side I can not step across the street on the chance of 'picking someone up', let alone being around a young boy, be he Karl or other – and so as in all things, our real selves dictate.

I'm feeling lately I want to come to tribunal and settle the affair practically. I feel the net closing in and a certain degree of unreality. I gather there may be a complete national male conscription into the Home Guard after Xmas to take over all home duties including fire watching. This, for me at any rate, brings a head-on collision. I feel the collision might be less personally hopeless if I were at least an accred-ited C.O. [Conscientious Objector] with a card – so if I see it coming I may try to force a claim to be examined first by a tribunal. The fascist net is drawing tighter and to stay out is to be a real job of work. I don't mind that in itself, it's the hateful business of putting one's music into jeopardy. However, it'll have to be.

Love –
Mike

[1942]

Dear Den,

[. . .] When it comes to the oratorio [*A Child of Our Time*] in fact, I think Schott's will pay all extras for the printing and I buy from them for distribution. Hugo has gone and old [Max] Steffens the real head of the firm is very friendly and easy to deal with – so when you are eventually ready, I'll discuss it with him.

Sackville-West abhors the spirituals, thinks they are 'phony' and spoil a well conceived unity. It does appear rather like that in the text, but I think the music needs them – and they won't appear so 'phony' in years to come, but will be judged as a historical fact. They are definitely the sojourn in a strange land and the uprooting from our tradition – do you think I am wrong to use them for that purpose? that is to show the shadow world by means of the shadow, or bogus, hymn-tunes. Perhaps we shall have to wait till performance – they can come out if necessary. They are put there frankly because of their associations and social implications. And as I wrote Eddy S.W., to the Dean of Gloucester they are the only intelligible portion! [. . .]

Till then –
Michael

10 February 1942

Dear Den,

I got non-com[batant duties]. It caused a considerable flutter in the dove cotes. As I may have told you, I cried like a child. This was all to the good. When I came up out of the pit I knew I could even put aside music for pacifism – it is that real. So I have the power to go backwards or forwards. Once this experience is past we can *then* allow the natural springs of hope to revive and to proceed back to one's work – because at the back is the awareness of the possible necessity and then of the power to sustain it without lack of gaiety. David [Ayerst] and nearly all others pitch into me to compromise and even hold that to consider prison be merely pettiness and spite. I think that's a measure of their own conscience! If I do a voluntary political act for pacifism, it is for the sake of the 650 lads in quod – why the hell shouldn't they have a good man on their side poor devils? And so they will.

[. . .] I'm full of beans again and back at work – ready for the rear-guard action too.

love
Mike

21 March 1942

Dear Den,

[. . .] I have grown beautifully lethargic as is proper between works. About the Tribunal I have grown dead also – the way seems ineluctable and leads straight to quod, as far as I can see – if with some delay. But I have no energy to go any other way. But I shan't like it. Heaven grant it that I have a short sentence.

When I am down with you all, I would like to try and discover the economics of Cambridge concert giving. Could you enquire ahead possibly the price of the usual hall, the possible takings, and the usual prices. Both these may be impossible to discover over the weekend, but only on the weekdays. I have a notion to risk getting [Walter] Goehr to Cambridge and perhaps Phyllis [Sellick] to play a Mozart first half, and Tip[pett] the next [Fantasia on a Theme of Handel]. Goehr hopes to start a baby orchestra of his own and by additional players perhaps from Cambridge itself we might make a possible venture of it.

I enjoyed Oxford, and then have been to Exmouth to my family. I feel a little starved of what the good Wilf [Franks] left me without all of a sudden – but that seems a permanent state, if generally asleep. I fall for soldiers in the train – and even they for me, but they get out at other stations.

Love –
Mike

[21] October 1942

[. . .] I finish the 4tet today [fair copy of String Quartet No. 2]. I may not get ink score done till Friday. I went to town Sat. to meet Britten and [Peter] Pears properly and to talk [about] the oratorio [A Child of Our Time]. Peter is a very lovely man in the best sense and quite obviously Ben's salvation. I'll tell you more. Peter wants me to write the recitative for him and it's possible I will [Boyhood's End]. I think you're right as to a dedication – we'll leave it be just yet. I don't associate you with Nature either with a capital or a minuscule. So don't fear. I don't think many others do either. Actually I'm still uncertain of the W. H. Hudson. I should like to see Peter a bit more and ask him how he feels. He has an odd mixture of warmth and Latin clear-cutness. But what gets one about him as a person, is the strength, the integrity, and the kindness joined to it. Ben is of course a spoilt darling – and Peter keeps him from spoiling worse. They are a nice pair whom I expect you'll meet some day when this nonsense is over. [. . .]

Love –
Mike

[November 1942]

Dear Den,
    You'll have to bring back the Stravinsky on Dec. 5, anyhow *Les Noces* – I'm going to talk on the radio one Sun. morning in the New Year, and about Stravinsky probably! and think of playing the final scene of *Les Noces*. Do you think Stravinsky a good idea, or is it too much off the common beat? Would like your opinion when we meet.
    It looks as if that weekend is still OK, because the summons hasn't come today, so it *ought* to be now, if it comes, for a court in the week after next. If it delay longer is it a good idea to come Dec. 12 weekend to Cambridge on the spree? Because 4tet [String Quartet No. 2] will be finished this coming weekend and by Dec. 5.
    [. . .] The man, Alec Robertson, who wants the talk on S[travinsky] (or anyone else) is a plainsong expert. Must get his book thereon – may enable one to find one's way.
    Want to talk to you about idea of setting a chunk of W. H. Hudson – it's a description of what he imagined his boyhood dream was, about to be shattered by contact with the hard, bitter world [*Boyhood's End*]. It's a statement of pantheistic faith. Fresca [Allinson] call it Wordsworthian – but it's a great deal better than that – nevertheless it's less her cup of tea because it's more extempore than formal. The questions are two: am I to reject it for that reason and practise declamation on a more formalised and stylised chunk; of Auden say? – am I to annoy the [Walter] Bergmanns and please the Evelyn [Maude]s, and the deep people of heart (as well as retaining the formal element as I am bound to do)?
    And thirdly and more important – if I do either of these, would you

like a dedication? and if so, would you like to say your bit as to your likes and feelings thereupon? or would you rather a later dedication on a more extensive work? dedications are always the more personal side of the thing for me, and have little to do with the public music, but lots to do with the private man. Thereby a nice confusion.

Love –
Michael

[December 1942]

Den –

[. . .] Work is going very well now after the intimacy of last weekend – and I don't mean that in any gross sense – there come times when some bond between two of us humans lets us enter a world of relationship, which often remains quite hidden to those around us. I mean that they don't observe it in the two experiencing it, certainly if it's a gentle imperceptible union.

Playing over the madrigals [*The Source* and *The Windhover*] for proof correction last night was horrified to realise how extreme they are. F[rancesca Allinson] thinks they are more difficult than anything, bar Alban Berg! Something must have gone to my heart – perhaps your playing of the *Les Noces* records. I think it's a heavenly sign all the same.

I'm beginning to hope I shall see the Dec. 5 out.

Love –
Mike
[. . .]

23 December 1942

Dear Den,

In some ways I was glad you didn't get to the concert, as it was not really my job to be doing it and it was a racket which taught me that I belong to the cottage and composition and Morley and not to this entertainment world where standards are non-existent. But it did no harm for once – and probably did the choir good, both in name and fact. Everything went without mess-up despite the no rehearsals – but unpolished. [. . .]

I've grown frightfully fond of you, but I think it's alright. By that I mean I think it's now back and can move from friendship toward love without a catastrophic cut-off of the way back – or I can put it better by saying I can love you as I do and it will last underneath the other side of any spring-like times that happen for us. And of the danger of that dark sinister world that was around Wilf [Franks] there is nothing – it's virginal and sensual at the same time and just the natural warmth that is love. And being you and me it's not in either of us promiscuity – for, as you're aware, that's never been the real me however much I might have tried to be like that. It's Den himself that is near and dear – and though the senses have their spring-time, it is not ever dislocated from the real person. So that the real person survives. I don't think there would be the ease of a springtime were it not so. It's funny writing you like this, but it's easier for me to write sometimes when the heart leaps – it's difficult to believe that the other person may respond but I always have need to say that I can be trusted and that there will be an immediate response the other way to any limits. That you can know by the curious fact that I can and have too so long shared a bed with you without sharing anything else. I do love you, I am human and warm, but I love *you* more than any expression towards you – and I've enough quality to live that throughout. So I don't suppose I shall tell you any further that you are as dear as you are to me – and just whatever mutual ground of love, that we will praise the Lord for, enjoy.

I want to see you and talk a lot about music (poetry would do as well) and what one writes to and for in the present day. I need to talk a hell of a lot. I've been a bit confused again – and the dream-like life of the artist too powerful without coming to expression. [. . .]

Heaps of love –
Mike

January 1943*

I've nothing but headed notepaper or official bits of things – the information on the back of this shows how necessary a radio talk is! [. . .] Fresca [Allinson] met me on the train from London – [. . .] she warned me I look like death, and sure enough [I] went down with an attack yesterday, Tues., and am rather grim inside today. [. . .]

Anyhow it's the usual warning – I must stick to the cottage for a bit, which indeed I love more and more. And I'm again in the odd dream

---

* Written on the back of a letter from Barclays Bank dated 11 January 1943 informing Tippett that his account was overdrawn by £4 15s 6d.

world which seems an important part of my existence – the world of half shadows and endless possibilities, and from which the real world seems pretty mad and indefinite. And it's a dream world where one is usually alone, and in dreams themselves where all the personages are bits of one's own interior. Mercifully for me this world doesn't have to materialise, as in the Hudson story [*Boyhood's End*], but happens within. [. . .]

Love –

Mike

10 February 1943*

The back of this tells you one bit of news – and the BBC really do seem to be interested in doing the Handel Fantasia fairly soon.

[. . .] I can't help feeling when this bloody war is over that, putting all our crowds together, we shall have a tolerably alive and dynamic lot of young folk – and if we keep ourselves straight, and don't go a-wandering after 20s debauchery and what not we may stem the tide of disillusionment and loss of good values. Anyhow it's a good thought to look forward to.

I've given up any idea of rushing the recitative [*Boyhood's End*] – I can't. But it's beginning to come alive – only it sets a terrific technical problem in the sustaining of formal interest during the long peroration.

Goehr has given over his idea to buy the Morley platform, as he wanted, and has been persuaded into 6 more Wigmore Hall concerts, of the same sort. So I suppose I shall have to put off my 4tet (1st) re-habilitation, and get down to my Chamber Concerto [this work never materialised] for him.

Come when you can.

Love –

Mike

[February 1943]

[. . .] I've been lethargic and with a heavy-beyond-normal cold, and struggling with the Strav[insky] and the correction of the *Child*. See daylight now and hope to start the 4tet movement [revisions to String Quartet No. 1] next Fri. when back from town.

* Written on the back of a letter from Alfred Kalmus dated 3 February 1943 requesting a copy of String Quartet No. 2.

Schott's are going to *engrave* the 2 madrigals [*The Source, The Windhover*] for Stainer & Bell. Did I tell you that? and seem like deciding to engrave in future always for me.

[. . .] The chap at EMG, John Amis, who has left that and is trying to get taken on in the LPO [London Philharmonic Orchestra] office with Felix A[prahamian] and Tim Hodge, is I think the best of the bunch and one you shall meet and know when you return to London. I fancy he's your sort (he's *not* queer – Felix is 1/2 – Tim is amorous!).

Incidentally he seems to have neutral musical taste. He's come to sing in the choir, as we were doing Britten's *St Cecilia* (which they read like birds). But Bergmann did *not* like it. Cheap – and last Sat. at Goehr's first concert, B[ergmann] heard a Bliss piece of hollow rhetoric – and said to me afterwards in his nervous manner – 'you know, Michael, I'm coming to the conclusion that you're the only hope of Eng. music' – and I replied in a low serious tone – 'sometimes, Walter, I think so myself' – his is a grand leg to pull. But he's also a true friend and a very sharp ear. Just the mentor I need.

Last night we had 2 sharp raids – F[rancesca Allinson] was much frightened by the second, at 4 a.m. I was singularly unmoved. Evelyn [Maude]'s mother had an incendiary float in through the kitchen window! [. . .]

Love for the present
Mike

22 April 1943

This grand paper because I'm in town and have been writing to Adrian Boult in an attempt at David [Ayerst]'s instigation to get the big boys to try and keep the Ministry from prosecution. But I've managed to face up to it again, meanwhile. Britten and others feel that in any case if I do time it will be a help rather than a hindrance to the music – and that's all I care about. [. . .]

Love to you – good Den –
Mike

18 May 1943

Dear Den,

Daresay this will cross a letter of yours. Coming to C[ambridge] this week-end is academic. I haven't finished *Boyhood's End* – and what is more decisive I have the prosecution here at Oxted on June 7 – the major act involving a year's maximum, but the means to have counsel for the defence: 'reasonable excuse'. So life's hectic, and with a feeling in the tummy, which is passing however. F[rancesca Allinson] can't get to town, so I propose to see her at Streetly End. This weekend I write like hell to finish the cantata [*Boyhood's End*] (that's the name now) – and when you think I have first performance of that at Morley June 5, and fixed a broadcast for Sun., 11 a.m. June 6, the day before the policeman came and handed me the 'contract' for June 7 – it's a good omen. So what I'd like to do is to come to C[ambridge] after Morley, Thursday, *next* week, and go to F. Friday morning. Various other plans for that weekend I'll tell you. [. . .]

Heaps of love –
Mike

22 May 1943

It was nice to hear your voice on the phone – and a great pity about this weekend, which would have been heavenly. But I am desperately hard at work. I shall get it [*Boyhood's End*] done, but perhaps with some details to be amended. I shan't do anything more than just get it done, and get it down onto Peter [Pears]'s score so that the performance can take place. And that will make me much easier in mind and ready to get on with the dubious business of the 'prosecution' – the lawyers are threatening to make it too much of an affair etc. I will tell you when I see you. I think we've got to play for a small sentence in order to placate the Ministry – they can't really allow one to get off completely – that would be too serious a precedent.

I've been reading the Byzantium book and enjoying it. That period has always had a fascination for me – different in kind from the purer and sharper one of classical Greece itself. It's still the core and source of nearly the whole western world civilisation – and a pity it isn't more so now.

Interesting in the book to see how passionately sex of all kinds enters into the life breaking the political world in pieces. I feel that artistic creation is often so nearly polarised as feminine, as against the pure disembodied abstract intellect, that it's hardly any wonder if artists turn out hermaphroditic in temperament from time to time. The real matter is to keep the polarity keen, and to learn to make value out of good sensibilities. I do get the repeated 'dream-wish' to be in on all the doings of the he-men and the womaniser, but it's really nothing much more than the wish to be everything, have every experience. And fundamentally I can't play a Don Juan part. The masculine drive goes into anything else but sexual activity – and in sex there is always the very profound and apparently basic feminine reaction, that comes up from within. It does not disturb me to know myself tender towards a man's virility – unless I precisely attempt to force myself to be shamed at it. And that seems less possible now. Why on the other hand in certain cases when a man is tender to me I can respond and have satisfaction which seem impossible from and to a woman I don't know. It hardly matters.

I hope, Denny, that the incarceration will be short, and sweet, and that sometime this summer we may have [a] holiday together somehow. I expect we will. But summertime is a soft echo of the Mediterranean and franker people – and it's a pity if it goes all by the board for the experiences of moral protest against the state of war. However we will see.

Till Monday –
Mike

24 May 1943

By the grace of God the cantata [*Boyhood's End*] is finished – and I believe it the 'goods'.

The swallows came to fly round the house 10 minutes later. Very pretty.

M.

31 August 1943 [after release from Wormwood Scrubs]
Exmouth

Dear Den,

John [Amis] and I missed you a lot in Cornwall – in fact we definitely want another do later with you and me and him and perhaps Adrian [Allinson] when J. gets another leave and when it's possible for you. Meanwhile I feel very much that someone's been missing from the home-coming – and I've thawed out of the prison and want to see you no end and hear all your news etc, etc. I posted you a pound a long way ahead for you to get a ticket and don't delay coming, please.

I wish the buggering war would end properly and release us from these goddam committees and what nots. I've heaps to tell you. Am at Exmouth – go Friday to Taunton to D[avid] and Larema [Ayerst] and children – and home on Thursday. Wildly impatient to see the cottage again after so long – to get back to music. It's a lot to be done there is. Would like a letter to say how it is with you.

Love –
Michael

3 September 1943

Dearest Den –

It's wonderful to be back – and coming into the cottage was heaven – didn't realise it was so nice.

I've thawed out now after the complete absence of all bodily affections in prison. And it's too bloody that our one chance of a longer time together than the so occasional meetings was sunk by prison on my part and harvest on yours. Frankly I'm longing to be beside you and no one else seems to be able to make up, and you're the only close friend I haven't seen since the release day. I want to come to Cambridge very much as soon as I've got certain commissions off my chest – and it can't be till later than the 18th – tomorrow fortnight when the first Morley happens. It seems a helluva long way off. Will you bring up again the grand piano? I wish you were here *now* but what's the good wishing. Johnny [Amis] will come over Sat. night tomorrow to talk out a possible class for him at Morley – but though he looks attractive in his blue corduroy pants he isn't you – pants or no pants. To hell! one might not be cut off from people one wants in this stupid way – but I'm absolutely stuck for the moment correcting oratorio proofs [*A Child of Our Time*] in a hurry and writing a Fanfare [No. 1, for brass] for a church in Northampton for the 21st of this month etc, etc. Come as soon as you can on the 18th anyhow – they're doing *Boyhood's End* at a tea night party next Sat. 11th, which I shall go to and anyone can go who likes – I'd better invite Adrian [Allinson]. I can scrimp up your fares when you elect to come so don't worry and don't hesitate.

Herzlichst
Mike

14 September 1943*

Dear Den,

[. . .] I find I'm really getting quite wound up in the masque [early drafts for *The Midsummer Marriage*] and think about it a lot. All the period of incubation is excellent. There's really no end to it except that suddenly the baby is born. I wonder if we could risk timing out 16 scenes now – because if that were done you might find yourself having a shot at one of them. In some ways I'm drawn to having the choruses in Latin, like *Oedipus Rex*. But that's really pointless unless the solos are in Latin too. But when it does come to the words for singing, there's everything there to be said for making them 'Indo-European', rather than very English – which boils down to the matter of *how* they are done. The choruses should be on the *Oedipus* method – single ideas, arresting words and repetitions. Some of the big solos may be of like manner. If we experiment by a madrigal or two, then I'm all for the sentences which, though jumbled up, somehow come out right in the totality. You want to imagine 4 or 5, or 3 or 2 voice[s] singing independently against each other and what you would expect or hope them to be singing – or whether you care at all. Madrigals really are conversations and hence partly visual: each voice should address the other – hence the endless canonic imitations, and the real reason why they won't broadcast. Therefore in concert room terms the conversation is, so to speak, also observed from the outside by the audience. Therefore, to experiment with an almost new form, you need to disentangle the polyphony, spacing it out, so that the conversation is more audible, and you arrive at even greater independence of character in the voice line, less imitation and the old-fashioned polyphony reserved for those remarks which all make. Can you conceive such an experiment? Actually it is in fact the ensemble of an opera – especially the Mozartian such. Only it's *a cappella* and more intimate. But it would be good practice for the masque?

[. . .] The Symphony [No. 1] goes well. It's terrific having an unexpected weekend clear. I've been reading Hölderlin. It's very lovely stuff – for certain words. The Greek elements in the masque need to be transmuted, not a romanticism. [. . .]

Actually the attempt to force the real ancient Greek feeling into Christianity fails, in my opinion inevitably. To wish a 3rd thing, a rec-

*Dated 22 September in British Library.

onciliation, unity of the 2, does not of itself make such a thing. The process of transformation is longer and less visible. If historical Christianity has in fact kicked out the hellenism of its neo-platonic tradition then it means that that element does in fact now live, and possibly thrive outside. If we are fed by it, then we are fed by it – and the consequence will be work of art in that tradition, possibly fed also by the tradition of Christianity protestantism. It appears to me in the masque that the Judaic element, at any rate, is small. I rather approve. But of course the true Hellenic feeling is not simple. All the contractions that belong to its drama return with it. In this Nietzsche saw deeper perhaps than Hölderlin – though H. expresses even better than N. the coming sense of the conscious world precariously balanced on a sea of chaotic unconscious and demonic forces. In the masque the laughing children appear to ride the storm out (while in the oratorio the child goes under and endures).

There's so much else *à propos* Hölderlin and whatever – but it must keep till I see you.

Love –

M.

[. . .]

28 September 1943

Dear Den,

[. . .] You'd better manage as well as you can while the bloody war is on, and accumulate what you can of your own stuff, which, without your expecting it, may help you in the end to the 1/2 time job – because it will be earnest of what is to come, given opportunity – and there are enough real people in the literary/publishing world to see what's what. If not, we'll find other ways through. In point of fact, it isn't the 1/2 time job that's the real problem – but the drive of the imaginative life. Because if that exists on such degree that most other things get, with struggles and loves and hates from period to period, put into inferiority beside it – that is to say, that despite the urges of the senses and the heart and political head and god alone knows what, the poetic impulse remains and enriched and strengthened and its loneliness increasingly and lovingly accepted – even if one at the time longs for the other things – that habit of creation and inner activity so proportions one's life that the rest falls into place and the sort of job or support is found and is morally acceptable, to fit the needs. It's very rarely a reality when it states itself: if I had this job I shall write (*vide* Wilf [Franks]); it tends to be – I write and I must have a job to correspond – and someone finds it for you – or one finds it for oneself because one knows what one wants, and if it's necessary creates that too (Morley!).

[. . .] I've just lately woken up to the realisation that friends (David [Ayerst], Johnny [Amis], Bryan [Fisher], et al) think I'm extra fond of you – not as blowing upon it, but as wishing us well. And extra isn't the right word. They imply they imagine you to have a special place for me, or in my 'shaking heart', to quote the poet. Perhaps it's after all time and I realise it not – so you'd better be gentle with me if I seem possessive or what not, springing from deeper emotions that I perceive. It won't matter an awful lot because there's certainly no fearful magic or evil split as when the Wilf were a constellation of all the planets. I don't think you'll come to much harm – and us both I dare say to much good rather.

I feel that Northampton [for the première of Fanfare No. 1, for brass] was rather like B.B. [Britten] taking his younger brother out – and I feel uncomfortable as his young brother, asked to show forth fruits of the high promise. There's an element of unreality, from B.B.'s own present make-up. So I'm better on my own slow way – recommending myself!

You know – the present rates for teaching at Morley are 24/6 a 2-hour night. I shall have a certain pull in that sort of employment after the war – at least at Morley. One such class should be a good addition to one's slender income for you. *Nicht wahr?*

Hope to see you soon.

Love –

M.

[. . .]

13 October 1943

Dearest Den,

The very little storm in the tea cup can serve to assure each other that we know where the permanent values lie – and that that goes for always. It's not quite so ironic either. Moral feeling is the most impotent-making thing in the world – and it's not unnatural that moral easiness produces physical easiness. Putting it crudely – if I were morally afraid of you – or for you, or for myself, I could hardly let myself practise enjoyment. (I don't think on the other hand Shakespeare got much of that out of the madness of Mr W.H.?) I imagine that we rate the 'divine madness' and all its complications higher in our scale than the delights of sensuality. Sometimes they happen to click – but I gather it's rare. I'm not afraid for either of us as to lust – it's a minimal thing in either of our lives – at any rate it certainly is in mine. So there's no need to get to an entanglement that Tip[pett] he's to have something he is having or bust – or even that I take the trouble to walk over the street to find it. It happens that you live graciously enough in the morality of the *Symposium* and that I don't feel it to be hurting either of us, because I've lived it the other way round, like you and know it to be a true expression of its kind. If it were not, I couldn't move. Please note the 'of its kind!' I don't leap to the conclusion that you are me or like me in other kinds, any more say than I did at any time over Bryan – or even over Wilf – though that was more complicated because he had such terrors about just that conclusion. At most this happens to chaps like me who are normal in a deep-seated sense, or shall we say, who don't make the abnormality the one virtue, the usual feeling of inferiority of being left out of some particular heaven that people have about all sorts of things, and which apparently no one is without. So that when Bryan seemed to imply that I might comfort myself as to the nature of the girl's and your relationship, it's a bit wide of the mark. I feel extremely little possessiveness, I dare say none at all – nor any jealousy or any loss – it's simply the old sore, or wound that is for a second fingered – a wound which of course in other ways I have learnt to be of mythological power. Nor is this particular effect to do with you Den. So that I don't get you, as you, mixed up at all in such momentary feelings – and they are very momentary nowadays. I can spit all this out to you just because it has become neutral and is dispassionately interesting to observe. (It's all in the *Child*.) There ain't going to be no sticky end in Lust and Rage. Can you really imagine it? Are you leaping to the awful conclusion that because I'm a 'sexy piece' with you, I lie with everyone? or even that I want to? Life of this frankness is something that for a while is possible with you – and it's not because either of us is wicked or debauched or sunk in buggery or what not and which not. Let us not worry. If I'm frightened of you it's probably a pity – as things are. Nor do I think we shall have to resort to that particular end. Nor will the term clash so much with girls and the proper pull to women as we could frighten ourselves into believing. Please do remember that I also don't take over that with you into life with Fresca or Evelyn – whose company I can't dispense with. We'll leave it be.

As to whether I get down to C[ambridge] on Sunday is still undecided. Work was frightfully good up to Monday – when it stopped. Then Tony [Hopkins] and Alison [Purves] decided to come from Mon. night till this morning. I have yet to see whether the thing loosens afresh. If it's a matter of detail work, then hours can be hours lost – while if it's conception then a break with friends may be hours gained. Factually, I've got the exposition of the new movement [for String Quartet No. 1] down, and it's a matter of the development which as yet I don't see. It's in a good vein. Hope awfully much the Griller [String Quartet, led by Sidney Griller] fall for it – but I just can't force things even to get a good première. I gather Goehr broadcasts the Double Concerto [Concerto for Double String Orchestra] – so Eddy [Sackville-West] opined on the phone last night. But I guess that to be Continental Service – 10 a.m. sort of touch. Still it's all to the good. *Boyhood's End* went down well at the [National] Gallery – and I've decided it's quite a lovely lyrical piece underneath the first effect of singularity. *The Windhover* and *The Source* still seem quite crackers. [. . .]

Love –
M.

21 October 1943

Dear Den,

Have *you* got my *Symposium*? not for the famous anecdote however. I've been somewhat bowled over by reading Hölderlin who had the *Symposium* Eros myth as his fundament and was Greece drunk. So if you have mine, please bring – or another. The ache of the northener for the south is nowhere better expressed than in German poetry of that period. Goethe's 'Kennst du das Land, Wo die Zitronen blühn?' as sung in connection with that weird creation, the boy-girl, Mignon, is a not to be forgotten experience of intense poignancy. It's in Hölderlin and much more. All this Greek business in a gayer way, is to be in the masque [early drafts for *The Midsummer Marriage*]: and what else besides! If it were not a rather suspect idea at this time I feel you will have to live along[side] me a day or two sometime, when I can gather all the threads together and try and get them across to you – sufficiently for us to project the gesture that corresponds. But that's a pretty problem considering the chorus of traditions I want to incorporate and refashion. I can't quite see how we shall ever get at much real correspondence and collaboration without a period of very close union in a particular atmosphere. I'm all for collaboration, but it's a helluva problem when it isn't a conventional opera text, but a new creation itself. However we can but try.

I've stopped feeling lonely and despite another cold outbreak and a general dopey state it's been good to be at home a few days on end. If only to ponder how to get out of commitments at Morley and elsewhere. I still feel I need to see you soon for all there is to say. I think that though perhaps dangerous, I'm relieved to find that what might have seemed lust is the desire we call love – and I feel it's better thus for you too. I find for me that this man-love is hopelessly mixed up with Greece and the spring-like feeling that idea is – though there's a strand of it that goes also to Hermes and the dark demonism (which is also an integral part of Greece). I have an idea too that the spiritual or artistic creativeness is of its own nature bisexual and it's useless to cry out against an apparently too concrete image of that fact. But it's curious that neither in the oratorio [*A Child of Our Time*] nor to any noticeable degree in the masque is queerness projected. In the masque it appears momentarily between 2 otherwise spliced males (and I suppose we shall have to show its counterpart), but it's just about as much as you have in yourself – i.e. no sexuality but candour and affection. And in the masque it stands as a gesture for a specific movement on the general dance – quite why I don't know. George [eventually Mark] kisses Strephon (the modern embraces the Greek!) to show his disregard of the conventional social barriers – from which the upheaval begins. And from that gesture he turns to Margaret [eventually Jenifer], who spurns his sensuality for 'heaven'. A pretty good 'gesture' for the modern boy–girl relationship! It's quite certain that I would never have been able to project with such certainty when I was younger, because I had perforce, through the violence of my own instincts, to try and live my Greek world as though it were the modern boy meets girl world. There's a certain excitement in holding (even if you have no choice but to do so) the personal Greek-ness when you have accepted the outer social fact – it's a symbol of the ageless necessity of the artist to be elsewhere than in the complete social environ-ment in order to create at all – as opposed to entertaining.

There – I haven't written so many letters for months – but as I told you, I'm in a dopey state and uncertain of my feet – and in fact as blind as never before. I desperately need to get the 4tet [String Quartet No. 3] out of the way and clear the air for the next big birth. The Britt.–Tipp. concert is put off to March and the Friends heaved out for the Wigmore. So the 2 songs [from *The Heart's Assurance*] will keep till later – and I shall begin the Symphony [No. 1] after a proper holi-day – part of it I hope with you.

Lots of love –
Michael

[. . .]

29 October 1943

Dear Den,

[. . .] It's true isn't it that you've had a 21st birthday lately?* If that's so, I want to give you £5 to buy yourself what you might want. A 21st only comes once.

You remember the name Roy Langford, the chap with whom I loved as well may be for some years – experimenting in sensuality, despite my virginal abhorrence of that time – he suddenly spoke on the phone yesterday, out of the past, and I see him tomorrow. It's very curious, but there's definitely a mellowness, even fragrance, in this particular past and person, which seems only possible from having paid thus the debt to the earth. I remember Evelyn once astonishing me by remark-ing that she put my unusual emotional maturity (of 25) down to the life with Roy – against whom I at that time had turned with almost disgust.

It's been grand to see Fresca again. She is taking my appearance in hand! New ties and new style of haircut.

Goehr gave a smashing performance of the Double Concerto on the radio. I was very moved myself, even by the slow movement.

The masque is still brooding. When at C[ambridge] we might risk a first sketch of the scenario, something to work on.

love from
Michael

* Newton appears to have subtracted two years from his age: the *New York Times* obituary gives his birthdate as 1920.

[1943]

Dear Den –

[. . .] You know – it's an odd thing to write down in a letter but for some reason of circumstance relations with you are more satisfying in fact than ever before with anyone. I seem to know more or less what I want and you seem to know how to give it me. I suppose it's easier for me because I'm fundamentally more susceptible in this way. I wish I could give you more what you wanted, as far as you know it. But nothing is ever exactly mutual – or rather the mutualities sometimes come a different way – it *may* give you a certain different sort of satisfaction satisfying me so exactly. And this may be possible till the proper person you're looking for comes along. But I fancy we are in a position not be afraid of each other – but frank indeed – so that were there anything more you could get from me, and we knew what it was, there would be nothing to risk as far as our general relations go. If we ever by luck were together longer it might come of itself – being partly an art like every other thing. [. . .] This apart from the matter of being intimate, because the real lasting friendship will never be dependent on it. It's just an enhancement that happens for the time being.

Don't worry yourself (I don't think you do) about queerness or not. The acts of love aren't altered or disturbed really by that problem. To live any intimacy never precludes another at another time. Satisfaction is the proper way to growth – and it won't be a satisfaction when it's a real perversion. Many people remain dual to the end anyhow. The real matter is of another sort – it's good to have a keen masculine intellectual, or aesthetic, or spiritual life. That is the distinctive psychological necessity. You may polarise in a feminine way physically against the tough-guy – as I do – but on another plane he is earthy and polarises as unconscious against my masculine discrimination. As long as your own life of the mind grows into the objective bents, then fundamentally you are masculine against the basic feminine subjectivity and dependence. Our discussion about books and music is only possible really between men. If this part is active and virile, then sensitivity, the feminine within us, becomes eventually a source of width and strength. Anyhow, follow the instincts however they come out and take the joy as it flies.

Much love –

Mike

[. . .]

10 November 1943

Dear Den,

[. . .] I'm a bit jangled again by trouble with Rose [Turnbull?] – and having had to withdraw and cut off – and so give her the hurt which I have sustained so often myself. It's so odd this affair of humans. Whereas with Fresca I have always been pleased and delighted to be with her – and we've always instinctively known just how much we are to each other and where we are not – with Wilf I must have lived a hopelessly illusionary but deep-going and passionate life, and so does Rose. And every time the imagined response from the other doesn't come, then it stabs through the stomach like a knife. Immortalised by Will Shakespeare, I might remark. I seem at present to be living a double if not quadruple life. I've never been more normal in general feeling, and yet never less upset by feminine desires. I suppose it's either a weird moment when we go over from one to another, or it's the platonic whole man with both sexes. Not that it much bothers me in any way to stop the music, for instance. I'm much looking forward to seeing you because it's not good to have too long [an] interval where there's any real friendship – or illusions begin. I seem bursting with talk and ideas – and longing to have too a break and/or holiday and get away from London and its commerce. It fingers everything so. It does me a bit of good to write some of it out of my system – and ever much more to talk it out of my system to you who are not in it – praise heaven. Mercifully it doesn't get much into the cottage here – and now to music.

Herzlich –
Michael
[. . .]

27 November 1943

Denlein,

[. . .] I wish I did not think so much – but that's like wishing to be someone else. I can't help analysing things and experiences, because out of that deposit seems to come some of the eventual artistic material – or some of the contact with it. It's only this central pole of creativity that keeps me going at all, or it's only when it's operating that I am at all whole and at peace – or what we call happy. So that these periods in between works are god-forsaken. The only thing that I realise is that they always pass and go over into activity again. [. . .]

However – love to you as ever

Michael

30 November 1943

Dear Den,

[. . .] I've more or less decided to polish off that wretched Canterbury thing [*Plebs Angelica*] before the big Symphony [No. 1]. It's also a politic move, to get on good terms with 'Canterbury' before the oratorio [*A Child of Our Time*] is done in town. It's just possible they might consider it for Canterbury festival after the war. The motet will also be a baby work to keep the public at bay while I deliver or am delivered of the Symphony. But they may both happen together – or rather the layout of the Symphony take place while the motet is being put on paper – and not much paper at that!

Much love – and send a p.c. if you can.

Mike

31 December 1943

Dear Den,

There's lots of things I've meant to tell you, but they're crowded out by the severe depression ensuing on an interview with the Min[istry] of Labour at Westerham this morning. All the old rigmarole. And I'm frightened somewhat to my surprise – and the self pity has gone so far that I've been crying – quite *à la* Eric Mason!!!

It's still possible we shall be able to reach some compromise before they decide, if they do, to reprosecute: that's the bright side. On the other you have the oh so well-known wheels beginning to grind in the official gear box: a sort of inhuman inevitability – what we call our 'fate' – so that it seems that either a loophole appears as I turn from side to side in the cage, or everything just won't come out luckily (as happened before) – and then one knows one is 'destined' to a certain martyrisation, and it's no good beating against the bars any further. And I lectured so well for Johnny [Amis] last night on the nature of this cage! I suppose it's the price to be paid for what little vision one has. [. . .]

Love –

Mike

1 January 1944

Central Board thinks it's only formal enquiry – that prosecution is *most* unlikely – so am a bit more 'manly' now! Also hope to get my position in bit sounder through some CEMA work [Council for the Encouragement of Music and the Arts].

Will write proper later.

M.

23 January 1944

What I dreamt at Ben [Britten]'s was that I put my hand on a penis that was fleshy and that bounded about under the hand like something alive in its own right. On a second attempt (uncertain what the person wanted) it was as though the tip were a fish's mouth and would nip my finger with the teeth. Apart from personal meaning concerned with the proper wound,* this is like dreaming [Paul] Goodman – which may explain why he affected me so inappropriately. Because it says that if the practical intellectual finger comes in contact with the semen-producing organ of sex, then the way is not open thereby to the world of the pure transcendental ideas, but to the world of natural history and the archaic animal past. In this connection the psychological technical regression in Don Juan to the classical mythology is correct – the regression to the period in which we were closer to the instincts, without our never to be disvalued, but dangerous intellect (a servant, but not a master, properly) – and where pederasty or bestiality were on much the same level as heterosexuality – a matter which *profoundly* offends our modern moral consciousness. No wonder Goodman writes with tears – for it's a horrible matter and terrifying shock – because of course we can't live as if in Greek times, yet reconnection with our instinctive past brings back all these age-old channels of pleasure (and horror, let us add). For me, as the dream will show you I only gradually realise these things, in dreams and thereby somehow in the body. I somehow both know I am worshipping a phallus, that I am shocking the ruling social morality and hence feel inferior, and that I have intense pleasure, and that in the naked light of day it sounds probably disgusting – as indeed all sex does. These facts – the inferiority, the archaic root, the pleasure and love – are simply one's actual

---

* At the age of 5, at his father's insistence and without anaesthesia, Tippett had undergone a second circumcision.

humanity as one is – not according that is to one's longing, but to one's history. To attempt to live at the level of one's longing is to deny the earth-bound quality of all life – to lose all connection with the instincts and to stymie. And yet the longing (for heavenly perfection) remains too a mystery. [. . .]

love –

Michael

What is the play you're writing?

1 February 1944

I've just received a book from the library called: *Orpheus the Fisher*, which I must say settles it. Not only connection with Dionysus from the wine – but the mythic milk pail, metempsychosis, scapegoatism – 2 fishes and a fig leaf for you (Chinese yin) i.e. outlining it. The fish-like thing in a remarkable condition with one heavenly Greek plate and a reproduction of a satyr balancing a pot of wine on it! Add to that the mere detail that Orpheus, besides the Fisher of Men and allied to our old friend Hermes the Psychopomp, was the god of music. Very queer!! I'll keep the book to show you.

M.

Christ was also knows as Ichthus – the Fish.

2 February 1944

[. . .] The phallic fish in the dream had teeth which puzzled me – such made me think of *Und der Haifisch, der hat Zähne** – but it did not click at all till I read a few moments ago: 'just as the sacred galeor (sharks) are said to conceive and to procreate in an irregular way, namely through the mouth'! (The fisher-god is a culture hero inventing the ABC etc – the 'Salmon of Wisdom' in the Shannon and heaven knows what else beside.) And now it appears that Emmanuel, 'God with us', in esoteric numbering is in *isopsephon* [equal in numerical value] with Orpheus, both adding up to the number 96!! That's a shattering one for you.

I've always known that queerness had, as well as its shame, its religious meaning for me, through the phallic symbol – also that it stood somehow for self-fertilisation, virgin birth and culture. But I never

---

* 'And the shark, it has teeth': the opening words of Brecht–Weill, 'Ballad of Mac the Knife'.

expected to have it thrust down one's throat (note the metaphor!) with such exactness.

Mercifully human relations aren't lived on this plan, and the phallus becomes the more homely object we ordinarily know. I wish I could bring you the satyr balancing the wine jar on it, but the book is too hefty. Some of the reproduced drawings are lovely – and a very beautiful fish alphabet from the dark ages, etc.

Finished Canterbury [*Plebs Angelica*] – sent it off there today – so am in holiday mood and also close to you.

M.

3 February 1944

I had no idea the 'net' is such a terrific symbol: in it are conflated the mystic oracle giving head of Orpheus and the wizard singer's magic lyre, the hidden image or phallus of Osiris and that of Dionysus; the image of the Tyrian 'Herakles', that is of the fisher god Sid, worshipped in Erythrae; the floating box containing Danae and her infant son Perseus, or the maiden mother Auge (brightness) and her child Teliphor (the 'Faraway light') or the heavenly twins themselves; the brass bottle with the juice of the Arabian Nights in it and the seal of Solomon's ring on the stopper; the barrel (sic!) which contains the infant St Gregory, the seamless coat of Christ, the gold mug, which the devil flung inadvertently into the greedy fisher's net; and finally the Apollinic tripod, cauldron or cup of the Eleven Sages, as well as the ivory shoulder of Pelops, the legendary counterpart of Parthenia's fabulous golden leg. Then follows an exceptional yarn in which a blind fisher catches a beautiful 'palamide' – to which a note is given that 'the name signifies the "hand-fish"' (from palamic–palm). The 'hand' is a well-known symbol of the semitic 'Mother-Goddess' – believed to be the mother of the Fish-God Ichtheus. It's the cylinder (Mark no. 31) in the B.M. [British Museum], where a goddess is represented standing between an erect 'fish' (sic!) and an open 'hand'.

Before I read this I had decided that Jack [eventually Mark, in *The Midsummer Marriage*] of course finds the barrel full of water – and that when he dips his hand in it to obtain the oracular object he is bitten by the hidden fish – and so refuses to proceed. But for Strephon, who intuitively approaches, then the ritual magical dance, the barrel is empty except for the magic net – ('Thy word, the great net encircling heaven and earth' (Babylonian mystic text)). Later of course, in the finale, the barrel contains the wine from the water. The stage problem will be how to keep this b[loody] barrel from getting in the way. I conceive Sosostris as on the upper stage, and the barrel on chorus level – perhaps when the resuscitated King Fisher is propped up on the regal chair at the very back, the barrel of wine is lifted up on to upper stage – but I don't know yet. You can't shift things about in the masque without fearful cogitations – because they will have catastrophic symbolical consequences. Think of that now! One can't be too careful.

12 February 1944

Dear Den,

Just had a letter from Bliss starting: 'I spent yesterday playing through *A Child* and was extraordinarily moved by the work. I do not know any music [of] recent years that has made so great an impression upon me at once.' Isn't that nice? As coming from him quite genuine. The broadcast may happen March 19 – and in any case he more or less promises a studio do, if not. Which I should prefer.

Leicester was a success. We drew a second audience! Seems a bit odd to me – and the Sonata [Piano Sonata No. 1] is goodish long and some folk went out, therefore. But she [Phyllis Sellick] played it with spirit.

I've actually begun to make the masque scenario [early drafts for *The Midsummer Marriage*] – but I shan't have much done by the time you arrive. At present anyhow it's only in pencil. But we can discuss it a bit nevertheless. [. . .]

love –

Mike

Symphony [No. 1] is begun!

2 April 1944

Dear Den,

I got back late Friday night and seem to be able to be here for a bit without visiting London. I had a mild migraine Thursday which kept me in the sunny room at home while Tony [Hopkins] did Morley. The Wed. before I had gone foolishly at B.B. [Britten]'s request to turn over at the 2 pf recital with Clifford Curzon and came back late with him, very tired indeed. I went to bed first and B.B. hovered about in loaned pyjamas, till I said: 'if you want to be matey you'd better sleep in the big bed *mit mir*!' So he did. Whereupon I got a fit of distaste, with-drawal, virginity, coldness or whatever, and tried not to make it obvious, except that there it was. And I spent a night of horrid dreams and nightmares, awoke with a fearful head – got up and shaved and dressed, and the telephone went, which was John Powis in trouble, consequent on a bomb on the house he was visiting, and the Friday night I was at Cambridge. So at this my stomach turned – and I said: I shall have to go into the bathroom and be sick: ring up again later. So I slept the whole morning – didn't hear B.'s opera 1st act – B. went to town and I was left sleeping in the sunny big room, happy in being alone and resting – and there was a very odd journalist interview on the telephone which is funny, but too long to write you. I'll tell it you over the weekend. B. came back late that night and of course slept in his proper place, and I had a lovely halcyon long night and a marvellous dream ending with feeding myself by spooning glorious peach tart out of an unknown woman's stomach! [. . .]

David [Ayerst] seems to find the masque story bearable and hasn't put his ban upon it. Even criticises it on its own right. That's a good sign – if his rationalistic mind can take it at all. I tried it, foolishly, to B.B., and I'm afraid probably made him envious, as against his *Peter Grimes*. But he tells me that the chance of production by Sadler's Wells is high. His own work will be for that this autumn, if ready in time. [. . .]

Heaps of love –
M.

24 April 1944

Dear Den,

[. . .] It's been a lovely June-like weekend and I'm wonderfully happy and at work in the usual meandering manner. I sometimes wonder how anything big ever gets done at all in this way. Why I'm happier is because the work is the 'complex' of the moment and London things are secondary – and the spring weather makes it easier I think, because more enjoyable here. I've even begun to tidy up the garden! I can't make out whether I feel this joyfulness will be killed before it lasts out the what I, in other words, feel to be a good year. 'June' coming so early: and a holiday (which didn't seem to have happened last year because of prison) not very far off. It's rather like Anglo-Saxon times, and Danish raiding. One lives, if properly adjusted, to the moment, and yet doesn't whine if the 'raid' breaks up the time. The swallows were back yesterday though I can't see them today.

As usual I look forward to the weekend, more than I care to admit.
Love –
Michael
[. . .]

25 April 1944

Dear Den,

[. . .] I expect holiday will be a bad time to attempt any exact work at the masque, *par exemple*. It's better to go on chit-chatting about it till the time to do it finally forces itself on us. Not only for our own reasons, but also because the war *might* have ended – or you somehow got free of Min[istry] of Labour. I shan't finish the Symphony [No. 1] till Christmas I'm afraid. Then I want to do anyhow a little piano work for Tony [Hopkins] and his like and perhaps the Chaconne for String 4tet. The masque therefore could not be till autumn [next] year – or conceivably laying plans in the summer. So the thing to do is to chew it over all this winter – articulate it further into relative timings etc. That ought to be done reasonably soon – and perhaps that is possible on holiday. Anyhow we'll take a script against a rainy day. [. . .]
Love –
M.

29 April 1944

Dear Den,

I like writing to you after a morning of business letters – otherwise I think I should think all letter writing suspect – perhaps indeed it is. I feel so much rested after the weekend and very happy about it also. It was a lovely time of spring – just suited Cambridge – and to quote the letter which must have gone astray – you aren't married yet and I love you in my funny way, and why suppress it and be shy of it in a world so short lived. It's difficult to know where I'd ever find the like and there's always many of things to talk about.

Britt[en] and Pears came down at 10.30 p.m. and went away at 8.5 a.m. next day. So like Ben – waiting for breakfast and seeing the streaming window frames of the door, I saw he had written in each

with his finger, P.P., M.T., B.B. It just expresses his small boy side.
[. . .]

  Love –
  Michael

17 May 1944

Dear Den,

   [. . .] I was talking to Evelyn [Maude] about the masque, as she hadn't seen its latest form. She thinks the 'Masque of Revolution' an unnecessary title and a confusing one. Perhaps it's better to keep the 2 very nice other titles [*Aurora Consurgens* or *The Laughing Children*], and then label the work opera or masque – or opera-masque – in so many acts, as per usual. E. puts out the idea that the indefiniteness of Strephon's girl really means that he isn't paired at all, that he subsumes her into himself. In one sense that's so. And the faun is the 8th character. But I have always had a pas-de-deux in my vision. Nevertheless I think it maybe right that she has no name and is always Strephon's girl – and I am pretty sure they do not pair in the general marriage, but are eternally separate. In other words, what I am trying to say, I suppose, is that Strephon and his girl are not biologically paired, to demand a final marriage, but are paired out of their selves – being both mixtures. Which makes Jack and Bella the fertile pair, and the Natural Man. Strephon reminds me a bit of Nijinsky – less sophisticated. If a woman forces copulation on him he is in the end sent off his head and destroyed – the balance of his creativeness being of another order. So we'd better leave Strephon with only a shadow partner. I don't want to have him so off his head or write another diary. We mustn't maltreat him so. Strephon, as I had forgotten till you reminded me, is half a fairy. The girl is the complementary figure, whatever that is – and if she has a name it ought to be indicative also somewhere of her function – or her ancestry: just as George [eventually Mark] is St George, King Fisher – the King, Bella the beauty, etc. Hers isn't necessarily a Greek name therefore. I expect it will turn up in time from somewhere. If we succeed in naming her, she will as suddenly have a role. Her name is very nearly Francezca. Or it may be Iolanthe. I suppose it will click in the end – or we shall not name her at all.

   M.

1 July 1944
12 Louisa Terrace, Exmouth, Devon

Dear Den,

Your letters came just at the right moment yesterday. Because knowing you were OK for the holiday made me feel completely happy and restored; so that it wasn't such a wrench to have to come away here. And we shall have to put it off a week. My father is dying and I have arranged to stay here right up to Friday week, and so I sensibly brought the Symphony [No. 1] MS with me; I shall find a room and work, and then come straight to holiday from here. Either getting J[ohn Amis] to go down to O[xted] and fetch tent and bedding, or going myself. In any case we'll meet in London I expect and travel down to Wales together: Friday week 14th. I'll send you later £3 (out of the P.O. [Post Office Savings Bank] book I have here) to get a through ticket from C[ambridge]. Save bother and time and money worries. You need not hurry too much about an occasional money demand. For the moment I have more than I need personally, and no one stands in fact closer to me than you do – though I may try to disguise the fact.

Hope you got the £2. You would have laughed. I had it in an ordinary envelope to post, standing in a long queue to buy the ticket to Exmouth, at W[ater]loo: when I realised I hadn't enough for that, so had to tear the letter open for a pound out of it, just as a rattle of rubbish fell on the roof, which was the Strand Palace Hotel in point of detail – shot up from over the Thames! The resultant scurrying around of folk left the little Strand P.O. empty, so I was able to dash from the train queue and get money from there and send off to you.

[. . .] It's been such a complicated time as you have realised. That is why the holiday begins to seem so good – as it will be. I'll tell you all about things bit by bit when we're together. You just mustn't mind my holding you so dear as I do. It seems I was born to be always thus, as out of abundance of warmth. But you're the best actual quality person I've ever felt loyal to. It makes it rather exciting. I hope it won't turn your head.

And now another set of emotions. Holding my father's limp hands in my strong and vigorous ones is like feeling the generation repassing into one's blood. It did him a power of good last night when I came.

Will write again soon. Drop me a p.c. here if you can.

Love –
Mike

10 August 1944

Sorry your air mail letter is so mucky – it's [the] blast, etc. Old cottages are destroyed – children including baby unhurt, likewise Miriam and Ben [Lewis] – Jack in hospital, but will be alright – Bron is dead. My cottage is unlivable for the moment. My address from tomorrow is c/o Shaxson, Elsted Manor, Midhurst, Sussex. [. . .]

Love –
Mike

16 August 1944
Midhurst

Dear Denlein,

Got your card this morning. The story is more or less the following. A bomb fell just on the tree in front of the double cottage at 5 or 6 on Tuesday morning. To begin at my own end – I woke to hear it chug-chugging to its end and just had time to wake up to what it was and put my head under the blanket as the ceiling came down and the doors were blown off etc, etc. I lay till certain incendiaries had finished pop-ping, fearing another crash, and then got out and mercifully the clothes cupboard was getatable and so got a dressing gown. Then over to see the other cottage in more or less ruins and Miriam who'd gone up to sleep in her bed just before, in a nightdress, having got out of the rubble while Ben was still in the steel table [Morrison] shelter below. But on the other side it was clear that Jack and Bron had been sleep-ing on top of their shelter (to give the children air) and of course the floor above had descended on to it as the tallest object in the room and pinned them down. Ian scrambled out into the arms of RAF balloon chaps who were there at once, and who were trumps, every one of them. Later Sheila [Wilson] was taken out of shelter by one, asleep! But Bron must have been killed instantly. She had fed the babe at 5 p.m. and thinking it all over had gone to sleep on top with Jack and both were sound asleep when it came. No one seems to have heard it in the distance. Jack was extracted after an hour but just when he'd nearly decided to give up the ghost. Miraculously he's unhurt in any organic manner. So the consequences:–

The double cottage is destroyed and will be levelled. The bungalow is cracked etc and eventually they will rebuild the front wall and a side, and redo the roof timbers, etc. For the moment they have put tiles on and plastered up the window with brown paper, and all the salvage from the other cottage is piled into mine. On Monday (Bron was buried Saturday) they all went to Wales, except Jack in hospital. Ben will come back in a fortnight and lodge with a Welsh family or elsewhere. Jack desperately wants them to make a home for them again, so Miriam will return when the bombing is over and they have lodging, and with Ian. Sheila will be fostered by a cousin of Bron's till old enough to join the home. I have told them they can rebuild a good-sized single house for the family, where the cottage stood, and plan and prepare ahead as if the place were their own.

I shan't go back till the bombing ceases because the place isn't safe from blast and I doubt if I shall get glass. They will put opaque white paper, but even then you won't be able to open the windows. The paper has to be fixed to overall wooden frames, in metal windows. But the windows of kitchen and bedroom are still there, because they were open and blast pulled them, not punched them. It drove the big window in tiny pieces of course on the whole floor etc. I shall make the cottage available though for visits and camping out in as soon as it's reasonable to do so. Because it's pretty essential to try and tidy it up and light fires occasionally and so on. I should be terribly lost without any home of my very own. So I dare say we shall be able to go there one weekend later on, from a Morley concert or whatever, just as soon as the worst of the bombing stops. (It may shift its directions east, when the allies clear N. France.)

At present I suppose I shall live here. There's an empty drawing room with a lovely Blüthner grand. It's almost ideal except that it isn't my own. But I'm thinking of a hangout in London. Pete [Pears] and Ben [Britten] are away from Sept. to Dec. and are going to give me (and you) a key so that we can live there if needed. This seems better then the expense of another place, until you know your own plans clearly. There's the Glocks' old flat in Well Walk going, Clement says £2 a week – and a young chap ready to take one room only at £1. But so far I haven't been able to get down to such things and I've wanted to get in touch with you first. There's so much I need to say as usual. I shall be thankful when you are nearer. You could help in so many ways in these sort of things when being single means having to do and think of everything. I haven't begun the claims yet. I've got to make a detailed list of all furniture, clothes, etc damaged. I just can't face it.

I'm going up to town to see F[rancesca Allinson] on Friday and talk all sorts of things over with her. I'd come this weekend onto C[ambridge], but I'd better get back to write I think because I have to go on Thursday (in next week) to London–Leicester–Reading on a sort of tour, and back Sunday. But Morley starts the first week of September, Monday fortnight. Suppose I come down to C[ambridge] the Friday or Saturday before – that would be exactly in a fortnight's time. I feel I must see you. It will seem odd not sharing a bed with you and shall hate it, as things are. But it can't be helped and won't be lumped like everything else. Perhaps we could risk some of the night together. I think this suggestion is probably just the effect of absence and the need to be comforted, not so much after the actual shock, though that's enough, but this singleness of responsibility which makes one a house owner and something like head of a communal family, when it's time for music one needs and somebody's arm round one from time to time where there is complete relaxation. (Incidentally I've begun to sleep again here without a perpetual ear awake, so to speak.) I suppose it's a weakness and imposition to want to be some-times in your arms and you're wonderfully gentle and good about it. I wish it didn't mean so much, but it's one of the few unadulterated things I ever experience. Because it's you, the pleasure is pure and unmixed and I lie on happy as a child. So you gave me more than you know. At the back of myself there is enough toughness and strength to do without all these things, just as one goes through prison or gets bombed on or whatever. So the childishness isn't fundamental – except that in another sense it is – being the secret of some freshness. So you shall yet be gentle with me for a while – much loved then.

I've yet a whole set of your poems now from Fresca – and will deal with them soon.

I've also the carol of Edith Sitwell written at Sackville-West's request for me to set for Christmas – BBC commission [*The Weeping Babe*]. I shall try to do it, even breaking the Symphony [No. 1], because I think it might be a memorial for Bron.

There's heaps more to say, but I'll wait till I see you.

You might try a phone. Make it a personal call if you like: I can repay you. I seem to have money yet. Let me have a card otherwise about the proposed weekend. Shall I come Friday evening or Saturday. Longing to see you. [. . .]

Heaps of love –
Mike

16 August 1944
Midhurst

PS. I spent the first 2 days practically fed by the balloon site* chaps.
Got to know them well and regaled them with the prison stories! They
hope to be there till end of war and to come to a concert of the *Child*
or some other, grand folk. And carrying baby Sheila down the road in
the morning sun, fantastic symbol of vitality ever-renewed. She's a
beautiful babe. It all adds up to what Yeats called an 'experience' and
will surfeit the biographers. But it was gruesome and frightening.
　M.

17 August 1944

I never seem to write 1 letter but I write 3. What has brought this on
since I wrote the letter this morning and dashed off a p.c. in Midhurst
P.O. when seeing to a new ration book for the one destroyed in
Miriam [Lewis]'s cottage – is that I have just elicited from Dorothy
Shaxson that I can't be here alone a week or two. So it brings everything into uncertainty again. If I put the possibilities out on paper I
may see more clearly for the best, and you might help to solve the
problem. Roughly the facts must be:

　1. The cottage at Oxted isn't livable until ceilings and glass windows
are replaced. And I don't think it really sensible to force the Council to
do this (if indeed they can) till the bombing ceases in that area. I'm not
really up to a second dose, at least, just yet.

　2. I must have a hangout in town, but I don't want to live there altogether unless, *par exemple*, you were permanently settled there and a
joint flat seemed called for. So the P.P./B.B. [Pears–Britten] offer is
probably the best for the moment. To have a key of their place, to use
at will.

　3. I need some place to keep my clothes and *live* in – and even more
work in. That is to say a room and a fire and a hired piano, so to
speak. If there were anywhere in Cambridge I'm rather drawn to being
there for a bit. It brings Fresca within reach, besides being near you for
company and chit-chat. What hopes are there, do you suppose?
Perhaps we can rant around when I come down in a fortnight, unless
you strike lucky before on a brain wave. I shall have to 'move' about
that time I gather.

* A balloon barrage had been set up on Limpsfield Common to intercept flying bombs.

Alternatively I might find F[resca] can solve the piano situation at Mill House and I go there for a while. It has its points, obviously – but it's not entirely my sort of household. Anyhow, I'll talk this over with her on Friday. [. . .]

Love –

M.

20 August 1944
Midhurst

Dear Den,

I saw Fresca yesterday for 2 hours in town. I hadn't realised that she nearly passed out at Mill House and had given herself mentally up to death. She's again turned a corner, but I'm beginning to have doubts as to her chances of really surmounting the 'thyroid', i.e. goitre trouble. It plays the devil with her. In full clothes and overcoat she weighs 6 1/2 stone!! [. . .]

David [Ayerst] was at the cottage the night before the bombing. He read the masque script [early draft for *The Midsummer Marriage*] and was converted to it. He doesn't think it ought to be called a masque. I'm inclined to feel now that if I do the Sitwell poem [*The Weeping Babe*] for Xmas – finish the Symphony [No. 1] – and do a small piano sonatina then I shall want to begin on the masque, sometime next year – that's to say in about a year's time – without any intervening madrigal work. I'm thinking I'd better do a fresh précis of the general ideas and associations in my mind behind each conversation, which you can read and discuss before trying to crystallise into a condensed image as suitable: or reject as too complicated or to be left unspoken.

I think it's mainly over the first scene between George [eventually Mark] and the Ancients, which takes the place of the Argument in the oratorio [*A Child of Our Time*]. And there's a similar place somewhere later – probably after the transfiguration and return to normal. I'm afraid it will mean risking a first draft in the spring. I don't think you need be frightened as long as we are not afraid to alter. In point of fact I would like the words well ahead – the first draft of them, so that one has time to consider the implications of their setting while there is time to alter. I mean the sort of sounds that won't sing well. Another reason to get on with the masque is because there's going to be a fresh attempt at natural opera, so it's now or never.

I'm reading Yeats: *Autobiographies*, with great pleasure. It's an excellent introduction to the poetry itself, which I hope to get hold of on Fresca's library ticket. [. . .]

Lots of love –

M.

20 September 1944

Denlein,

I'm actually here in the cottage, attempting to glaze the window! But have had the pieces cut too big – must retake them to Oxted – there's nothing but an open space, and it's raining now – Calor gas run out and usual carrier man on holiday – electricity people won't come to turn on the juice – meanwhile so much to do everywhere that there's nothing else, like music *par exemple*, possible so you'll have heaps of work over the weekend.

[. . .] The reason I feel you ought to leave Cambridge is because I sense that it is time for you to experience new adventures, even unpleasant ones like quod, for enrichment, and 'shadow', as it were. Maybe that's only an intellectualisation hiding the real feeling that I, personally, need you and badly want you to be near. It's very strong indeed just at present. I'd love to have you in the home a bit without the perpetual need to leave for Cambridge, so I hope it's going to work out that you can fit that in with London. *Without* the Lewises it's very solitary really, and you are by far my nearest and dearest and I love you far too much. It's the old business that never being long enough together it becomes an ache rather than a proposition and an easy warmth.

[. . .] Sorry to love you so much, but it's like that.

M.

25 October 1944

Denlein,

[. . .] Max Steffens becomes unexpectedly munificent – on Monday last: draws out a cheque for me for £103 3s and gives me also a fountain pen. The £3 3s is for copyright of *Boyhood's End* and the £100 the annual (!) retaining fee. Well, well! [. . .]

[. . .] I played [Peter] Makings the *Child* on Mon. He fell. Thinks to do it as a money making concert on behalf of all destitute and

orphaned children. Nothing could be nicer. It sounds too much like a
dream.

[. . .] You'd better dump what you want to here – and then we'll soon
get you the sort of place suitable in town. Possibly at Johnny [Amis]'s.
I need you to be tolerably near for a while, when there's so much going
on. Roughly you can somehow earn your essential keep say, and I can
be allowed to pay extra like some clothes, tickets to Oxted, Liverpool
or Paris, and expensive meals or taxis. Will write later.

M.

PS. It'll have to be £2 because I haven't a 10/- note. I'll send one
when I have one. I've just learnt that the workmen expect to be in
here by the end of next week and want me out of the way. I suppose
for several weeks too. They have to take down part of the outside,
and the inside walls. So I shall probably continue living in P.P. and
B.B.'s flat [. . .] So if you decide to come up at the end of next week,
that is to say the fortnight later as proposed, then we can very likely
be in London over the week-end; I leave for Liverpool from there the
Monday etc. [. . .] So that if it works out for you, make it next Sat.
week and I'll make it the same. It's a b[loody] nuisance thus being
out of one's home again for weeks. But as I said it's a bit more tolerable if there's nearly any chance of seeing a bit more of you. (Fresca
also may [be] in town round that time.)

8 November 1944

Dear Den,

[. . .] I'm still very lost without the cottage. I wander into it to telephone or get clothes. It looks very old now, with 1/2 the red outer wall
down and the inner white wall showing – and even holes right
through. But I have hopes again of being back by Christmas, when
(and if) we'll have a gathering for the festival. I'm roughly trying to
arrange it so that I'm away somewhere from each Tues. morning to
Sat. But it has to be London over the weekends more or less. So until
the cottage makes weekends possible too there, I suppose I shall tend
to see all London folk between Sat. and Mon. – including you. Sunday
week there is an American Red Cross concert to do somewhere in
town – and the Sun. after (Nov. 20) a concert in Tunbridge Wells (very
nice Vivaldi Concerto Grosso; Bach Brandenburg for vl, fl, pf, etc –
and *Stabat Mater*, Pergolesi).

I'm afraid the wretched Sitwell motet [*The Weeping Babe*] has become horribly romantic if not downright sentimental. I think it's taken on rather a provincial English flavour. Still – we can put it to the test. If that's how it strikes us all on performance once or twice, it can be scrapped and not published. The *Child* is romantic of course (if not a masterpiece) – but I'm strongly in favour of the other attitude. You can't *live* on an earthquake until it has settled down. But the process of 'settling down' in cultural quakes is one of digestion and assimilation; hence, in a quaking period, it's doubtful if you can be unmoved except on a balloon. The Symphony [No. 1] is rather like a huge engine to transform the vast energy into tolerable experientiality, it will quake less than the *Child* and perhaps more than the opera [*The Midsummer Marriage*]. [. . .]

Love –
Mike

April 1945

Dear Denny,

[. . .] I've been crying rather a lot [at the news of Francesca Allinson's suicide] and feel a bit better at least. I think it was inevitable probably but we shan't easily find the like again. Gay and gentle and loving pretty things and courageous and in the end grim. Poor sweet sweetheart. But if I write more I shall cry again.

One is selfish all through in my opinion. We cry like thwarted children. But if she were cold and level then I would have held her hand at least.

[. . .] I finished the deathly slow movement [Symphony No. 1] late last night, just after Cyril [Allinson, Francesca's brother] phoned me. Till tomorrow.

Mike

10 April 1945

Dear Denny,

I'm afraid I was rather inept and coarse fingered yesterday, forgetting how close you were to her [Francesca Allinson] and how grieved and sore you would be. I didn't mean to look in upon your privacy, so to speak, just because we share a lot of memories of her.

Her letter shows that she was unable to want to survive Germany's agony and live into the post-war world without a healthy body and active participation in the healing.

But deeper still lay her trouble that she had muddled her life because she had denied at times her love. Warmth and love were her natural world – and she strove to enter the dispersed love world of the saint, but couldn't not. It makes us even seem horribly cold fish beside her – selfish and abstracted. Yet it wasn't really so much love from another she wanted as strength to love and cherish. But maybe had I been less abstract, less manlike in fact, I might have helped her along to where I imagined we should end. Not that my love wasn't perhaps too severe and passionless and understanding to be of this life anyhow. One day when you and I went over to Mill House from C[ambridge] she said to me: As I saw you two come up the path from my room, I saw a vision of springtime lovers. I remember answering a bit bruskly and evasively – for I was a little shy, and a trifle distressed lest this conveyed a faint feeling of envy or jealousy. But it didn't. It was her vision of her loved ones at one with each other – the over-abiding love she wanted to pour on us all so that we were, she believed and hoped, to love naturally as she had not, without denial.

Then she spoke of you when I saw her last. She told me of the dream of her arms and wounds, and her feeling that she was forgiving herself for just this denial. She asked me of you fearing that you were not going that way, denying the love of the heart for social prejudged patterns of behaviour. I comforted her and told her that I felt it to be alright with you anyhow. But there her message is for us all, if for you particularly, whom she had close. I read the message for myself too, though it isn't meant from her for me just the same, because I became older when I was with her alone, and she had this illusion that I had not denied what she imagined that I had denied. But she did not deny, either herself or others. Only she remained to the end believing herself worthless.

Don't grieve, Den dear, and I don't write like this to make you cry. I don't tread this hidden ground to wring our hearts, but to establish a bit of a basis, sentimental, analytic or what you will, where we can talk of her occasionally, and where we can know that our own gaieties and light heartedness cover the inner sensitiveness to her memory – and that she wanted us to be so.

She wants you and me to finish the monograph for her. So we will. I've written to Veronica [Allinson, Francesca's sister-in law] about the MS and will go there to get it if necessary.

[. . .] David [Ayerst] writes the most sensible, pertinent, and rational letter imaginable – so exactly like him, the dear. All the same it covers something. I was writing him a gently worded criticism of his Christian war, which was the outcome of my agony of impotence at the lunatic state of things, just as she came toward her end, I suppose. However it's good to have the Davids – sensitive but sensible and with an even surer armour of abstraction. I am to the end, like the darling Fresca, a hopelessly double person – get over weakness is one's strength if we know how. Sitwell (E. and O. [Osbert]) invites you on the Sunday. Hope you come with Johnny [Amis] this weekend – being as you remain so near and dear.

Mike

The Auden is good. Comes from this same double world: Oh near your tribulation like a rose, a rose. That's a very good image of what she wanted so hopefully to do, but felt she hadn't. But to me, at least, she had.

2 May 1945

D-D,

[. . .] Most of the pile of F[resca]'s private papers was my own letter and one of yours. Between her bit of diary (with dreams) and my dreams and letter and bits of other things there's a curious chunk of 'shadow' biography, which I shall keep for a while at any rate before destroying – or leave somewhere safe for you to read or destroy one later day when I am also in the cold ground. Her inner life is just the chaotic febrile world of imagination which a poet has to inhabit at times for his sins. But a woman has greater difficulty to express it artistically as a personal satisfaction.

Love –
M.

10 May 1945

Liebes Denlein!

You'll be amused to hear that the opera [*The Midsummer Marriage*] has suddenly begun in earnest i.e. I've put down 1/3 to 1/2 of Act 1, at a sitting – with some beginnings too at musical organisation to correspond. As yet there are no lyrics. I'm not sure what will happen about them, because of stylistic problems if I do retain my own (further polished) version of the rest. I like particularly Bella's aria as you have left it. So perhaps that can be incorporated somehow. My intention is to compile this prose draft for type and then distribute and sustain the comments and criticisms. I've promised it to [Edward J.] Dent, Arthur Waley and Goehr, so far.

I've got down in prose an extraordinary aria, or 'scena', for King Fisher, which prevents the work effectively from performance in Russia. It develops nearly into a satire on *Boris* [*Godunov*], 'I have attained the power' – so it will upset the Russians both ways: e.g. Choir: Long live our leader King Fisher, Our little Father Fisher King.

I have suppressed the 'birth' of Jack, and given instead a new twist to the story by an earlier appearance. I'm also giving a further twist to the reappearance of the Ancients. But you'll see it all in good time. The style is much cruder than yours, but what is really happening is that the dramatic stuff latent in my own ideas of the work is now leavening to a froth – and I suppose would have been unable to function except by this aid.

What I need *particularly* if you could post it me, is the bit of yellow paper with my suggested final aphorisms for the Ancients. Have you got it still? I hope so. Would you be an angel and look and let me have it fairly soon.

Blessings –

Mike

What you did for me, which might not have happened otherwise, is to enable or force me to see the aria problem and how to solve it. In this version now there's more talking than expected and lots of recitative too.

June 1945

My dear Den,

The 4tet [String Quartet No. 2] went much better at the BBC. It was really a concert with an admitted audience and I got tickets the day before then couldn't remember altogether whom for. (Which shows how tired I must be and how glad I am to have 5 days off – tomorrow till Sat. – walking with David.)

I'm really pleased with the new 4tet [String Quartet No. 3] and rejoiced over what you wrote. I'm quite likely to do a new last movement – the same lyrical quality, without tension, but gayer, more

Mozart-like and without such an abrupt end. I have begun it – and if it doesn't crumple up on me, I shall go on and finish – the present last movement I should give a little introduction to, slightly extend the end and issue perhaps as a piece by itself.

I am now *at last* coming to the opera [*The Midsummer Marriage*]. I've had some funny and also disquieting times with it. Lastly, a few days ago, it grew a 3rd act. But it's too much to write by letter. I'll come and tell you of it. What is the most radical change is that the choir is a group of George [eventually Mark]'s young friends given an early morning assignation at 'the place'. The mythological appearances belong, like Titania and the fairies, and the Prospero lot, to the time and locality. The play between the humans and their mythological projections gives a new dramatic 'tool of the trade', which clarifies things a bit, and makes them less arbitrary. The new 2nd act is almost interlude. Jack and Bella just enter in time for her to see Parthenia for a second before she vanishes and the faun becomes stone. After commentary on her reactions to this (and the morning's doings) they come to their own personal problems – and their duet. King Fisher breaks in and is disagreeable (trio). He forces Bella to ring for the Ancients. (All the stairs and gates and doors are up-stage among the 'ruins'.) When they appear he is insulting and challenges them to produce his daughter or to appear at 6 when his own 'magician' will arrive to play magic against magic. (Dramatic recitative – and final, traditional 5tet ensemble.)

Last act begins (all on stage), with the operation of the challenge and is what you know except for a quicker movement of the mechanism. (There is no barrel of sea-water.)

The comic parabasis is taken away; end of Act 1, now. Too complicated. A real, serious parabasis comes at the end of everything. Jack has always known the Ancients from boyhood's and youthful wandering alone on the hill. Having no real parents they are his images. However, I hope to get a draft of Act 1 onto paper soon if it doesn't change anymore!

Love to you both –
Mike

[12] June 1945

Dear Den,

[. . .] I should like you to see *Peter Grimes* sometime. It's obvious that the masque will be so different it's almost frightening. I mean that we shall risk a serious failure to please because of our story's marked unsentimentality and so on. *Grimes* is nothing if not properly romantic. The emotional situation is pictured all the time in the music (not the action or gesture) quite like *Tristan*, but with less power. Two scenes are very good, but a lot of it is rather disappointing. Johnny [Amis] thought likewise I gather.

He by the way has in his gentle way been warning me that he opines you may at times feel worried that I shall grieve when the time comes for you to go off with your proper partner. There's no need to worry over much, even if I do let on occasionally how much I care, for you – not that you find the person. After all it's bound to happen – it's only a fact finally like Fresca's death and one just lumps it without ill feeling or self-pity. I've had the experience before – and though I may not know consciously all that may hold me to your image inside, I don't think an enormous lot is repressed, which could rankle. In fact I'm pretty positive. But I don't think you'd expect me, or want me to be the sort of guy that lives in fear of a future and has never any present joy as it flies. And also it doesn't look terribly serious. Both of us live most of our lives quite separately – and there are plenty of intellectual contacts to hold. I can believe incidentally that Fresca's going threw me metaphorically more into your arms, because I was suddenly very lonely (like Judy [Wogan] is now – I've had a long incoherent letter from her) and tried to grab hold of the nearest person.

I only spew things out rather like Fresca. I hadn't told you that a little while back I did have the opportunity (!) to practise what might be called sex without full affection. It was not a success and I didn't much like it. [. . .]

M.

17 June 1945

I have an idea the contact goings on may appear a bit worse because everyone is a trifle emotionally deflated by the peace and more subjectively because you can't make the holiday with us. So that part of the depressed mood will pass into its opposite sooner or later – or reach a new depth! I suppose a man's loyalty is normally functionally split between his wife and family and his occupation. The former loyalty often keeps him unwillingly at work in the office, and at other times

the office becomes a refuge from domesticity and female possessiveness. An artist gets all this less well functionalised because his work
(and all the loyalty involved to it) is so unpredictable, interior, illogi-
cal, and generally at the start unsaleable. Marriage can kill creative
work, as it can break a marriage – or it can occasionally pan out.
You'll have all this problem in due course. But earning always brings
some sort of struggle between undesirables and desirable and to a *limited extent* this tension can help creativity. I suppose I *may* have done
less composition than I might, but I've also gained depth, at least of
character, by the tenacity of other loyalties, even if, one by one, they
are outlasted by the music creation. Your land period hasn't been too
bad. [. . .] The business about earning or receiving money is just not
my strong point – whether of conduct or advice. I've never earned my
way and have never been unduly ashamed. Whether my father, or
Aubrey [Russ], or Evelyn [Maude] or Fresca, it didn't very much
worry me, because my own worth I never doubted and because I gave
tolerable service generally all round. So probably I've never fully
entered into temperamental attitudes which may need to get all money
by earning or whatever for various reasons of self respect, if from a
woman, or questions of queerness, if from a man etc I have known (as
with Wilf [Franks]) they can be quite basic – and so that's that. But
then Wilf is not finally a productive artist – marriage and money and
social adaption were pathological problems overshadowing the other.
That was his fate and he was right to go forward within it.

I shall have (or rather have) enough money to spare to help you as
I have been helped. But it's from you that the need and the decision
will come. I have learnt (or half learnt at least!) to let people be in
these matters and also not to try and make believe. Fresca helped me
for love as well as for her faith in the music. I have always been able
to accept gifts due to love, where I have known that the donor
(unlike e.g. the good Rose [Turnbull?]) is mature enough to be tolerably sing and dispassionate – just because I have loved so much one
way or another and had so much affection showered on my head. It
becomes a give and take which is fairly well understood of warm
hearted folk. So, thereby, money is tolerably neutral to me, repre-
senting just help and comfort from one to another and nothing much
more sinister. [. . .]

Love –
Mike

After a lot of experience I should say you're lucky not to be queer –
vide the sonnets. Be thankful for small mercies! [. . .]

18 January 1946

Den my poppet –

I think the Sitwell letter is just what you should have expected. She
is a very old hand at the game and must have a wildly acute ear for
imperfections of the type. You can't help being at the start as she can't
being at the end.

I can't tell always, if ever, for poetry. In music, so much turns on the
creative temper because so much else can take the emotional energy
away – concert giving to the public; teaching the student, etc, etc. Film
music and immediate success and so on. It's essential that the gathering of the energy together to that core, complex, or what you will,
which then eats voraciously everything else up in a sort of mastication,
later to be regurgitated or born elsewhere. It's the creative temper, and
it's part at any rate of the thing itself. It's not easy to say it is not there,
because it isn't manifested in typical behaviour, but one can usually see
it.

This is the explanation of my worrying about the opera [*The
Midsummer Marriage*]. I have got to the point now, when I am the
creature of this complex to a degree which may not be easily observ-
able to a dear friend who is used to personal attention and cherishing.
So that, where I *do* have more patience with the slowness of my librettist, because he is a dear (where I can't imagine I should have for
another and why?), there is an absolute limit beyond friendship when
the complex demands action irrespective of whether you have finished
it or are in prison. It's not difficult for me now to approach whom I
will, but I want it to be by you if you will produce it. We put end of
January for the date line for the draft of Act 1. I get horribly depressed
when there is failure. I begin to lose confidence. I can't help it because
months go by and at this rate of production it will not be in time. It's
no use my labouring the point. It must be in time if it just isn't in time.
What I will do in that event, I don't know – but it will solve itself for
me, as it always has done. I only trust it won't impair our friendship
which means a helluva lot as ever.

Forgive this moan – but I feel I was a fool, against advice, to turn for
collaboration to a friend – because this thing that drives me, that

makes me worried now, is so bloody actual, and so *final*. No one in the end can stand in affection against it, as the darling Fresca knew. It's only possible to humanise it, so to speak, when everyone is quite neutral in the sense that if an artist plays a work better he is given the recording.

Best of love, poppet, and I'm terribly pleased for you that you are having the experience you are; and may it be a true 'joy as it flies'.

dein treuester Freund

Michael

If you'd rather leave it at this stage for your own work, I should quite understand.

13 March 1946

Liebes Denlein!

[. . .] The amendment in the Lords to the C.O. [Conscientious Objector] release Bill means as I read it that C.O.s on the land will get no release date from the Nat. Service Act. Prosecution, if it came, *could* be under that act (12 months max.). I have no idea if it will come, nor if they will use that act or 58A. Should it come, and as I don't see much of you, my advice is to have a talk then with David [Ayerst]. He is very fond of you, will do everything he can to help and is very shrewd on social behaviours and misbehaviours. Secondly, see the Central Board as to the best legal means of defending a court case if charged with 'Non-fulfilment of the Condition'. If they want a lawyer they will provide one free, I dare say, apart from help of friends. They are the only people with enough material to give proper legal advice. I am out of touch.

If the melancholy prospect of a prosecution really appears, then it may cut the knot of the opera *faute de mieux – nolens volens*. You must not take it too hardly if that is so. Sometimes now I can't help feeling that the new happiness is of more importance than the libretto, to you, at present. I do like what you have done (I wish I might have the rest of Act 1) but it's no use disguising the circumstantial difficulties – and temperamental ones also! I have got a great deal myself out of your co-operation so far – in ideas and discussion. I must acknowledge that in any case: and handsomely as is appropriate. But I often get the feeling that it were almost better for both of us to leave straining and worrying and let me see what I can do either alone or with help between now and the summer. This indeed would be *easier* for me, if perhaps not a gain for the work itself. If we did decide now to leave it, I have more time to look around. If you decide to go on, then it will become a date-line question: leaving me with just enough time, I suppose, to get hold of a quick worker or get myself down to it.

Love
Michael

Benjamin Britten

Benjamin Britten (1913–76) and Tippett first met in November 1942 after Peter Pears, Britten's musical and life partner, had appeared as a soloist in Purcell's verse anthem My Beloved Spake *at Morley College when Tippett was director of music. The two composers quickly became friends, with shared interests in opera, English nationalism in art, and pacifism. Besides chronicling these concerns, the letters printed here highlight the ways in which they diverged, both personally and artistically; but Tippett's regard for Britten's musicianship and prowess as a pianist always shines through. The support Britten and Pears extended to him, especially at the time of his imprisonment, moved Tippett deeply, and he admired and envied the couple's devotion to each other. Some of his most heartfelt outpourings are found in the letters to Britten, to whom he often wrote about his experiences as a social and professional outcast and the frustrations of trying to compose in a shattered world. Their close friendship lasted until Britten's death, transcending artistic differences and paralleling the creative journey of these two leading English composers. Britten is the dedicatee of the* Concerto for Orchestra.

[1942]

Dear Ben,

It certainly is odd that we didn't come across each other before, but it's as certainly satisfying (at any rate to me) that we have done so now. There has been a spontaneity about the association and a general sense of comradeship which I can't help feeling makes a frightfully good basis for artistic grouping – that's to say for people around us as well for ourselves. It seems to me, at any rate, that the various forms of 'rebelliousness' we both suffer from are not entirely accident, but provide the necessary 'shock' to pure bourgeois life and culture, which makes for something new and counteractive. I also sense a very close contact latent between the newer generation and ourselves – though I can't put my finger on its basis. It's somewhere because we have a certain attitude to the coming society, a new mixture of acceptance and rejection, which is sympathetic to them – and probably more so a like new mixture in our attitude to the artistic musical past. It's decidedly complex, and needn't be analysed. I instinctively feel that its equality, candour and sense of comradeship are the most valuable emotional elements, which permit in some way the very much younger (in age and artistry) to come into fruitful contact – as well as the [Walter] Bergmann, and the Steins. For the moment it's decisively secular – because as I have learnt to realise, anthropologically, religion is the very necessary expression of individual and social fear – awe, and reverence, and its deeper, more courageous forms – but the young generation before us is not religious but much rather 'renaissance' – from *Wozzeck* in the same way. It will turn likewise from the oratorio [*A Child of Our Time*], as indeed it should as I do myself. That is a document of our fears – and *à propos* for the time being unassimilateable – (what a word!) – On this thinking track one can come at the obvious danger – that we get too much social and artistic success based really on a combination of fashionability of the new, and direct youthful hero-worship. *Les Illuminations* is quite alright in itself – but it's a pity when Rimbaud becomes a popular success or a musical setting – there is something in the core of Rimbaud which ought not to be there – or rather which thereby resides elsewhere – back in the French itself. I want to set [T. S.] Eliot – 'Coriolan' – I imagine I might equally run his poetry into that danger – and indeed it'll have to happen, seeing as I shall be writing for the coterie through whom one's music is performed at this time. So it's no good worrying about it, but to go about one's artistic business and not to be frightened either by success or hostility. For the moment there is a hell of a lot for us to do in gently shaping what is coming and to say it all over again. The goodness of it will be in the equality, candour and comradeship – and the tolerance by which we can assimilate nearly everything we need and more so, which the young ones may feel they need.

What I really meant to write about was how much easier all this present trouble is with you and Peter as friends – and how good a life it seems to look forward to coming out again to.

Sorry about the 4tet score [String Quartet No. 2]. You'd better hear the European broadcast from the studio Thursday, June 3, 10.30 a.m. I'll tell you later. I might ring you sometime about Monday evening next, if I have to stay over night after Johnny Amis's club performance of the 4tet, which I've promised to attend. Especially if the cantata [*Boyhood's End*] is finished – which is possible. Today I woke up singing and gay – and the feeling in the tummy is passing off somewhat, will return nearer the day I suppose. But in my heart I'm absurdly gay – and at peace inside.

Herzlichst –

Michael

[early 1943]

My dear Ben,

[. . .] I was tremendously pleased that you should suggest a weekend – because despite its simplicity, it's a nice cottage for friendliness and music and talk – and in fact any sort of real living. The weekends around the end of February and the first in March are the most possible for me – March itself is that fearful month when I do a row of spring performances with the little choirs – every Saturday. I up them all into one month to get it over! Then life becomes tolerable again after.

You know – getting to know you – and your consideration therefore – has been a much needed encouragement. It's not your fault that it has, but it is so. I have sometimes wondered whether I'm right up the pole because it's been such a hopeless matter trying to get things done off my own bat. It's getting a bit better now.

Don't frighten me over the 'recitative' [*Boyhood's End*] – as usual, it turns out a bigger thing than expected and this present rushing about sort of life is definitely not the proper one for its success. So we'll just have to hope that I don't let myself down – but good luck rather than good judgment. Actually I'm getting a lot of kick out of doing it – and it has an air of actuality because you two are in my mind and ear.

Peter seems to have made a tremendous impression – Seiber thought it the best voice he'd ever heard! Don't let that turn P.'s head. As to teaching and that palaver – we'll think about it leisurely, and pick up a group of pupils which he can do for so many weeks or months – in between tours.

[. . .] Try and fix a weekend somehow – and let me have the new address, so that I can at least write you if needed. I gather no phone as yet.

Love –

Michael

[early 1943]

Dear Ben,

I expect you've realised that the recitative just won't be done by Feb. 27, so it relieves [Alfred] Kalmus of all anxiety or any of the others likewise. I'm wound up in it now, which means it will go on steadily, but it takes me a long time to get exactly what I want, especially in an unfamiliar genre. I don't know what will come out later, but what you might call the 'adolescent crash' has appeared on the word 'want'! I think it will be rather like going backwards, in that it will get more innocent as it proceeds. I've got the first third clear in my mind, down to the 'bones uprising' – but the middle third eludes me still – at any rate formally. Whether to advantage or not I guess it would score very easily for small or large combination – but I don't think it that way and it's meant for you both. It can be arranged for orchestra after-wards if wanted. I hope to get on a bit faster when the Friends' concert on Sunday is over.

Love –
Michael

[May 1943]

Dear Ben,

[. . .] I've written Gerald Cooper today about this matter of con-certs, saying that if I am forced to decide between himself and Kalmus I've got to let the latter have it [*Boyhood's End*], because I did stupid-ly offer it him first, and I owe him something for the 4tet performance. But I have said that I have no legal means of preventing it being done, if Cooper gets Ibbs & Tillett [concert agency] to ask you and you accept. The trouble is that K. scents a good novelty and so does Cooper – so K. will stick to his rights (though he has not even got the work accepted by his committee) and Cooper will feel he has been forced to do inferior stuff. Anyhow I can't do any more. I've told K. I must have a definite fixture now, before I refuse Cooper with it. And the trouble is, that will be well on in autumn and it hangs things up – for Cooper is in July or August, and I fancy other requests will appear after June 5. If I tell K. I can't wait, then I suppose he'll take it ill enough to keep my name out of any further series – and I suppose that's rather stupid to court. On the other hand I just hate thinking in this way and won't. Which means that I will play straight enough and let K. have his rights, and leave any argument to be between Cooper and him and the real people that matter – the 2 artists. Because if the music means anything it isn't dependent on this or that occasion for display but how best it suits Peter is something on its own.

There was something that did annoy in my talk with K. He seems to hint that publication would ease the matter of performance – and this he let out after having forced my hand over the song. I just didn't like it, and feel that the whole matter is pretty uneasy. I don't grudge B. & H. [Boosey & Hawkes] their time for their own stuff and don't now feel it would knock me personally out, because there are other means afoot. So you see in some ways I'm sorry indeed that my impetuosity has given K. a means to have a novelty (which may well be the last with him) which would have been better all round to have done at Wigmore with Cooper. But as I say again – the people who really ought to be asked are yourselves – and we won't worry any more.

It's taught me one lesson – to leave handling my own affairs and let the young John Amis do it for me and properly. He's got the Zorians [the Zorian Quartet, founded by Olive Zorian] to consider putting the Britten [String Quartet] No. 1 into rehearsal – and it was his idea to have them learn the Verdi. And I have got them to do Purcell at National Gallery Monday week, and I will go and rehearse them on it. At present they're eating out of our hand and may become a tolerable ensemble. I can't help feeling that young folk like Amis and the girls of the Zorians, master Tony Hopkins and his clique etc, will create for themselves the conditions in which the music of their own composers is put across to the generation that wants it. This is much wider than Kalmus and his concerts, if less spectacular. But the idea is to feed concert giving groups with the ensembles that can do the stuff we want and like.

I'm letting Tony Hopkins set up his own Music Club at Morley to do in a more living sense what [Francis] Chagrin has buggered up by too much grandiosity and publicity. And I've suddenly realised the place for Seiber. Give him autocratic control of a composer-craftsmen group to meet regularly, but not too often on morning or afternoon at Morley, to discuss all matters arising out of the craft of composing at the present time. Analysis of major works, criticism of younger stuff etc. Open to anyone young or old interested in self-education of that order. Seiber has long wanted and hoped for this and it's taken years to realise that nothing stops him doing it, but just himself. Tony brought an RAF lad and his wife to choir last night – both composers. The fellow played wild 11/8 rhythm stuff on the piano afterwards – showing how deep-seated this feeling for accepting, assimilating and polishing the jazz-born rhythm is. Such a group as Seiber intends would be just heaven to him – the RAF of course keeps him out at present. For the autumn session I shall get Morley to print a syllabus of all the activities for use by us all. It's the luck of having a nice room with a damned good piano which makes it a good home for this sort of things at the present.

What a letter!

What a horrid throat Peter had, sounded grim in the extreme.

Herzlichst

Michael

[1943]

My dear Ben,

I had an interview with local Labour Exchange yesterday and things look up a bit. Kindness itself and very humane, and they have reopened the whole case in an attempt to have mine put on all fours with yours and Peter's and Clifford [Curzon]'s and Willi Busch etc and in this respect these have been high-up moves, which I oughtn't to put in a letter. But my pigheadedness seems to have fastened on fire-watching now. Could you tell me if you ever had dealings with local authorities in that respect and what was the outcome? I know Cyril Smith gets excused as being a professional liable to be called away at any moment. I hope to do the same. I find I draw the line (conscientiously) at training – which is what is the matter now here – in the depths of the country!

Listen to the 4tet [String Quartet No. 2] if you can on Thursday – Home Service, 10.20 p.m. I think it's the best 'pure' music I've put down, in the form that most interests me – combination and contrast of movements. I haven't seen Eddy [Sackville-West]'s stuff in the N.S. [*New Statesman*], but I've heard enough to distress me. *Times* man really got hold of what I was at. There'll be a National Gallery in a week or so – on the Friday before Good Friday I think – but I expect (and hope) that you'll still be away in quiet.

I'm going to do something about the oratorio [*A Child of Our*

Time] soon now. There's a *Listener* article to come out the week after next, I suppose – hope to see some dope on it there – then I think I shall approach either Sargent or [Reginald] Jacques – Peter, I think, favours the former. The publication delay is simply myself – but I make the final corrections with the good Bergmann at my side. Sunday after Peter's back at Morley – tomorrow week in fact. I hope to have another section of Peter's song [*Boyhood's End*] to add to the MS by then.

Love –
Michael

27 May 1943

My dear Ben,

I have just seen Counsel and am writing now because I cannot phone you tonight and if it is a long distance phone call tomorrow we shall not have time to discuss the matter.

The Counsel thinks that there is a chance for the case if we argue first of all that the changed circumstances do constitute reasonable excuse, and for that they want either Bax or Vaughan Williams (I would like to ask you if I can get hold of you which you think the better) and Mrs [Eva] Hubback about Morley work. Also Ayerst on the principle of 'colonel for colonel'.

But really more serious from your point of view is that he wants to argue on Peter's case and with Peter in court! As you know, [Ernest] Bevin has in fact stated that Peter's case did constitute deferment while mine did not, and therefore Counsel feels that Peter is perfectly safe. So he wants to argue that as Peter got the same conditions as I did and has since been deferred, then his work must have constituted in the eyes of the Ministry 'reasonable excuse'. They want to suggest from that that if the man who sings the songs obtains 'reasonable excuse', then it is a curious anomaly in British justice if the man who writes the songs does not.

I personally am rather worried at Counsel's request for Peter and was reluctant to agree, but they overruled me in the matter and are quite definitely of opinion that it would be of value. Nevertheless, you will know that I am absolutely honest when I say that I should not in any way feel distressed if Peter preferred for any reason not to appear.

Actually [Robert] Pollard will write to Peter, and that means that if Peter agrees, he wants a short statement which can be given to Counsel for his brief as to what Peter can say in this respect.

The case is on June 21st definitely so we have time to think it all out.

Yours,

M

August 1943 [after release from Wormwood Scrubs]
Mevagissey, Cornwall

Dear Ben,

[. . .] I'm at last beginning to thaw a bit and be less remote and able to think of music and work seriously. I think I shall come to, at last, when I search the cottage in a week's time.

I've decided to see if I can turn up the only early song I have kept – unless I destroyed it just before I went in. If it's there I'll copy out for Peter to see – and then set to and finish another which has one verse done out of 3. It's not very characteristic, but it will suffice I think – unless anything better pops up.

My original plans for the oratorio have bitten me again – to sink the family fortune and back a show in Friends' House – as being the only possible hall. To raise a special choir of 50–60 – use [Alec] Sherman's New London Orchestra augmented. Soloists of Peter's choice – myself probably to conduct. And to precede it with the *Sinfonia da Requiem*, which Alec would jump at the opportunity to conduct. What do you think? do you like the idea? I need for the *Child* extra cor ang. and contra fag. – 3 trumpets, so the extra flute, bass clarinet, 2 horns for the requiem, if you like the notion, you could probably make possible. If the idea matured at all (for after Christmas) we would put it all before Bliss and to get him to consider a broadcast. If not at least get a broadcast later – or a recording for overseas or European propaganda. The cost means backing the proposition up to about £300 some of which at least would come back in tickets unless we presented it to FWRS. It's rather a big present! But Friends' House is the proper home to bring the *Child* forth. I don't know yet if I can raise the guarantee but I guess it could just be done if it really seemed the right moment. I do really want to get it out somehow this winter season. I feel it's due.

I'll ring up Peter on Thursday next as I go through town home – or from Oxted. And I'll come in and see you both as soon as you're back in residence. I'll grapple with the song problem as soon as I've settled the fanfare.*

It was heaven to see you again and put hands on you in the flesh.
Love –
Michael

mid-September 1943

Dearest Ben,

Finished the goddam fanfare last night – 12 a.m. – sank in tiredness today – though been to Tribunal for a man in gaol, and helped to save him 7 1/2 months – he was in tears for his wife and family – and his wife likewise outside – so it'll be a great homecoming.

The fanfare is a funny noise – with one fearfully juicy bit.

Am due for rehearsal at Northampton, Monday 3 p.m. Am just doing the second song [for *The Heart's Assurance*] for Peter – will be ready sometime next week – but quite frankly I haven't your lovely gift of line – perhaps I shall learn from you bit by bit. *Boyhood's End* just hasn't got it – though I am always very moved by its atmosphere, and it's real enough for its own affair.

Johnny [Amis] thinks the Zorians have the Griller [String Quartet, led by Sidney Griller] beat for your 4tet. So as the Griller aren't doing the Berg for B. & H. [Boosey & Hawkes] I shall eventually have the Zorians with Schoenberg and yours too perhaps, at Morley – but just when. Am at present thinking of Bliss and the Frank Bridge – for February.

Now I'm going to bed to try and sleep round the clock.
Love to you all,
Michael

[1944?]
Elsted Manor, Midhurst

Dearest Ben,

[. . .] I'm here for a bit with farmer friends where I can work. Tell Peter I shall be sending him a second song [for *The Heart's Assurance*] soon. I expect to finish it today – and then back to the opera [*The Midsummer Marriage*].

* Fanfare No. 1 (originally called Fanfare for Brass), written for the 50th anniversary of the consecration of St Matthew's Church, Northampton, first performed 21 September 1943.

Aldeburgh, that is to say your home there, has had not only a won-derful recuperative effect on me, but it helped to settle my mind in what I want to do, consequent on the illness and other things. There is a plan, still in infancy, for John [Minchinton] and me and his mother to join together in a more gracious home than the Oxted cottage. If it can be managed at all financially I think it will come off excellently from other points of view. [. . .]

Love –
Michael

July 1946*

Dearest Ben,

I hope I wasn't too abrupt on Thursday. I was so pleased about the music that I rushed rather hastily to the attack on the other. I think I can make it clearer by discussion of the score: the arrival of Junius and Collatinus in the morning. Here you have various degrees of knowl-edge among the characters. Coll. knows that something is probably astray, but not the fact of Junius' perfidy. Jun. himself knows the fact of the rape but not the circumstances and imagines the servants know more than they do. The servants know the fact of Tarquin's visit but 1 only has a guess at the dreadful consequences. Lucretia knows all, in a sense, but knows also nothing of the wager etc.

Well! that is a classic operatic situation. I do not think it was artis-tically used up, so to speak: the dramatic qualities never really put *all* the characters or all the *character* of the characters into play (let alone the conscious artistry of playing with the extra knowledge that the audience has). Thus the benefits of Collatinus' remark 'why didn't you tell me this before?' is not merely the banality of the words, it is *really* in the banality of the response to the situation. 'Can this be the sort of man who has a wonderful love life with Lucretia?' It gives us 2 aspects of the same character which won't join: the schoolboy-witted soldier and the tender sensitive lover.

Then again – we are taken into the almost secret atmosphere of this love out of which happens the suicide. Afterwards we get a similar jolt over Junius. This Iago-like character suddenly brandishes a dagger and declares death to the tyrant. Is this the real Junius 'come clean', or

* Written after the première of Britten's chamber opera *The Rape of Lucretia* at Glyndebourne, 12 July 1946.

the old Junius 'jumping on the band-waggon'? We do not know.

You have written a preface, I gather, which I haven't seen yet. But you hinted to me that you thought high-thinking and good poetry were an aid to libretto[s]. Maybe that these things are a value to the present stage – I wouldn't like to say – it isn't my province. But the most striking thing lacking in English librettos is the knowledge of how to present emotions and characters in terms of dramatic situation and gesture whereby the words they actually sing withdraw a bit into the background. Arthur Waley wrote me a letter a little while back in which he gave his ideal of a libretto: 'one which we are not aware of, so that we come out of the theatre and say later "I suppose there *was* a libretto"' (this was the experience we had the night before at *Don Pasquale*). I have told this aphorism to many – and most find it good.

I spoke to Glock after he'd been twice and like me he thinks the music an improvement. I'm glad.

I have told you a lot of good things in this letter. Fruits of a great deal of discussion and meditation about this problem. I don't suppose they'll get all over to you, because our mental processes are so different. But I should feel lacking in friendship if I didn't hand you over all I have, as far as I can. You will write a lot of operas and something said to you now may work through unconsciously.

I shall be starting on my own opera soon – but I shall not face all the problems I have outlined above, because the subject is so pantomimic.

Hugo Hoecher, over out of the BAOR [British Army of the Rhine], was *very* impressed with the music of *Lucretia*, you'll be glad to hear.

Heaps of love to you both and all yours
Michael

3 March 1950

My dear Ben,

[. . .] I've heard a lot about *Billy Budd* and know you are just starting. I shall be finishing about the same time as you or a trifle later. *The Midsummer Marriage* will however wait till 52 before it leaps into the fray. I think [Eric] Walter White has some hopes that if the plans for *Billy Budd* mature and are a success, the good folk there might risk another English presentation.

I am just about to send Act 1 off to the printer (vocal score). Act 2 is all but finished. It's a kind of prolonged [*Prélude à L'*] *Après-midi d'un faune.* Act 2 is not as long as Act 1 so won't take such an age – but it's got some tremendous moments in it.

I find I suffer now from a deep-seated fatigue that's always round the corner, waiting to pounce. I have never kept so long at one huge continuous invention. It isn't complicated. I don't seem to use any-thing but common chords. And there's no counterpoint!! Though that will not prevent Howes (under whose skin any music of mine invari-ably gets) dismissing it as polyphonic. I sigh all the time for your won-derful ease of composition, and what I can steal I do. But it's less than I hoped! Though there's a lovely phrase from [*Albert*] *Herring* (not my favourite of your works as you know) which I've got into the most splendid aria I've written yet – for the heroine, Jenifer. But in fact I've never (since the *Child*) been so cursed by a work, which seems to live me, with all its stage trappings into the bargain. I've had to become extremely visual in composition. It probably wouldn't have take so long if I weren't venturing into such new ground and risking such a lot. I have to shake down such a mass of material of all sorts in order to come at a truly simplified image, that it seems to require hours of labour and forcing merely brings a crisis of fatigue. If I haven't got shingles, it's not from want of trying. Poor old Peter. But he really must take it easier.

I want to do some songs if I can and fancy have come at some poems, which I'm wanting to see. But I don't want to write second-rate stuff for you.

I'm very happy and cheerful, though I get depressive moments due to this so unexpectedly long wait – I imagined it would have been quicker. But there's been no stoppage, only a continuous high pressure of creation. It ought to be good one feels after all that. And that scares me a bit. There's some lovely music for tenor incidentally. A gay and spring-like love song at the very start of Act 1. And a rather bigger 'Dionysian' aria later in the act, after the hero has been 'below', in the catholic world.

It's just typical of my life that I can't even write you a letter without pouring out words about the opera. It's a kind of monomania. I'd love to see you. But I guess you're going to be shut up with *Billy Budd*. Should I though come and visit you? Or make a date in town?

Give my love to Peter, and my regards to [E. M.] Forster.

herzlichst

Michael

[1951]

My dear Ben,

[. . .] I'm only a few hours off the end of Act 2 of M.M. [*The Midsummer Marriage*] – and so very cheerful. [Walter] Goehr and I did a play- and sing-through of Act 1 to [Hugo] Strecker from Mainz last Tuesday and it all went very well. But we've seen 2 small, simple but advantageous cuts that I shall do at leisure. Then that act pf. score goes to the printer.

In 10 days or so therefore I shall take some kind of break. Perhaps to visit you? but not to disturb. Then I shall do the other 2 songs [from *The Heart's Assurance*] while drafting the pencil script of Act 3.

Meanwhile (again) I've decided to move, and to take my own mother under my wing. (She's an immense admirer of yours!) That is, that we shall have a home large enough to unite us and separate us. But financially at any rate this means a great help to me. For we can have proper care – whether John [Minchinton]'s mother will be living on my side of the house also isn't quite clear yet. There's been some problems around there. I've had to retake the key of my own door, so to speak – and to show a nasty selfish side of my character!

I may try and ring you sometime next week.

Blessings to you both

Michael

[late 1951]

My dear Ben,

I've actually now gone and done it and got an extraordinary house [Tidebrook Manor]. It's an old manor with an ugly Victorian frontage – imposing indeed. So that it has 2 very big rooms (one for me and one for mamma) either side of a hall, 5 ugly Victorian bedrooms above these, and then a congeries of smaller and smaller rooms in the old manor behind thinning down to a little wee half-finished cottage end. Then there is a bricked yard and behind again an oastery of houses. I've had to take 40 acres of pastures let off at a decent rent to the manor farm behind. All that is left is a 1/4-mile drive up the side of a hill, belted by trees, a small wood, and about 11/2 to 2 acres of garden – ending on one side in disused tennis lawn, belted by trees, which faces due south with a view over to the South Downs – the rest of the house faces west and has views over to Ashdown Forest. The Georgian part of the house is in roofage trouble as usual and there's no electricity. But Mother's heart does not fail her – although the permits business is so sticky. We shall not be able to do all that could be done, at once. But in a way that makes the financial side a bit easier.

I've finished a 3rd song [for *The Heart's Assurance*]. I hope your hair won't turn grey. It's a bit *schwermütig* and wildly romantic – that as you've heard, I've had to put in another gayer and lighter one, which I've just sketched out – a kind of tarantella. Then the most important of them will be the 5th and last. To a rather fine poem of [Sidney] Keyes.

It would be easiest for me now if you could get Elizabeth [Sweeting] to post me back the 2 you've got so that I can go through the accompaniments with a pianist and get some pedallings clear and notations and perhaps even simplify if we can. Then they can go off to an engraver while we can have a photocopy or two for use till the print comes to hand. Could you manage to give them to E.S. to post?

I've suggested to John [Minchinton] that maybe the regular allowance I let him have should rather be paid by me as a donation to Morley Concerts Society and then paid him properly for his organisational services for he really is awfully good at it. Quite a gift. If he ever went into that side wholeheartedly he could come out on top. What he'd better try for now is enough work of that sort and choirs to keep him going till chance offers him something bigger and unified. Between him and Goehr the Society has at last got into a more stable shape. That is, the work is all done by John, Goehr and an accountant. Then there is a committee to discuss and agree! John is full of ideas for raising money in regular and small sums.

I find that I've become unexpectedly close to my mother. There is now an awareness of a really strong pull, centred on a common need for tranquillity and room for the spiritual to flower and make its voice heard. So I do believe the new move to be a symbol of new life. Very exciting. [. . .]

Love to you both
Michael

[1951]

My dear Ben,
I hadn't realised I'd never told you I'd really moved. I flitted the

week before Christmas, in the snow, which lay in the pine trees for some time and was most seasonal. When you come back from Vienna and begin rehearsing do try and come down because it's a most lovely room to sing and play in, and it's tranquillity itself, besides being very lovely in situation. Wadhurst is just beyond Tunbridge Wells and it's a fast road – Sevenoaks, Tonbridge, T. Wells.

I think you'll like the songs [*The Heart's Assurance*], though I'm a bit close to them for the moment to assess them very dispassionately. Certainly Francesca [Allinson] could have thought of no lovelier memorial to her than the proposed occasion on May 7. The theme is so close to her own experience and the friends involved so near and dear.

Don't fret at the accompaniment problems Ben dear. You bring such sensitive musicianship to everything you do with Peter that shifts and turns of the hand to simplify anything will mean very little. There are no rhythmical problems as in *Boyhood's End*, just plain accompani-ment, so to speak. What matters to me so much is that you will instinctively know the kind of pianistic style and sound I've had in mind, and I can't help believing that that makes the matter of a fin-gered representation of the music easier than to someone with electric technique and little sensibility.

I'm going to try and make myself an extra (rough) copy for Peter to practise from temporarily (so that he doesn't have to look over your shoulder) until the proof copies come, which won't be long. The copy Schott's are making for you is professionally copied (I think) and should be clear and good.

In the last song, 'Remember Your Lovers', I seem so clearly to hear Peter calling to the young men in the fields of death, even though for-mally it may be supposed to be a woman. I can't quite tell why, but the man's voice seems right-er – and Peter's voice particularly.

There are one or two happy 'quotations' from you – turns of phrase which strike my ear as having been learnt from the master! Anyhow, Francesca would bless you for it. In the letter she left behind for me she wrote: keep a place warm for me in your heart. That's just what happened and what the song expresses – but for all of us lovers so to speak. I think it could only be possible now that the wound is healing and I can think of her death without resentment.

My love to both of you
Michael

[1951]

My dear Ben,

[. . .] You both did a power of good to Johnny [Minchinton]. He's grown up and developed in the last year or two at an amazing rate – but has to fight every inch of the way. With you and Peter so generous and candid he responds with his best – as of course he always does with me. Karajan and Casals have done the rest. I have no final fears now but that he won't be a fine conductor and a rich human being. But the turning and twisting in his efforts to get through will go on a long while yet – and each time one has to help him back to generosity and strength. I love him very dearly and am endlessly loyal. The gale last night blew a chimney into the roof.

   Love to you both –
   Michael

[1954]*

Dear Ben,

[. . .] I had news about the Divertimento [on 'Sellinger's Round'] at Aldeburgh, and was quite overwhelmed by the generosity. [. . .]

One of my intentions had been to incorporate a bit of your music, not Sullivan, into the last movement of the piece. But I abandoned it, because of my self-imposed secrecy. But if a second one ever came, say for a Mozart orchestra, I really shall ask you if I may. As you are the only English composer of nowadays I care at all about, it would be a way of saying so.

I want to come over to Aldeburgh for the Divertimento via and with the Allinsons of Streetly End, just over the west Suffolk border into Cambridge. (Where Fresca was when she died.) They are Fresca's brother and sister-in-law. John [Minchinton] and I would stay there a day or two as we long owe them a visit. My mother greets you. John sends his love from London.

   Michael

---

* Following the response to his contribution to the composite work *Variations on an Elizabethan Theme*, for the 1953 Aldeburgh Festival. Tippett later decided to write a longer variation-based work, incorporating quotations from several British composers.

3 January 1955*

Dearest Ben,

You should not have been out and about for my sake and so ill. I was deeply touched, but also deeply worried.

Of course yours and Peter's contribution stood so out, that that was all there is to it. Music only really speaks when performed thus. That got borne in on me every moment.

[. . .] *Boyhood's End* stood up well, I thought, from the far away and long ago days when I wrote it for you both; and Fresca was still alive.

Bless you both
Michael

January 1955†

Dearest Ben,

It meant a lot to have you there on Thursday; however the music takes you or not. Most deeply it meant an outward sign of affection. And [. . .], for better or worse, we two are the most interesting English music has at the moment.

I shall soon again try for something new for the theatre – and that will put *The Midsummer Marriage* into better perspective. The reasonable view that it's good music wasted on nonsense is a valid one. But for those to whom it speaks as a whole, it has a haunting and exhilarating power. They seem to be chiefly young ones.

For myself, I can't regret – for that's no use. It came as it came. The symbolic world is exhausted for the time being and I'm sure forever. I shall go down some fresh road.

Forgive my little confessional note. I needed to communicate with someone who can know where we kind have to stand. Don't answer.

Blessings,
Michael

* Following the 50th birthday tribute held at Morley College. The concert included a performance by Britten and Pears of *Boyhood's End*, as well as *Dance, Clarion Air*, Piano Sonata No. 1, String Quartet No. 1 and *The Weeping Babe*.
† Following the première of *The Midsummer Marriage* at the Royal Opera House, Covent Garden, on 27 January.

23 August 1955

My dear Ben,

[. . .] I had hoped that finishing my monstrous opera [*The Midsummer Marriage*] I would become freer to move about and visit the folk I really want to; like yourself. (For I realise I can't see and talk to you at Festival time.) But now I seem to have such a mass of music wanting to get put down on paper (slow and difficult always for me, as you know) that I never get away but to necessary professional occasions.

[. . .] Meanwhile lots of love, and to Peter.
Michael

[1957]

My dear Ben,

Sorry you've been confined to the house – but maybe it's good. For some months now I find that activities, especially professional ones, outside sitting on my arse composing here, make me slightly ill. And I don't recover till I get myself home. (The day I went up to [*The Prince of the*] *Pagodas* was no exception!) So I'm having to try to get used to just that. The only consolation is that the Symphony [No. 2] I'm working on, which is due out in February next year, seems to me one of the best pieces of music I shall have managed. [. . .]

Love to you both
Michael

[late November 1957]

My dear Ben,

I promised John [Minchinton] I'd write and tell you how much I was moved by *Hymn to St Cecilia* on Thursday. I've always liked the piece, but this time it spoke in a strangely moving way. I felt the Auden poem and the music in an unusual sympathy – and John brought us with a kind of emotional inevitability to the 'climax'. And the coda quite in place after. I think the being moved was pretty general. Naturally the performance is not technically perfect yet. But by the time he takes it to France you'll have as finished a performance I think as he now gives my little madrigal *Dance, Clarion Air* ([Christopher] Fry). Something toward the effect of a ghoulish string quartet.

For myself, on another plane, it was a very strange experience following. I was so much moved by the music – then there was a little party in John's top-storey flat. I was tired from 2 days adjudicating at my old grammar school [. . .] and by the time we went to bed Thursday and because of others staying, having to double up with John, I was desperately overexcited. I lay awake most of the night, which is unusual for me, with an ever deepening amalgam of the music and the verse, and the strange world behind it, and my own desire (John was sleeping). I don't think I've ever known so precisely how unbreakably entangled all our creative and expressive emotions are. Naturally enough by 6 a.m. I had made myself sick with stomach nerves – and had to spend the morning in bed calming down. But it was strangely worth the discomfort.

Your best (for me) music has always come out of this deep world. But not every performance can deliver it. The letter is not for answer – and hope the Red House is settling down.

Love to you both

Michael

[1958]

My dear Ben,

It was nice to hear from you, just how the old Symphony [No. 2] struck you. I'm still very much under the impact of it to myself – it meant a great deal inside. I have a notion you're right in that [movements] nos. 3 and 4 are less good absolutely than nos. 1 and 2 – but 3 and 4 will seem relatively better as someone else plays the piece adequately. So A.B. [Adrian Boult] proved woefully pusillanimous but P[aul] Beard was more than inadequate, he'd set out to make trouble – and succeeded. There's some long hangover there with regard to my music. Anyhow, we're busy trying to warn the supposedly unsuspecting Sir J.B. [John Barbirolli] ahead for the Hallé on April Fools' Day!!

I'm going to ring you Sunday evening on behalf of John [Minchinton]. It seems he's been a bit shy in telling you what he wanted – and what I'd told him to ask. Because he had wanted you more than much to appear with him at his first Festival Hall debut on May 21st, when he does *Agon*. (As you know [Ernst] Roth for some reason has entrusted its English première to him; and John's got a special late evening concert licence out of Beard and the LCC [London County

Council].) The idea is that you could do the motions of a 2-piano Mozart with Clifford [Curzon] or whomever – so as not to burden you – and to do at a blow all that I can't do for John. No motions of mine on a piano would effect anything!!

He should have asked you sensibly when he saw you – because he's got to fix things now or never. He's apt in any case to let things go too late, and I don't think he's right to do that on such an occasion.

The notion of the concert is: following on a recital of [David] Oistrakh, the Hall is cleared and then set for John and his orchestra. *Agon* comes first – about 20–25 minutes say. Then one other piece, i.e. if it's something like a Mozart concerto. The Hall is sold (out or badly!) at a one moderate price. John doesn't present himself for a whole concert, but in something he cares for, and very well done; he's been rehearsing bits already. But he needs someone like you to help him launch himself. That's how it seems to me.

Anyhow – you must say if you can or can't, Ben dear – and leave a message somewhere if I miss you on telephone.

Blessings.

Michael

[1960]

My dear Ben,

I'd meant to write you a while back. It's very personal, that's the reason for sending this letter via Imo[gen Holst] – in case a secretary opened it. It's about John [Minchinton] and myself. I don't want to go over any long story, because this news is only necessary to you (and Peter) because we are all bound to meet one day. The long and the short of it is that most unexpectedly (for I thought John's eventual marriage to be the first real break in our odd set of relationships, John, myself, Jessica [later Minchinton's wife] and Jean, his 2 girls) various unsatisfied desires in myself came to the surface (combining with a growing disinclination to find it so easy to accept John's need to bully-wrage his nearest and dearest, and I am too old), and these desires took or found an object. The moment of change isn't a pretty story, I suspect – but the outcome is that someone lives here with me, in a relationship as near to marriage as these relationships can be. And John has gone off into a necessary silence (after a period of dreadful non-silence). Karl Hawker is someone whom I knew when he was 18–19, and Fresca knew and liked. A painter. He was on the land in the war, at Cambridge, then felt he must get married (a long and complicated story). He was married for 13 years (the same 13 as I was entangled with John) and then it went wrong (progressively) and they parted. The wife has the 2 children (lovely girls) at Norwich near her father (a doctor at King's Lynn) and the other man. I heard of Karl's troubles, and had also once, 18 months ago or so, met him on the London street and felt the instantaneous pull. Eventually this June I wrote to him. A tremendous step as it transpired. The pull is quite mutual. Something I've never known before in this continuous way – and have consequently often envied you and Peter. So it's a totally unexpected flowering into a union I'd quite decided was due to me. We are very happy. My mother is also happy by it – and some of my friends find new life here, without John. He didn't please all of them. But I have no harshness myself towards him, though I guess he's still bitterly resentful. We shan't meet again until new life has developed on both sides. You always wished him well and were good to him and for him. It's possible he may have written you or seen you. I haven't told anyone what's happened except those who visit me. And Karl doesn't want much to go about in musical professional circles to which he doesn't naturally belong of his own right. But if, for example, we went up towards Norwich (he has a 20-year-old Morris 8, and is learning to drive!) to see the children, we'd like to have called at the Red House. Most of all we'd like you and Peter to visit us. Perhaps because, for me, there's never been an 'us' in this way before.

Much love to you both
Michael
[. . .]

February 1960*

My dear Ben,

It was nice catching a glimpse of you and Peter. And I still can't get over the pleasure of hearing such a fine performance of a work I still like. I know it always costs you such a lot to do concerts and perform such things, so I'm extra grateful.

Karl [Hawker] goes to get the children on Sunday, April 10th. What would be nice would be to get them from Norwich on the Sunday and

---

* After a London performance by Britten and Pears of *Boyhood's End*.

come to you just for the Sunday night, and bring the children home here on the Monday morning. Karl fell for you with a big bang, and had an instant sense that you can come as close to children as he can. So he wants to show you Susan and Sarah [his daughters] if and when it's possible.

[. . .] Returning to the performance I must admit I wish one day you and Peter could put it on to disc. The old recording with Noel [Mewton-Wood] is withdrawn. And somehow there's something extra from you (at least for me) which I can't explain in particulars, but which is just the very imagined thing itself.

Thought Peter was in tremendous form.

I've got back to the grind again. So I imagine have you.

Love to you both

Michael

[1960]

My dear Ben,

[. . .] The car got us home – big end gone. So we went to Cornwall in a garage car. A week after we were back and with the Riley anew, Karl left the brake loose and it tumbled down our fields into a tree trunk and is finished. I'm afraid too, an accidental but oddly symbolic image of Karl's deeply troubled state. He's moving back to London, to try to see if a home of his own there (within which I have at last a London room) will be a solution. And if it doesn't work, then he's not out any more on a limb. He has his own home. *Jedenfalls* – the essential is to get him steadied. Perhaps the divorce, which will be possibly final in Dec., will help to clear the air for him. Though it may as easily upset him further – as Anne [Hawker] is marrying again and happily. However, these matters are my (and his) troubles, not yours. (And incidentally I am astonishingly steady, infinitely tougher!)

We have tickets and hotel for the last weekend of Aldeburgh Festival – June 24 onwards, the last performance of the new opera. It'll be exciting.

Went over last night to Maidstone to see *Noye's Fludde* in the church. Very good it was. I see I used handbells in *Crown of the Year* somewhat the same, some kind of crushed chord. But I was much less skilful in other things.

Love to you both –

Michael

24 October 1960

My dear Ben,

Since writing to Ingpen and only making a tentative proposal, I think I really ought to make you, for the auction, a new ink MS copy of the variation of 'Sellinger's Round'. (Because the original pencil draft from which John [Minchinton] transcribed the ink copy you've got is lost or strayed.) So can you ask Imo to let me know her date line for receipt of – does it help at all if it's on 12-stave, say, or 24-stave paper – or whatever? I'll do it as soon as I get back from Vienna where I'm off to on Thurs. for 4 days.

I have been wanting to write you about MS in any case. And Eric White will sometime broach the matter with you. The point is I've been using his advice and help to try and sell an MS in America, in order to pay for Karl's analysis, which is vital but costly! Eric has a prospective buyer (with 2 Mahler symphonies already in his bag) who comes again to England in the new year. But he's said his priority in English MS would be Britten – naturally enough. And he'd only take Tippett in a package deal maybe. So Eric sometime will see how it is with you.

I won't give you all the ins and outs of Karl's troubles – but thank heaven he's in analysis now and at least he'll come out on a better basis for himself. Eric incidentally knows all that has been happening there, and he and Dodo, the wife, have been immensely helpful to both me and Karl. Karl is in a little room in town temporarily, and trying to build himself up again in his own right. It isn't being with me that's the cause – that's but triggered it off. Luckily enough just in time to act before it became too complicated and himself too alone.

King Priam progresses. On the last act now. A rather violent score.

Karl, by the way, thinks you almost the nicest person he's ever met.

Love to all

Michael

[1960]

My dear Ben,

I had a strange day last Thursday. I had lunch with Eric White, and he told me of all the MSS you've been offered for the Aldeburgh sale. I hadn't quite realised how (perhaps) inopportune my last letter may have seemed. Now I want to know how you think it is with regard to

211

an MS of mine in the collection? I would willingly offer one – but I am also aware I've nothing of the market value of what you've been promised by Bliss or Walton – or yourself. I don't mind being small beer but am wondering whether in fact it were better for the sale not to have too many but just those top knotchers. I haven't in fact got very many, because so much has disappeared. I think John [Minchinton] got away with some [. . .] but I may be doing him an injustice.

Anyhow send me a card or get someone to tell me – or phone or whatever is easiest. (I'm starting copying the variation [on 'Sellinger's Round'] next week.)

To return to Thursday. After I'd seen Eric, I found Karl at Schott's unexpectedly – gay and excited and happy and warm. He'd decided (through the first effects of the analysis) to go back to Anne and the children. Wonderful for them all. I have been overwhelmed by it, as you more than any other will know. We had 3 months when we chose each other and loved each other and by some transformation all seemed possible. Then the old life pulled poor Karl and the long descent into resentment and introversion began. Now, he at least feels new life again. I wanted a home so much (I've never found anyone before, I loved, who wanted to make a home together) that I've done a lot of crying – but that's passing. Everyone showers love on me, even Karl himself! – and I am only alone in the loneliness of an unfulfilled want. And there it is.

Karl still needs to finish his analysis – and I alone can make it possible. (He's certainly not really through.) So let's hope I can see an MS, or something for that, later on.

You and Peter are such a rare union. Thank heaven indeed that it sometimes happens. I'm always cheered and comforted by knowing it's possible, and that there in fact it is.

Work's been knocked off balance for the moment – but I'll get back. On the last lap now [of *King Priam*].

Love to you both

Michael

When the copying of the variation is done I'll try to get the next Achilles song onto paper [*Songs for Achilles*, written for Pears and Julian Bream]. I gather through William Glock they'd not gone right out of mind.

31 May 1961

My dear Ben,

The song for Achilles to a guitar has come out I think extremely well. Though I shall have to get the guitar part vetted [by Bream] – I've used a lot of 6-string chords. But the song as a whole really does express Achilles' mixture of sentiment and frustrated aggression, sulking in the tent. I feel, if Peter likes it, that I'd try to match it perhaps with 2 others from subsequent situations in Achilles' life at that point. Kind of parerga to the opera itself.

Karl's going to London, so far as it happened, proved a tremendous catharsis. He now knows anew that his problems can only clear gradually, and that he'd rather be in his home here when I can be with him. He may at last now get the bits of himself into better order – the art teacher becoming the painter, and the married father becoming the other thing. None of it easy – but it's more real than his life was before, and we are extraordinarily suited to each other. It won't all happen in a day – I mean his resettlement into a new life. But time will heal the older wounds, and the new will gain in depth. Do come in September if you can. It would be a kind of blessing.

It seems we shan't have a London pied-à-terre just yet. Financially it would mean Karl being tied to teaching again and unable to take the admittedly risky but exciting plunge into painting proper. We'll go in for a London flat when we're rich, if we ever are.

Living *à deux* has been a wonderful experience to me. Quite new!

[. . .] Glad [*A Midsummer Night's*] *Dream* goes so well.

Love to Peter and yourself –

Michael

[May/June 1962]*

My dear Ben,

Sweet of you to write in all the rush. And it's just as well you didn't get to *Priam* because we found when we went to W. *Requiem* that we were already overwrought and tired; exhausted from responding – so we got deeply moved still further, but could hardly fake it! (We'll come to another performance in a better building.)

* Following the premières, within a day of each other, of *King Priam* and Britten's *War Requiem* in May 1962.

Priam has been somewhat of a stunner, and a poke to all but the usual carpers.

[. . .] We're here (after Aldeburgh) then quietly (working!!!) till you and Peter come, as we hope.

Herzlichst and love to you both
Michael

17 September 1962

My dear Ben,

I have been grieved by news of your shoulder troubles, and hope that whatever regimen they have put you onto is getting results.

When I was in Edinburgh I asked George Harewood whether he would agree to a proposition that the Concerto for Orchestra, or whatever will be its final title, that I'm writing on commission for next year's Edinburgh Festival might have a personal dedication, if the dedicatee agreed. I want to know, at leisure, whether you will let me dedicate this work to you, in affection and admiration, on your 50th birthday year.

Just that, and please say yes!
Love to Peter and yourself from us both
Michael

14 December 1962

My dear Ben,

[. . .] Your Concerto for Orchestra proceeds by dint of hard work. It will certainly interest you, if nothing else. A kind of *musica concertante* – but hopeless to describe in words. 2 flutes, oboe, c.i., cl., b.-cl., fag., c.f., 3 horns, 2 tr., 2 trbn, tuba, piano, harp, percussion and a small body of strings. At times a mosaic of timbres which don't change for a whole movement. Then a re-grouping, and so on. For me a step forward, I think!!, formally. All this while I meditate on a 3rd opera [*The Knot Garden*].

Love to you both
Michael

3 April 1963

My dear Ben,

I imagine Russia was exciting and exhausting. Hope all went well there for you.

[. . .] I've been waiting till you were back to write you on another matter. I got called up to Schott's a few weeks back to try and help resolve a problem concerning Maxwell Davies. It appeared that Boosey & Hawkes have at last decided to launch out on new composers once again, and had, *entre autres*, made overtures to Max to buy him out. On the face of it, in that Schott's had not tied him with a contract, they are legally justified, but the money offered is fairly extraordinary – £1200 p.a. for 5 years – with rights to publish all works of course, and he couldn't at the end of the 5 years go elsewhere without refunding B. & H. the balance of costs of production of scores etc (not of the £6000).

The problem for Schott's was that to match this takeover bid they would have to reduce all their composers to 2 – Max and myself – because they feel they could not pay Max this sort of sum and not myself in some way commensurate. They would then try, by publicity and other means, to get returns from our music. They wanted my views, and whether I would like this. But I did not like it. I advised them to let Max go and to stick to their policy of publishing as many young composers as they could risk, and feel were worth while. (Priaulx [Rainier], Sandy [Alexander] Goehr and everyone else would have had to be excluded.) I suggested that they pointed out to Max that there was some moral obligation to Schott's who, through Hartog, had launched him. That as he was settled financially for another 11/2 years in America, he could reasonably delay signing the B. & H. contract till he was back in England, and could at least then talk it out amicably with Schott's. However, Max has plunked for this somewhat luxurious bird in the hand and is awaiting the formal contract now to sign.

I've written so that you can know how it seems from outside, so to speak. I would be sorry to see the inflation of unproven composers' financial terms go so far that the net effect would be to close the market for other young composers. (Chester's were in similar boat over Nicholas Maw, but at a much lower price.) I would also be sorry to risk, if that is the right word, a young composer's integrity by inflating the unearned rewards, to the extent that he was driven, perhaps unconsciously, to play safe. Though clearly that is a value which the composer is really responsible about, not the publisher.

I also told Schott's that, in my opinion, if B. & H. thought they had a new Britten in Max Davies, they were mistaken!

Not but what I'm delighted if B. & H. can take on really new names. I believe there is a third and quite unknown, other than Davies and Maw.

I really would love to see you in Corsham if you can manage. [. . .] I'm reckoning on that weekend to provide me a tiny respite from the tough going on the new piece [Concerto for Orchestra] for Edinburgh and you. All those ruddy operas in January and several other unexpected things got the whole schedule late, and I'm brutally pressed for time now. I have to go to West Berlin end of the month for a week, to conduct, etc. Things, as you know, get fixed up ahead and then prove hell.

And now I must return to the desk.

Love to you both dear dear Ben,

Michael

22 July 1963

My dear Ben,

I ought to have written to thank you for the long letter, which touched me deeply. This is really to say I've finished your piece for Edinburgh. But don't for heaven's sake judge my affection by the quality of the piece! [*The Vision of*] *St Augustine* on the other hand will be something indeed – I think.

You'll be tickled pink later by a short bit I've been writing about you and me (from the pre-*Grimes* days) for a magazine. I must admit I tried everything to refuse, but once down to it I've enjoyed doing it.

Herzlichst

Michael

10 October 1963

My dear Ben,

You've been very much in my mind lately, over the birthday. A small personal piece I did about our mutual friendship and esteem misfired I

1 Michael Tippett

2 MT's mother
3 MT's home in Wadhurst
4 With Jessica Minchinton and his mother, 1951

5 MT at Corsham
6 With Karl Hawker
7 With John Minchinton, August 1955

8 With Benjamin Britten on Tippett's sixtieth birthday, January 1965

9 With John Amis
10 With William Glock
11 With Howard Hartog

12 MT and Michael Tillett at Dartington for a performance of *The Vision of St Augustine*

13 With Meirion Bowen, Berlin 1989

14 With Colin Davis
15 MT conducting, probably at Morley College

16 With Colin Davis and Meirion Bowen at rehearsals for the première of
   The Mask of Time in Boston
17 With Jessye Norman in a performance of *Child of our Time* at the BBC Proms,
   1979

think.* Myself has got in the way. But there's a short strictly professional question and answer over which is better. Now I'm finishing off (that's how I feel!) with a biggish thing rather public. I think it'll be good, and worthy of you. I feel so close and intimate to you inside that this public 'showing' is difficult – personally – to refuse to those who are sure it's what I ought to do. And in another sense, when I overcame my personal fears and so on, it's exciting to be publicly among the celebrity.

Love to you both
Michael

17 March 1965†

My dear Ben,

What an unexpected and extraordinary honour! So that's that. Though I haven't heard or seen it yet, and it was to have come to the Bath Festival but there wasn't finally a church with wide enough nave. Then we tried for Wells Cathedral and so on. Anyhow, I do accept, somewhat humbly. And I can guess about notation. Shall be fascinated to see eventually what you do there.

I was about to write to you and Peter because it's borne itself inside me that I never thanked either of you for the bits in the book on my birthday. Yours, whose last sentence PS made me roar with laughter – and Peter's which is authoritative and candid – just my line. Anyhow I thank you both now.

Yes – am going to Aspen in July – then Karl follows me out and we have 3 weeks' holiday together. Madly looking forward to it.

Love to you both
Michael

* 'Britten by Tippett', *Observer*, 17 November 1963.
† Following Britten's dedication of *Curlew River* to Tippett for his 60th birthday.

David Ayerst

Tippett was introduced to David Ayerst (1904–92) in 1927 by Aubrey Russ, Tippett's flatmate in West Hampstead. Ayerst had recently graduated from Oxford in history and was working as a journalist for the Manchester Guardian. He and Tippett shared an interest in left-wing politics, education and literature, particularly the works of Samuel Butler. Most of the letters to Ayerst, in which Tippett seems to be writing down his thoughts as fast as they occur to him, date from the time when he lived in Oxted and concern communism, pacifism and his status as a conscientious objector. In 1934 Ayerst entered the teaching profession and by the late 1930s had become headmaster of Blundells School in Tiverton, Devon. During the Second World War he was a colonel working in the War Office, and helped Tippett prepare for his Tribunal. With his wife Larema (née Fisher), he remained one of the composer's closest friends.

[1934]

Dear David,

[. . .] I've retired into a musical shell again for the moment – also Wilf [Franks] has become a pivot point for me and it's got its touch of heartbreak – but I think probably invention on my part – I don't like his being away, because I torture myself with difficulties and moralities about him – and get long moments when I feel I'm hemming him in, like I did Christopher [Fry] – and yet he himself is so manifestly fond of me beyond the common lot – far worse of course, he has a habit of sharing beds, though not sexual commerce, with almost anyone who wants him to – his classic remark 2 years ago – 'I do this for your benefit' – rings in my ears – and yet what is one to do – I am by no means always the first to get an erection when we are together – well – I leave it to nature as much as I can – it's a bit of both – illusion, love, and altruism on his side – and for all I know it's much the same on mine, with greater accentuation on some one of the characteristics – I feel you see very clearly when you have people in front of you – hence my mute appeal – but don't think this is tragic – not a bit – I'm really happier than I've ever been – and the holiday was the happiest I've ever had – the 'Wilf' mood is only in spasms – I'm at work again at music and the season's concerts – BBC don't want the Symphony [in B flat] – I've polished it up a good deal and finally am going to hawk it for some outside performance – some of it is really worth keeping despite the BBC.

Michael

1934

My dear David

[. . .] Wilf went up yesterday to town on a sudden decision to apply for entry to the Royal Academy of Dramatic Art for a year's course! I'm thankful and hope he passes the audition. It seems such an enormous step for him and to me a great relief – he hopes to get paid work quickly thereby and get a door through to stage designing – it may be a strange way round to painting, but after all that may be illusion and at least the RADA means terms or hours and definite work and he will find that quite enough to manage. I'll let you know if he gets taken or not. Slowly but surely also we come to grips with the extent and methods of our friendship. I've been facing up to the veritable beast side of it and for the moment have relinquished things for a sort of compromise. Having spent a night walking or lying awake I have a fiendish cold on me but a lighter heart. I was able at last to talk to Evelyn [Maude] about it properly and that has eased a strain. The old story ever anew – but has got a bit further this time.

I shall be glad as the fervour of sudden physical desire dies away to something more placid – which it is doing slowly. Wilf is a hell of a mixture of love and altruistic friendship. Sexual expression has to be wilted away to its least sensual because that's the only bridge between our difference in intensity and it also leaves least aftermath – and gradually even my impulsive release of emotion will tend to grow rarer. But I do not think we should have got to where we are without travelling this path, either for Wilf or for me – we are both of us less 'repressed' if you like – remembering that Wilf broke a 4-year continence of mine – consequently more open and frank to one another and with a great deal of give and take and mutual forbearance at the back of things by now.

Will write you later about the Labour Pageant at the Crystal Palace which is turning out rather fun. All luck to the new work.

Love from Michael.

1935

Dear David –

To be clear about things I am now a member of the C.P. [Communist Party] – with 3 others (one only known to you), I belong for the moment to a street cell in Camden Town. For some time I have been preparing the next move – formation of a cell here [Oxted] etc – but all of that will tell you later – the three of us (extra the party) are putting down or out a pamphlet on the position of the 'educated class-es' in the class war which will put our rather heretical case – actually we are Trotskyists and enter the party with few if any illusions and with direct intent to move things in a certain direction.

1935

[. . .] I am also getting extremely mixed up in Labour Party organisa-tions (I may even have to join the party here) to do with music, speak-ing-chorus schemes and ballet Alan Bush and I are in the process of setting on foot – he is not a C.O. [Conscientious Objector] member.

Now the other one of us 4 you know is Phyl [Kemp] – but she and the other 2 are all in the party under other names (a quite normal method of joining) for various reasons – I can't obviously keep you ignorant that Phyl is implicated so it is much better to have it out here now – it is really essential that in no way whatsoever this information (really serious for a particular reason) reaches anyone's ears at all – whether known to her or not – my trust in you is implicit and explicit and that is why I can be so open – speak of her as an anarchist or a Trotskyist or some name people would regard as 'dangerous' and suit-ed to Phyl but too unknown to be real!!!

I am quite happy about this decision though the thing may wear off – I am diligently reading Marx and getting to grips with what aspects of modern political and social life I can with my limited knowledge, experience and interest. Incidentally, I am trying to wrestle with 'bour-geois art' and the absurdities perpetrated as proletarian music, etc, – the Left Theatre, the 'Workers' Theatre' and the 'Workers' Music League' are officially a cover and an occupation for the Bloomsbury arty lot who are unfortunately allowed membership – as you know the whole organisation is very tiny and that is one of our reasons for joining – Wilf – as far as he knows what I am doing – is distressed – he feels that I am a real person led into folly by a sham revolutionary Phyl – but in fact I voluntarily associated myself with the other 3 at a later stage and unexpectedly to them – and as I say it is some relief to be able to canalise my bitterness about social injustice into even a ridiculous form. [. . .]

Michael

1935

As far as I am concerned I am in 2 minds about spreading the information that I am a member [of the Communist Party] – so far no one knows but Stanley [Fisher] here and Evelyn – or will – but in cases where I sense a hesitancy of people to join because of social stigma I am quite prepared to give a lead – but for the moment it's all feeling my way and feet and learning the jargon etc, etc.

[. . .] My 4tet [String Quartet No. 1] progresses and is good, it will be better than the Symphony [in B flat] – more modern, better wrought – very personal – in some way the outcome of the Wilf affair – which cannot be entered on in any way now! And therefore any time after [. . .] come here – perhaps Stanley will be here too, in any case can be a longing to see you and hear all about your ventures and adventures – it seems ages since we met.

[. . .] The dearest love to you David.

Love

Michael

1935

David mine –

[. . .] You're quite right – I am intensely interested in social structure – making up for lost time – it is a reflection too of my own social behaviour – I can't get in without some small local background – the working class people of my immediate district [Oxted] are now taking the place of the school – and the C.P. cell will be its social nucleus – frankly I am not cut out to be a revolutionary agitator and can leave leadership to those of us (not Phyl) who really have it in mind – I am only interested in talking (endlessly as usual!) to young people of a different social standing – we both get a great deal of rich out of it – but underneath my pleasant exterior and charm is a grim nut of fire somewhere which burns all the time – so that I shall be happy selling the *Daily Worker* and doing the odd menial tasks of the party – canvassing house to house – I've lost all my shyness now – it's the harvest from the Wilf burden (he's being the dearest possible person just now – though he hates my communism) and the general move or snap after leaving the school and refusing Dartington – so left – but much more of it I admit has changed – but I'm quite clear I should be unhappy if you, Wilf, Evelyn and Stanley were on the same tack, except in the broadest sense – I do not see the goal as large party membership [. . .].

But it's good to be among non-talkers – as to me one of us said 'it's like having a clean bath' – after the 1st cell meeting I'll expect you Jan. 5–6 or whenever you like. Yes – you can tell Ruth [Pennyman] about my communism now – now the first flush is over it became known gradually. I saw Mrs [Eva] Hubback of Morley and found it won't prejudice my work. Stanley has 'rewritten' Harris Psalm for me.

Love to you
Michael

March 1935

Dear David –

[. . .] Hitler's move is now a fait accompli and the first obvious result is a big military rearmament. Of course we want the middle and working classes to stand out together against it – but not by plastering over the vital distinction between the pure humanitarian pacifism of the public school father and the desperation of the undernourished out of work – that way is betrayal – the middle-class father has got to face the social connection between his pacifist fears and the economic misery that will drive the working class to agree to rearmament and war – just be honest enough to keep your eye on the righteous pacifist taking it out of the down and out volunteer – can you not see David that pacifism alone is just a hypocrisy and as such can never have the moral force it thinks it has – it's simply false ethics and no amount of counting up the rises in wages, the factory acts, etc, etc will make it principally correct – conditions are set up, or allowed shall we say which put a material value on military service, armament, employment, etc, etc – and the answer to this is to mobilise public opinion to collective security, or pacifism – and when country after country goes under to the terror (Russia in this respect is not communism – I mean can never get out of it until world communism) all we can do is to appeal to humanity, freedom, justice, pacifism above the stink of our own slums and colonial empire. How can you ever turn me back to a view which will not, refuses to, face up to the direct implications of this. It's false on its own plane of feeling – and false on the plane of materialist conception – you cannot put a convincing case for it on any one of these planes – you never have – you only show by your resistance that you shut up on two of the planes and that on the plane of feeling you go neck and crop over on to my side. A perfect example of the condition of the period – so you should be – I am only another sort of example – that of the humanist turned full circle in order to save the humanist values by cradling them, there where they will survive – in the persons who survive the social change that is coming, who have enough sympathy to teach them not sabotage them in pique (there were both sorts in Russia).

I can't continue though I'd have liked to discuss the question as to the worthiness of defending the S.U. [Soviet Union]. The answer to me is – yes – but only by working class action not by capital military intervention – I am a Trotskyist not a Stalinist. [. . .]

Much Love –
Michael

March 1935

David mine –

[. . .] I am not interested in what appears to me as the academic discussion on the 'causes of war' – they are as you say manifold for each occasion – I am interested only in estimating a prognosis of an actual war, warning the working class, clean conscious element in time to organise themselves to use the beginning or end of the war to seize power – quite categoric – you see at once the difference – well, my prognosis is a war within 5 or 10 years, contingent on certain happenings of course – I am clear that the pacifists are powerless to stop it – now that is the pivotal point – the League of Nations is gradually becoming the entente-sterling-bloc – if Italy leaves and Switzerland (!) follows suit, the naked truth you have so long denied will be shown clear – this has been my prognosis all along – and consequent upon it

I deal simply with the question – what sort of war, how, when, where – there is no time to deal with anything else – the next step is to try to realise the movement of 'public opinion' during the event – the amount the true blue-ers fear revolution is the measure of its possibility – of course no European (except perhaps Hitler) wants a European war – take what colonial mandates you like, but not a general war – because they are genuinely probably anti-war in itself and more so, frightened of the result of another European conflagration – consequently I am openly an advocate of revolutionary action during the next war – I say and those like me, 'by all means prepare your white paper and when we get the guns so built, we will shoot you with them' – it gives them to think as you might say – this alone could perhaps keep us out of the war, only I am quite certain my views will never prevail in time, especially when you and your like oppose them on humanitarian grounds – divide and rule – the pacifists will be annulled by the revolutionists – but at the end of the war things will be different – during the war my like will do all and every sort of illegal propaganda for revolution – that is if we are worth our salt – (I may say this is not probably the C.P./G.B. which is going opportunist – I mean the left Revolutionaries gradually crystallising out of the C.P., the ILP [Independent Labour Party] and the C.L. [Communist League] – the tiny band of 4th internationalists). There is no time to discuss psychology except individually as school masters, lovers, etc, etc – as you and I do all our time – when social changes bring social convulsions, I mean bring them on the nail, we have to meet them with a dedicated mind or get left behind – you will not adapt fast enough otherwise – at the end of the next war there will be the same touch and go situation – armed people with months, years of killing behind them – the stage is set for the operation – the logic of this is impenetrable – there will be a war (if things do not break beforehand).

Reading your arguments again I see I haven't flatly denied them enough! It is what happens in the coming war which is important – the causes are too deep to be analysed in time – I mean in time to use the analysis for a liquidation of the psychological condition. I don't care a damn almost what are the causes of this coming war – my energy is directed to, 'what can we get out of it' – the answer – the final collapse of a disgusting state of affairs, a fine civilisation grown overripe and decadent and crying out for the new syntheses – an appalling simplification – I know – it's dreadful – but then bombs and guns are simpli-

fications of life! Grim ones – so are malnutrition deaths, and stratifi-
cation of all the lively hopes and courage of the children – little though
I think Russia has got through, at least the young ones will have their
chance of making their own worlds. Of course Stalin is in the group of
the world war – he will 'sacrifice' Russia's sons in the same way (to
defend Russian soil) – but there the war will be a continuation of a
revolution – only waiting for the revolution in the attacking country to
stop and be friends from common man to common man – to one who
believes in liberal, metaphysical, true values, this means nothing – to
the materialist, or realist it means a lot – and finally it will be the
deciding factor – it doesn't follow that wars will cease after capitalism
– but capitalist wars will and what is more, capitalism will have gone,
with its gains and victories handed over to the economic-democratic
community – you don't see that step as historically inevitable or rather,
internally desired and wished for – I do – and I fancy I am nearer to
the Zeitgeist.

And a war will be followed by a revolution – what would you do
about it? That is all – of course I do not feel or think this convinces
you – the convincing is a thing quite irrational and impulsive – and
even after the conversion there are continual doubts – but the new
vision of the world today, the new aspect of the present cross-relation-
ships given by conversion, can never apparently be broken – it is so
curious because everyone gets it in the same way and quite independently – I have just read it beautifully described by a French pacifist
writer, Jean Giono – the servant worker saying 'la première fois que
j'ai vu . . .' – just that – 'j'ai vu' – that's all there is to it – of course you
see you are quite as clear that you also 'as vu' your point of view – all
well and good – that seems to me only to mean that your function is
slightly different – but on the rational debatable ground between,
there is the possibility of testing out our subjective ideas in the objective world – and I fancy I have the best of it – (!?). There we are – we
shall see – but every move of the world political gambit proves my
prognosis, and leaves you psychological-communists up in the air –
when Fascism comes in France because the pacifists won't arm the
workers, perhaps even you will feel the East wind of armed reaction
which is beginning to blow – with far worse revolutionary storms
when its bloody terror exhausts itself. [. . .]

Michael

1935

Dear David,

As you foresaw, it will not be long before we are out of the C.P. Again – not quite for the reasons you imagined but nearly – I think our difficulty is that from the inside the Comintern [see p. 123, note] is clearly Russia's foreign policy and that none of us is satisfied with Russia's internal affairs – we are all Trotskyists – that is we believe in the continual proletariation of the party before and after the coming to power – a wider democratisation through some sort of Soviet system and consistent struggle against the ever recurring bourgeois tendencies of the necessary bureaucracy – in fact exactly what Trotsky got levelled out on. But this does not mean we give up the revolutionary idea your point of view seems to me fundamentally a hypocrisy – I held it for a long time and it was the growing awareness of its moral contradiction that brought me round – to a new set of contradictions, but more tenable ones.

[. . .] I can't resolve the entanglements of the sacrifice of 'bourgeois' standards for the common good. Our great difference here is that I can't take bourgeois standards seriously – I think because they are self-righteous, built on a slavery; economically and morally. Here is the real revolutionary kernel in me – sown by Blake and more disastrous than Marx–Lenin because it thrusts the luring branches up through the most sacred institutions of the whole kingdom – church, state, law, morality crumble before the child's tear.

> The poor man's farthing is worth more
> than all the gold of Afric's shore.
> One mite wrung from the lab'rer's hands
> Shall buy and sell the miser's lands
> Or if protected from on high
> Does that whole nation sell and buy.

The last two lines are tremendous:

> The harlot's cry from street to street
> Shall weave Old England's winding sheet.*

carry the argument deeper to the superiority of morality going nasty on your hands – all bourgeois comfort can acknowledge it as 'Spectre' and rekindle a state of brotherhood and innocence by regeneration –

* From William Blake, 'Auguries of Innocence'.

otherwise it's the human energies driving the human machine backwards – capital debt in a mental abstraction called minus – minus so
many pounds I lent you – hire-purchase art – to put it plainly all balls
and bloody hell and futility and no intellectual reasoning or poised
judgment can save – 'it's getting late'. Wystan [Auden] expressed – I
don't know about that – it's a historical judgment I'm not qualified to
make! 'It's getting rather smelly' is another remark which I understand
more – I would of course in my coarse mind. You belong to this truth
– that I'm sure of – you may make intellectual reservations and obviously clearer judgments but as a conservative you can't because things
could be better and sweeter and kinder and wars could cease – and
Blundells couldn't be undergoing transformation merely for intellectual delight in rearrangement!?!?!?

I've been writing a lot of long letters lately – could you send this
back to me. I'm trying to find means to save my activity in the flesh –
Wilf will understand what I mean by that – I don't mind if I can't
because there's music – and how I must begin to work again.

Much love – and treat this effusion as a 'flash in the pan'.
dein
Michael

[1935?]

Dear David,
[. . .] I can agree that the real collective experience is that of the soldiers etc. Behind the C.O. business is the refusal of the individual –
both the pathological escape from the social responsibility as well as
the refusal to enter a de-individualising existence – like the German
confessional pastors. In a collective Germany or Russia it must be virtually impossible to stand at all. Here, I do think there is a traditional experience of refusal, in itself almost a collective experience, but by
its very nature more individual. I know my own true support is that I
am wholly 'within the experience' of musical creation – if that is
taken away however the collective experience of the war can not
manage to take its place, but a certain sort of passion, which I associate with my internally catastrophic reaction to *The Enormous
Room*.* The figure of the man in prison is an archetype for me – that

* Novel (1922) by E. E. Cummings describing his experience of being mistakenly held in a
French detention camp on suspicion of expressing treasonable views.

is to say it is an image which reaches down into the undifferentiated levels of the collective psyche, *à la* Hitler if you like. It is not mine, but ageless. The archetype of the warrior won't act as a connection for me at all, while the archetype of the prisoner, scapegoat, crucified, and so on, is the totally powerful one. Naturally this archetype is not usually a general one, though it is so in Germany today – hence I suppose the strong tie-up between the PPU [Peace Pledge Union] and the German experience.

I'm reading Bayner's *Germany Possess* – unequal like all his work – Churchill is positive for him, Hitler and Stalin the shadows – but I guess that Stalin is positive now, because for all his insight he reads as completely within the collective experience on this side and not neutral, or properly straddled between the opposites in good Jungian style. See you Wed.

M.

[. . .] I came across a grand passage in Burcan's *Cromwell*, from Isaac Pennington: 'All truth is shadow except the last truth. But all truth is substance in its own place, though it be but shadow in another place. And the shadow is a true shadow, as the substance is a true substance.' That about sums up my views on militarism and pacifism and what not. In a world battling for its Atlantic charters and new orders, it isn't difficult to point out the minorities and negatives. But when Hitler and Roosevelt begin to seem like squirrels in a cage, the strangest things seem positive *à rebours*. Paradoxically I find I can view the thing dispassionately, and feel it yet passionately, at the appropriate moments. Appropriate to what, I cannot say. But I am quite prepared to be shadowy on one score and substantial on another and enjoy it as being the sort of three-dimensional life I think to be the best and fullest. Its obvious danger is a mere relativity and the next step seems to be a religious one which give values to values. But that may not be possible to do in our 'shadow' age.

M

[mid-1935/6]

David mein –

[. . .] Wilf has been for some weeks now on the old tack – he comes here nearly each weekend, but we sleep apart – I think I am getting used to it now and though it has flared up, it gets nearer each time to

my being able to make it permanent – which is what he says he wants
– and though I am incredibly active just now, the whole question is
rankling very much – I am spending my last Wed. night in town
tomorrow with John and Doris [Layard] – I want to put the case
before someone who does not know its ins and outs, because I'm absolutely lost. Suffice it to say that physically I'm very turned in on myself
at home, very lecherous in the street after handsome young men,
apparently longing to be married and with a home, but none of these
things stops the work [String Quartet No. 1] which is at high pressure.
All goes well, and will be glad to see you August 1.

   Much love
   Michael
I'm turned in on myself emotionally which is the real thing – turning
away from Wilf to some balance deeper than sex questions. The BBC
will perhaps do the 4tet!!!

[1937]

David mine –
   I had a strange 'flare-up' of a mild sort in a letter to Wilf [. . .] – you
know I was put back a long way by the intensity and pain of that experience and made less sure and happy about myself – a condition which
is gradually healing – it was all symbolised by Wilf's public address on
a returned letter of mine 'To Mike, Bugger' – it has put a false taboo
on relations with him, because I really keep apart as much as I do
because he doesn't like it – at least he doesn't like it very often – but it
intellectualised itself as the other thing in a long rigmarole – Wilf being
quite solicitous these days, and obviously (if he could but make me
and himself feel free of this 'must be warned' dogma) content to enjoy
a very very close intimacy – Wilf being all this took my letter to heart
and acted in a usual Wilf way – he asked me to come with him to visit
Sari and Paul Dienes – met me just outside the house and explained
that they were people of no taboos then read Sari's hand after supper
and said 'by a certain line you are just as homosexual as Mike' – Sari
asked me at once without any shadow of 2nd motive – 'how much are
you Mike' – 'quite considerably' – Wilf was a trifle worried by this
exchange especially as I said later on 'Wilf's quinquennial plans don't
always come off, though they are always from his heart' – so he went
further and himself began the discussion – in his Wilf-like way he

acted very well – these Hungarian internationally cultured people had no shadow of 'bugger' taboo and gave advice courteously and humanely, after asking all sorts of sensible questions – 'could I have children biologically etc, etc?' – eventually Paul 'I don't see then what is this irony you speak of' [. . .]. Paul gave us a résumé of the *Banquet* and put unbiological-sexual love on the Platonic pedestal – but then he is half Greek – however he was entirely sincere and was of such calibre that it did have the effect Wilf intended or hoped – you see, David, I am the only one who had grown with and watched Wilf's development – the boy who now lives his own life in London, discreetly and fairly happily turning his hand to this and that as it comes, is so far on from the boy who tramped to Manchester to see you and way to Dorset, and came down here overnight – it hardly matters if my life does get buggered up a bit in consequence and I have also gained in width and love during the experience.

[. . .] I think the trouble about Wilf may simply be that I gave the impression that he (Nick) would only be allowed friendship if Wilf gave his consent – you might be an angel and get this straight – what I tried to express was that Evelyn and Wilf are constant poles in my life and that Evelyn has already a sympathy because of her saint-like touches, Wilf a sympathy for his rebel-like twitches – not that he would see either of them except casually – he, Nick, is of himself from first to last, be a dear, and give him this if it's the cause of the trouble – if there is any trouble I can't see that it can be a sexual taboo though I suppose it may be – you of all people can teach Nick to discount my remarks about Wilf because I have loved him so much – that shouldn't grieve anyone with half a heart – I feel exceedingly quiet and sure as far as Nick is concerned – a response to his own virtue and innocence and faith – I don't really know what I have said about Wilf – it's simply intuition which makes me think it's the notion that Nick has to take Wilf as well as Michael so to speak – that would be worrying – dispel that if you get a chance – So far, angel, I don't think the sterile breath of theory has come freezing the human growth – nor shall it – perhaps Nick won't meet Wilf till much later – there's already a side of Nick which Wilf won't accept – the R.C. taboos – you see what is meant – I'm curiously happy and obviously much invigorated by the visit and full of songs. Till Christmas.

Michael

[1937?]

Dear David –

   Don't worry what wild letters you write – and Larema I feel won't be upset by anything very much – she's much too understanding as nearly all women are – may it all go well and god bless you both – she is to me indeed a darling creature and nothing could be more satisfactory and comforting it seems because one feels so close to both of you – and I hope without in any way coming too close or offending or begging.

   About my own affairs – it is really somehow true that the Wilf business is ceasing to be emotionally so all-enveloping – that is really why I am happy – I'm on the other tack at long last and it's a bit of a relief – you see, in the summer it all reached a fantastic climax and exhalation which is now dissolving into the sort of friendship which will allow complete independence emotionally to both of us – of course there's some way to go yet but as I almost never see him and certainly never live with him except as an echo, my body and self have to shut down again and be self-contained till the time comes to reopen if it does. And then Wilf is seriously considering going to a school – he has apparently already got permission for a 2-months visit to one from the headmaster and he knows I want him to go, now – so you must not really think I am holding him for present comfort – that is over – he wants to see me in love with another he thinks, a woman may be – this is his sort of mission – but that springs from the muddle we all get in – Evelyn says that to her we all seem to get marriage on the brain as a sort of magic symbol – that we look for it and work for it in a way she finds at times comic, at times foolish – in other words the relationship to anyone, as we really all know inside, comes like the gift of tongues – she deplores for instance the effort to straighten out Wilf say by us who are ourselves but half out of the wood which our nature has born us into. She says that my 'shame' is much older than Missenden – it's simply the sensitiveness that I didn't have with Christopher [Fry], which has grown up with the awareness of the social life – that it springs really from the distress that the inside reality doesn't correspond to the outside social judgment – that she went through the same about me, as a younger man kept in tow by an older woman – to her it is growth all the time, because it's got to be wrestled with – such and such is the nature of us – let us make what beauty we can of it – the

231

real happiness with Wilf for the moment is this sense to ourselves that we have refound the internal validity of ourselves if indeed on terms which are less sexual – I guess for myself that only when the whole past love with him seems completely valid again and lively will I be really ready to love anyone else (even if I want to) man or woman – true, Missenden was a mistake – I could have avoided trouble by staying here – but by the mistakes also we grow.

I know I want companionship from very deep – it remains to be seen on what terms – it is not on the terms of living with Wilf – *tant pis* and it is useless regretting – when the Nick was with me and I liked having him feeling quite at ease about it now – I made one or two mistakes I'm afraid of the sort Evelyn foresaw – but not serious ones I think – anyhow I see more and more what she means and will learn to control myself altogether with young people. It's the provoking of preconscious disillusionment and emotional difficulties – such as telling him too much about Wilf and myself you see.

Much Love –
Michael

1937

Dear David

Things have settled down again – but with real intention and necessity on my part to live more than ever of my life outside the Wilf entanglement – of course after his excess of argument and so on he comes down here for 2 nights and a day and comes very close and very friendly – I'm coming to believe in the end that this is, partly, all that he complains of in me – I mean jealous, possessive, self-centred, interested, etc – because try as I may I can't really make these attributes fit my case in anything like a relative importance to my neighbours – e.g. I am not jealous over much – and keeping Wilf is not an attempt to balance possessiveness but quite natural. These moments of extreme misunderstanding when I appear almost a master of double dealing and when I become too unhappy to care whether he goes or stays he invariably returns to a curious warm affection and there we part again. I am clear now that it is never going to be straightforward as I would like it to be – that being what I am it will be a long time before successive misunderstandings break down the love – though that is almost gradually happening – certainly he has made sexual relationships into so self-conscious an intention they are impossible and arise only from his own needs and my immediate response – and yet with all this almost brutality of treatment there is Wilf himself and a quaint tenderness of a peculiar sort – I am going to run away from him when such periods arise again – subjects which he prefers to misunderstand will have to be left unresolved and undiscussed – it is I suppose David the thin edge of the wedge – I am coming to my senses and dreadfully reluctantly giving up the game in certain particulars – it is what he has asked for all the time – for me to turn my eyes elsewhere that he might be able to come closer himself – I have no faith in such subtleties of mind and leave him to himself – inward twinge of unhappiness is really that alone – that, as it were, his is still unreclaimed – that the only one who has loved him through and through must turn away beaten – but don't think that this is all – there is now a 'friendship' if you will, an intimacy which is of its own value to us – we go to films together, we talk out a general hodgepodge of art and sociology in a way pleasing to us both – for instance this time he spends an hour or so with me here on the Blake I am going to set, and with a surer instinct for poetry than mine tells me where to get off – in point of fact I am therefore only setting the 'Song of Liberty' from 'The Marriage [of Heaven and Hell]' and not the wad of stuff from 'Jerusalem' only intelligible to myself and disconnected – Wilfred Owen he knows almost word for word and draws it out for me, its meanings, its divine pity and so on – that will stay as long as it means something to us both even if his strange compulsions finally shut down the sex life – my friends get a jaundiced view of Wilf from me because they only tend to see me in trouble and anguished over him – the constant meetings and say the one heavenly walk together in Yorkshire are things of our own – and Wilf in response is jealous of you all – you, I believe, especially – I think he is afraid of you, or rather afraid of your influence on us as he calls it – I think he has given this to Lissie also over Stanley [Fisher] – I think it is Wilf's own thing and not hers – and foolishly mentioned your letter as having said something about him – at once his excessive self-interest is aroused and comes out as jealousy – 'I don't want to come down to the cottage, to all your friends – David, Stanley, Lissie (!), etc – you and all your clique of trim boys' – and so on – this is Wilf in his bad moments – he does it to provoke me to say where I stand – mercifully for us all, I have you so much nearer and dearer than anyone else, and the others rather little – so it all passes off and Wilf becomes all the other way – you will have to be generous with him for my sake – but nothing out of the way – I only mean continue as you are and leave him to me, without if possible despising him more for being let in on his Wilf-ful moments of pique. Also you will have to be generous with me who am obviously much under his influence – perhaps for that I didn't take to Lawrence enormously – he is living something very like the Aubrey [Russ] life – I mean an out and out town bugger life – I have somewhere bits of taboos – or rather I feel oddly out of place because to tell you the truth David I am not interested in young men as young men – I now see what Stanley meant in Wales when he said he saw a choice for himself between two distinct lives – it is precisely the destruction that is the limitation – and if one has to choose, we go eventually with the overwhelming majority. [. . .]

Much love and excuse this rambling letter
Michael

1 September 1939

Dear David,

It seems to be going over the edge. I lose all my jobs in London. Composition isn't a social possibility in war. So as long as I am allowed I can only be an educator of some sort, and preferably with children. I cannot take part in the destruction. Possibly in the picking up of the bits. But as long as I can stand out for it, I feel I belong to the future generations only. I want to take a school job. If you get staff called up or volunteering or hear of such will you do what you can for me. (I promised Paul [Dienes] that I would, apart from war, mention his [younger] son Zed – now a Britisher – a Ph.D. in mathematics – looking for a teaching job, academic work of some sort.)

Forgive my putting my personal problems before you – but communication may be difficult later. We are having children [billeted] on us.

Best love and luck
Michael

7 January 1940

Dear David,

[. . .] any feelings about the Symphony [in B flat], now? Eliot says in his critical essays: 'but, the more perfect the artist, the more completely separate in him will be the man who buffers and the mind which

234

creates'. I have come to realise that at last. The Symphony, Quartet [String Quartet No. 1] and the Blake [*A Song of Liberty*] all suffer from the reverse operation. I was too involved with the idea of the direct expression of the emotions the 'man' suffers, and too little conscious of the terrific problem of adequate technique. The Piano Sonata [No. 1] begins the new *Einstellung*, and art begins to become impersonal, as well as personal. I dare say the oratorio [*A Child of Our Time*] will take this process a long way further – though it is a dangerous work to write, because of the constant trap laid for the 'man' in it.

I enjoyed seeing you and taking stock of how this goddam nonsense all around affects you. I have for the time being begun to live for periods in a considerable degree of serenity – whether specious or not, I don't know. It is a necessity, of course, for the production of the oratorio, and may be no more than that – however something has healed inside and I feel less wounded than since adolescent days.

Enough of myself – all good wishes to you and Larema.

Michael

1941

Dear David,

[. . .] I've grown very fond of Karl [Hawker], but I can't bear the thought of the intensities of cross love affairs and jealousies. I find that after Karl was here over Whitsun I had re-reached a sort of gay and sensual notion of sexual life and the darkness of Wilf had receded into the past. I don't know if it has any sense but I'm inclined to dream of a more prolonged liaison of this sort if Karl were to be in such circumstances as made it convenient to make here his chief home for a bit. In fact I've more or less proposed to him! – all providing he has some outside job and isn't emotionally dependent entirely on my attending to him in the daytime. Meanwhile the good Sheila [Busch] nosed this out a long time ago and 'warned' (!) Evelyn as she said. I was almost annoyed and Evelyn came down at once to straighten things out. It's not easy to talk to Evelyn about a liaison which isn't on a high plane and very moral because she doesn't have such frivolous needs – but she knows that when all is said and done she has a husband and a home life, so that some allowance is to be made for that, as well as for my own nature. Also she has continual confidence that the music isn't really balked by my personal flightiness. Sheila unfortunately thinks of me on some terribly high Evelyn-ish pedestal and is, I dare say, unconsciously jealous. I haven't told Evelyn yet that Karl might be here more completely – because I don't see how it's likely to happen under the present circumstances. I've mixed feelings about it in myself, but I know I 'want' very much and enough, I fancy, to take the consequences. It's quite true as Evelyn deplores that I entangle myself not with people of Paul [Dienes]'s calibre, but with anything but. However the Fresca [Allinson] is going off to Cambridge herself, I get a little fed up with the singleness of the cottage, though during the oratorio [*A Child of Our Time*] it seemed an imperative necessity. For the moment things are very gay inside and it's odd but true, that I have never lived a gay sensual life since Roy [Langford], and never at all one in which I desired and my desires were accepted. It seems all rather in the air – but I think I'm right in guessing that Karl has been toying with the idea from a long time ago, while I was still kicking him out. I don't quite see what it means to him – though I realise what you said of the romantic appeal of a sort of 'celibate' artist!!! I think Karl gets a lot of kick out of drawing the sensuality so to speak out of someone very, from his point of view, ascetic and severe. Well, well, I'll tell you if anything really happens – at present it's the over treasured, because rare, weekend – and that's too like the days with Wilf. I would like to be the other side of satiety for once – meanwhile the music may knock it all to blazes – who knows?

By the way – the records* are well advanced. I've been settling questions of copyright and royalties to Schott's (mere formalities) – a photo and lots of dope about the work and my ideas thereon. Initial sales will be possible quite soon – so I'll send you word when that is.

I had a good time with Aubrey [Russ] – funnily enough he appeared on Taunton platform just as you went on interview at King's School. But he refused the job for reasons I will tell you by word – too long in a letter. This came to my mind *à propos* of the records because he played my set 3 times (pre-sold a copy to a blind organist-pianist and an Anglo-Catholic Father) and I admit the music stands up astonishingly to repeated playing – and is good. I have much less shyness in recommending it. I like it in many ways the best of anything I've done – for its coolness and clarity and force without over emphasis. My

---

* Fantasy Sonata (Piano Sonata No. 1), played by Phyllis Sellick for Rimington Van Wyck.

dream is to get the strong Double Concerto [Concerto for Double String Orchestra] out on records and see if that wears as well. It's a deeper going work and on a trifle more dangerous an emotional scale. Some of it is alright I know, but over-emphasis may betray other portions of it. The oratorio is too monumental to appreciate as yet. It may be of some significance in the welter of present day cultural problems, or it quite well may be up the pole. I don't feel very personally involved – it wrote me rather than I it – but some of the music is very intriguing technically – ideas which I shall work out more extensively in purely instrumental works.

I'm just restarting on the piano–orchestra work [Fantasia on a Theme of Handel] for Phyllis Sellick – gay and gaudy – very great fun.

I think Bryan [Fisher] would rather La[rema] didn't know too much of his escapade. So far his blood family don't know at all.

Dein –

Michael

25 April 1942

My dear David,

This letter from the lad in the RASC [Royal Army Service Corps] seems rather *à propos* – as it is clear one can have both representative and witnesses [at the Tribunal]. So there is a great deal to be said for your being there in person, if the luck has it that you are available. If not, I dare say a letter on the added matter of the struggles in my conscience since the local Tribunal would be a sensible move – because you have been the person closest to me during that time.

Will you let me know if you can, if you are not at 31 on Wed. night – because I would probably then try to get home – Otherwise I shall see you then.

Fresca has not arrived – another relapse of some sort.

dein

Michael

Seeing the matter of a letter if you are not personally available is important one, I'd better ring you myself to make sure. More on Tues.

10 May 1943

My dear David,

[. . .] [Ernest] Bevin has answered all the letters and press cuttings etc, as per his letter to [Stafford] Cripps: so there is nothing to do but await prosecution. Personally I am glad. We had begun to lose sight of the actuality, responsibility indeed conscientious objection. Turn about how I may, total war and such particular attributes of it as the Br[itish] (or Axis) might – bombing, and the square miles of terror involved, is as far removed from the life of the gospel as anything I can imagine. Archbishop [of New York, Francis Joseph] Spellman blessing the American bomber which carried out the Antwerp daylight raid and its attendant horrors is a mockery which organised Christianity must atone for if it can. The Casablanca conference demanding 'unconditional surrender' and 'no compromise' shows only too clearly how power corrupts and the old evils return. The United Nations are pledged to fight to a catastrophe. The promulgation (and action thereon) of the whipping that in India is so alien to anything I know that I am ashamed for my country, as I am ashamed for Germany. The unconditional surrender policy ensures a state of affairs where the political and economic and emotional problems out of which the war arose will be both unsolved and further exacerbated. Any more, however small, that can hold a portion of human spirit steady in this holocaust is something I know which Christ would have understood. I don't profess to be a Christian and to speak with knowledge – I can only feel my way and believe that such way as I go is not alien to the fundamental forgiveness and gentleness of Jesus. This is subjectively right, I am sure. It has the glimmerings of objective right also – because the fatal round of bitterness and attribution (that retribution which the Archbishop of Canterbury asks for) can only be broken by a more fundamental reorganisation of society, similar to the impact of Christianity upon the Roman Empire. In order for some *point d'appui* to be made from which a new moral and critical attribute can be levelled at the errors of ourselves and our State, there will first be a period of voluntary spiritual withdrawal. There is nothing truly frightening in that – nor even in the highlight of outlawing it may occasionally involve. The real thing is the spiritual struggle and search. At present the issue is a coarse and brutal one – for or against the 1000 bomber raids – and the answer is against. Where this central refusal lands you depends on temperament and other considerations. However I feel very much at peace and ready to go.

Herzlichst
Michael

June 1943

David mein,

[. . .] if you can keep the possibility of June 7 morning free I would be grateful – at least till I've seen [Robert] Pollard – 10 a.m. this Thursday. I've had a feeling that your appearances in fact do a lot to turn the case, but that may be just because I'm personally sustained by your presence. So we'll take the counsel's advice. Similarly over Vaughan Williams. Evelyn feels we oughtn't to overwhelm the Bench. I'll probably ring you after I've seen Pollard. [. . .]

dein –
Michael

Have heard from Fresca and will have to visit her next Friday.

31 December 1943

Dear David –

I had an interview at Westerham today – with Ministry of Labour official – nature of work. I persist in refusal. I'm very frightened, to the extent that I've been crying – the usual bout of self-pity. It appears a lot more the second time.

The dossier now returns to the London people who decide on prosecution or not. It seems it will turn on whether anyone can manage to penetrate into that august body and get across my willingness to do anything within my vocation, my qualifications – under CEMA [Council for the Encouragement of Music and the Arts] – or factory concerts with ENSA [Entertainments National Services Association] – or perhaps teaching in a school again. But if, as I feel more likely, it's just not going to fall into place like that, then one's 'fate' is a grim one and will have to be endured whether I like it or not. It is unfortunately what the world, in England as elsewhere, is now. The Ministries have dictatorial powers and no one can say them nay.

I feel pretty rotten today – it will pass – but I have very little strength or motivation to fight about it.

love –
Michael

[1944/5]

I have always found [Eliot's play *The*] *Family Reunion* fascinating – and I think the experiences it describes are fundamental to humanity – or to certain people who are 'called' and have a long tradition – both in East and West. At present they are possible outside the church as well as in. And I don't think we all quite realise how consonant such poetry is with the nebulous world of mythology that I so dubiously inhabit. I admit I am caught in a way I could not wish to go. To over-simplify it: as it is to all observation Christian civilisation which is destroying itself, then the new thing will come from deeper sources once more. This notion led [Eric] Gill to realise that the break would have to come within the church and its membership. I am less san-guine of that, because I feel that churches are so entangled in the nexus of the materialist distraction that all they can do is to attempt to sanc-tify it – which will involve them in the nemesis – though it may not involve the deeper-seated idea of the Christ-like life. I've had to realise that I admittedly no longer expect healing from this quarter. No doubt many fine men and women will feel called towards the church but I don't think it will avail. The Christian ethic no longer guards a man for example from usury or from handing his humanitarian conscience over to the military authorities – we bomb if they think fit, not if it is Christian or the reverse. Naturally enough the military care little for the episcopal blessing and much dislike the papal stand against them. But then the Curia plays another hand in Spain.

I have of course not the slightest idea where healing will come because the moment of complete dereliction (for the Christian civilisa-tion) has probably not been reached and so the moment of God's voice from the whirlwind has not come. Though perhaps the whirlwind has come! And that is the only kernel of truth I see – that God will be found in the refuse bin as of old – the stone that is thrown away. It is not easy doctrine for our reasonable, civilised selves and our modern comforts and our enlightenment. The idealised figure of Jesus gives way before the physical actuality of the seamless cloak that was never probably washed – to use a rather violent metaphor. However I doubt if we shall see much further in our own lifetime. The soil needs to be dunged yet!

dein

Michael

[1944/5?]

Dear David

Sorry to have thought on to paper with such dogmatism. It needs really a whole gloss on the nature of symbolism. I doubt if I am ever very sound when I draw conclusions and make statements because my proper life is always the exploration of possibilities towards a new formation of the material. And what I am really describing is my own inner state and attitude. Not but what such a state often has to correspond with the true conditions of the time – having a touch of the prophetic madness in me. It is not pleasant, incidentally, because you only learn the conditions by suffering them.

The argument would run something like this: for thousands of people now the Christian symbols no longer have mana [supernatural force attributed to good fortune or magical powers], while the Eastern symbols have mana. Jung opines that this has now reached the dimensions of a collective experience. I fancy most of us have met it in one form or another, its influence is insidious and widespread. But these lovely, subtle symbols from hundreds of years of cultivation of metaphysics and the inner worlds are not ours by any right except of theft and conquest – and will not help or heal us, but complete our disorientations. For those who see this matter as a responsibility then the prime need in the Western world is to break the ice of rationalism and release the imaginative life once more, to dig the ancient soil from which the symbolising function grows. This is a spiritual adventure fraught with real dangers and can doubtfully be done within the security of a traditional faith whose symbols have lost mana – even more so when the guardians of the symbols are not aware of such a fact. Nor therefore will it happen among those who luckily possess the peace of such faith. But the general climate of opinion will alter by the adventures, catastrophes, mistakes and victories of those driven on the ancient way. I do not think it will appear as a decisive break and perhaps after many generations the traditional and the tradition will fuse again. The text on the oratorio cover [of *A Child of Our Time*] is a nice example – 'the darkness declares the glory of light'. It is both effective for the faithful and effective for the Jungian analysts. It has the typical syncretistic touch. The interest in Hermetic philosophy, Greek mystery religions, Mithraicism, gnosticism, has perhaps seldom been so continuous. But the final symbol in *The Family Reunion* of the cake and the candles and the anti-clockwise circumambulation is less effective. The masque [early drafts for *The Midsummer Marriage*] will be an attempt to deal with this matter of the healing symbol, or symbol of healing – a symbol in this sense being something which cannot be picked to pieces either intellectually or from sensibility and is by its nature a pluroma. As far as I can guess the material in the masque is rather more pagan than that in the oratorio. Syncretistic of course, but leaving more to Apollo than Dionysus – or rather a fresh attempt to divide experience between them according to the needs of the dual flesh. Union therefore is part of the final symbol – but I hope it won't get too transcendental.

See you Wed. week, Café Royal, 7.30.

Michael

8 April 1945

My dear David,

I am too out of mind to be very coherent just yet. Fresca seems to have reached zero point and felt herself unable to go further and drowned herself in the Cam [correctly the Stour]. I can't adjust to it easily. Her gaiety and gentleness and even her waywardness and her love of pretty things all seem irreplaceable values. I love her more deeply than I knew when she was there. The memory is extremely sweet and fragrant. Her going out has turned everything topsy-turvy. I got myself into one of those black moods of *Weltschmerz* on Friday and wrote you as a whipping boy – but naturally later destroyed the letter. The nightmarish quality that hangs so easily over or just behind our present life. It isn't her going that seems wrong or unexpected, it's that the manner seems to enter with one this nightmarish world. If she were cold and afraid I would or should have been there.

We were both marked as so many of our generation have been – but perhaps my career especially got in the way and she is part of the price. We never learn about real loss till it's there in our persons. Her going is less perhaps than the maiming and deaths of so many young folk, children, mothers, in this lunatic power-driven world. But I know it sharper. She was a lovely lovely creature as I feel, and lived her birthright out with courage – poor lamb.

dein –

Michael

One is exclusively selfish whether over life or death. We can't accept anything or venture anything with grace. So it seems to me.

10 April 1945

My dear David,

Thanks for your letter and its sensible and pertinent remarks. I have come to my own senses again now.

As I guessed, her letter shows that she was tied up with Germany's agony, did not want to survive it, or into the post-war years without a constitution to take her there (as she felt necessarily practical and energetic) in the healing.

My letter to you about all that and general agony of mind on the Friday seems to have corresponded with her own – poor sweetheart. She would have liked to have talked it out with me, but that was impossible to prevent my responsibility. But I am sorry she didn't do so. I would not have wanted to prevent her, but to express the love I felt and the help I might have offered.

We are singing anthems at the [National] Gallery, midday on Thursday.

Michael

29 October 1945

My dear David,

Things have intervened which postpone my visit. I've agreed to do morning teaching temporarily at Hazelwood till term ends Dec. 2. (This because of call-up of the headmaster on the officers' reserve.) Also I'm taking Morley College Sunday work in music – the music director being 'bombed out' to Sheffield. (Did I tell you that Morley was bombed to the ground? 50 dead – it was used as a rest centre for bombed mothers etc.) We work in LCC [London County Council] school building, which being on top of the st[atio]n at Waterloo I don't think will last long. One of my works went west in Morley, though some things are being salvaged now. The only other copy is in Mainz – which is good.

I am proposing coming by train on Sunday afternoon, following the classes at Morley, or Dec. 1. I shall go back in time to take the Friday orchestra in that week. It's a nuisance not making it a weekend, but that's impossible now – and by Dec. 1, I shall be terribly glad of some days off – I work at music under great difficulties at present – but Part II [of *A Child of Our Time*] will get finished before Dec. 1.

Hope all is well – I have a system now which [means] I am not so consistently alone at night, or rather at the beginning of the night raids. It's much better.

All the best
Michael

12 September 1948

Lieber David,

My plans and news more or less is following:

I go to Hungary Oct. 8 till 22. Am looking forward to it a bit more as I gather I shall hear a lot of Bartók including the operas. Will conduct Double Concerto [Concerto for Double String Orchestra]. [. . .] though Oct.–Nov. are months for Morley and various public things, they won't be too dreadful. For I'm not drawn yet to anything except the opera. Have just written the new words for final scene of Act I [an early draft for *The Midsummer Marriage*]. I shall show them to you when we can meet. The usual night before travelling won't work I think, for I have a recording session with the choir to redo some of the Tallis. And I travel with Professor E[dward] J. Dent. But a lunch – unless you felt like a visit this way. Am in town Sept. 20, 22, 27, Oct. 3, 7.

A book coming fortuitously to my hand has repeatedly plucked the chords of our race-old memories, in the proper [Maude] Bodkin: *Archetypal Patterns in Poetry* [1934] manner – G. R. Levy *The Gate of Horn.** Palaeolithic, Neolithic stuff most absorbing – also Old Testament. (Gave me much more than your little book because it put it in a way that fitted) – Mycenaean and Greek: very good. Helped me no end to deepen the opera and traditionalise the imagery. Particularly for the 'hell' aria. Have been reading the Greek plays with fascination. No other word to express it. Even Gilbert Murray *The Four St[ages of Greek Religion*, 1912] can't finally spoil them. Most other better translations (and Loeb) are out of print. I'm toying with the idea of learning how to read Greek with a crib. Or rather I get to know various lines of the poetry, where I've got the Greek to hand, and a truly

---

* Gertrude Rachel Levy, *The Gate of Horn: A Study of Religious Conceptions of the Stone Age and Their Influence upon European Thought* (1948).

percipient book *Euripides and Dionysus*, just published nicely in time for me, had some lovely translation that led always easily back to the Greek. So far it's been Euripides *Bacchae* and *Hippolytus* and Sophocles *Oedipus Rex*, *Oedipus at Colonus* and *Antigone*. But I've had to send for Aeschylus, *Septem contra Thebam* and *Eumenides*. Funny to think how this old passion of my father's, which I've had on and off since I can remember, is now fulfilling itself. Have sent (from Switzerland) for a biography of Burckhardt which will I think be afterwards a book for you.

Love to you all
Michael

1950

Dear David –

[. . .] I've sketched out some songs [*The Heart's Assurance*] for Peter [Pears] and Ben [Britten] to present at Edinburgh this year. From a new anthology from poets killed last war – *For Your Tomorrow*. A gentle flavour of young spring promise cut short. Nothing hectic. Because opera [projected première of *The Midsummer Marriage*] is definitely postponed to 52, Ben's *Billy Budd* will be at Edinburgh in 51. This all suits me very well. It's relieved too constricting a tension. [. . .]

Michael

[1953]

My dear David,

Just to forewarn you that K[arl] was vomiting and in a dreadful state – he thinks indeed he's slowly dying! and we drove home late last night – a warm and candid talk most of the journey. Today he's asleep all day – I wake him for meals, and he's eaten proper food at last.

I shall behave on Sunday as if your knowledge goes no further than his move to town and for treatment. Because the latter is important – especially as he's back to certainty the whole sickness is physical. I'm not worried about the coming to me at Tidebrook on his non-teaching days – but I do hope he'll stick to treatment when and if offered.

Also – I am not disturbed for myself – feel very calm and serene and strong. But I do worry of course for Karl himself.

We'll try and bring apples and eggs.

Love –

Michael

His Mayfield doctor comes to visit tomorrow and I really thought it better some professional person saw him and relieved some of my responsibility.

[1953]

Dear David,

K[arl]'s cardiograph showed nothing. It brought everything to a break. Indeed apparently to a breakup. From this agreed end we found, at K.'s suggestion, a kind of compromise, that he would have a place in London as his, and from that try, slowly, to refind some shared life. But he is very down. Everything seeming to fail at once – and with all the resentment over onto Tidebrook and me and dependence and what have you. However, because we're so far gone, we have at least been talking when he wants it. And he's trying with psychiatrical help. Problem now to find a room in town. Tom (Stallabrass) has been very helpful, and would tell you to phone much more detail and his opinions (he saw Karl in town alone).

I'll keep you informed. But don't worry. Somehow I feel able to go ahead, because the London plan has a practical timetable and should take K. away and out of here. Yet, yesterday, when he had planned to go to look for flats, he felt too ill! and decided that was a sign he didn't really want to leave Tidebrook!! However, I'm sure he's got to – at least temporarily – and he says the agreement as to London place his, country place mine, has given him relief. [. . .]

Michael

William Glock

After successful early appearances as a concert pianist, in which he first came to Tippett's notice shortly before the Second World War, William Glock (1908–2000) settled on a career as a music critic, writing for the Daily Telegraph *and then, from 1934 to 1945, for the* Observer. *It was during the latter period that he and Tippett became better acquainted. Glock was involved with the BBC Third Programme from its inception in 1946, and his influence later as Controller of Music (1959–73), particularly in promoting contemporary music, was immeasurable: his Proms series became a byword for imaginative programme planning, combining the old and the new to the advantage of both. He had already been associated with a number of related initiatives, founding the Summer School of Music at Bryanston, Dorset, in 1948 (and remaining as musical director after its move in 1953 to Dartington Hall, near Totnes, Devon, until 1979); he started the periodical* The Score *in 1949; and as chairman of the music section at the Institute of Contemporary Arts in London (1954–8) he championed modern music during a fallow period by mounting a groundbreaking concert series. He sat on the board of the Royal Opera House, Covent Garden, from 1968 to 1973 and succeeded Tippett as musical director of the Bath Festival in 1975.*

7 February 1943

Dear William Glock,

Hope you've got the script anew from [Alec] Robertson.* I am not you know a Stravinsky 'fan' and at Morley we do a great deal of early music of all sorts as well as contemporary stuff. Perhaps that's the best way of esteeming the moderns. I can't help feeling what we want most is an artistically discriminate public somewhere, even if a small one, that has some sense of a much larger and more living tradition than the usual notion of a few great names down from which, as it were, we

* For the broadcast of *Portrait of Stravinsky*.

scale to the small fry. I am sure the way around is to have a sense of a tremendous tradition within which the great men are great; in part or virtue of which they are great. And when it comes to the moderns I just feel it's impertinence on our part to try and 'put them across', like a disagreeable political policy. No – they are there, and praise heaven there are such active minds alive – let us be thankful for them and do our best to see what they are up to – their works will fall into place soon enough, and if they are of the true tradition, then they will ever so little alter our view of the whole mass of stuff gone before. Stravinsky, Hindemith, Bartók are all of this and I'm pretty certain to speak of the living. And each of them without exception has the strongest sense of tradition and the music of all sorts of pasts. This is how we get at it at Morley, in our tiny way; to train a discriminating audience to have a sense of loving style, not a hotch-potch, where late Purcell can be sung like Dowland etc. [. . .]

Michael

3 April 1943

My dear William,

So glad you actually heard the 4tet [String Quartet No. 2]. I feel it's perhaps about the best thing I've done in that sort of form – which I care very much about – e.g. combination and contrast of movements – bringing 4 equal types of movement to birth by procuration of 4 (or less or more) techniques which will be able to handle 4 sensibilities – hence the snatching of madrigal technique for the 'lilt' and flow – the unifying form of fugue – the very deliberate formal repetitions in the scherzo (and the 'jazz' vernacular turned to more fastidious uses) – and the Beethoven traditional drama of the more complex material in the final movement. The *Times* chap whoever it was seems to have sensed this. [. . .]

Yours –
Michael

[November 1943]

My dear William,

I got the article off by 8.30 a.m. post Thursday then went off to Leicester to a lunch hour concert, to introduce my Sonata [Piano Sonata No. 1], *entre autres* – [Phyllis] Sellick playing – and where they had almost their record audience! I left word on the article to ring

John Amis of LPO [London Philharmonic Orchestra] if in trouble. Ivor Brown did so to remove a somewhat sweeping sentence running something like: 'In my opinion nothing can now stop the vast out-pourings of treasury money on mass-culture – the inevitable conceit of the all-providing State. I do not want this spent on the new, if we could find it – for public money rightly caters for the masses: adding up end-less figures of concert attendances, appreciation of music classes, always furthering the style that is about to decline. An attitude that would be fatal to the new'. Or something like that.

Brown feels that this would give a handle to reactionaries and on that I perhaps agree with him. But I'm sorry to see go my tilt at the 'mass' numbers etc. What I am trying to say is: patronage (which is no doubt materially essential), just as much if it be State patronage à la Russia, has to be fought with one hand, if sought with the other. The dangerous view has appeared that State patronage by the 'left' is there-fore good in itself. I write you this so that if you wanted you could put 'my' case for me, by re-formulating it in some such way. As the article reads now it's probably less dangerous for my credit with all the cul-ture pundits – and perhaps less opinionated too, and conceited. So I dare say it's all for the best. I don't really want to annoy because, if I feel, as I say I do in the article, that mass-culture can only be permeat-ed gradually by good work in small fields, then it's manifestly my job to work away there, and not tilt at the other side in a naturally hope-less cause. For that's the usual paper romanticism. What I'm really writing for at all is the young folk – who may at the turn of adoles-cence get drawn to 'our' side of the fence and join in the field digging. And that's the value of your own articles, though you may not see that value to calculate or demonstrate it. [. . .]

Herzlichst,
Michael

1 January 1944

I gather I've rather unduly frightened myself [about the threat of being prosecuted a second time] – least that is the opinion of what we, my lot, call the Central Board – who handle all the cases and the records – nevertheless, am going to suggest work with CEMA [Council for the Encouragement of Music and the Arts] – and still would like to see you when you come down on leave.

Michael

[January 1944]

Dear William,

First of all I had an accidental meeting with Eric Walter White of CEMA and heard of your kindness in writing to J. [Reginald Jacques, director of CEMA] – ever so many thanks. As far as I can gather it's not the general practice to re-prosecute and it will turn rather on how 'official' they can make my work seem. Hence J. may be of great help in trouble if it comes. Suffice to say on that point that I feel a lot more 'manly' once more, less lost in horrid self-pity, and will therefore survive what is my lot. And the result of re-reaching this point of feeling, is that I can make decisions for the best – for my work and my general integrity, and not to sell my soul for an avoidance of another term 'in'.

See – Amis of the LPO just phoned me to say that he'd got agreement with Harvey Grace for a 'puff' of the oratorio [*A Child of Our Time*] in *Musical Times*, Feb. issue: and that he had suggested your name to H.G. who had concurred. Can you possibly do it if we send you a full score and/or an MS vocal score.

First: it's up to 1500 words, with a few musical quotes, preferably melodic. It has to reach the office first post on Jan. 24.

Second: copies are promised (?) for end of year – and there has been so much press that I think we can rely on that now – which means you can treat it quite as review and can put the 'Vocal Score pub by Schott & Co.' at the end of the article.

[. . .] I shan't send any MS of oratorio to you till I hear – and if it's easier (or worse) to wait till you come down, then it'll stay here till then – and you can certainly have the expanded vocal score proof for a period in town. Much much easier to read. [. . .]

All the best

Yours

Michael

An addressed p.c. [enclosed] just to write on it 'yes'? – save you bother any further.

[January 1944]

Dear William,

[. . .] I am now so deeply enmeshed in trying to get the oratorio brought to birth – and to production – that I've much less time to worry myself. If they seem bent on re-prosecuting, in other words that they actually serve me with orders to go onto the land, then we shall make a fight for it. If they are determined to pick me out (as that will be) for example that the law must go on on one or two guinea-pigs, then all one can say is that it will morally rebound on their heads and make the protest of the oratorio (for the outcast whoever he be) peculiarly immediate. It will also put the BBC in a tricky position if they are tied to a broadcast.

This moment I'd just had a phone call from the people who run the Arts Enquiry which if you don't know the lowdown of I must give it you, so that you may be well informed on all that is toward. It's possible I might do some advisory work for them and it means probably a satisfactory box for the Min[istry] of Labour to have me in. I hope I have enough courage now to make up my mind for the real best and not for the avoidance of discomfort. Perhaps I might go into a 'box' for a while at least, especially as the work is decisive for a helluva lot of music making after the war. (Roughly it's ensuing into the proper one of continued Treasury grants.)

There's a real fight to be fought after the war. Over the Ralph Hill *par exemple*. This insufferable attitude of pseudo-scholarship and gentleman musicians, and mental annoyance before the real thing. It's the distinction between 'poetry' and 'literature' as [Jacques] Maritain discusses in one of the essays in *Art and Scholasticism* [*Art et scolastique*, 1920] – which arose *à propos de* Rimbaud. Art as entertainment and relaxation or mental gymnastics or diversions or what not – instead of the pure shock either of exuberance or horror or at times mystery – or gaiety: of something so old and beyond morals or brains – given us through the nourishment of the senses – hence a possession, an engendering, and therein at times a shattering of emotions before something deeper than our outside lives. Well, well!

Much love –
Michael

[March 1944]

Dear William,

Have seen *Observer* and like it very much – and I thank you. What you give as your opinion *à propos* of the [Osbert?] Sitwell *Horizon* article I think is about right, and I share it. I think it may be possible that a long-lived composer of nowadays might work on into the period of maturity in the newer style much in the way that [T. S.] Eliot thinks Shakespeare combines two processes in his own life work. a) The exploration of a new verse tuned to the vernacular b) the exploration of the subtleties and complexities possible within the new verse. Quite obviously we have not reached the latter in music or will do for a generation. I think the healthiest sign of the present is the number of youngsters of all sorts who want to try their hand at composition and are not afraid to limit it to their capacity, rather than fly to all the more grandiose forms etc. In this way Britten is a very good influence, because of his gift for the actual in music. Because neither he nor I nor any one of us can really get anywhere decisive at all without a whole school of activity. That in itself won't be decisive of course either – because the next matter will be the level of taste within the school. But if we all arise B[ritten] and I and the like will encourage everyone around us (the younger ones I mean, which is what is happening to both of us now) and direct our influence towards improvement of taste, rather than a moaning and groaning because it isn't a talent of Purcells. This is your job, William, too, ever more as a critic, as you are well aware. It's a funny position we are all in in this period. We have to create style, taste and audience! But there is no other way.

All the very best.

Yours,

Michael

28 June 1944

Dear William,

Have come to a sudden and complete break in composition [Symphony No. 1]. I had 2 such in the *Child*. It's the natural end to the long season. But it does mean that the symphony is desperately slow. Most of my personal problem is to keep a proper balance between the music making and feel I have to do all the laborious days of composition. I can't really contract out of work at Morley yet.

[. . .] Am hoping to go away on Friday for a weekend to recover myself – and avoid the flying bombs which are caught here and blow our windows in and out. Then on Friday week I have 2 weeks away properly D.V. and so back to (bombs and) composition. See you sometime.

Michael

[late June 1944]

Dear Clement and William,

It's all a beautiful muddle now and it looks as if in the end I shall decide to stay here and lump it. Ever since these last raids began, coupled with end of a busy season, other personal peculiarities, I seem to have fallen into an odd sort of inner nervousness, and to which my father's deathbed seemed to fit appropriately. It's a sort of time of disruption, very similar to what I felt during periods of blitz in 1940–1, but which were all mixed up with and discharged into the *Child*. Now, it's baulked, because the symphony has the exposition of the first movement completed and I can't move forward in little bits, that's to say not at details, an hour at Exmouth, an hour elsewhere, because the next section needs all of my faculties collected up together. So it's held up, and now I need a holiday. But I don't like this stoppage, and I get into almost moral attitudes about it – and it isn't really artistically satisfactory to have such big breaks in the middle of movements. So I dare say this first movement will be a miss. All of which is not completely subjective. This just isn't a good period for artistic work – either in peace or in war. And modern war is an accentuation of the whole confusion. Perhaps when I've been away on holiday I shall recover some of the poise and I guess too that the symphony will take a move forward. Once past the 1st movement it will come easier. I am much less sure than I was that it is tolerably good. It still gives me the sense of what I call 'middle period' music: not now the freshness of real early things, nor the finer simplicity of a later style. But I suppose it's got to be lived through. And again, I can just believe that the technical problems and slow building of this wretched symphony are objectively consonant with outer events of the period.

Still, to leave such pointless speculations for the day to day matters. The point is that I write best at home here, with my own associations. So far these few days I've been here have been dangerous but possible. I've got to about till July 31st, so I think I shall wait and see how it's like then, and all being well just sit here and get on with it. Canterbury asked me to sing tenor as a lay clerk while their chap is ill, but that means my only free consecutive four weeks in the whole year (some lost last year in gaol) so I'm trying to refuse.

[. . .] Actually the thought of getting back to work at the symphony is so exhilarating that I dare say all that's the matter with me is merely the need for a holiday – which Exmouth wasn't, because of the emotional complications.

My wild pamphlet* for the pacifists on artistic problems is about to go to the printer, so I'll send you both one when out. It will only cost 1d to anyone, anyhow. It's merely a plea for young people to learn to stand upright instead of crawling. Also, as soon as I can get Ben [Britten] to let me have typed the notes we last made about the masque [early drafts for *The Midsummer Marriage*], I'll paste them into the copy and send or bring that too. [. . .]

Love –
Michael

[1944/5]

My dear William,

[. . .] I feel I have been sailing rather near the publicity racket lately and am in danger of psychological inflation. Or to put it another way: there is a fresh adjustment to be made between the larger public 'persona' and the same petty individual at home. Also, this increased publicity means a lot of rushing around, until such time as it goes its own way. As ever, the next *Child* do ties me up with every sort of social consideration to the Poles and Poland and the wicked world at large. Perhaps one can't ever escape it – to write a bit more each year, then less. The Symphony [No. 1] is difficult going to write. It tires me very easily. But there's also the general tiredness of the war and the strain underneath. I can't quite make out whether the new sense of assurance I have is merely the publicity 'inflation' or fresh, or greater power. The symphony will tell the tale.

Love –
Michael

[early April 1945]

Dear William,

I am very jangled and sore – and silly sentimental tears (which will pass). Fresca Allinson, whom I don't think you ever met, [so] felt that she couldn't go on with the protracted and wasting illness she had that she took her life by drowning.

* 'Abundance of Creation: An Artist's Vision of Creative Peace'. London: Peace News, 1944.

I can't explain by letter all this really means. I'll tell you one day. She was ever gay and gentle and fond of pretty things and with a deep-going courage – perhaps this lunatic power-driven world has no place for such at present.

Men with careers are often just masters it seems to me. Everyone can go to the wall.

I finished the slow movement [of Symphony No. 1] late last night, just after I'd heard the news. I used to think its death was my own. Well it just wasn't.

Love –
Michael

[1945?]

Dear William,

If you were able without inconvenience to give Priaulx [Rainier] the typescript of the opera-masque [*The Midsummer Marriage*] – or whatever – on Friday evening, she would bring it to me here on Saturday. For I gather Den [Newton] has begun to make notes for it, and I want to get a libretto out now in words before he goes to prison or gets entangled in other things. Then the libretto can chase around a bit for common criticism. I can't afford to make a mistake, as I shan't write operas by the dozen. *Aurora* [*Aurora Consurgens*, an early draft and the original title of *The Midsummer Marriage*] is to be in every way a conjunction and deposit of all sorts of ideas and interests and traditions – and somehow contemporary or artistic/symbolic even, into the bargain. Still that sounds grim and priggish – but I don't mean it like that. But one knows that certain sorts of art works one does are of a bit different order – both impurer and more imaginative. The *Child* is horribly impure, *par exemple*.

I miss not seeing you, but I can't do anything but sit here and write the Symphony [No. 1]; last movement. I am still very anxious about finishing it on time. The spare score of the 1st 3 movements is now being corrected. So later you can see it if you want.

LPO [London Philharmonic Orchestra] seem to want to do it the first in London – at the Stoll.

Dein –
Michael

spring 1945
Maldon, Essex

Dear William,

[. . .] Last movement [Symphony No. 1] pursues its course. And I have got inklings at last now of how the form problems might take a move. That is to say, that I feel at length, that I have rooted myself substantially in the traditional forms (a big problem for an Englishman) and may be in a position to enter 'transition' – which is I suppose about all we can hope to do just yet. There is nothing new formally in the symphony. That is not quite true of course – there are new elements, particularly in the scherzo – an unusual method in the slow movement – a sort of orchestrally translated fugue for the last. And incidentally, for better or worse, it's laid out in a substantial scale – despite my view that English music shouldn't go that way! it has . . . perhaps to its doom once more – we shall hear. Anyhow, it had got to come, as far as I was concerned, because these sort of overall problems occupy me all the time, and I have to put it all to the test – even to that of a huge form like opera. It's a sort of process of gathering into oneself all the strands in one to try eventually to take a real step forward – or the sort of step which makes someone later to see round a corner. I calculate that you will see this process first in the 3rd 4tet which I am pondering over – but which won't be written till after the opera [*The Midsummer Marriage*]. [. . .]

Love –
Michael

summer 1945

Dear William,

[. . .] I've nearly finished the great work [Symphony No. 1]! any day now – I'll send you a telegram when that happens. Roughly – I've been so shatteringly tired with the coming inertia of the end, that I find it difficult to force myself to get the last notes down on to the paper. But I did manage to move at last today. Ideas for the opera, further to do with the story, bubble up early, on the other hand.

I've just been reading the new *Tempo*. It has an odd effect – very subjective I'm afraid! When Fresca died, it was found that she had kept all my letters to her and there is one which is tolerably interesting. (For the rest they are wildly unfeeling – there is nothing whatever in them, except occasional gentleness to her, but everlasting accounts of the music: reads like a monomania.) It was written apparently as an answer to some letter of hers fearing for my temper in the newly appearing success. I reply that the experience of going to Northampton after I came out of prison to hear performed the Fanfare [No. 1, for brass] which Ben [Britten] had so kindly commissioned for me – and finding that I was looked on as a sort of minor Ben, the younger brother. I seem to have gone through some minor internal struggle and once for all relinquished competition in success as being foreign to my proper nature. But obviously I get momentary return-ings and twinges of adolescent envy – only being me, it's all pretty mild! Unfortunately we never do anything without *amour propre*. It is healthy to destroy it occasionally, but in order to create at all it has at once to be rebuilt!! I get moments when I do wish I had Boosey & Hawkes' terrific organisation behind the *Child* say – but it doesn't last for long. And oddly enough, things seem to transpire of themselves. The *Child* has drifted (I think that must be the word) abroad. However – even that would not have happened I fancy without your championship and others' friendliness and belief. Not being inhuman and cold I certainly depend a little on men like [Walter] Goehr to sus-tain my belief in myself.

[. . .] As a matter of interest, too, your characterisation of Ben as the professional par excellence, and of me as something other I can't remember how you phrased it (I saw it only in French at 21) is correct and is to me a satisfaction. I am, whether I like it or not, totally involved in the whole present social and cultural process, wherein the immense social, economic, collective value of specialisation is seen to have produced a drastic poverty of the individual, whose accidentally (because socially, economically useless) 'inferior' sides are never per-mitted conscious vitality, which vitality would force a lower degree of specialisation for the gain of a wider and richer human being in its own right. (Our discussions on virtuosity, etc, etc, are all subsumed under this problem – brilliantly stated in the 2nd chap. of Jung's *Psychologische Typen*.) I have to gather up every bit of my nature, developed or underdeveloped ('My shadow and my light') towards a richer outcome if less immediately *glänzend*. You will appreciate what all this has to do with the opera. In fact Jack ('of all trades') is going to be nearly a caricature of the modern man who is only understood as his job, his social value, and has no rounded human value permitted by the nature of our society. And though the music I dare say will be paramount in the end, I am ceasing to be frightened by the amount of whatever else is going into the padding.

What is happening to it at present, is that the story is taking on more naturalistically human dressing and the allegorical and mythological element is receding behind. It constantly gets warmer – but is as unsentimental as before. That merely means that the authors are still sufficiently detached emotionally to give the feeling of the dramatic, overall outside viewpoint without which good comedy can't be made. In fact it's turning out fascinatingly well!

Expect a telegram soon – shall be glad to hear of Clement's successful delivery.

Love –
Michael

[late 1945/early 1946]

My dear William,

I have not seen the *Times* article, but I gather amongst other things he thinks the work [Symphony No. 1] 'drab'! That is not how it struck Goehr whose opinion luckily for me means more. At least I have the dubious pleasure of not having a chorus of critics echoing praises! It means I suppose that it will be a long fight after all. There is a passage in a letter from the wise Evelyn Maude which is well said, I think: 'but I don't think as things are at present the ordinary, even cultivated, public so in a mood to take any pains over music and I expect if the truth were known the fact that you are in the public eye now counts with a large number more than the actual music.' Bartók had this experience to an even sharper degree, as you know. In an age which more than ever does not want the vitality of clarity and precision and formal design and that mixture of passion and intellect which produces the seeming complexity in the artistic image, then if one is doomed to that way (even though one fumble) one is doomed to the support of the *Gemeinde* around one, and scattered hither and thither and not the public mass. It is time for the opera [*The Midsummer Marriage*]! were it not that *Child of Our Time*, through outer consideration and inner innocence, did actually come to the public at large (if not as large as *Grimes*. I remember telling Fresca years ago that the symphony had to be got out of the way before the opera could proceed easily and publicly, so to speak. So I am not too discouraged.

I shan't change a note of the symphony because I can't and know it to be also stupid to do so. There is an element in the first movement of in-success. That has to be admitted and I knew it when writing it. It is not probably and finally quite up to the others. But that difference is not a great deal more than the usual experience of nearly every symphonic work and is scarcely to be avoided except by occasional stupendous activity – and it is not possible to come at it by re-writing. It doesn't really work unless the discrepancy is very obvious. But there is also another element of experiment in the sort of material for symphonic purpose. As [Hans] Redlich writes to me: 'I think it a grand and new idea to fertilise symphony by ways I mean of a "madrigalian" polyphonic style. The result is thrilling, especially in the first mov[ement]: with its clear sonata structure and its complete absence of harmonistic (*sic*) pivots.' That quotation is not proof of excellence in the 1st mov but merely of this element that we have yet to decide upon. If it be a failure and a *Sackgasse*, then I wish it to remain such for us all to see. Because, to repeat back to the first element, the amount of failure is not of the dimension that demands its suppression and non-publication.

Your point about complexities etc is very absorbing. I shall ponder about it. It has I'm sure an absolute truth, though I am not quite so sure of its application to this movement. The actual performance did transform many of the difficulties into continuity. That process will go on till the limit is reached. There we can form a better judgment. Meanwhile I have further whims in my head of how to proceed. But it will be years before I take them up in that medium. What I had hoped to do was to write a real symphony – big and strong and un-intimate as against a 4tet. Not too far away from a possible public, but never to sentimentalise to achieve one. For the moment that is enough. I need all the concentration I have now for the opera!!

Love –
Michael

[1946]

My dear William,

[. . .] I am now on the last, 5th, movement of the 4tet [String

Quartet No. 3], which goes fairly easily. It's a quiet finale, with the stress *schon vorbei*, so to speak.

You know as well as I do that there must be some absolute points in music as in social life. Technical progress gets so far away from the rate of walking, breathing, gestation and what not, the consequent spanning brings widespread neurosis and recoil. In a sense it is so with artistic 'modernity'. It tends to strain against even the limits of instruments and voices, apart from the question of 'dissonance'. If the overvaluation of technics has produced a consequent impoverishment of the imaginative and spiritual life, then the way out is through an exploration of the neurosis which only appears neurotic because of the preconceived undervaluation. Out of the neurotic resistance can be cultivated the renewed imaginative life. Which will be of another order. Presumably then, something analogous has befallen in the world of artefacts. It is not the 'neuroticism' so to speak which will survive but their imaginative vitality, and this way bear less violent a relation to musical absolutes. Also, the day of great tensional dissonance may be passing. But not to sink back into banality. It can only pass, or be transcended, by being transformed into a greater imaginative variety, if less specially intense.

I am getting wound up in the opera [*The Midsummer Marriage*].

Love –

Michael

September 1947

My dear William,

[. . .] I found I have my own form of the general depression or malaise. I think I must have pitched myself too high lately, and that some necessary adjustment is being made from inside which I resist and don't like. Perhaps it's really the first recoil from what limited success I have had – learning my place again! Or it may be tied up with this long new work. Or it may be a flooding of one's feelings by a general inertia and lassitude. Anyhow, I have singularly little pride in myself at the present moment. In Holland I may be able to revive myself again that it's not as bad as I know. Maybe, on the other hand, the *Child*, which is more naive in some senses, is tolerable, because it's close to people in an 'impure' way – while the 'pure' music one writes has all the disadvantages of its 'purer' imperfections.

Incidentally – all this moan is quite beside the question of the opera, which I want to know properly how it strikes before it's finally too late. [. . .]

Love –

Michael

September 1947

Dear William,

I've just finished copying to the end of the scene [from *The Midsummer Marriage*] and will take the score to Schott's tomorrow to have posted to you, at c/o Deas. If I can't find a fresh script copy I'll send you up mine – but for God's sake don't lose it and I shall want it back without fail in 2 weeks' time.

I find that really everything depends on getting the script right, each scene, right from the point of view of the music to be composed. It's fatally easy to start setting any words and to try vainly then to force shape on the ensuing music – let alone relevance to the music of scenes before and after. It's this labour which takes the time. And I'm beginning to begrudge it less. [. . .]

Michael

June 1955

Dear William,

I've now seen *The Score* and *Encounter*! I find the criticism just and perceptive, and the only criticism that has said anything useful to the point.

I had a curious experience a month or so back, for I went to Germany to hear the Symphony [No. 1] played.* (This is *à propos* of your remarks about orchestration etc.) It sounded an intense genuine musical experience, but very clumsy in expression, though the slow movement was overwhelming. There has really been a lot of improvement in the presentation. Harmony still remains for me a quite empirical, almost guesswork affair. I can't *schreibe* either like Hindemith or Schoenberg. It doesn't ever work – I can't think musically that way. The best (I think) is when I can use fundamentally simple harmonic progressions in a new way. Maybe I'll come back to chamber music

* Performed by the Städtisches Orchester, Dortmund, conducted by Rolf Agop.

again soon and see what purification one can make. But I'm getting wound up in a new big (choral) work with an apocalyptic theme [contemplating material for *King Priam*]. I remind myself of all the great poetry my beloved Yeats wrote after his marriage at 52. Maybe all the best is yet to come!

Do bring yourself to make a visit one day. You would be more than welcome.

Love to all,
Michael

1957

Dear William,

Oddly enough I'm planning to write a song for voice and guitar, as part of commissioned music [*Crown of the Year*] for the centenary of Badminton School next year. (Words by Christopher Fry.) But I shall have to wait till the Symphony [No. 2] is finished in October before I dare start on it. So you must tell [Julian] Bream what a joy he may have in store by the summer of 58! (How I wonder if Badminton would or could amplify him!!)

Many thanks indeed for asking me.

herzlichst –
Michael

6 October 1961

Dear William,

Although this is a professional BBC matter I'm writing to Connaught Sq so you can keep it all under your hat if you prefer.

It's about a conductor for *The Midsummer Marriage* next March [for the 1963 Third Programme studio broadcast]. I heard from [Howard] Hartog that [Peter] Crossley-Holland wants it to be Stanford Robinson (Mackerras now being unavailable). I'm inclined to say that I'd rather in that case call it all off. However, I want to find out how you really feel about my conducting it myself. Hartog first suggested it to me and was pro and then became con, and I don't quite know what's in his mind. And he said you were 'not much in favour'. But I have not spoken with you direct.

I feel that given the support I would undoubtedly get from the BBC – I mean your department – I could give an accurate and exciting performance. I assess myself saying thus: I am not as good and gifted as Ben [Britten], but I'm better than Henze. I could and would give the piece with considerable panache and make it an occasion the BBC would be proud of. And I am disengaged!

I have not told anyone I'm writing to you. For it's no good going into the fray, so to speak, if you're really half-hearted. You'll have to be ready to take the risk and back me, as you unfailing will, if you think it finally good.

King Priam s'achève in about 10 days! Quite extraordinarily exciting. Everything at the end is fallen into place.

I've been already in long conferences with [Sam] Wanamaker. I think we'll have a vigorous and powerful presentation.

I was in the train, returning from one of these conferences when the Third Quartet was done from Glasgow. It got such a good notice, I thought, in *The Times*, that I feel the performance must really have been good at last. Sorry now I didn't have a disc made. Is it still on (BBC) tape? But don't bother about that – I'll find that out without bothering you.

Heard from Priaulx you both had a wonderful time in Greece. I'm extremely pleased. Good holidays are vital.

Herzlichst –

Michael

15 October 1961

My dear William,

I finished *King Priam* yesterday!, in full score. So it's very exciting – and I'm extremely pleased – as I guess you will be.

I've had Peter Crossley-Holland's letter about conductors; and have replied today. I bow to the judgment concerning myself.

Of the list of names he suggests, the one I hadn't thought of, Maurits Sillem, is the one I plonk for, I feel he may retrieve the situation in a fine way. So, seeing he's agreeable to all of us, I hope Peter [Pears] will delay no more to see if he's available. I'd rather have him than [Manuel] Rosenthal – English-language work and so on. Or maybe that's no matter, in fact.

I'm ringing Peter tomorrow to see how it is.

Gather you've been laid low. Ever so sorry – just after a holiday too.

Am looking forward to my little go with Divertimento [on 'Sellinger's Round']! All fallen just pat and so fine.

Herzlichst –

Michael

11 March 1964

My dear William,

Before I get to my own affairs may I say how exciting the Boulez concert was last Wednesday, and how fine the orchestra sounded. Hope you were pleased, as you must have been, to see the substantial (and fairly eminent!) audience. May it prosper.

In your 'plan', if that is the term, is about a TV project, that next year they make a film of *A Child of Our Time*! I think, with composer alive and appearing in person as conductor (though only in the 'spirituals', the solo numbers to show the studio) and ensuring that the film is decent, simple and in good taste (without loss of power), that the venture could be one to be reasonably proud of. It seems that, naturally enough, money is a problem. But also perhaps there might be co-operation financially with Schott. My plea is therefore (if you feel, honestly, as I do) that should it be a question of priorities and where you have authority, you give it sympathetic consideration and if possible active help. There now – a mouthful!

Herzlichst –

Michael

5 April 1965

Dear William,

I really would like to conduct the Piano Concerto at the Prom on August 19th. This is *à propos* of a phone call last night from Malcolm [Sargent]. I had somehow got it into my head that a) date was impossible because of Edinburgh, b) that the BBC Orchestra would not have gone to USA with the work till the autumn. But I am free for that date, and with the orchestra familiar with the piece I could give a better performance I guess indeed than Malcolm, who has never been any good at my music, for various natural reasons. I'm also very keen to do a good and exciting performance with [John] Ogdon, whom I 'trained' in it, so to speak, for the EMI recording.

So here's to it!

Michael

Will be writing in a few days again to you with good news of end of [*The Vision of St*] *Augustine*!

3 May 1968

Dear William,

I've written off to Peter Pastreich the manager of the St Louis Symphony Orchestra and suggested he sent the tape to you for approval. I did a double concert, same programme. I hope he took tapes of both and makes up the tape from the best of each. I don't think the Purcell Fantasias made great sense except the third one, In Nomine, 7 parts, which was rather splendid – 6 violins (2 parts) 4 violas (2 parts) 6 cellos (2 parts), the In Nomine plainsong on horn, flute, cor anglais, unison same pitch. Had a fine baroque sound.

My own Concerto for Orchestra had great moments in the fast movements (though I turned two pages in one performance and there was momentary confusion). The slow movement not as good as I did with the LSO [London Symphony Orchestra]. The Holst was brilliant on the Friday, two mistakes by the players on the Saturday. The Ives lovely both times, and Elgar excellent.* I doubt if such a concert – English/American – has come off so well before, or happened at all, in the States. There is much more scope in this field than appears, if one has the courage to do it.

Yours Sincerely,

Michael

PS. Two critics have just come in from N.Y. [John Ardoin and Ivan Davies, the latter a pianist]. They're rather wild! I doubt if the old take will match the warm and excited concert.

8 August 1969

My dear William,

Please excuse the 'business' notepaper – can't find any less formal. It's about an idea of Colin [Davis]'s (this letter is) for next year's Prom. He heard the final set of pieces of the enclosed programme, i.e. the 3 bits to date of the eventual 5-movement set [*The Shires Suite*]. He was fascinated by the new bit, the fast instrumental Interlude, because it has a furious vitality and virtuosity which the Leics. kids [Leicester-

---

* Tippett conducted a programme of Holst's *The Perfect Fool*, Ives's *The Unanswered Question* and Elgar's 'Enigma' Variations.

shire Schools Symphony Orchestra] performed in a stunning manner. (There is a BBC2 videotape of them doing this bit after 3 days' rehearsal. It's very remarkable.) He conceived the idea that if I completed the 5 movements he would like to have them as an item in the final Prom next year. He thinks their directness and immediacy and gaiety just right. (I might say that George Harewood, at an earlier occasion, fell for the Epilogue and had asked for a London première with New Philharmonia – which I didn't grant as I hadn't intended to finish all the 5 till a year or two off.) Colin has told me on the phone he's spoken to you about his proposition. Is it real for you? Because if it were I could compose the other 2 bits this Christmas.

The Leics. lot, who have commissioned the piece, must have first performance – which would be at Leicester next May – unless Colin was meaning that the kids themselves were to perform in the Prom. The orchestra is stunning – but the choir would have to be students or grown-ups. The small bodies can't produce any true resonance.

Drop me a card if you think the proposition sense, or phone, or I'll get someone in Schott's to try and contact you meanwhile.

Herzlichst –
Michael

5 November 1969

Dear William,
[. . .] *The Knot Garden* – I'm afraid the score does not lend itself to any concert preview. It's so intensely operatic in a somewhat new quick-change style; short highly characteristic scenes and so forth that will only make sense in a visual stage sequence. In absolute contrast, for example, to the flowing lyricism of *The Midsummer Marriage* (which comes back next July so that it can be commercially recorded between performances). So I'm sure any Prom preview would be ineffective and mistaken.

But I do think privately you ought to manage more representation than a horn quartet [Sonata for Four Horns] for next year! Why not Symphony 1 (a fine, tough piece – known to Norman [Del Mar], Colin [Davis] and Ted Downes) or even the naive but moving *Child of Our Time*, both Prom premières!

These of course are 'real' pieces. The new 5-mvt suite for the Leics. kids [*The Shires Suite*] isn't of this reality – obviously. So I've no doubt what I would prefer. But for your files you probably know already that the Leics. lot are giving a concert for [John] Manduell in the Cheltenham Festival in July to contain [Richard Rodney] Bennett's new piece, mine, and (for good measure) Bliss's Piano Concerto with the composer conducting!

How I wish, meanwhile, that you were free to help me with ideas for both. I'm already through into the 1971 [Bath] Festival. Not bad.

See you 13th.

Herzlichst –

Michael

9 November 1969

My dear William,

I don't see how I shall get to the meeting on Friday. The trouble is that consequent on taking on too many non-composition activities in the 6 months since finishing *The Knot Garden* I have developed a medical condition which produces frequent and repeated 'crisis' of 'nerves'. In order to get the body out of the vicious circle I am taking medicine to comfort the autonomic nervous action and should stay quiet, composing when I can, for a week or so. (The doctor's advice today.) But I do want to see you. What about a lunch with me on Nov. 27th – a Thursday? I have to be in London then. Any good? I'll get someone to ring your sec. at BBC to see.

Love to you both

Michael

29 June 1970

Dear William,

I feel I must write to somebody (forgive me) having gone to London yesterday to hear Lawrence Foster do my Symphony 1 with the RPO [Royal Philharmonic Orchestra] – since it hadn't been performed in London for 25 years! The performance was stunning – and a tremendous vindication. Not of English music promoters, but of the dedicatee, Walter Goehr, who did really know what's what even in MS (and you yourself were one of the few who gave it a good crit. all those years ago). But what an irony! I have had to wait till a young American forced it through the RPO management. It's a funny world . . .

I'm well into Symphony 3 now. Richer, I suppose – and sometimes deeper. But not with more intellectual and emotional drive than I had then. I was just 40.

Last night's experience was of course very personal (I think Sandy [Alexander] Goehr alone shared it absolutely). And it can only come with age!

Herzlichst –
Michael

17 December 1970

My dear William,

There's been a shift of a sort in the Bath Festival. A month or so back, after a longish meeting, I had such a bad 12-hr 'tremble' that my chairman, Mrs Robertson, and the 2 young men who will run the office from next July got a bit worried. So they took Philip Moore into their confidence and asked his help to allow them not only to run administration without reference to me, but to initiate Festival programmes to be put to me at convenience; for they want to have me 'around' name-wise and even in fact, while making the fullest use of the present Council of Management, who are of the region and of which Philip is a good attendee member. And also, the gradual build-up of Philip's own Bristol Proms and the Festival's large use now of the Colston Hall has all tended this way. So we shall see how this works. And if it does, I imagine they'd want it to go on for some time.

I write you this because I do not want to have lured you down any garden path. You must read the future as best to suit yourself. God knows, though you badly need, I should think, some prolonged rest after the BBC, you have more than valuable gifts for the continued service of music. But you know this in yourself better than I can tell you.

For myself, I find the threshold of my 'nerves' (I don't mean immobility of course) unhappily low. The inner tension of *The Knot Garden* (though I only went to 2, final, rehearsals in all) played me up like hell.

I have to go on plodding away at new scores as near to a vegetable as I can manage, to steady the inner obsessions. I am all set, for a new Symphony [No. 4], a piece for [Georg] Solti in Chicago,* and a new

---

*This commission, which was to have been a setting of Robert Lowell's poem 'For the Union Dead', was never completed. Instead, Tippett wrote the Symphony No. 4.

opera [*The Ice Break*] for Colin [Davis] and Peter [Brook]! The last, indeed, is well into the brooding stage, as I would call it.

Then I'd like to return to some chamber music. And that should see me through.

Love to you both –

Michael

1977

I began the quartet [String Quartet No. 4] after I spoke with you and a week later had such violent nervous attacks that I've put it aside. And more important released the sense of pressure for a B.F. [Bath Festival] 78 première. Also, it would be stupid to be 'pressured' at all, on my winter–spring 'sabbatical'. But I'll talk to you again soon and make a visiting date.

herzlichst –

M.

Edward Sackville-West

Tippett's letters to the writer Edward Sackville-West (1901–65) are concerned mainly with the composition, première, casting and reception of his first opera, The Midsummer Marriage. *The author of several novels and a volume of critical essays, Sackville-West worked in the Features and Drama Department of the BBC from 1939. He shared a house in the village of Long Crichel, Dorset, with the music critic Desmond Shawe-Taylor.*

[early 1942]

Dear Sackville-West,

[. . .] I played the new work for pf. and orch. [Fantasia on a Theme of Handel] to [Walter] Goehr on Sat. at Schott's – and he wants to include it in a series of adventurous concerts at Wigmore with the LSO [London Symphony Orchestra] Classics and Contemporaries and spiced with box-office artistes. The moderns to be: Bartók, Schoenberg, Stravinsky and myself – of all people. The artists: Solomon, Ida Haendel, John McCormack (singing Wolf) and of course Phyllis Sellick, if she agrees. A very nice piece of good fortune and I was somewhat too excited by Sat. evening to conduct or sing straight. But the concert was a great success nevertheless. I've written in the oratorio text [*A Child of Our Time*], because it's a first and tiny private printing by schoolboys with Gill Sans type – I hope you aren't put off by that. Please remember as to the text itself that, as [T. S.] Eliot remarked, it should not be too good.

Yours sincerely,
Michael Tippett

24 November 1947

My dear Eddy,

[. . .] The score of the Symphony [No. 1] is corrected and returned for printing. It'll come off the presses soon now. I'd like to hear your recording – because Goehr did a very good job that time. I'm sure the work is a grim one and I dare say it sprang more than I knew from the experiences of general catastrophe.

The opera [an early draft for *The Midsummer Marriage*] has so far no polyphony at all – hence I think its slowness in composition. But I'm entirely absorbed in the matter.

As to the experience of exhaustion – I find that when it comes in this time, the objective, general debasement, disillusion, catastrophe can very easily flood over us (when our defences are weakened by exhaustion) and overwhelm us. But that does not permit us to give up the struggle.

There is a lot about this in the *Four Quartets* – and much better expressed!

I've been wanting to see you, but I can't see how on earth I'm to get down to Long Crichel – at any rate till these talks are over and I am relieved of earning my money, by accumulating enough to go on again. Because after weeks of no composition (as at present), no one at all can drag me from my room. But when I get into the rhythm again I can afford to consider some personal life.

I not only support myself and help some others, but I had to put money into my concerts last year – and will do again. And I have to conduct in them. So I am a horribly overworked man. Until the family fortune, such as it is, passes to me and my brother there is no escape. Personal life takes the line of least resistance. I see those I see and move nowhere.

Isn't that depressing and distressing?

[. . .] I have a lot to talk to you of about the opera. Do let me know if you propose coming to London.

Yours
Michael

[March/April 1948]

My dear Eddy,

I shall certainly go and hear *Falstaff*. I was sorry you needed the score back as it has been, and still would be, my vademecum. If you have less need of it later on I would much value its continued loan. At least a year more! The matter of transitions in opera is endlessly fascinating. Naturally I can't emulate the great master, but I am having a good shot at pulling something off on those lines. I find I scarcely ever descend as far as real secco because the matter spoken seems to need a greater emphasis and big sweeps of the voice even. (King Fisher always seems to rant and shout and I have difficulty in controlling him.) On the other hand some of the arias spring from such clear 'aria-like' situations that I imagine even fools will know that they have reached one. Also – I find the arias very necessary musically to give length and stability to the music. The repartee of recitative, however musical and lyrical, soon becomes tedious.

However mad the scapade may be into which I have plunged it's unbelievably exciting to do. To work on more than one plane at once is exciting in itself – at least to my temperament – So that [*Lady*] *Rohesia* [opera by Antony Hopkins] (which I had to go to see, like you), that isn't on a plane at all, is operatically futile. Actually I got a lot of amusement out of watching how a non-music could be given stage substance by production, décor and acting – which were on a high level, if the planes mixed to the recipe of *Hellzapoppin*.

In a month or so I shall have finished Act 1 [of *The Midsummer Marriage*] and will send you the script as set on the act – and later pf. reduction and score if it interest you.

I'm off on Sat. to see the *Child* born in Lausanne – a French birth. So it will be interesting to hear how the language may change the flavour – or not. [. . .]

Love
Michael

1948

Thanks for your kind letter and invitation. Maybe I can, if luck holds, avail myself of it. I'm considering recuperating a bit at Aldeburgh in Ben [Britten]'s house, for the sea air, when I'm fit to move. Am still at present in bed, with John [Minchinton]'s mother nursing me. The worst is over now and the bilious liver beginning to behave. Italian holiday is quite certainly postponed.

Love to you all
Michael

2 September 1948

My dear Eddy,
[. . .] I've been in hermitage all these summer (?) weeks writing, and

I'm about to start the final scene of Act I [of *The Midsummer Marriage*]. That doesn't sound much but really it's a lot. I could have hardly worked harder. The whole thing has deepened during work, and clarified itself; the music always remaining lyrical and uncomplicated. The text has taken the course you advised, and though still at times nearly colloquial, is in general on a more 'rhetorical' plane. I have been reading masses of Greek mythology, anthropology, and the plays – all of which has been substance for this curious imaginative world in which I'm moving. The hard work is always to reduce everything to the simple clear and lyrical image. I'm learning the technique of juggling with words and music at once, but naturally words don't leap so immediately to my mind. I use much a thesaurus indeed! – but the peculiar world I am creating seems to preclude, *ab initio*, any collaboration with another. A nuisance – but one which being there, must be made a virtue of, as far as one may.

It will be another 2 years before completion. I have not the genius to toss works off like some of my colleagues. I must needs plod.

Much love
Michael

30 December 1949

My dear Eddy,

Thanks for the nice card of Long Crichel – which surely I *must* see in the flesh soon! Perhaps this spring. For I'm bowling down the straight (I've mixed metaphors) towards the end of Act 2 [of *The Midsummer Marriage*]. Which has turned out much more sentimental and romantic an interlude between the bigger gambits of Acts 1 and 3. But I'm still living in deep seclusion so that the work really gets done. I don't go to Morley this year. And am most strict about going to town at all. But today I go to Amersham to have another session with Goehr on the piano score of Act 1, before finalisation. [. . .]

Michael

1952/3

My dear Eddy,

Finishing *The Midsummer Marriage* is like coming out of a long dream into a grey reality. At first there was a tremendous sense of achievement. Now I'm in full retreat and I can't imagine what it was all about and what drove me that stony way. But my stomach is releasing its tensions at last – though they all came back with a final 'gripe' when we tried to play some of the music to [Günther] Rennert last Sunday. I felt it was all rather premature. But he'd expressed interest and knew the script from before and is only in England for a while. He seems to have told my publishers that he thinks it to need a bigger stage than he has at Hamburg, but he isn't certain: that *he* takes it to be the most significant stuff in the operatic field *he* knows of to have come out of England, and quite appropriate to Covent Garden, so far as he knows that. He raised a possible objection that the *Problematik* of the book [libretto] might not be properly matched by the lucidity of the music. Perhaps he's right. But it was quite deliberate on my part, because I felt strongly that to make the music recherché, or too unromantic, let alone dissonant for dissonance sake, would be to put its 'message' out of any relation to the young people portrayed in the story on the stage. I *think* it will be seen that I am right when the orchestral score and the voices are heard in their fullness. And *en passant* it was interesting to note that Noel [Mewton-Wood]'s playing, so much more conscientious and pianistically capable than Walter Goehr's, let alone mine, didn't convey a score nearly so well as either Walter or me. So that if *you* want a play-through, you'd much better risk the composer's idiosyncratic touch and voice, when the print is available (quite soon) and I have recovered from the nausea that follows *Fertigkeit*.

Meanwhile, before I put it all out of mind, so that I can start on the new work for Edinburgh [Fantasia Concertante on a Theme of Corelli], I tried to overcome my slight self-consciousness with David Webster by writing a little personal note to him that it was over. And I told him what Willy W[alton] had suggested: that he, Walton, would be quite glad to see *The Midsummer Marriage* on the stage before *Troilus [and Cressida]* – which I take to mean that the latter is still a little further off than supposed from real completion. But just as *A Child of Our Time* seemed to need 3–4 years of 'rest' before its première was felt to be rightly timed, I have always imagined the opera would need some space when it is known to be complete and when bits of it become known as music, and the whole in print. And, Eddy dear, can you write Feb. 18 in your diary of next year for the première of the Ritual Dances with BBC Orchestra and Goehr, Home Service.

(Or Feb. 19 Third.) But if possible come to rehearsal and the trans-
mission in the studio. [. . .]

herzlichst, herzlichst

Michael

PS. All the vocal score of the opera will be engraved by Christmas
and then printing will follow straight on proofreading. Schott's will
make a fresh well-written full score, so that they are doing me proud
and if Covent Garden really *did* consider the thing in the terms Willy
[Strecker] suggested, all is ready. Maybe when it's appropriate at
some future time you can make the substance of these facts known?
You know me well enough – I have a composer's natural impatience
to see and hear what he has done, but a deeper-seated patience that
bides its time in reasonable confidence.

7 August 1953

My dear Eddy,

I had meant to write you the day after you came just to say *how* I
enjoyed your visit – and how welcome you *always* are. And that too
something you said about piano concertos in general reminded me of
a necessary ingredient, and helped to settle a further formal point in
the middle movement. Thank you!

[. . .] Webster saw [Howard] Hartog of Schott's, and they seem to
have planked for January 55 for the great première [*The Midsummer
Marriage*]. (My 50th birthday is on the 2nd day of that month.)
Probably the Piano Concerto will be released round the same time. I
think you'll approve of it. Lyrical and clear and classical, with terribly
little counterpoint and singularly simple harmonies. What more could
you hope for?

The final printing and issue of the vocal score is voluntarily being
delayed by Mainz till nearer a première. That's their usual policy.
Some specimen study copies will be available any time now in
London and Mainz. That is, there is one on the way to London now.
And Schott's London can have another at need. Maybe also now I
shall let the final libretto be set up in print in the same way, against
an eventual issue. It is quite definitely not a libretto for previous distribution to people who find it difficult to imagine the possible
transformation that music can make. And there is some shuddering
doggerel in it, here and there. But so little of the total experience

can be guessed from the libretto (not only for the general reasons of all librettos, but also for the added difficulties of unrealistic situations and techniques) that it would prove a confusion rather than an aid.

I learnt so much in wrestling with the whole matter, that I haven't really assimilated it yet. It will bear fruit again at a later time, in another big-scale choral piece I'm beginning to meditate upon [*King Priam*]. But that is some years ahead. A kind of odyssey – that is, a series of situations, where the topography, so to speak, is part of the image of the situation – as well as of course various musical imagery, appropriate. But, not yet, the *Odyssey*, so far as I can see. At any rate; various landfalls. We shall get there only very gradually.

Love –
Michael

1953

My dear Eddy,

I'd heard lately, before the Philharmonic Concert, a good performance of the [Ritual] Dances in Liverpool ([Hugo] Rignold) and a better one in Munich ([Eugen] Jochum). It's now got to such a point that I feel I must avoid them until they reach the stage itself. Because my own stage pictures are so vivid, and I can't communicate them of course to others, so I begin to boil inside.

Anyhow, Hartog (of Schott's) and I had lunch with Webster last Monday, and Jan. 1955 has been once more agreed as a kind of funding date. For the string piece I wrote for Edinburgh this year [Fantasia Concertante on a Theme of Corelli] had its creation in Germany a week or so back, and Schott's here had a letter to say that the Herr General Direktor of the Town Drains (or somesuch) was so struck by the 'euphony of the polyphony', that he wanted to secure the German première of the opera for *his* town. So – although it may well never happen – i.e. he'll recover from his giddyness in time – we had to let them have a funding date in Germany, beyond which with the agreement of Covent Garden, it wouldn't be held up.

Actually, what cheered me, as the composer, in this, was not so much the possible German performance, as that such an impression had been given through just some conductor and orchestra just from the printed notes.

Anyhow – it's becoming now, so that my German performances will soon be my greater income. All of which is helpful, if strange, and I'm sure accidental.

What am I writing? I'm full of music. I'm well on in the first movement of a Pf. Concerto: to which you added an ingredient, when you were here last. As I told you then, a warm, poetic work.

Then I'm extending my 'trick' of the variation (for Ben [Britten]) at Aldeburgh, and writing Sacher (on commission) a Divertimento [on 'Sellinger's Round'] for chamber orchestra. Then I'm potentially doing a big choral work for Edinburgh 1955 (this *strictly* confidential) to open the Festival. Some setting of the sentiments, maybe even the words, of Pericles' funeral oration. That is to say – the Festival in the City, as the possible mirror of the humane virtues, so singularly latterly neglected. A work after your heart, I think, if I can bring it off.

I go to London again at the end of December – to hear John Minchinton's Christmas concert, *entre autres*. When will you be in London? I'd come up specially if I knew? Meanwhile – just love from
Michael
I do flourish like an improper bay tree.

1 January 1954 [after Noel Mewton-Wood's suicide]

My dear Eddy,
[. . .] Yes – it was difficult not to be despairing about Noel. Both unexpected and incongruous; so it seemed to us all. And so we none of us ever guessed or suspected such an inner violence. [. . .] What a waste! Those records become precious. The songs in any case were to the memory of a very gentle, lovely person* who went the way of Virginia Woolf, into a river.

But turning to cheerful recordings: I have heard now officially from Columbia that the Ritual Dances (Karajan–Philharmonia) is agreed on by the company – for this summer. So it will be a great send-off to the whole opera, which should come then at the crest of a wave.
à bientôt
Michael
[. . .]

* Francesca Allinson, dedicatee of *The Heart's Assurance*.

277

[early April] 1954

My dear Eddy,

[. . .] Yesterday after a Br[itish] Council meeting I was chatting with John Denison. He asked me what I thought about conductor. I had imagined this settled. But he said 'no' – that there were doubts of Pritchard's ability to handle so exacting a score. He asked me again my opinion. I stated it at once: Sacher. I said I knew Webster thought Sacher had never conducted opera. But Sacher himself, with whom I have most candid and satisfactory relations, told me later that he had done so – but that he understood quite clearly how for an English opera an English conductor might be preferred to a Swiss – though he was always at the service of the music which he thinks so highly of. And there I left it.

But Denison did not seem to wish to leave it – and asked my permission to give all this as the composer's opinion and preference. I said that I would welcome any move that he made, that I would find out and inform him exactly what Sacher's experience was, that should my luck be in and Sacher eventually assume charge, that I could guarantee Covent Garden a fine and accurate performance by a conductor who would know the work note for note months before rehearsals began, whose resource was in no doubt at all, and further I should then guarantee as successful a reception for the whole opera as was obtained for Ritual Dances at the Royal Phil. I said this all in no mood of bravado, but just as fact. Because I realise it is so. But I have never supposed that Covent Garden can arrive at such an opinion in time to obtain his services, before other commitments. Perhaps though my luck is holding. This latter part of the letter is confidential in a manner. I just have wanted *you* to know. [. . .]

Love
Michael

8 April 1954

My dear Eddy,

[. . .] I saw something which *I* think might be an alternative to [Graham] Sutherland [as designer for *The Midsummer Marriage*], if he's not tractable. I went 10 days back to watch [Barbara] Hepworth put her Whitechapel Gallery exhibition together. I was struck by a very big canvas, which was of a long 'avenue' leading straight into the background, with, on the left, a row of typical Hepworth monoliths. What caught me at first is the curious effect of looking in Sicily down or along just such a dead straight avenue of a Greek town, with one side a series of temple pediments and broken columns – and with the sky and sea in the distance. Even the colouring in the Hepworth picture was similar.

I didn't say anything at the time but thought a lot about it. For I realised that the stage *set* of *Midsummer Marriage* is an assembly, a sanctuary, of wood and stone silhouetted against the sky, and that Hepworth had caught something of this age-old but new – fresh – in the light feeling. And I've since discovered that she has done stage sets once for Old Vic. [. . .]

I have not said anything to her yet – and I don't know at all about costume capabilities. It's only that I've kind of seen a possible set there on a wall. [. . .]

M.

PS. Jochum, in Munich, did the Ritual Dances with a heavy Bruckner hand, that took or tended to take out the gaiety – and clarity – and that's what I'd be sorry for. [Schmidt-]Issterstedt monkeyed about with them at Hamburg and I had a row with him. Goehr tried to recompose them – [Hugo] Rignold, at Liverpool, did a very good job. But Sacher was just 'it'. That's all I know from experience to date. Clean, clear, accurate, and every note known and every point discussed with the author ad nauseam. Result – the best presentation of a *new* piece I have ever had. M.

13 April 1954

My dear Eddy,

[. . .] I agree with you as to Sutherland. Please do pursue him – if that is not too horrid an action. I think I just caved in and pessimistically decided he'd never agree.

Meanwhile the conductor. I think chiefly, you know, I wish it had remained settled; if indeed it ever really was. Sacher means, in any case now I should imagine, a long postponement, and that I should find terribly hard to bear, after all the years of work and waiting. I do really believe it's going to be an exciting occasion comparable, I *hope*, with the never-to-be-forgotten first night of [Peter] *Grimes*, different though it all is in temper. So, as with *Grimes*, I comfort myself that something gets through however limited the means of reproduction. i.e. *Grimes* remains in a way [*Billy*] *Budd* and *Gloriana* don't, despite the more lavish conditions. Now Covent Garden can and will do more for M.M. [*The Midsummer Marriage*] than [Sadler's] Wells could do for *Grimes*, especially if there's any sense (as there certainly and rightly was at the Wells) that it's an occasion. But Covent Garden is such a big affair, it gets bogged down, I guess, in its own administrations. Ideally we should have got beyond possible conductors and producers by now, because the better ones get booked up and need firm engagements *now*. But they won't get them out of C.G., and I doubt if it's any use anyone's fretting. I shall be so excited for the thing when it happens, and prepared to hope for every best out of whatever is finally bestowed.

But I shall be nevertheless more than pleased when decisions are really to be taken.

Love

M.

Blessings on you for your patience and help.

[July 1954]

My dear Eddy,

I've been living in opera houses – viz. Covent Garden and Glyndebourne – for a while now, and am exhausted and dead. But it's not about that I'm writing, but to tell you news of Graham Sutherland as far as we know.

[David] Webster arranged a joint meeting a few weeks back, for lunch here. It was a lovely day and all was gracious and leisured. I thought him a *most* engaging person – so that quite apart from any other motive, I enjoyed his visit exceedingly.

The talk about the opera was severe – on my side – and exhaustive. When he went, after tea, he told me he would like to do it, providing a) his own professional commitments didn't interfere unexpectedly, b) that he felt able, as it went on, to do justice to my own general conception. He said he was due away a week later, but would like to see me once more before he went. Next day I sent him a card with my few committed days – and got Schott's to send him a galley-proof of the libretto.

Meanwhile David was arranging some personal meeting at

Brighton, and for this Mrs Sutherland was to phone Covent Garden.

However, none of this happened. I did not like to be importunate, and did not try to ring him. He and she just left for Venice, and no confirmation or declination.

[. . .] I am torn between wanting to write and always preferring to leave people of his quality be. And what I really want to convey to him is only of course that I do *so* much desire the collaboration and shall be so relieved when I know it's a certainty. My impatience is solely of that kind.

Incidentally he told me that the real effective thing that swayed him was a letter from you. So I am grateful.

[. . .] It's too long in a letter to tell you of all the comings and goings as to cast for *The Midsummer Marriage*. Two names will displease you. But the male one I *had* to decide on my own, as against the alternative offered and preferred, and I must trust my judgment – and my eyes and ears. The female was shifted on to choice of her from David. Yet I think too it's right.

There is no international star *à la* Walton. David wouldn't concede it for the 'Pamina' (but a hard moralistic one) role. It's to be [Joan] Sutherland. I think, from the outside, it might have helped to go right abroad, but I don't know. Will folk feel the Tippett isn't considered so valuable because it hasn't a Magda Laszlo? Ben [Britten] never went whoring after such names. And in some ways I can accept the challenge that the M.M. has to come first forward in native dress. But if the great other Sutherland is with us, that will enormously help. One voice – Sosostris – with a huge extravagant alto aria – is uncast. No one can think of a singer! Have you or Desmond [Shawe-Taylor] names in your heads? [. . .] Maybe here a furriner?

herzlichst

M.

26 July 1954

My dear Eddy,

I seem to be letter mad! I'm sure everyone will wish I had never been born. But I'm naturally very wound up over the gradually forming cast etc – and don't wish to let anything down by lack of my own interest and attention.

I've had some 'mad' (as he says) suggestions for Sosostris from

Michael Tillett – who made the vocal score – and alone knows yet the opera as I do.

Margarete Klose
Hilde Rössl-Majdan
Martha Lipton
Marian Anderson
[Kirsten] Flagstad

The last two seem odd. But as he says, Anderson sings Sibelius and Mahler besides spirituals – and *she* would 'draw the crowds'.

Of Flagstad, he just wonders if she'd return as a disembodied voice, which now has no top, but always had wonderful low notes. But I'm still inclined to plank for [Maria von] Ilosvay.

You mustn't get any idea that I want *The Midsummer Marriage* to be thought of as in rivalry with *Troilus [and Cressida]*. Hartog rather put into my head the notion that it might look from outside as if C.G. didn't value Tippett as much as Walton. But *for myself* such considerations don't really ever enter. Objectively it's quite possible that Cressida's part has to carry most of the Walton show, and that needs a star. But as certainly M.M. needs a good cast all round (because no one is really a cipher) and as much *Vorbereitung* as I can accomplish by cajolery, force, or politics. Then to add what first-night excitement that they are all capable of.

As to the public viewpoint – I feel the only truth is simply that with Berkeley, Britten, Walton and Tippett all on the stage within 6 months, this is a season of good hope for English opera. I would have liked to get that view across to all I can. Because I believe it, subjectively and objectively. And I know you do too.

herzlichst
Michael

[late July] 1954

My dear Eddy,
To keep you absolutely informed, here is the cast to date:
Mark [Richard] Lewis
Jenifer [Joan] Sutherland
Jack [James] Johnston
Bella [Adele] Leigh
Ancients [Michael] Langdon

[Edith] Coates
King Fisher [Otakar] Kraus
Strephon (dancer) [Pirmin] Trecu (? name right and not fixed I believe)
Sosostris uncast

I hope the dancer comes off, because Strephon is a real role. And I am playing hard to have a fabulous second act, which shall have spectacle and sentiment only – and thus appeal at once without any *arrière-pensée métaphysique*! For it has only an off-stage gay chorus – Bella and Jack's love affairs – and the first 3 Ritual Dances. All to the more elaborate orchestral music so that if we have a really fine Strephon, and a good display of gauze and lighting effects for the transformations – then this act, conceived as a kind of elaborate [*Prélude à*] *L'Après-midi d'un faune*, should be as direct as of any other opera.

As to Sosostris; you will see her considerable aria from the score. What she says is, I'm afraid, a plagiarism from [Paul] Valéry 'La Pythie'. That is, a gradual movement from a kind of self-pity of her own strange fate to be woman and yet no woman – to acceptance of her pythic role, and eventual possession by the God. It's the most Verdi-like of the arias, I think myself. What you see on the stage is a huge over-lifesize veiled figure (containing of course (unknown to the audience) the divine *hierosgamos* [sacred marriage] of Mark–Jenifer *verklärt*) – whose veils wave in fantastic shapes and swirls in a surrounding night. Round the figure actually, stand the singing chorus, ready to move with the aria from a naturalistic group of young people to a more mantic Greek chorus – and beside or in front of the figure is Jack, masquerading as a bardic 'magician' in green cloak and Welsh conical hat, holding ready the white marble bowl, which when he lifts up to the figure, at Sosostris' command, will steam as though the vapours from Delphi's cleft have got into it. The actual voice should eventually almost resound from the whole stage – for when she says: I am what has been, is and shall be etc – the orchestra is let loose! Because afterwards is to come the simple line of 'You who consult me', put in E major to remind you of 'In dieser heil'gen Halle' – or whatever the German is.

Clearly – *if* I can stand pat up against David [Webster] on some fine, star singer here – then it would be a great help. And I'm really quite serious about Ilosvay. She's making the grade in Germany rapidly.

As I told you on the phone 'Covent Garden' had set its collective heart on the girl [Joan] Sutherland and it was vain to struggle. Very well, then. As Lady Bracknell once said – if we have to change both the house and the fashion then we must do it. Sutherland must be made to appear a star! Or seriously, I shall do everything in my power to *help* these singers to do what is wanted. I've already been up to hear the chorus – and to make myself known to them. And I've won over the chorus master to do all in his power to get it as good as can be. On his request, I go again in Sept., to tell them the story!!

But in the same way I shall try to get to know them all well and easily – and the same goes already for [John] Pritchard. It's not ideal – but it's professional – and terribly ready to do all in his power.

I'm still worried about producer. [Frederick] Ashton wants to do it, but may well be too committed in ballet. I know you wanted [Robert] Helpmann. But I admit I don't. I'm afraid of his pantomimic streak. I need something harder. I don't see the way round yet. The important thing for me, is to have vigour and gaiety and directness. Everyone is young – except King Fisher who is violent and rhetorical. It's vital to get the tone of youth and vigour and directness (musically stated unequivocally at the curtain of Act 1) *against* which the Ancients stand in their temple. In the great moments of *Offenbarung*, then of course everyone becomes still – 'Turn the face before the face' – but plainly and simply. I can't make this add up and come out as Helpmann. I would rather have a double-harness effort with myself and a stageman, or dramatist even. Enough, enough.

Love to you all –

M.

[late July/early August 1954]

My dear Eddy,

I was just going to send you a card to say of course Grace Hoffman is the answer [for the role of Sosostris] – when your letter came. But whether the egregious David [Webster] will do anything in time is much to be doubted. At present I'm too miserable to be of use. David sent a letter as his parting shot – sufficient to spoil any holiday I might contemplate – but my terrible answer to which he will only see when he returns.

He misreads me enough at the start of it to imagine that I really care whether Willy [Walton] has any better singers or not. Our minds just don't function on the same plane. And that is to guard himself because he says now that Kraus is too busy and will I take [Frederick] Dalberg?! We – Pritchard, Webster and I – had an arduous casting conference 10 days ago, where Kraus was exhaustively discussed because I would not have [Howell] Glynne. Now just why can't he have the common (or uncommon is it?) candour to say straight out that Kraus has too much and isn't available? That would have saved time and argument. And now he suggests Dalberg who isn't even the right voice! He's too much a bass – let alone being the wrong role. What's so depressing in it all is that after hours of explanation it's clear David hasn't taken in what King Fisher is, and is just determined to go his way sense or no sense. I can only say Eddy dear, that if he manoeuvres, as I think he will, to leave no one but Glynne, then he'll be doing the opera a great disservice. I would like you to know anyhow that I go down fighting, and that I have said not once but many times (with a copy of my last letter) that this is a disservice.

I have told him now the sensible possibilities as they stand, if he won't release Kraus from other work in order to *help* the opera. They are:

1. [Marko] Rothmüller (who is free of course, but unavailable to Covent Garden it appears for reasons of relationships: what I don't know)

2. Geraint Evans. I heard him recently as Escamillo, as the Music Teacher in *Ariadne* [*auf Naxos*], as Abbot in [Busoni's] *Arlecchino*. As the last he shows he can do a character part if pushed to it. He isn't anything like so good for me as either Kraus or Rothmüller. But clearly David isn't going to care.

For the next thing in his letter is the statement that Ashton has taken engagements elsewhere and isn't free, and so in 3 weeks he proposes to offer it to [John] Cranko! Perhaps this doesn't seem so distressing to you as it does to me. Just whether Helpmann has been approached I don't know. All I know is that I've stood out all the time from the beginning for a producer of authority and maturity and not for a second-rater. I have said that sometimes flair and gift can carry immaturity, as I think it does in Peter Brook. But Brook is taboo. But of course I have always asked for Rennert – and Rennert was willing. But in March David talked me out of Rennert in favour of Ashton – by late July he has booked up Rennert for *Tales of Hoffmann* and let Ashton go loose. So, as I said in my letter – 'We (but I meant he) have muffed it.' And as to Cranko he couldn't have chosen someone less personable to me. I happened to be at Aldeburgh when he was seeing Ben about *Grimes*. His arse-crawling just made me take very much against him. Perhaps I'm unjust. But here we go out to get someone really in the first rank like Graham Sutherland, because we know the opera to have quality, and we (or David) then thinks the producer can be a Cranko! As I've put also in the letter 'such confusion of values is beyond me'. Why not Helpmann? I suppose David's made his mind up, or just let him get signed up elsewhere. At least Helpmann is one's equal in age and experience etc. But the diddling (for so it seems to me) over Rennert makes me feel unutterably depressed. Rennert really has quality – to go his own way – to argue with me in his own right etc. Authority and imagination and *courage*. I'm too upset to be sensible. I've written David a letter, right from inside. But he won't see it for a month I presume. And he won't care. So we are going now down-hill. This I've also said to him – and that it isn't allowed in any way to depend on me.

I shall pick up the bits as best I may – and do what I can. Though how to work at all with Cranko I really don't know. Why couldn't I be given just a real theatre man with whom I could work? – and I would work too. The technically equipped is always easy to work with, if one knows what one needs. It's the young lightweight blown up into a producer on a fashion wave, that gets my goat.

I just feel I've been sold down the river. My relations with David were, till now, one of reasonable trust and confidence. Not that it would have helped if I had distrusted him. He doesn't care in the same way. I don't mean that it's personal malice. I simply mean that he can't be what he isn't.

Midsummer Marriage needed just the producer of authority and imagination and the *weight*, to match the subject – even if the young people on the stage are to appear young and vigorous and unsophisticated. The moments come when the very much deeper notes sound. Of course Graham understands. Because he is a wonderful artist – if also a fashionable one. David maybe even sees this. But then why has he not the wit to see how dangerous in such a set-up is the weak producer? I can hold up the weak conductor, by dint of great perseverance. I can't do a thing against a weak producer – though I shall try. I just feel and say to myself: what a pity!

My love to you

M.

[August 1954]
Chy-an-Goverrow, Lamorna, Penzance

My dear Eddy,

Excuse the rough and tumble paper – but rough and tumble holiday conditions!

Graham [Sutherland]'s letter makes me imagine he's *very* unlikely to retract; unless he can work M.M. sketches very quickly and easily indeed. So we mustn't entirely forget alternatives as time is getting on. I can't see that it's much use saying 'so and so has never done scenic design' if they are first-rate people – because Graham himself told me he'd only once done it before. Then too the question of abstraction shouldn't fuss us too much. [Ben] Nicholson has all the necessary talent to be representational – and you can't have an abstract temple! If he won't play, then he won't. But many wonderful artists who have had cubist phases have done lovely sets. I can't get myself frightened by labels, or we shall get nowhere. What I'm trying to do is to get some idea *for myself* as to what degree of representation is right or wrong. The talk with Graham made that quite clear. He needed the answers from the composer. So if that is so I must use my friendship with the excellent folk at St Ives at least to clear up these points by the proper process of discussion and trial.

Am home by 9 p.m. next Sat.

Yours
Michael

[1954]

My dear Eddy,

Please, please, please will you agree to do the article on *The Midsummer Marriage*, which is looming on the horizon, in *Opera*? I'm so terrified it'll get treated all wrong – e.g. 'an esoteric fantasy' (Antony Hopkins), 'all very problematic, but we shall see on the night' (some other name). There are probably problems, but I hope, hope we shall surmount them. For the people who can do it all can be counted on the index fingers of both hands, and one hand is to me invisible.

Just the sense of excitement at something possibly new and original – something not really arbitrary, but with traditional breeding – for the Quest story, the search for the precious thing to be fetched, or the thing to be seen, is maybe nearly the oldest of all.

And I would offer you anything and everything that could help – by letter, or voice, or in person.

Incidentally things are settling down wonderfully. I dare say I've bullied and bullied – but now there's a real chance of something good. [George] Harewood told me that, though I may not think so, 'no opera has ever (in C.G. [Covent Garden]) been so much discussed by so many people so far before the day'. I've hated doing this in many many ways, but it did seem necessary at the time. Now I am relieved and relaxed.

Love
Michael

[late October/early November 1954]

My dear Eddy,

You are a great dear to do it* – and I bless you for it. A libretto should have gone already to you. It's difficult for me to see, myself, all the problems because the 'story' is for me so ridiculously old and traditional that I have the firm belief it will not seem eventually so arbitrary or strange, if once the music is accepted as carrying it successfully. Not only because of the immortal *Zauberflöte*, but also because in various guises it *is* so old and tenacious – from the Argonauts and the Grail, to *Divine Comedy* and *Faust* – that it's bound to force itself through us poor suffering creators in its own time.

Incidentally, Sosostris' predicament (taken from Valéry 'La Pythie') of being permitted no womanhood, because of her divine but exhausting gift, seems to me absolutely my own (and many others') as composer. Hence I was more strangely moved in that scene than maybe at any other time. And maybe too that's why it appears to be the bit of music which has most excited Covent Garden.

I'm going to Switzerland on Monday, for a première of a Divertimento [on 'Sellinger's Round'] at Zürich, under Sacher (commissioned by him), and to have a few days complete break. But I shall also hope to hear Grace Hoffman sing 'Sosostris' on the Zürich stage to me, if she can be given leave of absence at all. Shall be back about 12–14th, and will be ready to meet you when and how you like.

Love
Michael

* The article for *Opera* mentioned in the preceding letter.

4 Dec 1955

My dear Eddy,

[. . .] Passing through Switzerland and staying a night with Paul and Maya Sacher, I found Graham [Sutherland] and Kathleen there, and the Sacher portrait at the initial sketching stage. Was a pleasant surprise. We spoke of you, and felt it was odd you had not met Sacher personally.

Lots of love, Eddy dear
Michael

1956

My dear Eddy,

[. . .] I've written one movement of the new Symphony [No. 2] – the finest allegro I've ever done, *I* think! It's somewhat different from the [Piano] Concerto – athletic and very vigorous; with powerful (2-part) lines. I'm now on movement 2 – in the poetic vein. All in all I feel so full of music that I just go on wrestling with it for all the hours a day I have strength for.

Was nice seeing Desmond [Shawe-Taylor] on Sunday morning. I realise on such occasions how I isolate myself on behalf of the music.

Much love to you, dear Eddy
Michael

Ernest Newman

Although he had no formal training in music, Ernest Newman (1868–1959) became the music critic for a variety of newspapers, including the Manchester Guardian, Birmingham Daily Post, Observer *and* Sunday Times. *Best known for his monumental* Life of Richard Wagner, *in four volumes (1928–47), he published several studies of composers (mainly late romantics) and numerous collections of essays and opera analyses. His correspondence with Tippett, while brief, shows how Tippett invited a few select individuals to act as sounding boards for his ideas about works in progress.*

12 March 1946

Dear Mr Newman,

I have just seen your article in the *Sunday Times* of March 3rd *à propos* of the good Mme Gueritte. I have not seen what you wrote further, if you did, last Sunday. I thought it just worth while getting clear my own relations to Mme Gueritte (as she seems to have used my name to you) from whom I got an effusive letter after the Britten–Purcell concert which I assisted at on November 22nd last. Her letter was of much the same tenor as the one she appears to have written you. I replied at once that I had no idea what 'liberation' of English music meant in her sense. That I esteemed Purcell because of his music, not because he was English, and because I had a great interest in Monteverdi, Schütz, Buxtehude and the whole period, of which Purcell is a shining light. I pointed out that Purcell took the English fantasy, as he explains, and taught it to be European with the aid of Italian models and that I was in sympathy with his 'manifesto'. That any opinion I might hold on Brahms (which I did not disclose anyhow to her) was arrived at by the same aesthetic, empirical test. That Lully had written an opera with a display of Italian and French technique; that Schütz had studied under [Giovanni] Gabrieli and Monteverdi and had begun the fruitful musical collaboration of the once called

Axis, which reached such a height in Mozart, whose Viennese characteristics in no way remove him thus from the tradition of German–Italian music, any more than Haydn's Croatian blood (if he had that) did for that master. That the only ground I knew to stand on now, was the necessity to work within the tradition of the whole of Europe as we generally understand it. (Whether Russian or Magyar or Bulgarian rhythms, tunes, etc are to be assimilated I can't tell. It is not my problem.) That finally I considered the dangers of provincialism, arising from chauvinistic tendencies, far greater for English musicians than eclecticism arising from a European outlook. English genius, if I may risk a generalisation, is wayward, and wide, rather than intense and severe (Shakespeare as compared with, say, Racine). Hence, if we would produce from our stock and our circumstances figures (artistically) of European standing, who, like Beethoven, Wagner, Berlioz, Mussorgsky, have spoken to the condition of us all, then we must learn, even with effort and attention of the will, to add those qualities to our waywardness, gentleness, Celtic exuberance, and 'faery', our humaneness, which will round out our natures to their full dimensions: intellectual, emotional and sensuous disciplines, whether we have to learn such from Germans, Frenchmen, Italians.

Yours Sincerely
Michael Tippett

13 June 1946

Dear Mr Newman,

You should not have bothered to type such a long letter and I did not mean to impose any explanations on you. Quite the contrary. Thank you anyhow very much for your consideration – and for your encouragement.

Schott's I gather have sent you a min. score of the Concerto [for Double String Orchestra]. I rang up just now to see whether, in view of your unfortunate eye trouble, they could not better spare you one of the printed full scores. There are less of these of course – but I have settled it that if you should rather have one they will send you one most willingly on request.

As to the Symphony [No. 1] – actually the MS is a very good copyist's hand and photo-printed. But meanwhile the score is being slowly engraved and will eventually appear. The MS original went off to the engraver last Nov. – but as Schott's have no printers etc here (they were, and are, all at Mainz) they have to wait on everyone else's convenience – so Nov. means nothing. However – [Walter] Goehr and I have decided to risk the invidiousness of putting a big work of my own in next season's Morley programmes and propose to repeat the symphony next March!! along with Purcell and Monteverdi probably. But this is also to ensure that the min. score will be available for previous study and which will help a lot. So, unless some other organisation propose to do a performance earlier (broadcast *par exemple*) then I suggest you let Schott's let you know in time for such an eventuality and send you one of the photostat scores then. I don't like the idea of your using your eyes too much now.

I am going to conduct the Double Concerto [Concerto for Double String Orchestra] myself with the LPO [London Philharmonic Orchestra] at the Stoll Theatre on Jun. 30 and again at Cheltenham on July 5, where it will have a Midland Region broadcast. It is also due from Hilversum on June 25 and Beromünster (Scherchen) on June 21. Can you get their station because I could probably run the exact time to earth: to mix the metaphors.

Our trouble with concerts' days is mainly the Hall and the orchestra and the artists and the conductors. It usually comes down to such and such a day take it or leave it. The July 5, Friday is of course designed to be as close as may be to the Int. Festival one. We are doing at St Cecilia's Day festival Purcell next Nov. 22 at Central Hall and the Saint is responsible for another Friday.

A quite different matter. I am very slowly (after years of cogitation) sketching out a libretto for an 'opera' [*The Midsummer Marriage*]. I put the word in quotes because the genre is rather that of *Zauberflöte* and so a mixture of pantomime, Aristophanic comedy (as conceived by Cornford)* and ritualism. A dangerous mixture. It's a sort of complement to the dark, over-compassionate score of *Child of Our Time*, which I have got to give forth whether I will or not. I think I'd like to take a risk and send you later on the unfinished, I mean unpolished, text.

(Here I must interject on myself that I had no intention of writing such a colossal letter, and my handwriting is appalling and I can't type.)

* Francis Macdonald Cornford, *The Origin of Attic Comedy* (1914).

Wagner's advice on how to construct a big-scale opera seems to me to be definitive. I could not move till I had, accidentally, come across it, though at second hand. But I have deliberately turned from the sung drama to a stylised type of stage musical work because I judge it necessary at this time, and certainly a sine qua non of my own schemes.

However that can all keep till I can get to London to a secretary and write you, if at all, by type.

Yours Sincerely
Michael Tippett

5 September 1946

Dear Mr Newman,

I have been meaning to write to you, but waited always in the hope that one of the Symphony [No. 1] scores would come from the binder so that I could fulfil my promise to you regarding the work. Meanwhile the proofs of the first movement have come, and I am correcting them, and I think it won't be very long before it will all be engraved in full score and then that will be so much better for your eyes that it is worth waiting a bit longer.

A Child of Our Time is being broadcast by the Germans from Hamburg tomorrow Friday night at 7 p.m. on 332 m. (904 kc/s). It will be done in German and I hope and believe very well. I wasn't given permission to go over. *Aber es hat mir nicht viel Leid drauf getan!* [But I didn't much mind about that.] Hamburg is not very pleasant either for the conquerors or the conquered. I read your articles about Ben Britten's [*The Rape of*] *Lucretia* with great interest. This libretto question exercises me now indeed a great deal. I have sketched out the details of the stage action, of the work I propose to write [*The Midsummer Marriage*], and it has been thought out as far as I can operatically rather than merely dramatically: if that makes sense to you. It has, I mean, a 'sound' pattern as well as an 'action' and a 'thought' pattern. But some of the technical problems still baulk me badly. I may have to resort to *Singspiel*, in the sense of a complete break in the music for dialogue, rather than recitative or an attempt to draw 'up' the dialogue, or more argumentative parts of the opera, to the level of the higher flights. Anyhow I shall have a shot at putting down some sort of continuous words with indications of how they are to be treated and that I shall have to take advice on.

I am just finishing a 3rd 4tet which will come out at the Wigmore on Sat. afternoon Oct. 19th and be broadcast on the C[ontinental] programme on Oct. 29 some time.

I do very much hope you are better. It is most distressing to think of you so troubled.

Yours Sincerely
Michael Tippett

11 September 1946

Dear Mr Newman,

[. . .] If I may offer you advice, to one so *erfahren* as yourself, in return for all you have written me – it is that ailments I'm sure are organic as well as particular. I mean that proper holidays, in the joyous, carefree sense, as well as physical recuperation, are also a real regimen. Even the eyes take a turn for the better. Leastways that is my experience, precisely about those sensitive organs.

I am meanwhile more than grateful for the wise words about opera. Actually I had only since I wrote you moved away again from spoken words. I have been rereading the 1st act of *Fidelio* and was struck by the amount of incoherence produced by the speech, the breaks in the music – and on the other hand impressed by the power of the coherence when he used dramatic scene and recitative. So I am probably going to try to have a shot at a solution (though necessarily not markedly successful I dare say) rather than an evasion.

In some ways, what I want to do makes it more difficult, though easier in some other directions. I have had to 'reach back' to the more formal categories in order to articulate the business at all. Partly because I know I have to work through that way, and partly because the pantomimic element in the stuff I am working with has started by an appearance of *Singspiel*. It is only now, as I go over and over the 'stuff', that I can begin to conceive of the problem as of transition. I am well aware of this point. I talked a lot with [T. S.] Eliot about it once, because he has been preoccupied with something similar – e.g. language which could rise from colloquialisms to the poetic apparatus for allowing us a stage vision of the Eumenides. It is just this which I have to grapple with, and it is the colloquialisms that are the present troubles.

Further – I have conceived a rather quicker tempo of stage incident.

So the transitions – as often in my own more symphonic music – need to be quick as well as (I hope) joltless. So – I have found that the first step has been an articulation of operatic machine, a sort of clear consciousness (which I did not posses a priori) of functions, e.g. recitative, aria, ensemble. While this was going on, there was little possibility of imagining any deviations, but only clearer and sharper divisions. Hence, even now, I can't plunge into Wagner for example, because I can only come at the *idem in alio* by almost deliberate avoidance of the one solution. But I am going to look now at *Die Frau ohne Schatten*, because I am told that [Richard] Strauss and [Hugo von] Hofmannsthal made some approach to some problems peculiar to the sort of ideas that have been gradually taking, at least, gesture, action and character in my head.

This question of 'setting words' must I think be of such difficulty for me. I remember how in *A Child of Our Time* I found with pleasure that the rhythms of the words I had invented were specially suitable to the music. That indeed I had the music unconsciously there subliminally when 'discharging', as it happened, the word pattern. I am hoping and believing that something of the sort will come again. In fact, I more or less know it will. What makes me quail is rather the greater degree of purely literary imaginative resource required for this newer venture. Yet – as it appears to me now, I am forced to proceed in this way and to take the plunge myself.

For the *Child of Our Time* there was a lot of polishing of the text with advice from a great many different sorts of people because I sought a poetical 'deposit' – a sort of common denominator – except for those few chosen moments when I deliberately left that plane for a record of individual, more *innerlich* experience, which could not be so reduced without caricature.

I know I shall have to do the same sort of things now again, when I have made a first draft. I fancy the eventual opera itself may show too many traces of the articulatory period to be quite satisfactory to you. But that I think is to be expected. I am not supposing I have the power to solve the problem at all. I am rather aware of the need to clarify for the purpose of later, more integrated efforts. I have almost contradictory sympathies to *Wozzeck* on one side and *Porgy and Bess* on the other. In this wretched opera of mine I am deliberately separating experience and characters into a form of 'higher' and 'lower' as happens between Tamino and Papageno *zum Beispiel*. And there are other 'castes' than these to be handled. It all takes a 'helluva' time to digest. But either I have a shot at it, seeing that is how my own odd mind works, or I do not all. And certainly I shall.

Yours Sincerely
Michael Tippett

13 November 1947 ['/49' added in binding]

Dear Mr Newman,

[. . .] I am deep in my opera now [*The Midsummer Marriage*]. I find that having laid down a libretto scheme, with even words to read like one, and with of course careful consideration of the musical layout, that now the music of each scene requires an alteration of the details of the words because so often the mere writing down of a sort of libretto has produced a sort of 'play' texture, which won't disappear nicely with the flow of the music, and further that the word rhythms one invents in this haphazard libretto stretching are too repetitive and banal, and effectively hamper the musical imagination unless readily changed and reinvented as we go. So that, while I'm not much changing the strategic design, the tactical design is having to be the clearest and most unequivocal imagination of music and words together. It's laborious, difficult, but fascinating. Would it interest you later to see an act when completed? (I compose always onto full score.) It would not be till late spring – and this is no offer to be lightly accepted! Think of your eyes and wait upon a proper première.

Yours Sincerely,
Michael Tippett

20 June 1948

Dear Mr Newman,

I have been away in Hungary and only just seen your recent articles on 'Making of an Opera'. I must thank you for both of them. They were fascinatingly interesting to me.

There's a small personal point I am writing about in this letter. In fact I agree with your estimate of Stanford's opera [*The Travelling Companion*]. I introduced it for I'm afraid subjective, emotional reasons. I had been annoyed by the tone of a circular from my friend Britten, appealing for the English Opera Group, which seemed to imply that until his and my generation (or till *Peter Grimes*) there had been no English opera. This seemed to me to fail to distinguish between the success of *Grimes* here and abroad and a just estimate of all that our forebears have attempted. So that I decided to take Stanford, example of a period which in general my generation turns its back on, and show that in my own 'history' I must, in honesty, recognise how much I have been influenced by the sounds of his English setting. Also of Sullivan, of course, and probably [Hubert] Parry. I should have liked, had there been time, to show that English 'patter', shall we say, has a certain unmistakable tone that is both in Parry's cantatas e.g. *Pied Piper of Hamelin* and *Grimes* e.g. first scene in the court. My fastidiousness in manners made me drag in this matter, which was not really fundamental to the talk – and did, I'm sorry to say, cut out hereby a discussion of what *Die Oper und das Wesen der Musik* had taught me. But one can never get everything into an hour's talk, and I have read and pondered too much about the operatic problem in the last years to be able to digest it all into a perfect quintessence, partly of course too because I am still in the practice of the theory.

I have (in my opera text) reduced the verbal statement to the minimum, eschewing 'imagery and similes' and trying to avoid unintelligibility when that has to be accepted. I mean, by taking account of purely technical hindrances. But I fall down on not being able to use the orchestra so frankly as Wagner, to help dissolve the words. I believe, even, that my passion for correct English accentuation adds to the difficulties, because trochaic words like 'bitter', 'little', 'open' (from really hard to softer) if set as such must tend to break the musical line, and I haven't Purcell's genius to cover them always successfully. But the other way, of disregarding the English accent, I'm unable to go. It offends my literary ear too sharply. (I have to use pure vocalise on simple vowel ejaculations, to help the line – and sometimes of course, in more lyrical moments, vocalisation on open vowels in the better-suited words.)

What is interesting is that as I proceed (very slowly) I am forced to abandon the 'speech in song' for the Italian trick of speech superimposed on orchestra line. This of course only suits a light, gay speech and situation. And means, as you can easily see, that I am narrowing down the speech-in-song to as few scena as I can, and very carefully sandwiching these between full ensembles or lyrical songs.

My chief danger, I know, or think I know, is that I have left romantic verismo (whether foreign or native) for the example of *Zauberflöte*.

I expect I've read too much Goethe! But as that is my own tradition, I have to take myself as best I may. The great excitement is managing (or mismanaging!) the transitions. The chorus begins naturalistically, and only at two big moments (the two Agon) goes over into manic behaviour, when (as I learn to see from Nietzsche) the 'drama' seems like a projection of the choric imagination. I am just coming to the first of these now. Whether I shall succeed at all, as you say, 'we can only wait and see'.

I imagine you understand that I really only write to discharge myself of some of the emotions excited by this whole matter, and because I know of so few people who have any sympathy or knowledge of what is going on in me at this present time. I get a kind of reflex encouragement by writing to someone as informed and intelligent and generally sympathetic as yourself. But I apologise for doing so.

Yours Sincerely,
Michael Tippett

22 July 1948

Please do not think me too egotistical if I say that it did me at any rate a lot of good to know that others have a like prostration after work. My own experience, for what it is worth, is that it just has to be endured, and that to stir it up courts a much more fatal collapse. Even a cabbage may I'm sure become a cauliflower in one's dream inner world.

Yours Sincerely,
Michael Tippett

Evelyn Maude

Tippett met the Maude family when he moved to Oxted after finishing his studies at the Royal College of Music. Evelyn Maude (c.1895–?) helped him find his first home, a cottage at Hazelwood Preparatory School, where he was employed to teach French and to play the organ for services. Her husband John Maude, who as Permanent Secretary in the Ministry of Health later helped establish the National Health Service, played the cello in the amateur orchestra of the Oxted and Limpsfield Players. Their son was a pupil at Hazelwood, and Tippett was godfather to their daughter Stella, who later worked as secretary to the theatre director Peter Brook. The four letters addressed to Evelyn Maude were written while Tippett was in Wormwood Scrubs. During this time he was allowed to write only in reply to letters from an official contact of his own choosing. These letters have been published in his autobiography, Those Twentieth Century Blues, *and in the 1977 exhibition catalogue* A Man of Our Time: Michael Tippett. *I have included them here to show them in the broader context of Tippett's correspondence. Evelyn Maude is the dedicatee of the Piano Concerto.*

21 June 1943

Evelyn dear –

   No letters allowed except an answer to each one I send out – every fortnight. Write V.W. [Vaughan Williams] if you will and thank him from me. If the *Surrey Mirror* has a write-up of his evidence let John [Amis] have a copy to show Schott's, Boult etc. Ring [Phyllis] Sellick and wish her luck for Sat. and July 4. Tell John to wish Tony [Hopkins] luck for his Prom July 7. Cis Bennet will contribute to the case if you write. Tell John to get the message about Eric Mason's Appellate from Peter [Pears], and to tell him and Ben [Britten] to give their recital to us as soon as possible. Send a message of encouragement to the good Rose [Turnbull?]. Visitors will be in a month. Would like to see John and the [name omitted]. I suppose Den [Newton] and Tony would talk same language. If not, David [Ayerst], Fresca [Allinson], Ben, you? As to holiday – it seems I shall be out Aug. 21st all being well – early morning. If John can wait I suppose it would be nice to have a week in Cornwall with the 'children', and possibly some time with David after. Otherwise shall be rampaging to get back to work. It'll be a desire to be with one's own again and perhaps a need for fresh air. Please send me in as books – *Art of Fugue* (on the piano), *War and Peace* – any good work on astrology – the Cornford* etc – 2 or so at a time, the sooner the better. I think I can have up to four at once – but I'll let you know how it goes next letter. They remain in the prison library. Shall want if possible 3 or 4 more Gillette-shape razor-blades. My father would spare some I think. Came from Oxted chained to the young soldier whose case we heard first, and with one of the lads who stole the rabbits. Wasn't that curious? It's rather like the first days of term before the days begin to move. In the good mood it's rejoicing, it is – as you can tell everyone – comradeship, peace and a full heart. On the recoil it's somewhat of a waste, negative and like being unwell in a foreign hotel.

On second thoughts tell John as to the various plans suggested at Eric Mason's Appellate etc that they're better left – and in general not to worry about me – this includes the visit of Mrs Mason. John will understand, and tell him straight away. It is only gradually that one takes on the new life. Write straight away if you can. I'll get it quickly then.

Tomorrow is Quaker meeting which I look forward to. There's also a baby orchestra I hope to be allowed some time to help on its way.

Love,
Michael

5 July 1943

Evelyn dear –

Your letter was a great pleasure to get. I will reply to its contents first. Books – I got the 2 Devotional books, but haven't yet read them. In fact I read little. Cell task occupies a lot of time, and there is a baby prisoners' orchestra here which I conduct and try to improve – and that takes 2 hours out of possible reading time. It's a sort of light café

* Francis Macdonald Cornford, *The Origin of Attic Comedy* (1914).

orchestra, and with instruments all of different pitch – in fact throw-outs. But we manage – and I hope to get in better music. On Sunday we are to play in chapel, in the middle of a recital by Peter Pears and Ben Britten – all very amusing. So don't worry to chase after books. But there is a text-book I'd like (I've got the Bach) – will you ring Alec Robertson and ask him from me if he could spare me a copy of his book: *The Problem of Plainsong** – on the art of which he is an authority. If and when you get it, take it to Friends' House as you did the Bach. I shouldn't send the Cornford just yet.

Tell Mother if you're writing any time, not to wonder at the letters about me to her – I'm sort of a general favourite. As to getting down there, I might manage after the proper holiday on way back from Cornwall if it's to be there – otherwise I think to write the long delayed 1st movement of the old 4tet [String Quartet No. 1] and then take another break away, at Exmouth perhaps, and then start the Symphony [No. 1] – which will be a big thing.

I agree with you completely about press hoo-ha – no interested party should write at all.

Holiday – I'm quite as ready to go with David [Ayerst] first. The point is anyhow that I come out Sat. 21st Aug. and will make the 4tet performance at Wigmore [String Quartet No. 2] the public meeting ground for all and sundry. Rose [Turnbull?], choirs etc – then come home and get things together etc Sunday.

The question of my getting something from people, like books, is difficult. I don't know for instance how much I really get from David – sometimes I'm rather repressed by him. I get a great deal from you – but that is a more subtle business, and in this case must wait till I'm properly home and at work again.

Keep the Hölderlin, [Jacques] Maritain etc – they're for my library and the autumn.

Haven't read any Paul [Goodman] yet. It hasn't worked out quite as I expected. One gets not only fallow but sluggish. We're all the same. You can't manufacture the proper conditions and there's a lot of internal strain – a great deal of dreaming and inner adjustment – and the weeks inside seem monstrously lengthy and disproportionate, so that you fail to realise how easily they pass to those outside or how little one might oneself get done outside.

* Correctly *The Interpretation of Plainchant: A Preliminary Study* (1937).

As far as I know there is nothing against length in letters in. Write on thin paper perhaps. You might send some 18- or 20-stave score – a few sheets – with the Robertson book. I shall probably get permission to use it. But 12-stave will do, if the other is too big.

And now messages: a special one this time to Ben and Miriam [Lewis], who use after all my home and my own. Tell Miriam to use the tin of sugar in the larder which Den [Newton] gave me, for jam. I shall have forgotten the taste by the time I come out. I have already. Is anyone in the cottage yet?

A message of greeting to the choirs; 1o [first] Tolworth (book under T.): hope they're managing. Write if you will to the deputy Tanner – and say he must choose music to suit himself – and that I shall probably take at least September clear away for my own work – (if not give the choir up altogether). Ask to pay for those times he deputised for which I signed the register – and generally to try and solve the payments, claims problems of that choir, via the Sec. of the WEA [Workers' Educational Association]. It is done terminally, and so quite soon. 2o [second] Tooting (under T.) Just send them greetings, either via Tony [Hopkins] or the Sec. Will see them again next term of course.

Morley. Give them best wishes for the concert on the 17th, and hope they do well. Will be thinking of them. You can let them know sometime that I shall make my first reappearance on 21st Aug. at Wigmore.

Fresca: Give her my love – tell her I'm managing fine – that I came across a typical Irish ABBA tune in *Songs of Praise* masquerading as English Traditional Melody. If she thinks to come to the 4tet on the 21st, would like to lunch with her beforehand, and go with.

If this gets you in time ring Peter and Ben, Primrose 5826, and wish Ben well for his Prom on Sat. evening – and tell them not to be distressed by the 'orchestra' in Handel's 'Largo' and Bach's Chorale on Sunday. It's for the sake of social progressiveness, not to rival their artistry. If they're still at home on the 21st would like to breakfast with them and bath.

John Amis: Not to forget 6 tickets for Tooting choir via Tony for 17th – and if to spare send a couple to Wilf Franks c/o 45 Holmesdale Rd, N6. To send my love to the two Walters: to Goehr, not to worry about the 17th, but that he'll probably gain by all the publicity – and good luck to him and it. To Bergmann my love – and could he possibly begin to look at the printed church music of Weelkes for Morley next session. I think 'Absalom, my son', or some such title, a very fine one. To Schott's in general, Cheminant and Steffens my regards and good wishes. John can do all that. As to visit: the order is due on Mon. 19th, but it probably won't reach John till 21st or 22nd. It will have 3 names on it: his, Tony's and Britten's (?) – is that OK? Otherwise we must invent. All the 3 come together – 2.30 at the prison is a good time. You take a no. 7 bus from Oxford Circus to the door (1/2 an hour) or Central London to Wood Lane, 11/2d trolley bus a minute or two to Du Cane Avenue, and walk down 2 or 300 yds. Quite quick. Ring the bell and ask to see me and show the order. Should like to see read to me any press notices etc.

As to the [2nd] 4tet movement (please keep these notes): I think the 2nd subject needs a longish bit (B) and the repeat of A to lead straight to the constricted portion: perhaps by using some of the old material to reach the same chord before cello up-going cadenza as before – then a possibly contrapuntal development of which the reprise of the opening themes will form the climax – and a recapitulation as varied as the material allows and leading by the same coda material to the down-going cello cadenza.

So far I've only had this one 'thought' about my music, as above: I don't think it's any good trying to make things move when the circumstances forbid any real output or creation. Prison is not a creative experience at any point – except perhaps in human contacts. I dare say it will seem less wasteful when one looks back – perhaps it may be a real holiday mentally. It's difficult inside not to give exaggerated importance to its actual length of days – and to brood on them so that they go slower. In fact I am pretty active and the time passes somehow.

Razor blades – we are allowed to change the permitted one each week. I have 4 only in 'property' – if you post some more (not with your answer) to me, they'll just be put with the rest and I can either use them or bring them home. I like to keep shaven and as clean as may be. It's better for one's self-respect. Any blades that fit a Gillette – 3-hole type – or slots.

I've experienced a lucky chance with eye-exercises that may be helpful afterwards. It's very hard on the eyes here. Sewing etc, and a bad light in the cell and little time to exercise at all. I shall just about manage to keep them no worse than they are.

One has moments of nostalgia, but not too many. I shall come through. It's boring of course. It is good to know things happen out-side. Much love to all friends – and especially to you.

Michael

I dreamed of a green flowering olive tree in spring last night. Good.

19 July 1943

Evelyn dearest:

Have been hurrying up my cell task so as to be able to write at leisure. I sent off the visiting order with the one envelope, so this may be delayed while I get hold of another. I'd better answer your letter first. Tell Morley if still going that I got their messages and thought of them hard at 6 p.m. last Saturday. And will you ask Miss Cowles there what the date of next term is – because it may curtail the holiday away to 10 days. I'll come back on this.

Please write [A. L.] Rowse – say I am so glad to hear he's written, I will look forward to reading the letter when I come out. Sorry he's been ill again. Tell him plans to be at Portloe and shall I look him up on way back. Does he know off-hand a pub, hotel, that would break-fast the 5 of us on Sunday, 22nd, at St Austell. When I come to holi-day you'll understand why.

Betty Hamilton leave.

D[itt]o the Greenwoods and others, but tell John Allen if you think fit where I am obtainable when I'm out.

Holiday: I'll write it you, though I intend to ask John [Amis] to do the trains etc on visit. But you can never be sure of anything in prison! If the Sat. night train is OK, we shall go to St Austell and bus to Mevagissey – John must check the Sunday buses: we need to be at Mevagissey by lunchtime (I believe it gets in at 1.30 or so) and there-fore take food for Sun., and walk along the coast to Portloe getting in to tea: though it's a good step. If this won't work we must go to Truro and walk over Malpas ferry and Lamorran woods. J. needs to get £10 out of Britten (?) in cash for me: get tickets for Den [Newton] and myself and let me have the change. The ration book etc I would have to get you to do and send after me. It may be rather rash to plan so hasty a departure: but it feels good. I'm hoping that a day's good food will recover me: I'm as weak as a kitten: and we shall have to carry packs. If John has no pack he can share mine: or have you a Bergen of Evan's [Evelyn Maude's son]? I don't see how I can be away more than

2 weeks at the most because of the Fanfare [No. 1, for brass] for the church [St Matthew's, Northampton]. If Morley first do is Thurs. 2nd Sept., then I'd better be back for it and so home. You'd better settle this and warn David [Ayerst].

I suggest you advise Mother of the fanfare commission, and that I will come 1 night to Exmouth to see them, or 2 if possible: and put off the real visit to October. It would be advisable therefore for D. and Larema [Ayerst] to be away already so that I can go there on Monday the 30th. But it won't be for long if Morley is open. Otherwise I would like to get home by Sat. 4th *for certain*. If Rowse suggests that we all breakfast with him, then I could cut a visit there on the return and travel to David on the Sunday. But if Morley is not opening till the 6th Sept., then I'd enjoy a night at Rowse's, Sun. 29, some days with D. and L. and 2 nights at Exmouth and travel home morning train Sat. I'll write you next time the clothes I would want in the pack – apart from a pair of flannels and a jacket to replace the suit I've got here, and will wear at the Wigmore. I think, by the way, it might be worth putting a nicely worded advert in P.N. [*Peace News*] for the Aug. 14th issue, that I am coming out all being well, and hope to be present at W.H. at the perf. of the 2nd 4tet in order to do Cooper a possible fillip for his concert. Or is this too publicity-like? I think actually the CBCO [Central Board for Conscientious Objectors] would put it under their notes. I'm hoping in any case to make it an occasion of public return, so that the more it's broadcast around the better.

Tell Mother also that I'm so pleased to hear of my nephew John's successful operations.

Cornford was a book I meant to buy so don't worry. Will be glad of the Robertson I think. Ring him and thank him if you will and give him a cheerful message from me: he's a very nice chap.

If you have time write a note to Emily Borner, Fred May's sister, and give her a kind message and say I'm so glad to hear Fred is joining the hospital staff. Hope to see her at W.H. on 21st.

When writing to Mother tell her I wrote Phyl [Kemp] before I came in, but no reply.

What you wrote about 'endless patches of time' was extraordinarily helpful. I do believe in it, and it gives strength to endure the apparent wastage. (Incidentally the Symphony [No. 1] is gestating alright, almost consciously. I shall have the whole form mapped out in my mind by the time I come out. It's going to be a big thing.) I am only really close to you, B.B. [Britten] and John Amis – no one else. And while John is simply a projection of my musical self and therefore often in my mind, Ben is very near, just because he is himself, I sense, so moved by my imprisonment. You of course are something almost eternal!! and the closeness is more to be expected. Everyone else is nowhere. The concert here was a terrific success, and to be next him at the piano was absurdly deep-going. The orchestra did not function. I'll tell you all the story sometime. I haven't been to practise this week either. It matters not, except where I can be of service. The 'library' is musical comedy selections and very tiring. Later this week I go on 'association' as it is called, and have meals at tables in community, and move to another cell – the Upper School! and that marks my exact half-way, which will seem better afterwards I think.

Could you get me a fresh tin of Calverts tooth-*powder*, and send in for me.

I have my specs in fact – but the truth is that the strain of the eyes is very great, and I shall have to do exercises in all seriousness this autumn to try and undo the damage.

You might suggest to Fresca, if she is still at Mill House, that she bottles a few things, extra, for me. I shall be sorely in need of that sort of food, at suppers and so on – and generally the Allinsons have quantities. I want to try and get a better supper arrangement for a bit anyhow to try and feed myself up – I'm very thin and long – if not haggard!

Fresca has the Irish Folk-Song Journals.

Would like you to cheer Steffens up if you see a way. I can't help feeling that wrongly or rightly, the publicity has done good not only to the cause but to the music – and he need have no fear. And please write Hugo – 2nd Lt H. Strecker, c/o Schott's – and give him my love and good wishes and tell him I'm gay and surviving brooding on a smashing symphony: and give him news of the various nice things said by V.W. [Vaughan Williams] etc.

Would like you to ask Rose [Turnbull?] if she managed to get any of Cooper's handbills for 7th and 21st to send out – and to get them via John if not.

You will let me know of course about Pam's [Evelyn's daughter] new babe, when and what sex and name. Very pleased about Gillian [Maude].

You know the thought of your being whisked to Oxford is somewhat shattering. I can't quite imagine what becomes of the cottage without you nearby. I am not in the least ready for such an eventuality – oh dear. But we won't cross the bridge before we reach it.

Wish I could have seen the ceanothus and the jasmine. But will next year. What they want if La[rema] can manage – is good earth fetched to them from elsewhere because they are really bedded on the clay foundations of the house and with no proper soil except what is brought them. I'm sure she'd do it if you explain.

The MS [music manuscript paper] has come, but I haven't applied to have it yet. I just brood mentally on the symphony – and have the plan for the Fanfare [No. 1, for brass]. Would like to know the exact date required, if you could ask Ben.

If I apply to get my next visit (due in my last week) put ahead, would it amuse you to come and see me in my prison clothes and I'll send the letter to Mother, say?? (This must not interfere with meeting me at 7.30 on the day. You'd better come and breakfast at Ben's too.) It won't be worth seeing the others really, as I should see them all a day or two later in freedom.

Please get the watch and bring for the holiday.

All in all, my dear, I am *very* close to you and your letter is a great excitement when it comes. It's all very dreamlike – as indeed freedom often is to me. But here it's stronger. I, actually in prison, sense something so natural and yet so like a dream existence. That's enhanced, you see, by not feeling or being a criminal. I got terribly excited on Sat., the 17th, thinking of the music outside. And there are whole days of impatience – days also of boredom. Wonderful moments like the hundreds of men's voices singing the Old Hundredth – and that brings tears. One is rather emotional, naturally: and fearfully self-conscious. We all are. That takes a bit of time to go afterwards I believe. Quaker meeting means a lot. One is also closer to the spirit in here, by the act of cutting off. I've never felt it more strongly, though I can't as yet go the violent ascetic way – but I have sense of clearing the grossness by means of which the spirit shines clearer through one – it may affect the music, I think; gradually. And I think the Symphony [No. 1] may gain by this enforced rest. I'm pretty certain of it itself anyhow, and think I shall pull it off. But I've decided to get the 4tet movement [revisions to String Quartet No. 1] done first. Give my love to all and at this moment I am at peace – god bless you.

Michael

15 August 1943

Evelyn dearest –

At last the final letter and few days to go. Am ever so sorry to hear of your pneumonia and hope indeed it is as slight as you suggest and that it was in the nature of a rest and that you're back now at home. John [Amis] on visit last Thursday told me you were still in hospital then. Shall be so delighted if you're at the gate on Sat., but I don't know how sensible an early rise will be for you, and if you can't come will you let Britten know – if you still feel I ought to be met by someone – failing B.B. – John would be preferable. For you to get here you go from Chiswick by tram or bus to Hammersmith or Shepherd's Bush and get on the north-going trolley buses, which go from the former to the latter and on to Wood Lane Und[erground] Stn at the White City and then next stop or so is Du Cane Avenue – you ask for that – straight along the road about 1/4 of a mile. I believe it's 7.30 to 7.45 or so, release – but will wait for you. If Ben B. is to come his quickest way, other than cross-going taxi – is tube via Oxford Circus to Wood Lane, trolley bus to Du Cane – (2 stops?).

Hope John gave you message to add my leather belt to the clothes list – and the watch. Now about my final and proper homecoming. I'm so impatient for the cottage and work that I am not staying away longer than I planned, but will definitely travel up from Taunton (and David [Ayerst]) on Thurs. Sept. 2nd, and try and get the 2.30 down from Victoria. Perhaps you could meet at the Halt – 3.35 or so – and come over to tea. And bring some margarine if you could as I may not have much rations after sharing between Mother and David's mother – and the week-end to go. And ask Miriam [Lewis] if she could keep me some eggs for the week-end for suppers and then we can start normally the following week. Give my love to Miriam and say I'm dying to be *home*, and that even Cornwall is only necessity and good sense. And let us all pray that I shall be left in peace now, because I'm so full of music. Also, Felix Aprahamian, who came with John and Bergmann on visit, wanted to pencil the LPO [London Philharmonic Orchestra] for the first perf. of the Symphony [No. 1], subject to publisher's approval – and for the spring! Well – they will have to wait. Yet it's great fun to have offers through the glass window of visiting box! and shows how the publicity and performances are beginning to tell.

John told me the Morley choir, who will earn 20 gns from BBC for the Seiber recording, want me to have the balance after singers' expenses etc, for my holiday. Isn't that a nice gesture? So we can all have a good time – and excursions across the Fal by ferry and such cheerful holidayish items.

I've written Mother about Rose [Turnbull?] – just to tell her that of course I'll go to Exmouth whichever way it goes, but that in fact it will prevent any real family intimacy, and put me on edge – and after 9 weeks imprisonment, quite the worst thing for Rose, or me. She had better face up to the fact that she will just spoil my (and her) home-coming – for the old usual mother-ish moral reasons which spoilt so much of childhood. I had a fearsome, but illuminating, dream on that a night past. It must have been quite the most decisive emotional influence of my upbringing. It's as well to attempt to assimilate it now that the possibility has arrived at looking at it dispassionately, as far as the personalities are concerned.

I don't think I've quite reached the point of being ready for memories and their refreshment – except occasionally. But I anticipate it. As yet, it's still plans and the future – only not in so youthful a manner or matter. The music particularly is fairly concrete and serious – though apparently much more ahead to be done than already created. That won't alter for a year or more – and a fair number of good launchings, like the oratorio [*A Child of Our Time*].

Bergmann told me by the way that he's nearly completed the first reading of the proofs. So that goes forward and will be out in the autumn – a good time. Meanwhile I hope to get Steffens to print the *Boyhood's End* – which had good reviews, and unexpected ones.

Sept. 11th at Morley is a Bergmann concert – choir is not till Oct. 16th (Weelkes). Though that means a lot of work already. Mrs [Eva] Hubback rather jockeyed me (or I did myself) into giving Wed. evenings to a Morley orchestra – but since then I've given a message to John at visit to try and keep it at bay – at least for the beginning of term. I just must write and everything else must and will have to wait. The November concert B.B. refers to is a proposed Britten–Tippett do, 1/2 financed by LPO lot. Clifford Curzon to play my Sonata [Piano Sonata No. 1], and 2-pf. work of Britten's with him – P.P. [Peter Pears] to sing [Britten's *Seven Sonnets of*] *Michelangelo* and *Boyhood's End* – perhaps also something else of Britten's. A nice show? I gather that [Alfred] Kalmus is toying with letting Goehr repeat the Double Concerto [Concerto for Double String Orchestra] at a Boosey &

Hawkes concert – I do hope it comes off. Sellick is down to play the Sonata at Nat. Gallery on Sept. 21 or 22: forgotten which. So things are not too bad – and John decided to begin negotiations with Bliss to redeem his promise and do the Fantasia [on a Theme of Handel] broadcast after the Prom season.

Yes, perhaps it's better I breakfast with Peter and Ben *à trois*. And lunch? It looks like a crowd, and not really your crowd. I fancy if you can but make the early morning that's nicer and then tea on Thurs. Sept. 2nd in our proper surroundings. Oh, that will be a good day.

As I feel now, I'll go to Mother's on Sunday 29th – move to David at Taunton on Tuesday afternoon 31st – and leave the same on the Thursday morning – two nights at each of them – and the Wed. David can plan an expedition. He will think I ought to take more holiday as I can, but he can't have it. I know that after 10 days of holiday and differing company, decent clean food and fresh air, I shall be champing to get back and let out the dammed-up stream of sound. First the Fanfare for Brass [Fanfare No. 1] – then the 4tet movement – then a short break and revisit Exmouth probably – *hoffentlich* all this by mid-October – and then the real thing – the new symphony which is very much getting up steam.

As this letter tells you, I'm already living outside the prison – I try not to get in a fever – but occasionally I do; though not for long or seriously. By the time this gets [to] you, if it does in time, the thing will be virtually over – and I have little wish to repeat it – but of course will do so if driven.

Have made some very good friends and seen a great slice of life so to speak. Extraordinarily childlike, if not frankly childish. But all of a piece with the army, factory life and all other mass phenomena. We are indeed 'such stuff as dreams are made of [*sic*]' – I become more drawn to Shakespeare and his viewpoint – only in another age's setting.

Love to you, my dear, and perhaps will see you Sat.
Michael

Covent Garden Collection

The collection of letters to Covent Garden is addressed primarily to David Webster (1903–71), to whom The Knot Garden *is dedicated, in his capacity as general administrator of Covent Garden (1945–70) and to his successor, John Tooley (b. 1924). Most of the letters focus on the arrangements for forthcoming productions of* The Midsummer Marriage, King Priam *and* The Knot Garden. *They give evidence of Tippett's enduring determination to find artists able to meet the theatrical and musical demands of his compositions, and clearly show his dedication to the highest standards in every detail of the productions.*

29 April 1946

Dear David [Webster],

I have written the enclosed letter to [Victor] Hely-Hutchinson [see BBC collection, p. 7] recommending the young conductor who did *The Child of Our Time* in Brussels [Léoncé Gras], and it saves me writing it all over again if I enclose it for you to see, because I think you might also be interested in him either for Covent Garden concerts or for Liverpool. He is a very good chap.

I want to come and see you soon about my own opera plans [for *The Midsummer Marriage*], because it looks as if Den [Newton] is unlikely to be able to do what I want for the libretto, and that I may have to make the first attempt myself which will bring me at once to quite serious problems and in particular the movement of dancers. So it might be that I ought to talk to some choreographer before I go too far, and certainly before I write any actual mime-or-dance music.

For your information the Symphony [No. 1] will have its first performance on June 6th, Thursday evening, at the Central Hall, Westminster, with the National Symphony Orchestra, under [Walter] Goehr, and promoted by Musarts and Reynolds News, or whatever their proper title is. Do come if you can and hear whether [Reginald] Kell is an improvement on the Liverpool clarinet.

I fancy the young fellow, John Minchinton, came the other day to get something from you. He is a very nice young student and we have just had a wonderful week's holiday together in Mevagissey.

Yours sincerely,

Michael

The Monteverdi is a most lovely work.

6 November 1949

Dear David,

I'm writing to you before I get once again immured in my solitary cottage and lost to any world but *The Midsummer Marriage*. I've so few dates in town (or anywhere) that those rare days get very preoccupied with demands – especially from my publishers – on my attention. So I've been looking in my diary just to see what is what and I see that I'm having to be up for evening rehearsals on 3 days of the week Nov. 20–27. Monday 21st, Friday 25th, for certain and Thursday 24th probably. Could you get your secretary to look in your diary (full to the brim though it be) to see if any of those are possible and to grant me a time 'in pencil' shall we say, which can deepen to ink when I ring up very soon after this letter. Would you care to lunch with me, or are you destined to be host? I'm in the middle of writing love music: the Afternoon Interlude.

Yours

Michael Tippett

13 October 1950

My dear David,

It's quite time I saw you again. You'd better come and lunch with me – perhaps with me and [Howard] Hartog of Schott's – whom I want you to know sometime. However this letter is just to tell you chiefly that I finished the music to Act 2 [of *The Midsummer Marriage*] last night. So I'm very tired but very pleased. I shall go away on Monday for a week's rest (or more) and then make the great effort needed to put down the pre-final version of the script of Act 3. While that's being vetted and considered (in typescript), I hope to finish the little song cycle [*The Heart's Assurance*] which was due at Edinburgh this year, but got postponed by my illness [hepatitis, contracted two years earlier]. It's due now in the Festival.

Act I piano score of *The Midsummer Marriage* goes to the printer in Germany on Monday. We had a big session, with Goehr playing and me singing, with the head of Schott's, English and German, and the act pleased but needed 2 or 3 minor cuts, which I've done.

So what with Act II music and score also completed, I begin to look toward the end of this extraordinary undertaking. As soon as there's a decent script of Act III, so that you can read the whole opera text, then perhaps you ought to hear 2 acts of music? What do you think?

Yours ever
Michael

11 March 1953

Dear David,

[. . .] I thought you'd like to know that we've had a conference in Schott's, with Wilhelm Strecker, the Mainz 'boss', about the opera [*The Midsummer Marriage*]. It appears that consequent on the terrific performance of the *Child* by Karajan at Turin, the Italians made then and there enquiries as to the possibility of doing the opera at the Biennale. And that meant that Munich, who have had, because of their long-standing interest, a kind of first refusal, have had to be told to make up their minds here and now: within weeks.

So the conference was partly about ways and means of making material etc. It's been decided that the opera is worth putting all they've got on. Which means that not only will they finish the engraved piano-vocal score (and the last pages are due on 20th of this month) but they will engrave the whole of the full score (!) to match the existing engraving of the Ritual Dances. So that when we meet I shall not bring you Act I full score, because that goes back with Strecker senior to Mainz this week. But I'll bring you a printed full score of the Ritual Dances and a MS of Act III. All the most difficult things are in those two scores. (Ritual Dances are chiefly from Act II.)

Anyhow, I am extremely pleased with this Schott decision. For the result will be top knotch for all scores and parts. But it can't be done in a hurry. So the Biennale is off anyhow, whether they want it or not. All very exciting.

Yours
Michael Tippett

18 October 1953

My dear David,

I'd hoped to see you at a party last week for [Günther] Rennert and to tell you then that *The Midsummer Marriage* was finished the day preceding. But now I can write and say that not only the composition but the ink full score is all done and copied, and the printing of the whole thing is not far behind. It may have seemed 5 1/2 years ago that I'd in mind the smaller house, but insensibly the work has grown under my hand and the 3rd act has the splendid kind of sound only possible in this country to hear at the Garden. So there we are! W.W. [William Walton] told me on the phone that as *Troilus* was delayed and in any case not possible at the period originally intended, then he hoped to put into your head a suggestion that *The Midsummer Marriage* might precede it. But he probably didn't say anything, as many things else were agitating him then.

Meanwhile I'd very much like to see you just to celebrate the completion. As you've already heard, it's a strange plot, but the whole thing has more than an ephemeral substance, though it will probably take its time to make its impact. It's quite a fresh venture in opera and that's the long and the short of it. It seems absurdly different from most of the modern works I know because its chief note is its youth and gaiety. All the serious side is embedded in that atmosphere.

I'm going to have a rest now before I do the commission for Edinburgh [Divertimento on 'Sellinger's Round']. So I would and could come to town any time to see you if you were at all able to give me a date before. In any case I'll ring you soon, dear David, and see what can be. I very much want to see Rennert's *Ballo* [*in maschera*], so maybe I could make it fit – at least for one of the performances.

I hope this letter doesn't sound too 'off the earth' – I'm just very excited and want to share some of it with you.

Yours,
Michael Tippett

April 1954

My dear David,

This is a confidential letter, in that it relates to a conversation with John Denison, whom I haven't consulted before writing to you – and to a matter which I haven't discussed with my publishers (they have been on a German tour) and if the matter is vain anyhow I shall never discuss it with them. But I should have liked you to know what I have said to Denison. It may be that I am that innocent I take everyone and everything as they themselves would have it. But I said something to him in all seriousness and meant it. He was driving me away from a Br[itish] Council meeting and asked who I wanted to conduct *The Midsummer Marriage*. I told him I thought it was settled, and with whom. He said 'no'. And pressed me for my answer. I said I had answered you this question once before – [Paul] Sacher – but that he was felt to be someone without sufficient experience in the pit. A few days later (I told Denison) I saw Sacher who asked me who was to conduct and I told him what I knew and the reason, as I understood it, that he himself was out of the running. For Sacher is, at any rate with me, candid and we have no problems of avoiding the exact facts. Sacher then said that he had had operatic experience of course, but that he quite understood how it seemed in England, and that probably an English conductor was the more obvious than a Swiss, and that he remained at our service at any time if it happened that way. (This was just after his very successful Ritual Dances with Royal Phil.) The conversation only took a minute or two, and there it was left.

All this I told Denison, and he asked my permission to bring Sacher's name forward again as the composer's choice. I said of course 'yes', and getting rather excited at what seemed to me 'luck', I said further.

If this man were to do it he is not necessarily the best there is, but Covent Garden would have a clean, clear, accurate performance by someone with great resource (especially in new music) who would know the score by heart 3 months before première, and I can guarantee as good a reception to the opera under his direction as to the Ritual Dances viz. practically a 100% good press.

Now I said all this, David, not out of bravado but because I just know it to be so. And not even because I think it might happen or even wish to try and convince anyone sceptical. If it were to happen I should be in luck again, as I was with the Royal Phil. do.

However I have gone so far as to ask Sacher to tell me his more recent efforts in the pit. And he wrote: Honegger *Jeanne d'Arc* at Scala, Milan, [Heinrich] Sutermeister *Black Spider* at Zürich, Stravinsky *Oedipus Rex* at Basel. Denison knows this, as I have written it to him. But it does seem to me stupid that I haven't spoken or written to you direct, so here it is. But again if it is all vain anyhow please don't worry my publishers with the story.

Now that I've finished proofreading to master the score in the proper sense (and one would have helped with some tolerable inclination to newer music) then the opera will speak for itself – as the Ritual Dances have spoken for themselves. Not only to critics but to public.

The summer recording, by the way, is Karajan with Philharmonia – in July. Liverpool offered it ([Hugo] Rignold) but Columbia went all 'glossy'. Suits me! For Karajan does make a wonderful sound. So with luck the recording will be out in the autumn.

Best of wishes dear David. Invitation to the country in the spring.

Yours ever

Michael

[April/May] 1954

My dear David,

I hope I shan't have to write any more letters to you (not for my sake only – I hate writing letters in general – but for yours), because my publishers are back from the annual tour abroad (with a nice sheaf of dates!) and I've been able to put everything relating to M.M. back into their proper hands. For the meeting with Denison really only unsettled me. After all the years of work and waiting, and with all that mass of new music yet to be sounded, one gets an impatience which colours judgment too easily. I really wish it hadn't come unsettled, if indeed it ever was. But here's to some decision.

Blessings,

Michael

[summer 1954]

My dear David,

The enclosed letter is entirely confidential between you and me. I received it this morning as a consequence of an impulse on my part, and send it you on impulse. Because in any case it gives me a great kick to see how an intelligent youngster follows everything that's done at Covent Garden. This is the generation to come, and as he's a teacher too, it's hopeful. He's really Michael Tillett, who used to be a student of mine at Morley during the war (medical reject) spare time from RCM, and is now on the staff at Rugby. He made the vocal score of

The Midsummer Marriage, over 5 years of arduous work. And is the only other person in the world who knows the music as I do – or even better! Now I sometimes get afraid that talking to folk and discussion makes my mind a bit coloured and subjective. While I have always known that the best for me and my music comes when we get a genuine consensus of opinion. That's difficult about this opera casting because the music and the notes aren't known equally to us all. So I suddenly, under impulse, sent your letter and proposed cast to Tillett, and asked for a candid comment – giving him no word at all of what I felt. Just asked him to let me have his opinions and without prejudice. For we used to do this even with the composition. I never told him my own musical doubts about places. But when he expressed a like opinion, then I reconsidered the matter – because I could see that it at any rate came from someone whose knowledge of the music had become equal to mine. So I decided to use this excellent test once again. His letter is the result. It helps me to know where I can trust my instincts, even if it doesn't do anything else. But when you read it please don't hold it against him for the forthrightness of his style. He's heart and soul in the business of English opera and opera in England.

[. . .] I am not with him in his slight doubts about [James] Johnston as Jack, I think. I feel indeed that probably a Verdi–Puccini tenor figure gives Jack something of what was also in my mind. So I still hold with Johnston.

What he says about the possibility of casting Michael Langdon for the He-Ancient is worth consideration. I mean, for the good point he makes about his build and stage presence. But also too a possible switch of [Howell] Glynne?

Then it's curious that he comes pat down on an old hunch of mine – that the She-Ancient really is [Edith] Coates, and no mistake! He puts my original sentiments exactly – both about Coates in other parts and here! But I could yet prefer to be guided by you in this matter. The She-Ancient cuts a ridiculous Coatesian figure. And the stage moment Tillett refers to, when the She-Ancient comes down to the footlights, and then suddenly, like a jolt out of the stage picture, she points at the audience and for a few seconds accuses them is a thousand dollars for an actress. But also a very beautiful moment of singing! Say it as should. And there's the rub.

You'll see that Tillett almost echoes my voice about Glynne as King Fisher. Putting the matter I think on the most sensible basis. That his very popularity in certain parts is just the problem. And I'd quite forgotten about [Bliss's] *The Olympians*. Yes, yes, yes – to echo him.

But as to his own suggestion you alone can counsel me, I think – and I am willing and ready, David, when you tell me, to go wherever I must (except America) to hear what I should.

Meanwhile I feel very much I'd like a chat with you alone. If I stayed up Monday night could I see you? Or go with you together to Glyndebourne on Friday? Because I need some quiet counsel, from you, and also some quite practical information about stage transformations. That is I have some sensible questions to put to you, now that my mind is clarifying itself point by point. So I'll ring Monday morning and hope to get you, to see what you feel.

Bless you,
Michael

21 July 1954

My dear David,

Just to recapitulate our casting so that we have not confused ourselves, it runs:

Mark [Richard] Lewis
Jenifer [Joan] Sutherland
Jack Johnston
Bella [Adele] Leigh
Ancients Langdon
Coates
King Fisher [Otakar] Kraus
Sosostris?
Strephon [Pirmin] Trecu (? name I haven't seen spelt)

Comments. I'm glad I held my ground about Kraus. It was a frightening thing to do, deciding without the support of others – a thing I endlessly hate. But the vision of King Fisher ordering Jack to put a kind of SS uniform on, and then himself unveiling the goddess, made me see my own sense again. It must be. The oracle spoke.

Giving way to you about [Joan] Sutherland doesn't have the same sense of certainty but I can see that it isn't so musical, so artistic a worry. I think that at the back of my mind is the nagging fear that to the outside it may look as if the second of the 2 new English works isn't given so much value, because it holds no international name (except [Richard] Lewis, who is that in my opinion, now). But I haven't the temperament of my distinguished colleagues and cannot, when it comes to the real matters, remember these other considerations at all at the moment of decision, so that if it is in fact a price to be paid for my own kind of temperament, then I must, as I have always done, cheerfully pay it. You, or John [Denison], would have to watch for me in matters of that kind . . . So being quite and congenitally incapable of remembering or thinking of such things at the time, I have mildly to rue it afterwards. And accept it too as a kind of challenge. The god has clearly spoken again. This work clearly has to come fair and square before its fatherland's public in native dress. (Though we might yet do the other thing by a stronger name for Sosostris.) If, if, if, we have the other and international Sutherland [Graham], that will be a lot. And if, in an even more sharpened time, we can but play a real, real, real card for the producer, then maybe the challenge will be gloriously met. My old plea to you. For someone of authority and quality. Still that has to wait.

[. . .] Question: shall I write a little note saying how much I value his possible collaboration? or leave it that what he said to me goes, and one trusts his sense of propriety to have let us know 'no', if it were so? Will ring you tomorrow if I may for the answer.

Blessings,
Michael

27 July 1954

dear David,

Your letter makes me unutterably depressed. It's nothing whatsoever to do with the Walton. A possible Tippett–Walton rivalry is of no interest to me at all, and is a red herring. I take the view that this coming season, with 4 new English operas by composers of my generation, is worthy of comment and congratulations. I hope even to be able to express this view publicly. That I am really fussed or interested in which one gets this or that better singer is absurd. It's not my character at all. Good luck to Berkeley, Britten and Walton, and may they get as good as can be given to them. No – my interest and my responsibility indeed, is solely to try to make the best use of what we have got available for *The Midsummer Marriage*.

Now I have written and spoken with you a lot on the subject of the role of King Fisher. Need I go over again the vital importance of our not miscasting this part? [Hermann] Uhde may indeed be the ideal King Fisher, but it is not about him specifically that I have even spoken. But about what is here to hand. Let me try again.

[Frederick] Dalberg is not the role at all. He is not, to my knowledge, demonic, rapid in his movements, flamboyant, hard, rhetorical and finally iniquitous. That all this has to be said again is horribly depressing. But seeing that Kraus is likely to be too busy I will say now, for the record, what I take to be the next here in England.

There is no doubt, after seeing [Jerome] Hines's part taken by him at Glyndebourne this year, that [Marko] Rothmüller could be as good as Kraus and in some respects better. His Nick Shadow [*The Rake's Progress*] is well on the way to being a part of King Fisher. By one of those curious accidents Rothmüller sat beside me at *Ariadne* [*auf Naxos*]. Naturally he expressed his desire to be in *The Midsummer Marriage*, that he was free, that he wanted to see a vocal score. Not only did I not comment, I did not let him have a score. Though this may be accounted to me for rudeness. I bent over backwards to keep faith with you all, so to speak. Because I not only supposed Kraus to be available (though you and I and Pritchard had not had our casting conference then) but I had reason to suspect that there are other difficulties of relationships, of which I was ignorant. Nevertheless it would be most irresponsible not to say now that Rothmüller could do a fine King Fisher. I myself naturally have no problem of relations or dealing with him.

The next downwards on the list reading Kraus, Rothmüller is Geraint Evans. His Abbot in [Busoni's] *Arlecchino* showed that it could be possible. But not generally advisable.

I can only say that if Covent Garden can't, for other reasons, take Rothmüller, then if it wanted to do the best for the Tippett opera, it would try to release Kraus from other things. There is no question in my mind, that on Covent Garden's decision to do or not to do this a very great deal will turn for my work. We are now going downhill. How far downhill we shall go I can't say. It does not depend, it seems, any more on me.

Production by [John] Cranko is downhill to the bottom. I am not supposing that you are able to control [Frederick] Ashton's commitments. I agreed in March (I wish I had not!) to your view that Rennert might make the opera too philosophic, and that therefore Ashton were the better. Rennert is now doing something else for you – Ashton turns out by end July to be unavailable. Both at least are mature figures. Cranko is a lightweight who has no idea at all what this opera may be. I know him and do not get anywhere with him. How could I? He is not only immature but for me at least, not so imaginative and exciting that he overcomes his youth and reaches out toward real flair and gift. The only English name that has this gift, though young, is Peter Brook. So back we come to the root problem. Rennert, whom I deeply deeply regret, you talk me out of on behalf of Ashton who proves unavailable, Brook you do not want in your house. So that here we have an opera with a tremendous need for imagination, depth, maturity and courage in production, just coming to rest in the half-baked and the second rate, and the little. While Rennert, who is my equal, who has the strength and the authority and the imagination we need, is given *Tales of Hoffmann*!

My depression is deeper even than my personal distress. As I have said before – we are prepared to have Graham Sutherland, again right clear out of the second rate into the first rate – to do scenery. And we think to match Tippett and Sutherland by Cranko! This confusion of values utterly defeats me. I feel terribly let down about Rennert. I can believe that Ashton now being unavailable is in no way your fault. But we've muffed it somehow.

Yours
Michael

1 September 1954

Dear David,

Thank you for your letter. Yes, I am better in that I don't feel so impulsive. But I could not get the matter out of my mind, and spoilt my holiday therefore. I had no idea such things could worry me so much as to make me physically sick. I had a bout again on Sunday and Monday, which I have managed to overcome and force my mind on to my new work. But as I am free either of the days and times you suggest, I think I would prefer the first – Tuesday next, Sept. 7th at noon.

Another side of myself is of course distressed in a different way, that the absolute nature of one's creative needs and the consequences that may spring from it, make one temporarily different in one's person from what one wishes to be, driving one towards difficulties of relationship with others whom one would dearly wish not to distress, maybe, and who may not even be the voluntary author of the troubles. Nothing but the imperative needs of one's work ever accomplishes this – and the price, for me, at any rate, is a very unpleasant nausea. Which will all go, I know, when decisions are at last made, for better or worse. But for better I am sure!

Looking forward therefore to seeing you

Michael

[late 1954/January 1955]

My dear David,

Although I'm not immediately ready (nor is anyone else) to clean up the opera (particularly of course Act 3), I have a reasonably clear plan of campaign.

There are the purely musical cuts, which I more or less already know and have mentally completed.

There are other minor cuts specifically to suit Christopher [West]'s production – even in Act 1, as he will tell me in his time.

There are some musical matters, particularly off-stage chorus, which are not doing their theatrical job, so to speak, and which I need to wrestle with, helped and advised by Reggie [Reginald Goodall] and Pritchard.

Nevertheless all that will not amount to what we really hope, unless too we can give ample reconsideration to some matters of theatrical movement alone. In my opinion the set gained us so much, that I can believe we have now lost too much, in that we have no sense now of the 'temple' magically reconstructed for a day, and 'disintegrating' into natural ruins at the end. That is my view there. But the central disaster, as I see it, is what, for various reasons, has happened to the Sosostris–King Fisher drama in Act 3. We have gone so far from the text (of a huge veiled woman–goddess, whom K.F. 'violates', and who 'gives birth' to an immortal couple, who display a series, exactly annotated by me!, of hieratic gestures, as the music changes from power, to mourning, to ecstasy) that we have brought a complete new confusion into the matter. And by the same token destroyed the drama. I am absolutely clear that if we don't put our theatrical heads together to resolve this in terms of the drama, then it won't matter how much we cut, nor how much fact Sosostris displays – she might just as well move around – and so on. I am of course willing to cut Sosostris' aria to the bone, in order to have restored to me the dramatic situation between her and K.F. And that is as the text says – a struggle between a veiled woman–goddess and a proud mortal. Somehow K.F. must verbally seem to unveil her – otherwise there is no *frisson d'horreur* at all. I still believe that my own 'vision' is the better one, even for its stage movement.

'The sacred veils are flying, torn by King Fisher's violent hand. Black snow flung up against the moon!'

I shall see Christopher sometime at leisure about all this, because I do want to do the clarification in theatrical terms, cutting, or even changing, to help the situations to speak for themselves. Not merely cutting to cut.

Agreed? Agreed.

Michael

1957 [on the revival of *The Midsummer Marriage*]

My dear David,

I was much moved by Thursday night – not least by [John] Lanigan's generosity in singing under such conditions. I went to thank him afterwards, but will also write him a little note later today.

For the rest I must be content with the chief fact that my own very developed self-critical ear was not disillusioned. (Though of course I am already imaginatively in new worlds.) To some *The Midsummer Marriage* can never be acceptable sufficiently to let the thing work. To those who accept it most easily, and they seem to be the younger ones, it works its magic ever again. I've had a note from a young musician who went to every performance last time: 'was completely bowled over by the actual hearing of it again – strange, rich, powerful and beautiful as never before'. I think it a triumph of both Christopher [West] and John P[ritchard] that it did in fact 'speak', to those ordained to hear, 'as never before'. Christopher (for all the reservations I may have about this or that) I am particularly grateful to.

I have sometimes thought that, if the occasion ever offered, I'd have liked to conduct the piece myself. Which is what Morris Smith would like, for his orchestra's sake. I haven't of course P[ritchard]'s accomplishment; but have a more sensitive hand for orchestra accompaniment; and for choral singing. I have felt the Covent Garden chorus in general to be often too coarse and insensitive, even for an opera stage, which must of course have punch. But all this may be momentary dreams.

Chiefly, as you may probably know inside yourself somewhere, I have drawn comfort and strength from your being there in your high office. Like many creative artists who have to live deeply and desperately within the imaginative worlds they are creating, I am fundamentally timid over public relations. Though I am old enough to know how to wear the particular public mask that is appropriate. I project onto you all the hidden admirations for people whose responsibility and gift it is to manage public things and elaborate institutions. And I am aware that only our gifts in this respect could ever have brought onto the stage such a strange work and given it such a generous and authoritative backing.

Naturally enough there are times when I wish the imaginative world of this opera had not been so strange and therefore so hampering, shall we say, to the work. I feel it will never quite fall into place until other theatrical works of mine put it in a kind of general sequence. And it can never appeal fully to, shall we say, [Frank] Howes of *The Times*! Who speaks for a quite real point of view. The other point of view, of those who are deeply moved and who rejoice in it, is less publicly expressed, perhaps even less expressible. But when the opportunity is given to them to experience the experience, they are like me, very grateful. To them, as to me, the piece has a strange exhilaration and compulsion.

Michael

1957

My dear David

John [Minchinton] and I will be at *Grimes* tomorrow, as you may know. This letter though is just to tell you that I've heard at long last from America that they agree to the new opera as being their commissioned work [*King Priam*, for the Koussevitzky Foundation]. They also write:

You mentioned the fact that no stipulation has been made concerning first performance rights. This is quite true, for the Foundation does not take responsibility of arranging a first performance, neither does it place any restriction whatsoever on the composer in this respect.

All in all it's a very nice letter from them – and they wish 'your exciting undertaking' well.

I also have had a helpful session with T. S. Eliot. And when I've got soon now the first draft synopsis down onto paper, I shall see him again. You shall also see the draft if you will.

Eliot is quite convinced that the composer has to sort out his ideas (even musical ones) as far as he possibly can before he goes to any literary person. (He thinks, for example, that Auden baffled Stravinsky by putting over plausible Audenesque ideas onto the composer.) So on the whole we are looking at a fair consensus of opinion between yourself, myself and some others. Having cleared the Symphony [No. 2] out of the way, and through the press, I shall draft the synopsis in a week or so.

All the best
Michael

1957

Dear Muriel [David Webster's secretary],

I've written out the synopsis [of *King Priam*] on separate sheets of paper, and it looks much longer than it will be when typed. However the real point is that I believe all these kinds of things are quite public, and so I don't mind how the material I've set out, scene by scene, is condensed or shortened (for instance, at this stage we could leave out all account of the Interlude between scenes, but I leave it to you and David).

The only (public) other facts are that the text has been worked over constantly with Rennert, who approves. That Christopher Fry very much approves. That the idea of the story etc is approved by the Koussevitzky Foundation people, who've commissioned it. Though of course that sounds better than it is. For, where Rennert and Fry really have examined and helped, the Koussevitzky people have just said yes.

Complete typed texts, in their form to date, will be available in about a week. They are so far near the final to be composed text that I don't mind who sees them, although in many ways opera texts are not always helpful to unknown operas. But in this case the story is such a story in itself that little harm can be done.

If David wants me to condense further, then I could come to town perhaps and have a go with your or his help. The next thing for me anyhow is to get the right title. And there David's advice is essential.

Yours
Michael

7 September 1957

My dear David,

Just a PS to my last letter (which you may not yet have seen) to keep you up to date. I saw Fry: very helpful. Then I went to Edinburgh to have a long session with Rennert; most helpful. On the lines of his advice (especially where it coincided independently with Fry's) I am redoing the text [of *King Priam*], particularly of Act 1. Then I shall go to Hamburg in October to see Rennert again (I may see his *Lulu* in Berlin en route). I think all this will see me in sight of a final text for Act 1. So then I can begin at last to compose. Fry, incidentally, is sure that I must complete the text in my own words, myself. He has already commented on various tricks of style and echoes of Eliot.

Rennert is much impressed by my long and careful preparation (this time). As he says: he has no fear at all about music; the problems are all form in the deepest sense. Operatic form; material condensed into lucidity; the important things forward, the subsidiary things behind. I won't recapitulate the decisions we have made to amend the text as you have already seen it. It's quicker to send you a fresh one. But what I would like soon is a 'session' with you about voices and orchestra etc; particularly voices. That is: what kind of voice to fit these roles, which are now becoming substantially clear and known. Orchestra is smallish, I think, but unconventional. Chorus not more than 14, it seems; with 4 playing semi-roles. Formalised, uncomplicated staging. Saw Rennert's [production of Adalbert Lortzing's] *Wildschütz* and liked it. Saw Eliot, his play.

Michael

14 May 1958

Dear David,

Surely you've been to enough parties by now, and can go to the one on May 21st late, say 11.45, and come with me to what will be a stunning performance of *Agon*? Whatever magical something Karajan gave John [Minchinton], it's now breaking out. I had one of the best performances ever of one of my works, during John's first broadcast a few weeks back. It's a conducting talent and temper we haven't seen in our country for a long time. I'm personally extremely proud. So won't you come?

For the rest I've been meaning for weeks to write to say that I took a draft scenario [for *King Priam*] to Germany to show Rennert. Most exciting talk. He liked the material, and the shape, extremely. Gave me version of the advice from you and from Eliot. I'm day after day, in intervals from finishing my children's piece [*The Shires Suite*], working at a deadpan script. I shall want you to see it fairly soon. Because, when I finish the children's piece in 3 weeks, I shall try to get the draft script far enough on to be typed, and then to see you, and go again to see Rennert – as to actual stage details.

This deadpan script will tell us whether I am to embellish it myself or some other. Providing of course we feel that my creative work at the material is done.

It's fantastically different from *The Midsummer Marriage* though that will grow in esteem gradually all the same, though I may have moved away.

Lots of love and congratulations for *Don Carlo* at Covent Garden. I want to go, May 26.

Michael

1958

My dear David,

Whatever the outcome I was much moved by yesterday's meeting. Despite my reticences I am deeply attached to you personally and inescapably loyal to Covent Garden and what you have built up there over the years. I went to the microphone so relaxed the girl at the knobs thought I would finally begin to sing an Alleluia. (The talk is called: *The Music of the Angels*.)

During the winter I shall hammer out a text of the new opera [*King Priam*] and you shall see it as soon as seeable. I've already had a further inkling of how to manage Act 3 since I saw you. Then I shall compose like mad. It must be finished well within your span.

I must accept I think that *The Midsummer Marriage* belongs where it always has, and that a perceptively imaginative production will prove that one day. I learnt in the BBC they are relaying their fine

[Norman] Del Mar tape of it again (the 3rd time be it noted!) the day after my birthday Jan. 3rd and we may relay it simultaneously to Munich. So it goes.

Herzlichst
Michael

22 July 1959

My dear David,

I expect this will find you on holiday – as we shall also be, Karl Hawker and I, in a few days. Just to say that I'm halfway through Act 1 – having finished a big dramatic monologue for Priam, which has great force. I am still up to schedule – i.e. end of all by this time 1961. Also haven't yet made a mistake, I think. Still has the drive, clarity and simplicity I wanted to find, to suit the subject. All that seems slightly unexpected is that Priam, so far, is the central figure entirely. If this really keeps till his death in the last moments of the opera, then at least the title will settle itself.

Rennert and Mrs Rennert and Ita Maximowna came over recently to supper. Rennert was suddenly gay and frivolous – but we had a few words about my own affairs with him. He would like to produce the opera, and in England, but said that if for any reason it helped the work for it to be produced by anyone else here, he would entirely understand. Which was nice of him. I saw his *Fidelio* at Glyndebourne and like it very much for the simplicities that I feel would suit my own work, when it comes to it. So I remain very much of the opinion that he is my man. Of the Maximowna sets we liked 1, 2 and 3, but not so much 4.

I've missed [Teresa] Berganza for various reasons. But I shall hear her somewhere.

The music and the composition flow now with assurance – all seems to be falling into place. End of Act 1 by Christmas. Hope to see you in the autumn.

Michael

[1960]

My dear David,

[. . .] I hope to finish Act 2 in about a month's time and then have a fortnight's good holiday with Karl and his children in a Provençale *mas* near Les Baux.

We both enjoyed our weekend at Aldeburgh immensely – though we got a little less than we expected from the [*Midsummer Night's*] *Dream*. I guess it's because *King Priam* is such a different and tough world and kind of fighting through toward new experiences; so that its own intensities prevent my having receptive ears at present.

I had a nice time checking fingering etc with Julian Bream over a fine (I think!) song for Achilles in the tent to a guitar. It's a kind of Hylas-like nostalgia for the homeland, but with Achilles' frustrated aggression given into the guitar part. The small sound comes suddenly after a tremendous racket of the war itself. Very effective!

Greetings from Karl and myself

Michael

29 May 1960

My dear David,

Thursday's run-through [of *King Priam*] was most successful from my point of view, and I'm grateful. Ted Downes in particular was more than helpful. We had a good discussion about voices, and he had sensible observations to make. This all means that I am not now the only person who knows from the music what the voices should be to compass what's written. And except for the few to be found outside the house all is very well in order and ahead. The 2 outside the house seem to be [Geraint] Evans and Meyer. I'm a bit worried as to Geraint, because he's being sought after everywhere. He has a new role for the Henze at Glyndebourne next year [*Elegy for Young Lovers*]. He says 2 new roles a season is his limit. I should be relieved I must admit, if we knew he'd committed himself to Priam for the season after. It's going to be the devil (as Downes admits) to find an alternative – because it's a tremendous part for a fine actor-singer. It lies a wee bit low for Fischer-Dieskau, incidentally. Though that might be circumvented. Anyhow, I shall trust to Geraint just so long as we dare. And that's where I shall badly need your advice. How long can we leave it before we ask for a final yea or nay? My guess is that he won't want to commit himself till this *Wozzeck* is delivered. Can we wait so long? I must say I get a trifle agitated; because I don't want us to fall down by my own illusions. I mean, illusions that singers are loyal to their friends!

After you'd gone (Thursday) we tried a scene of Act 2 and thought

329

therefrom we could cast Hector with Forbes Robinson. Paris with [André] Turp is, as I surmised, a bit worrying for that I've done a particular kind of 'high' effect to express the irrationality of his love. Downes saw immediately what I was after. Says Turp couldn't do it now, but could in 2 years he thinks. And so on . . . it's very exciting.

As to length – the music will be under the 2 hours. If Act 1 is 35–40 [minutes] (the latter I think), Act 2 is 20 at the outside. Act 3 is perhaps 45, for it's just that much longer than Act 1.

I'd like to slip in to see you one day before the season ends. Just to take stock. This rather long-scale preparation is a bit of a nuisance to you all I guess, but it will help us in the end.

Yours ever
Michael

14 September 1960

My dear David,

Bits of news and I hope you won't feel I've been up to no good!

I've just finished copying the ink full score of Act 2 [of *King Priam*]. Act 1 score and parts and vocal score is going into production soon, as we have a German translation ready at last.

Act 3 I begin tomorrow. I am tinkering and shortening the text, after further considerations and meditations.

As to the (to me) vital matter of producer, as you know I've wanted theatrical flair and some 'tough' quality – even willingness to use the flair to find how to produce the toughness with a minimum of theatrical fuss. But the underlying tragic violence of the text must not be sugared over – or decorated over.

Rennert, [Peter] Brook, [Tyrone] Guthrie have all been unable to tie themselves despite (in the case of the first two) great pleasure in the subject and text.

We then wrote to [Oscar Fritz] Schuh, and had no reply. Nor shall we have one. Which in my opinion, isn't good enough.

Now I have taken up an unorthodox but serious suggestion of Pritchard's, to wit Sam Wanamaker – of whom Pritchard has great esteem, and with whom a successful friendship. Hartog saw Wanamaker for me, and I see him myself tomorrow to hear what he says. He has had the (private) discs of the première of *The Midsummer Marriage* and a text; also a text of *King Priam* and a vocal score of Act

1. When he has studied these by tomorrow, we will meet and talk. (He is as knowledgeable about music as Brook or Guthrie, and he's produced musicals. But you know all about that.)

I've taken this unorthodox step because I consider it a good one. There is the quality there I want – and a figure with plenty of public face. The latter side is not to be dismissed either, in my opinion, when launching a really new work. But it is you who have taught me that.

If all goes well I'll come in to see you as soon as maybe. It would be a tremendous relief to me to get a strong working conductor and producer team settled, as we are not so far off any more.

Act 2, by the way, is about 20 minutes I should think. Did I tell you Brook was asked by Coventry to take over the whole artistic direction of the Festival for them? – but refused on the same grounds as he refused us.

Sosostris came over splendidly at the Proms. It's difficult to believe it just yet, but one day not only the music will be acceptable and considered firm, but the music will 'straighten' out the theatrical problems to the extent that performance in the theatre will be considered the proper one.

I'm seeing Glock too tomorrow, and want to discuss with him possibility of a more considerable chunk of the music as a concert piece. Perhaps the end of the whole opera.

Michael

23 March 1961

My dear David,

I've been meaning to write you for a while, chiefly to thank you and everyone else concerned, both for the generosity in letting me see so many productions in Covent Garden, and for the unfailing patience and co-operation everybody I have to deal with shows me. I feel I'm often impatient – I hate being so, if I am. In any case all will soon be in order.

I've had an enthusiastic letter from Wanamaker from America in which he hopes to have some conference with Jo Mielziner, when he, Wanamaker, reaches New York with his Broadway-bound show; next week or so. This all sounds very exciting. A fresh mind.

King Priam itself races along as never before. Extremely moving.

331

I'm so far ahead of myself, I'm taking a few weeks off to do some songs for Peter [Pears] and Bream, for Aldeburgh this year [*Songs for Achilles*]. I'll finish the opera end of summer.

Fidelio was tremendous.

The BBC will probably do a studio performance of *The Midsummer Marriage* next new year. A kind of send-off to new one. We hope they'll ask to use Covent Garden orchestra. I'll have a word with you about all this when they fix a real date.

It's difficult not to get over-excited by the way *King Priam* goes. If David Ward does the name part it'll be a triumph for him. A colossal role. I'll slip in to the Garden when I'm up next in the hope to see you for 5 minutes.

Yours ever,
Michael

11 September 1961

My dear David,

At the back of my mind is the following: especially when I get riled about Pritchard. But I guess he will climb down, so it may never come to such a point. However, as probably there may be a moment where there really is a question whether John [Pritchard] can manage rehearsals and dates willingly and not as a perpetual favour, I tell you what's in my mind as a basic position, so to speak. But you must talk to Morris Smith about it, because he knows that side of my capabilities professionally and practically.

What's been in my head is that, given the clear 'piecemeal' kind of orchestration and score to *King Priam* (i.e. simple instrumentation at each point, very few complex ensembles), given my knowledge from seeing *The Midsummer Marriage* production from the inside, of just how much a house like Covent Garden sustains things by willing and capable repetiteurs and sub-conductors, knowing my own experiences as a youngster with the burden of bringing amateur opera to the stage single-handed, I would say that before we went too far into unknown or mediocre hands, I myself could manage an exciting and accurate performance. I'm not as gifted as Ben [Britten], but more experienced and capable than Henze.

For the rest, I've had Wanamaker on the phone and am dining with him and conference following (with Sean Kenny too if available) next week, 20th, and that he will get in touch with you to meet you immediately after.

Returning to the first matter of this letter, you can see how my mind has been working. I've already done so much preliminary conferring, casting and so forth, get on so well with your own folk, and with producer and designer, that I begin to weigh in the balance the effort and trouble of a late coming conductor; even John. When I can do the whole bloody thing with verve and knowledge – providing of course I were sustained, as I really would be, by Covent Garden staff.

Michael

June 1962

Dear David,

First of all, to thank you and everyone for the tremendous effect and success of *King Priam*. It's difficult to express all I feel as to the co-operation, kindness and hard work of all concerned. But you must know all that by now.

I'm just finished in a preliminary conference for a TV appearance next week; and Karl [Hawker] is driving me now to Aldeburgh, where I conduct for BBC on Thursday – and then we rush back to Corsham, where I conduct English and Russians for Menuhin in the Bath Festival. And after that a bit of quiet, and back to composition.

Now – I gather that it's possible *King Priam* might return next season. And presumably earlier (for its public's sake) rather than later. But John Pritchard is not available. So I've been thinking about alternative. I would have said Colin Davis, as first choice. Norman Del Mar as second – though some way second. Someone has suggested [Charles] Groves (who I fear might be too heavy-handed – thinking more in a big 'choral' terms) and there's Meredith Davies – again, to me, very unpredictable.

At some times I feel I'd very much like to do it myself, just because of the huge goodwill everyone shows to me, I mean the singers and the players, and the staff.

It's in some ways easier to take over and add my own values to John's performance, than to discuss it all with someone else.

However, I suggest this possibility with some diffidence. You, I think, are the only possible final judge. Good for public relations – and if I worked hard, and responsibly, good technically. It's only really come to mind because I can believe that it would be good, if it's to happen, to bring back *King Priam* soon – if there are spaces in the plans. And it's certain that good alternative to John P. won't be easily free – and I wouldn't want things to break down over that, if you agreed.

Once again my very great thanks.

Michael

PS. Karl asks me to thank you for himself personally for letting him attend rehearsals and come with me to performances.

4 December 1962

My dear David,

I've told [Bryan] Balkwill, Charles Taylor and Morris Smith that the Karlsruhe people, where I was Sat.–Sunday, and who give first German performance of *Priam* on Jan. 26th, intend to do the score as the composer wrote it – i.e. with violins, not piano substituted. The conductor, [Arthur] Grüber, played me what he thought it should sound like and the result is as magnificently exciting as I imagined. So I thought everyone ought to know. Because a German provincial opera orchestra isn't really better than Covent Garden. But the conductor is more in sympathy with the score! I have written nice letters, I hope, but I do mean them.

I also worked out in Germany a kind of fiddling with harpsichord stops which produces an alternative 'guitar'. This I've passed on to Balkwill and Morris.

You will be invited of course to Karlsruhe for Jan. 26th, as they want to make a splash, and your presence would mightily cheer them. I saw incidentally a *Pique Dame* [Tchaikovsky, *The Queen of Spades*] of Hainer Hill, who told me he is in London soon to discuss *Lohengrin*. After the opera everyone as usual (in Germany) went to a hotel (luckily mine) and settled down for drinks and food and talk. We finished, or rather I got them to go, at 3 a.m., by which time Hainer Hill and Grüber (the general music director at Karlsruhe) were shouting at each other over the vexed question of [Walter] Felsenstein. The wives tried to calm them down. They are a turbulent lot sometimes, but in small doses stimulating.

Yours ever,

Michael

15 January 1963

My dear David,

As you may have heard by now the production of *The Midsummer Marriage* [broadcast] on Sunday night was terrific. And in some ways, I feel, a vindication of your own perception with regard to the opera so many years ago. But this is not what I was specifically writing to you about. I really want to say a word in your ear about Norman Del Mar. He knew the score in a way which, for large-scale opera works, is pretty rare. And at the same time he gave a performance which had an astonishing sense of the theatre. This was felt and acknowledged by many of the players and singers. It made the broadcast so tremendously exciting.

I feel I want you to know that I'm sure he is someone who is worth more in opera than only to have been used by Britten for *Let's Make an Opera*. His stature is in my opinion growing all the time.

Returning to the *The Midsummer Marriage* for a moment; when I am in Germany next week for Karlsruhe I hope to take up the matter of a German production with my publishers at Mainz, because I feel after Sunday's broadcast a kind of vindication myself, in that this stream of continually exciting and lyrical music has begun to sweep away the difficulties and obscurities which people imagine were inherent in the piece. It all appeared so lucid and so consequent.

I am certain now that when we can give it a production as imaginative, simple and accurate as Sam [Wanamaker] gave to *King Priam*, there will be a public ready. It will be seen to be a winner one day!

I will probably write you a note as to how *Priam* goes in Germany, though it would be much more exciting if you were there. (Karlsruhe January 26th)

Yours ever –
Michael Tippett

12 September 1964

My dear David,

I feel I'd like to see you for a short moment, if you can manage. Nothing special – but a third opera [*The Knot Garden*] looming up (if that's the right expression!) and some other like matters that are confusing me. I feel I need you to be in 'the picture' if you will permit.

So – I'll ring Muriel in a day or two and see how things are. I can always pop up to London, and it would be a welcome break indeed from arduous and prolonged composition (Fischer-Dieskau, BBC Chorus and Orchestra, Schmidt-Isserstedt: Jan. 66) [*The Vision of Saint Augustine*].

Affectionately,
Michael

10 January 1965

My dear David,

This is just to put on record to you, *à propos* of Dizzy Desmond [Shawe-Taylor]'s article in today's paper regarding *The Midsummer Marriage* ('that extraordinary opera'), that I'm quite unrepentant. It simply could not have remained so fantastically alive (compared say with *Troilus and Cressida* or *The Olympians*) for all these years in limbo, quite disconnected from the stage where it first saw light. So that one day it will return to some stage with a producer (this the crux, as I see it) who can do for it what Sam [Wanamaker] did for *Priam*, and it's going to have a lasting public, that's been growing in limbo years and is nearly ready to act. But – dear David, I wouldn't think it sense to slap down a *Priam* revival for a *Midsummer Marriage* new production. For heaven's sake let's see that back – as it's a glory to your house as well as exciting to its author.

I gather BBC have decided to put Act 1, *The Midsummer Marriage*, into the Proms. And if a recording company actually takes Desmond's advice then the disinterment from the limbo will be ready. Of course it's flawed – but it only thereby enters a big group of truly fascinating problematic pieces. But this one you fought for – and hence my unbroken sense of gratitude.

Love
Michael

1 December 1965

My dear David,

In a few days you'll receive a type copy of the libretto [of *The Knot Garden*] to date. First 2 acts are probably in their final shape, if verbal details will still get improved. Act 3 is nearly final, I guess. It has proved very difficult to hammer into shape. Many folk have had to take a hand. The metaphors are certainly not all in order yet. But enough to see what is in the wind.

Title is as usual to be found or chosen between various possibilities. As before, I'll set them all down soon and ask you to help in the choice. I regard title as very much a 'collective' operation. Public that is.

I leave entirely to your discretion how soon you show it to [Georg] Solti – or not at all. It will be at least a year before we have to consider seriously conductor and producer. (I can't help feeling though already the designer is [Sean] Kenny.) However, you'll see there's a Negro baritone needed. I gather Covent Garden is hearing one such at audition in the new year. May I be present? I've forgotten his name.

And last, I meant to discuss with you a method of commission payment which the Koussevitzky generously adopted for me last time, and which helps my tax. I'll get Richard Hawkins of Schott's to talk with you later. Again, that's at least a year off. Good luck to *Boccanegra* tonight!

Michael

27 July 1966

My dear David,

I hope Hartog didn't cross over lines. I didn't feel it is Cranko – nor does Colin Davis. He and I have discussed it exhaustingly and we both feel it really is now Colin Graham, with a good choreographer and a designer who has also designed for the ballet. (Act 2 is 2/3rds dancing.)

I'm recovering [from prostate surgery] very slowly – one day off one day on. The off days I get deeply depressed. (And then I'm fussed and bothered.) I've also conceived a new choral work [*The Vision of Saint Augustine*] so bitter it's quite frightening. Perhaps it'll vanish with health and vigour. Karl [Hawker] is very gentle and very good and keeps me on an even keel.

I've re-begun work at the new opera [*The Knot Garden*] – 1/2 hour a day or so.

Much love
Michael

30 November 1968

My dear David,

I went to see Joan Ingpen on Thursday to try and sort out if and when my new opera [*The Knot Garden*] had a Covent Garden première. I recognise all the financial problems you have concerning new productions. So though the vocal score will be printed and published by the summer of next year (1969) I am not in violent haste. However – it seems that the 70–71 season is possible, and 71–72 season is possible. It turns on Colin Davis, at least in some measure, for a commitment to use one of the new production spaces for such a première. Much as I love the house (and you and I have real and mutual understanding of all that means) I can't withhold the new opera beyond the 71–72 season. I have written to Colin, in very gentle terms, on these lines. I have never had personal dealings with him about performances of my music, and have been generally ignorant of his intentions. He did in this respect ask this summer to see a libretto of *The Knot Garden* and we supplied him one. But this present matter isn't really of course whether Colin conducted (that is secondary) but whether as prospective musical director he can engage Covent Garden (or you and Solti have in principle done) to produce the work by the 71–72 season, seeing it is completed in print by summer 69.

Speaking personally to you, and as a composer, I'm not afraid of going elsewhere but shall be mighty sad.

Love
Michael

29 September 1969

My dear David,

Many thanks for your letter. Oddly enough I had myself gone back to the view you hold. And was going to tell you so. Most of the she-mozzle over Colin Davis and Jack Phipps was really over the financial and artistic nonsense of running a fine regional festival from London (it was just the same problem really, *au fond*, with Menuhin and Ian Hunter). So having got the (very efficient) office running well in Bath, I've got to find the right figures hereabout, before I can hand over to someone younger and less tied to other matters e.g. composition! And I'm thankful to say I'm back in harness on new pieces. Mind you, this is always an odd period for me, when I have finished a major work like

The Knot Garden and have to await the proper and necessary preparations for the final event. Especially when the new work is so fascinating and strange. But by the time the opera does reach première I shall be deep in a new Symphony [No. 3] for the LSO (commissioned at a fee I dare not mention – and I'm sure is undeserved) and then I'm going to do a biggish work for Solti in Chicago.* In fact another 3 years hard.

So you see, the Bath Festival takes second place!

Michael

21 November 1969

My dear David,

This letter may not be in order – but you will bear with me I know. I have not been well lately – plain overwork and consequent strain. A continuing series of nervous crises, lasting some hours – after which I recover. Obviously the doctors prescribe some drugs, and I try to keep strictly to composition on good days, and resting on bad ones. It will pass. But the publicity locally through the Bath Festival has forced me to decide to leave this town and go into the country proper. I have bought a marvellous secluded house and with a swimming pool for the vital muscular relaxation.

Now – the crunch of the letter is simply this. When you and I first talked of *The Knot Garden* (though it had no title then) you thought it should have a commission fee, and that to be £1000. Maybe this has all gone down the drain. And please understand that I am not complaining of anything from Covent Garden to me. I am royally served. But if the commission had not gone quite down the drain it would be a great help at this time.

But I have contracted to buy the house anyhow!

And don't be alarmed, but rejoice, in that I see already the subject and scope of a 4th opera [*The Ice Break*] – presumably my last.

When I am better I'll come to London and we could have a lunch together and I'll hear your news so far as you can see ahead.

affectionately,

Michael

* This commission, which was to have been a setting of Robert Lowell's poem 'For the Union Dead', was never completed. Instead, Tippett wrote the Symphony No. 4.

[December 1969/January 1970]

Dear Muriel,

I've just had another of these 'nervous attacks' and there was a mild one before Christmas too. So it's clear I'm not ready to make visits to the opera just yet! A great pity. So will you let them sell the tickets you had got me for Wednesday. And forgive my having troubled you.

These 'attacks' aren't serious but off-putting. The doctors merely say that the 'autonomic nervous system' is misbehaving. It begins with a fluttering of the heart and a trembling of the body and then a loosening of kidneys and bowel and takes 4 hours or so to go over. I think it will give up and be sensible again come the spring and the new house. But I shall all the same make a date with D.W. soon for a lunch together.

    Yours
    Michael

23 October 1970

Dear Muriel,

Thanks for your letter. Could you pencil in Thursday, Nov. 19, for a possible lunch with Sir David. I'll confirm in a little while.

And could you take up gently for me another fairly personal matter? This is, the second half (£750) of the commission fee for *The Knot Garden* is due when the rehearsals begin. My hope is that they are considered to have begun! But I don't know who directs payment, so to speak. I shall be very glad of it when available. (But I see, on re-reading your letter, that I am probably previous.)

My inner excitement over the coming première is now rather too strong. I try to keep it at bay.

    Love –
    Michael

3 October 1973

Dear John [Tooley],

The Midsummer Marriage in Karlsruhe was good. On a much higher *niveau* than *King Priam* therefore. Musically, often quite splendid and very moving. Scenically, gains and losses. Gain was the way by which the temple moved (filling the revolve – which forced it rather far forward, as the stage is so small) when turned into a fresh position for Act 2, refracted the light so that it itself, though necessarily solid, became magical. This is what Ande [Anderson] never really managed. And all in all the set-up and setting was simple and good. Production seemed to me simple and good too – but maybe I was very aware of the tremendous hard effort that had gone to get the chorus to act at all etc, etc – as well as the necessity of getting maximum speeds of exits and entrances – for the music was driven pretty fast, and the bits of music for large stage movement and display cut every time.

Loss was always the limitation of a small stage for a work which was conceived for space. But I think the whole performance and production quite overcame this. I forgot it all in the event (as did the public).

Peter Heyworth was there from the *Observer* and I gather in one of his grumpier moods. He seemed to feel he was judging a performance in Hamburg or the Met! But I dare say he'll recover his balance before Sunday.

Best of all was an outstanding King Fisher – the Belgian-born baritone, [Jef] Vermeersch: and the favoured Wotan in Berlin, where he's housed; trained in Karlsruhe where he's still on guest contract. He really was the best I've seen. I asked him quietly if he spoke English. Only school English, but thought he could sing in the language. Might come in handy one day.

On my way home via Mainz I met the wife of one of the men in Schott, Mainz. She is your Elektra in November. Remained very quiet and contained in a wild German–English evening, a house wine-drinking party. I spoke to her a little. Will see you sometime.

Michael

Barbara Hepworth

The abstract sculptor Barbara Hepworth (1903–75) designed the sets and costumes for the original production of Tippett's first opera, The Midsummer Marriage (1955). *Although Hepworth was not Covent Garden's first choice – the painters Graham Sutherland and Ben Nicholson had been approached but were unable to accept – Tippett had come to know her as a friend and was familiar with her work, and he knew that she would be able to realise his clear visual conception of the opera. The letters show the close attention he paid to the essential details of the production, while also allowing us to glimpse the workings of his mind in connection with theatre matters and his idiosyncratic approach to opera. Hepworth was one of a colony of artists in St Ives, Cornwall, where she died in a fire in her studio. From 1938 to 1951 she was married to Ben Nicholson (1894–1982), to whom one of these letters is addressed.*

[March 1952?]

Dear Barbara Hepworth,

Thanks so much for your kind letter of welcome – and of appreciation of those talks. *Moving Into Aquarius* did I think just what you say – and it's for that reason it's been worthwhile.

I do very much want to come down to St Ives. Though I wrote on Friday to Priaulx [Rainier] to say that the end of April was seeming to be the better now for me, if that was alright for others. Because 'flu and various other things have forced me to rest for a while now, and I'd have liked to try to get another scene of my last opera act [of *The Midsummer Marriage*] finished before I have the long awaited and long needed real holiday in Cornwall. To which I am enormously looking forward. I have been hoping to get to know you.

Yours Sincerely,
Michael Tippett

22 June 1954

Dear Barbara,

[. . .] Tomorrow Covent Garden bring to lunch here their, or the, fashionable painter and his wife. To wit [Graham] Sutherland. So you see what they want – a glossy name to help publicity. As I've told Priaulx, one must hope that he's wise enough after all to enter into some different vision; and that if Covent Garden do sign him up then they must give us a good singer or two to match! But if he doesn't like the proposition at all – or doesn't like me perhaps – then I shall presumably have more of my own say. But the composer goes for little in the operatic world – and in some ways I'm glad. I've so much new music to write, and the endless toings and froings of that theatrical world are a nightmare. I entered into them for about a month over the question of a conductor and got quite overstrung and 'difficult'. So I just relaxed and let go and let be. The public world belongs to the public and the socially minded. Nevertheless there'll be plenty of nightmare to come and as the rehearsals progress.

Love to you, dear Barbara,
Michael

13 August 1954
Chy-an-Goverrow, Lamorna

Dearest Barbara,

I need to see you rather badly if you can spare the time, and if I am not going thereby to impose a strain on you, because of asking for too high a degree of objectivity. For none of us artists can go, or should go beyond a certain amount of purely objective judgment, and it's advice of that kind I need, because I am not a visual artist myself. I know now you see that Graham Sutherland can't do the scenes for me because of his portrait of Churchill! And Covent Garden's second choice is another painter [Ben Nicholson]. Very close and near. I need very badly to talk to someone who *knows* what is what in this field, and to guide me with wisdom as to how much I say to Covent Garden in my *own* right and *own* judgment. But I suspect, you see, that my judgments in this field are subjective altogether. I have absolutely no trained eye – only a very general sensibility, easily coloured by my relations with people.

I'm going to ring you tomorrow morning to see what you feel about my asking wise advice from you in this way. Maybe it's quite wrong to ask you, or maybe I just take it too seriously. I fear I'm being inconsiderate because so much is involved for myself. The worst kind of artistic selfishness. [. . .]

Luv
Michael

19 September 1954

Dear Ben [Nicholson],

Thanks for your letter. I've noted all you say about *time*, and all your dates. But I shall need to know more exactly about Barbara. That is, I wasn't clear from talking with you, whether Barbara should maybe do the costumes in her own name or helping you, so to speak. So when I spoke with C.G. [Covent Garden] I have made it possible to be either. But clearly to get fee and so on settled with C.G. I shall need to know how you and Barbara would prefer it. I spoke with Barbara already on the phone about it, and shall ring either you or her in a day or two to see what you advise.

Then I will send you some records at once – because I have here in the house a private record of the Ritual Dances from the opera taken off the first English broadcast – not very accurate as to the speeds but sufficiently so as to get some idea of the music from it. And I'll have sent you from London a string concerto (early work) [Concerto for Double String Orchestra] and a song cycle (late work) [*The Heart's Assurance*]. (The song cycle is an LP.) Then more important still, the librettos are promised from the printer on Thursday. I'll get [Howard] Hartog (of Schott's) to send both you and Barbara one. Then I imagine I see to a model of the stage being put in and for you, but that we keep that here till you are in London, end of this month – when, as you say, we had best come to grips with as much as we can. That is to see both C.G. stage as it actually is – and to meet the head of the stage mechanics part of it (John Sullivan) and Clement Glock – who has already worked with [André] Derain and [Christian] Bérard and seems confident. And as you will see from the libretto there's in fact fundamentally only one main set. That's the thing to keep hold of.

Yours –
Michael

21 September 1954

Barbara dear –

Many thanks for your letter and the cheque. Yes – your copy of the libretto should have gone to you today. Meanwhile I wrote last night and sent this morning a letter to Ben [Nicholson] which I asked him to show you if he approved. For I had had kind of 'visions' about it all, through trying to think of the huge proscenium of Covent Garden as the frame to an immense picture of Ben's. And the vision, or illumination, was simply that I realised that I had in fact by the story and everything divided up the stage as between natural and supernatural in quite a specific manner. So that therefore if the Ancients and dancers (immortal, supernatural) come first out of the temple (the centre point of the supernatural magical sanctuary) then their dress too will correspond in some way to the place they appear from (however much in the libretto I have called them ancient Greek), just as the dress of the singing chorus (mortal, natural) will reflect that they come first from the nearly naturalistic wood. So that all the transitions between the 2 worlds which I have so carefully calculated and placed and shuffled about, will have visual counterparts – some mobile (the mortal and immortal roles, characters) some immobile (the natural and magical places on the stage).

But I see further than my letter to Ben, that my very late idea that at the end, at the second dawn, if the mists were to rise again a second time, one would see no supernatural place at all, but only natural landscape, isn't probably right. For the music most certainly has both worlds. I suspect it means simply some simple rearrangement of the 'supernatural' spatial relationships, tending to mute the magical somehow. I must get down to St Ives to hear all about Greece!

Love

Michael

PS. As you will see from the libretto I already instinctively 'saw' the meanings of dress. Because as Mark and Jenifer undergo their initiations their dress changes. In the first act I visualised it (for myself) as allied to Greek mythology. Towards Athene and Dionysus – towards white and red – and (historically) wool and silk! (Dionysus upset the austere Greeks because, coming from the East, he was dressed in silk, and rather effeminate.)

In the 3rd act I visualised the Sacred Marriage as Indian – yellows and golds.

I had to have these 'visualisations' to help myself. I've put them into the text only as footnotes. Because they are only potential guides. But I can *see* now, now that I've been imagining into it a bit as I might guess Ben would be doing, that if the places on the stage are clarified (to ourselves) into their respective functions of natural and super-natural (e.g. foreground–background = wood–sanctuary, and Right heaven, sky – Left, hell, earth = stone staircase–cave mouth).

Then the folk who correspond will immediately make sense, without intellectual explanation – and that when Mark and Jenifer disappear in natural dress and reappear in super-natural (the first time partially transfigured the second time wholly) then it's addition-ally obvious (other than by what they sing) what has happened. And similarly for their return to themselves. Clearly the production will follow from this quite naturally and easily.

1 October 1954

Dearest darling Barbara –

I came back on air – because I think the costumes absolutely right, and very lovely. It seems to me we're set now for something really remarkable – and I'm too grateful to be articulate.

You seem to have too a marvellous way of dealing with folk – so that all we want and stand for imposes itself without violence. I think *you* will do this with [John] Cranko also. But I'm trying to get a joint meeting fixed between him and me and Christopher [West], as soon as possible. Then I'll send him down to you, if that's the thing that's sensible.

I had a message for you from Schott's that they were making what sounded like an 'offset litho' (?). Colour as nearly exact as they can do – in very great haste in time to go abroad on the post and mail.

After the high-water mark of being at St Ives again, I'm down below the surface a while. The time draws inexorably near!
    Love
    Michael

[early] October 1954

Barbara darling,

I shall see [George] Harewood on Friday and I shall put your case to him – i.e. I will ask him to see Webster as soon as he returns and explain that he'll get a letter from you stating that you felt the fee offered [for work on *The Midsummer Marriage*] was inadequate, after due consideration of your expenses and earlier commitments. That we hope C.G. will see their way to raise it to what you need, without demur. But between you and me alone I'd like it to be understood that whatever Covent Garden does on that matter you will receive it (I can see to that) – so that while you are negotiating with C.G. we don't either hold things up to hold them to ransom, or have to fret ourselves into emotional haggling. Because at this hour and in this matter I don't feel equal to pretending to jeopardise the opera in order to force Webster's hand. I would prefer to negotiate with him quietly, in the belief that he will accede in his time, in the knowledge that from some unstated (and publicly unacknowledged) source the missing £50 (or even the £100) will reach you.

I have thought this out very carefully since you phoned – and talked it over with my mother. She wholeheartedly agrees. I think she knows that the fear and worry of further indecision at this stage (for *me*) cannot really be measured by whether C.G. pays all or nearly all – so long as the project proceeds and you are recompensed as you know you should be. You must remember that by one of the accidents of our present social life the composer's economics are inextricably delayed. That is, he does not have to negotiate an immediate recompense once for all, but puts down a kind of capital value which *may* draw income till his death and after. So that what I do is absolutely right for me. I live at present on *past* works. The opera is still entirely in the capital-making state, and this or that more or less at this final moment is not a principle to be fussed over, unless one is *very* short-sighted indeed. But I still suspect that if you go on gently negotiating with them by letter, or word – they will agree.

All this means to me that please get up to see John Sullivan as soon as you can. I'm going to pave the way on Friday – and given all the good will that seems to be flowing in Covent Garden towards the piece, we should succeed – even if some anti-elements must be lurking round corners I never see. The most exciting thing to me is that Harewood tells me the music itself, as they rehearse, is beginning to make its effect. The kind of 'official' view is that however strange and odd the libretto appears on reading it will all fall into place and seem ordained when the music articulates and orders the whole piece.

When you said to me did I realise the decor would be abstract, I suppose I had a momentary jolt on the word, as of an old battle-ground. I'm so sure that the issue has never taken on in music so sharp a form, because music was never representational in the crass sense of some periods of painting etc. I don't especially want to do battle in the opera, though I'm getting used to the idea that the libretto itself will force this on me to a limited extent. 'Representational' scenery – whatever that extraordinary nonsense should be named – is not so much anathema to me as an impossibility in this piece – if the work isn't to degenerate into pantomime. But the music (as I see it) isn't involved in this particular problem – because the music shifts and turns (in time) as the situations and characters shift and turn, and the worlds interact; so that the music is much more immediately connected with the specifically human element of the personages on the stage. I think that that is one of the reasons why Priaulx, for example, practically rejects opera. While I don't reject the theatre at all, though I have deliberately chosen a tradition which has ritual and spiritual elements in it, as well as the old comedy element, if subdued. In fact the latter was always the most difficult. To give rests from the big moments (because in a long work in *time*, there have to be these rests corresponding to the normal rhythm of life) I needed all the art (and artifice) I could command to descend towards the common or garden, without banality. I did not always succeed – as indeed Mozart and Schikaneder did not entirely succeed in *The Magic Flute*. The comic humour is too gross, maybe. In *Magic Flute* they designed and composed for a late 18th-cent. theatre of high pantomime, so to speak; with masses of machinery and real animals and what have you. So that they tried, in their way, to correspond scenery with scene – the high with the high and low with the low. Therefore, when I rejected the high pantomime (as I feel I really did, however unimaginative my own visual sense may be, and however conventional it was as I composed) I certainly cut off any possibility of changing the scenery with the dramatic sense of the scenes, except for the transformations of the Ritual Dances where I ask specifically *for* transformations – partly to give a rest even to the eye looking at one set, and partly for absolute needs of the 'story'. There will probably be an almost unintentional extra irony in the comic scenes – e.g. King Fisher talking to the Ancients through his secretary. That is to say, King Fisher's contemporary artificiality will be directly counter to the magic artificiality of the 'place' (what kind of place is this do you think? It's very odd for a house).

I am sure therefore that there will be attacks on the 'story' – and on the non-representational set. Yet I can conceive that it will all be so accomplished that the rightness of the strangeness, so to speak will gradually sink in during the long time that the audience looks at the one main set. Because there is here an advantage to place against the disadvantage – that representational and non-representational in vision is, or has been, the place of the fiercest battles. I would hope that the glory of the whole combination of varied, gay and warm music flowing over and in the visionary set and strange 'story' will still the old desires to do battle. It won't altogether, but it will for many. I suppose therefore that I'm saying the music will contain much more that has been quite clearly transformed from all the high pantomime and imaginative opera tradition, then maybe the sets can, because the old clichés in that field lag so far, far behind – and no one maybe has seen how to transform visually the high pantomime back, or forward, towards its pristine state of ritual and illumination, with the gaiety and vigour of the ironic and comic intertwined. [. . .]

Luv

M.

PS. You must be seeing more clearly than I am that I write (as I always do) to clear my own mind. Because I am in fact very slow to see. It seems indeed now that we are bent on transforming the theatre to the imaginative level we need. By the very fact of using music (opera not drama) and the traditional 'story' of two worlds and moments of illumination, I took the initial steps. For you, I suppose, the complementary step, the new adventure which Ben [Nicholson] (I think) was frightened of, is to use *your* gifts and sensibilities also *in the theatre*. And this is quite another thing from painting a backcloth!! Or even really a picture by Ben in depth. How slow I am to see [. . .]

But it all means that I *need* you much more now that the question of what is seen becomes the matter in hand. And I am with you heart and soul.

17 October 1954

Dearest Barbara,

[. . .] I don't know if Ben [Nicholson] ever let you see the letter I wrote him about my efforts to try and visualise the set as a huge picture by him in depth. Maybe not. And maybe that was not very helpful. I've had a short talk with Cranko who is to do the dancing, and find that it's the fact of 2 worlds, natural and supernatural, that boggles him. He doesn't ever seem to have apprehended that this is the tradition between [*sic*] *A Midsummer Night's Dream*. So to get clear what I call the transition in time that is the inter-action of the 2 worlds during the 24 hrs of the story, I have to explain in detail all the time just where it has got to. But the scenery, the stage habitations, are in a way stranger and more exciting because the transition from world to world is almost made (in space) once for all, without change; except that the audience doesn't see it all immediately. They see first the wood near the footlights, which would be as near to the natural world as we can artistically go. Then as the mists rise from the buildings with the sun, the habitation of the immortals corrects, or contrasts, and adds dimensions to the wooded hill, towards something imaginative if at the same time a 'habitation' of a certain supernatural manifestation. And I suppose the Greek part of it is simply because with the Greek world I always felt the extraordinary power of the natural backed, transformed, by the supernatural.

I was in a house yesterday and saw a copy of a wonderful head – a candid direct girl's face looking down, and a Phrygian cap with a mask-like schematic face looking up. It just depended whether you saw it first from below or saw it as Priaulx and I did (for it was on a table) from above. But what the extraordinary secret of the inner relationship between face and cap I can't tell. There is no jarring – yet the 2 worlds are there together in stone.

In the play of the plot the worlds so to speak come and go, and that's how I worked at the music. It's more than exciting now to realise that I must all the time have visualised the stage like this face and cap.

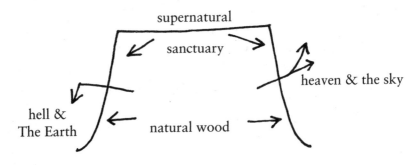

Or rather that the face and cap is the almost exact equivalent of Bella and Jack in love, against the background of the animal ritual dances. The relationship between growing wood and stone sanctuary is analogous but on a wider and deeper scale – more public and monumental, so to speak. To express indeed by stage illusion the kind of force that drove Stone Age men to erect Stonehenge and Woodhenge – the circles of 'dead' stone and the circles of various kinds of 'living' trees. I'm sure, with the immense size of Covent Garden, and the huge numbers of folk involved at moments on the stage, that we need the illusion of the monumental and the spacious – so as not to get the human element produced by the living actors and dancers, too overweighted against the spatial dimensions, so to speak. But I won't write more, but wait till I see you.

I haven't told you that my mother prayed all the time that it might come out as it has – and she feels her prayers have been answered! She feels, intuitively, that Ben is enclosed in some kind of perfection, shall we say, that cannot adventure easily into the big world. She liked [Graham] Sutherland *very* much, but still has the feeling that he got led away to his portrait because of some fear. But I wouldn't be sure of that. I think her intuition of Ben is sounder. I don't myself condemn Ben at all. I'm inclined to echo the comment made (not in my presence) by Herbert Read, which was simply: 'He's a b[loody] fool!'

Ben's written me 3 letters now in which he seems to be excusing himself ever and again. So I suppose something is worrying him under his skin – and I can't help him to exorcise it because it's in himself not in me. But I have gained so much out of my tiny experience with his book and his work, that I bless the way it has gone – tortuous though in some ways it may have been.

Blessings darling Barbara
Michael

20 October 1954

Dearest Barbara,

I was still radiant yesterday after the 2 night journeys because Monday was so rewarding. In the train after, Christopher [West] made a gesture to me which was gentle and dignified. There had been a problem for him (and for me) because the producer I had really wanted, [Günther] Rennert from Hamburg, is here now producing *Tales of*

Hoffmann. (My bitter letter of the summer was about that.) C. and I ran into Rennert last Friday on the stage – and it wasn't too easy. In the train after C. led the conversation round and then said: 'I know that Rennert would have done better for you, Michael. I apologise for my limitations.' I found this very nicely done. Did he write you a little note? He wanted to. He's afraid that I have forced you too much to consider the limitations of the theatre and he had found no opportunity in our so factual and necessary talk to get across to you that he hopes you haven't got an inhibitory feeling in consequence. For he feels there should be no bounds to the free play of your own characteristic imagination. The sense of his questions as to whether you saw sky behind the sanctuary was: if you wanted to draw our eyes *through* the curve of a Hepworth monolith, then he was all for it! No limitations on shapes, as might have been necessary and appropriate for e.g. Agamemnon. I think he will learn now very quickly that his relations with us can be candid and strong. There's been a not so candid tradition set in Covent Garden, I should guess, from their experiences with Britten on the one side, and the merely lesser figures on the other.

Cranko is a different kettle of fish. I'm glad Christopher decided that all the main lines must be laid down by us 3 alone. All we can do with Cranko at the moment is to bring him down to these limiting essentials where they are going to affect his necessary contribution. He's at present at complete sixes and sevens. This isn't mattering yet because it's so clear that we shall have controlled the style of our conventions and will necessarily have to carry this style over into Cranko's choreography. [. . .]

Love
M.

21 October 1954

Barbara dear,

All is set to see [John] Sullivan tomorrow and then begin work with the joint producers, Christopher West and John Cranko. In a way it's a bit of bad luck for them – especially West, the resident producer – because it's only just now it's got round to them, and they must feel a little bit that the odds are heavily weighted, with you and me already working at it. But I am not going to begin by trying to overwhelm them, but to draw them out and up. I find this necessary patience and

is to come – the light that raises the mists over the 'eternal' sanctuary, the light that lets Jenifer see 'further' – the light of the 'summer morning' that even effects King Fisher – and the afternoon light that in the dazzle between moving clouds allows Bella and Jack to dream the ancient rituals. Then, by the first chorus (taken from Aeschylus in technique) of Act 3, the wood is changed from sunset to moonrise – to the white Goddess and her night journey, airborne in the summer night sky.

Now I never was willing to visualise the eternal set more than I had to, in order to proceed at all. But I put down the names of the symbols that seemed necessary: wood, stone, cave, 'steeple stair', temple. Images that have the oldest antiquity of all. The tree, or wooden pillar, that became everything up to Christ's tree; the stone pillar that is equally old – the sanctuary of wood and stone – intertwined, as it was in Stonehenge (the wood circles have rotted away) – the caves in which Ice Age men went on hands and knees to paint and draw and chisel; the 'staircase', allied to the going up to the hill-top – all these things which are divine numen but use all the human imagination. And, the key to it all, is that they have always been an occasion for ritual. So that it was thus that I was brought to the theatre, to opera – which began as ritual – and where personages act the ritual and the 'story'. And once I'd got that far, I became incredibly fascinated by theatre – by this age-old art of representation – so much so that I was prepared to change my musical style (which I don't think my darling Priaulx will like at all!) and to begin to play with all the complex patterns of roles and situations and gestures and passions – tempting the audience by every artifice to rise every so often to the timeless moments when the action is nearly pure ritual.

You know I am now coming to feel that B.N. couldn't really have felt all this – while you my dear can – because of your own great human warmth. For theatre, thought of in this way, is a great richness – the 'ripeness in all' of Lear. The movement from the bottom to the top – and the return to everyday! – so difficult indeed that was at the end – even now I can believe it will border on anti-climax. But at no point did I reject anything of our rich, even muddy, humanity, till it rejected itself. And then I placed it on midsummer day, in the light of sun and gaiety and youth and vigour ('everyone shall dance for me') – and I suppose colour – whatever I can possibly mean by that. (That is more indeed how B.N. came about.) And I *think* I imagine the greatest sensation of colour to be allied to the sense of summer – and the young people who have been 'beguiled' by summer – and so their costumes. But I can't see anything clearly, for I'm visually very blind – and I'm holding back till we can talk, and till we, or you at any rate, can confer with the producers. For we must somehow draw them to us and indeed in the human drama draw from them what gifts they have to give.

Please forgive me for my occasional use of a kind of caricature of Ben and of Priaulx. I do this only to draw sharp distinctions. Priaulx, indeed, is a rich personality, but does not project this richness in the Shakespearean sense through her art. But theatre, once one leaves the drawing-room story, for the 'ritualistic', is to be thought of as huge-hearted and embracing all – the heaven and hell as well our common life. I'm *sure* Mozart was right in *The Magic Flute* to give this 'story' such lucid, translucent, gay, warm music – ordered but luminous. Such winning music that it has carried with it that impossible pantomimic theatre of machines and live animals. Naturally I could never emulate his innocence – but I have emulated his clarity, I think – and had to use of course my own richness of invention to carry me where I had to go. I don't want to pare away the spectacular either and because that must always have been part of the illuminatory theatre and ritual – the darkness and the blinding light – the Pythia on the tripod – the ritual dancing – the clashing of cymbals for the young men dancing – the *korybantes*. It's *only* theatre (by embracing that age-old art) that can join thus a huge number of 'contemporary' people into touch with the 'great memory', the secret universe behind all phenomena. By this extraordinary technique of using the very passions of our humanity to unfold at chosen moments some revelation. Even Jack's and Bella's love, which trembles on the borders of the most common or garden expression, suddenly, at the kiss, goes over into the timeless and the eternal – and by that 'trick' even for all those who may in the audience be lost, *everyone* will have suffered the experience as it happens before their eyes. But that 'trick' is probably only possible just because we have to turn the set in such a way that the 'glory' is slightly put out of sight round the corner – and yet even then, the drama seems to say, the magic happens because sexual generation is divine too – if, seen from another angle of a dark and sacrificial ritual. If I've done my job right, when the kiss comes, and with it the crash of universal music, then Bella's 'Let's go within the shadow of the wood' will have the effect of incantation – so that the wood, the wood in the theatre I mean, has all the ancient conventions that have been there since the primeval forests. The whole thing is this curious play between our sense in the theatre (what we hear and see) and shall we say, the collective uncon-scious, that given the symbol (not the fact) rises up to greet the image; and the timeless moment is created; from which it later again recedes.

[. . .] But enough! I must do some commonplace correspondence now. And I'll phone you tomorrow evening 10 to 10.30 (don't get back till 9 p.m. and then have supper) with all the details I can manage.

Blessings –
M.

26 October 1954

Dearest Barbara,

[. . .] a request from my publishers via the stalwart Howard Hartog – would it be possible for them to have a tiny line drawing from your hand, either of or akin to the decor, or portion of it, to be used for their house Christmas card? It would, from my point of view, be a *very* happy possibility of good publicity – in the sense of decent and come-ly. The cards go out to all reputable musicians and organisations at home and overseas. It should be more or less a case of the sooner the better. But could wait till I come.

I might say Schott's have never gone to town in this way for one of their English composers before! And I'll tell Howard to write or ring you.

All my love and all my thanks and blessings.
Michael

1 December 1954

Barbara dear,

[. . .] On Friday evening is the Walton, *Troilus and Cressida* – all set for social success. A shambles artistically from our point of view – and ill prepared even strictly musically! The M.M. will be *much* better sung and played – quite apart from the fact that it will be a unity of eye and ear. Which is so rare in England as to be almost non-existent. Though maybe in their own world it has come once or twice from [John] Piper and Britten.

I might say that Christopher [West] is now 'wild about the costumes'; to use his picturesque phrase. And he does now know what he has got – and what this unity is. So that I am quite overjoyed. He comes to be with me over the weekend.

I am a bit foxed still by Jenifer's wedding dress. Maybe Christopher is too – I'll ask him. I'm not sure that is that we haven't gone too far towards 'wedding' in the pantomime, realistic sense, to match the dignified simplicity of Mark's own clothes. Will you think round and about it for me?

I heard Bella sing yesterday – it's quite lovely. (And the He-Ancient – excellent.) Bella and Jack will fetch everyone. Their duet is quite melting in its innocence.

Love

Michael

I hope Barbara darling you *are* resting?!

29 December 1954

Dearest Barbara,

I've been writing letters to you in my mind, but never done so – having been in a curious kind of disarray – half physical half mental – and I didn't see how I was going to write without turning all into a self-piteous moan! It began with a fiendish tooth extraction that sent me to bed, and produced a very long enduring nausea. Not only physical but mental. Just as though all the continued strength of the period since the summer at St Ives had drained away and left a wrung-out rag. It *has* to lift today, because I go to London in an hour to begin the last lap.

Nevertheless I feel God has been good. When there seemed a last difficulty over the last costumes I was *very* near breaking point. The relief when that was settled was really I suppose too great. I felt so thankful, but so inadequate. I blessed you in my heart, and then plucked up courage to go to the dentist – and then collapsed. I feel conscience-stricken now; because very unsure of myself. I felt instinctively that you too must have been stricken back by all your fabulous hard work, and that somehow I should have found means to be helping you, comforting you – instead of just being crumpled up like a child needing its mama. I knew of course you'd be as understanding as you always are. But nevertheless I'd have wished to be stronger. I'm not yet!

But I fancy, on the other hand, it's some deeply preservative instinct which is forcing me into this nauseous lethargy, so that I shan't crack up when it finally begins.

I think the relief of getting such an extraordinary degree of artistic sympathy and collaboration between us both has played its part in so knocking me out. I have the underground impatience, of so many months, years already, flowing like a great river. I want to *see*. I want to *hear*. But the wanting is so powerful it gets from me a complementary violent repression, which plays its part in the disarray, when once one relaxes.

Barbara darling, I can't say thank you enough – but you know that. I do so trust that it's meant something to you too. But I know too that it has done.

I'm beginning to count the days, in an odd sort of dream. I hope I don't become too stupid!

I thought of you with all the children for Christmas. I had a wonderfully quiet and tranquil time here – with the first tiny sounds of the spring birds, in this curious mild December.

I shall probably ring, when this will have got you – and our life begins to reawake.

Love to you all, beloved Barbara
Michael

1 January 1955

Barbara darling –

[. . .] *Everything* is happening at once now – stage rehearsals and music – in different places! And costumes and scenery being done like mad – I haven't had a moment to see any of that, and must pray that all is well. Shall be thankful when you are there to cast your professional eye on it all! But all that I have been in on – rehearsing, and press interviews and what have you – is good. Am terribly pleased – and I think the omens are good. [. . .]

Love
M.

6 January 1955

Dearest Barbara,

John [Minchinton] brought me your letter to Schott's yesterday where he is tied up in a day and night crisis of orch.–parts–production. First orch. rehearsal is tomorrow morning at 10! I saw a stage rehearsal and Christopher [West] at work. All very exciting. I managed to see John Sullivan and Clement [Glock]. The particular problem of some days past was too technical for me. But Clement is a tower of commonsense and strength, and she said she would be speaking with you last night. It seems that some decisions had to be taken on the spot, which, had you been there, you could have seen for yourself. It did not *sound* crucial, as Clement explained it. But she said that *I* wouldn't understand it anyhow! She's gloriously frank and straightforward.

Today I'm doing a special commentary for the BBC – for broadcasting. Too long to explain by letter. And this evening I entertain a critic, for a profile in *Observer*. Tomorrow is all day in town with stage and orch. rehearsals at once! I hope to have Sat. and Sun. resting, and then a fortnight, I think, at a stretch. Because I shall certainly be at the lighting rehearsal on Sun. week – and I imagine you will be there too, as you say. It's a matter for eye.

Christopher works slowly but tremendously continuous and serious. I feel he knows now what he's going for. I rarely intervene; sometimes choose between musical and visual where they clash.

Love
Michael

27 January 1970

Dearest Barbara,

Anthony Adams sent me the 'Pictorial Autobiography' and really nothing could have been nicer. I took it to bed with me (I take a lot of bed-rest for present health troubles) and read with great delight the whole lot. I was very moved by coming upon the generous pages about *The Midsummer Marriage*, and of course I entirely echo your hope of the last sentence – and indeed, in a 4th and final opera slowly gestating now [*The Ice Break*], I feel I may come tolerably near to this dream. But it will be some years before I can start the music.

Many, many thanks and heaps of love.
Michael

Anna Kallin

Anna Kallin (1896–1984), called Niouta or Niuta, left her native Russia for Germany in 1912 and studied at Leipzig University. After moving to London in 1921 she spent twenty years in Britain and on the Continent as a freelance reviewer, translator and publisher's reader. She moved in a wide circle of European artists and intellectuals that included the painter Oskar Kokoschka, with whom she lived in the 1920s, and Isaiah Berlin, whose radio talks she later produced. In 1940 she joined the BBC for wartime intelligence work and served in various capacities before being appointed a producer of talks in 1946. She was associated with the Third Programme from its inception. In his autobiography, Those Twentieth Century Blues, *Tippett described their working relationship as a 'stimulating partnership', and his letters to her, which range over literary, artistic and philosophical topics as well as music, are at the same time a testament to the strength of their friendship. While naturally focusing on the talks he was to deliver, Tippett kept Kallin up to date with progress on his new compositions, as well as writing on a more personal level to commiserate over her health problems while sharing details of his own physical, financial and artistic hardships. She is the dedicatee of Piano Sonata No. 3.*

April 1952

Niouta dear,

I oughtn't to be writing this letter to you at all, because I want to involve you, if ever so slightly, in a different kind of matter of mine with the BBC. My music. And it's Karajan over again. There's been a scheme whereby the next broadcast *Child of Our Time*, due early autumn (3rd Prog.), might now be done by Karajan. At first Leonard Isaacs was sympathetic (with my publisher, Schott & Co., London). But now it transpires that the 'Committee', whatever they may be, turn Karajan down, for the reason that they know 3 English conductors capable of performing the work adequately. Of which we (my publishers and I) suppose the first to be [Walter] Goehr, second Sargent (a *dreadful* performance once at Leeds – this comment 'off the record') and third we can't guess. (Perhaps the composer!) Anyhow, the real matter is this. If an English work begins to get an international status and suddenly shoots upwards, so to speak, with a conductor of Karajan's 'reputation', through a performance in Rome, is it always to [be] debarred from an English broadcast with the status of such a conductor's performance? To put it now more personally: can I not enjoy in my own country the 'luck' (I won't say 'merit') of being played by Karajan? And if the BBC a few years back *themselves* asked Ansermet to conduct a symphony of mine, to help it on, can they not be willing to put a seal to some other rather more successful compliment or esteem, or whatever it is, of one's work?

Now this moan isn't for you, dear Niouta! I'm sending it to you only because I'm unsure if I ought ever to moan at all, in any matter which touches myself. What I *hope* you can do, is to distil the moan into some less offensive essence, and have a gentle exploratory word with Christopher [Holme] or Harman [Grisewood]. If I wrote direct, then they would have to write me the kind of letter which Harman has just said I do myself so admirably (*à propos* of Hans Keller). Of course I could also enclose such a letter already composed. But if you were to speak from outside any publisher's or composer's griefs, games, gambits and so on; then they can speak off-hand and unconstrained to you.

I dare say the difficulty is really English musical chauvinism in a disguised form. And if I've got to have an English man then we'll be back at Goehr again (just when we seemed to be escaping). But I suppose I'm momentarily disappointed. The 'Committee's' decision seems as yet to me rather narrow and ungenerous. But probably it's me who is ambitious and grasping. Because, indeed, why should the accident of a Rome performance with Karajan affect the BBC at all? So if that's how it seems to your sober mind, put the letter in the basket.

bien des amitiés – je viendrai vous voir – à bientôt –
M.

spring 1952

Niouta darling –
[. . .] My publishers, viz. the representative, Howard Hartog (good-

hearted English-born Dutch Jew) went rushing off to Eric Waugh (?) [Warr] about the opera, in order to go right to the top – and the first remark on broaching the subject is a gem. 'Why doesn't [Schmidt-]Isserstedt and the Hamburg Radio do it?'! I don't suppose E.W. realises how odd that sounds for an English work – and it's the old old story why the music got to Schotts Söhne Mainz before the war – refused all down the line here – even and particularly the string piece [Concerto for Double String Orchestra] that's now metaphorically leaving the Third for the Home [Service]. But I tell you this in confidence: re Waugh (or is it Warr?). For Leonard Isaacs won't react that way. Personally I'm not impatient at all. But of course it's much more of a nightmare to Schott's who are investing at least £1000 to £1200 just to have printed vocal scores and orchestral hire material. They'll recover it in the end – but not at once.

Anyhow, what I meant just now is that if a tone of resentment, let alone bitterness, crept into my letter on the surface, it isn't inside to any depth. I tell you the story for 'BBC politics' not because it piques me – if it did. We all get put into boxes in public life. For some reason my box is not an officially royal English one. Very definitely Third Prog. 'cosmopolitan', with such odd eccentricities as being a specialist in Purcell and the Elizabethans – (instead of Elgar, I suppose). And that was the irony of the [Schmidt-]Isserstedt performance of the String Concerto in Festival Hall. It was done so well that *The Times* revised its niggardly opinion of my music and put the work beside Elgar and Vaughan Williams!!! (All the Karajan nonsense has come through that – for the *Times* crit[ique] decided Walter Legge, and so it goes.) But there's a long hangover: even in the BBC. What *will* happen gradually is that certain works (like that one) will slowly force themselves onto H.S. [Home Service] because they come through even into provincial repertoire – but the fresh things will go on being put into the proper Tippett box – for after all didn't the Schoenberg talks show just the kind of mind that lives in that box? And as so many really first-class folk are somewhere in them kind of boxes it's where we would be.

Now really, that's enough meandering about my own affairs, which seem to have got under my own skin again.

I've got Mr [*sic*] Frankfort's curious book *Arrest and Movement** –

* Henrietta Antonia Groenewegen-Frankfort, *Arrest and Movement: An Essay on Space and Time in the Representational Art of the Ancient Near East* (1951).

though I haven't finished it yet. He (Frankfort) is rather drier and probably much sounder. Did you ever read Rachel Levy's *Gate of Horn*?* But maybe my passion was subjective? I was reading such a lot at that time – 2–3 years back – when the opera [*The Midsummer Marriage*] was growing its leaves and branches. And so often it was the women anthropologists who did most. Harrison's *Themis*,† for instance. A decisive book. But then I went all Greek and amassed a lot of Loeb bilingual texts and read the *Iliad* in that way – and Aeschylus and Sophocles and that oddest of Euripides, the *Bacchae* – and paid £20 or more to have A. B. Cook's *Zeus*‡ on my shelves, for it has reproductions of nearly everything that exists Greek. And then, as usual, it died of its own excess – the discharge being fulfilled – and the last book was this one of Zimmer on Hindu mythology and iconography¶ – which is nearly finished and has provided the last flower. After which I've borrowed English 19th-century poets and am being refreshed by George Eliot! And truly refreshed. [. . .]

I'd better try and do some music.

Michael

May 1952

Dear Niouta –

Such a lot to say, but I can't remember it all. Anyhow, the inside is settling down again – thanks to the sofa and various other aids. And I've decided I think to go to learn muscular relaxation# from someone. Whom? I have no name yet. Then my amanuensis, called Michael Tillett, who makes the piano reduction of *The Midsummer Marriage* started his last letter off (before a string of technical suggestions) with such confidence in the freshness of the music that some of my temporary depression lifted. Because B[*illy*] *Budd* made me feel terrifically lonely – i.e. working away for 5 years at an opera that just flouts all the fashions; of the psychological study; of the *Neues vom Tage*–Menotti–*Consul* touch; of the neo-Verdian Schiller–

---

* Gertrude Rachel Levy, *The Gate of Horn: A Study of Religious Conceptions of the Stone Age and Their Influence upon European Thought* (1948).
† Jane Ellen Harrison, *Themis: A Study of the Social Origins of Greek Religion* (1912).
‡ Arthur Bernard Cook, *Zeus: A Study in Ancient Religion*, 3 vols. (1914, 1925, 1940).
¶ Heinrich Robert Zimmer, *Myths & Symbols in Indian Art & Civilisation* (1946).
# For his gastric problems. Tippett believed their source to be the mental turmoil he experienced while composing, manifesting itself as a physical ailment that affected his stomach. The condition was aggravated by sitting for long periods.

Shakespeare grand drama; of the frank love story. And so what is left (not being a communist) but this dreadful inchoate* world of mythology, anthropology and god knows what. Though the opera isn't like these long words sound but gay, and fresh and only occasionally numinous. Then a few evenings back I got a fillip from listening to G. R. Levy on the 3rd [Programme]. Her *Gate of Horn* was vital in spawning out the background for the opera – and I'd like to meet her and tell her so one day. Is she nice? I hope so – for it's her kind of folk and mind that will shape whatever conscious audience the opera may one day have – apart from those who *may* find the music fresh and good in its own right. Meanwhile my publishers are beautifully despondent of getting it on an English operatic stage and are going to try for a 3rd Prog. performance a) to recover some of their colossal cash b) more seriously, because they think this may make the sound, the music, begin to carry the dubious text. So there it is. And instead you will be able to see at Covent Garden a big Meyerbeerish opera by Sir William Walton [*Troilus and Cressida*] and another and another of the curly cherub's [Britten, *Gloriana* and *The Turn of the Screw*].

All this curious despondency may lift again yet – and the music does go on and on, and *will* get finished soon.

Your best date, I should think, would be to see the month of June from here. [. . .] I have a *very* good sherry in the house – [and] a cheap, but good, Hungarian white wine. My Thelma and Jimmy [domestic helps] are longing to see you and will do all that their simple selves are capable of to show you of their best. You shall have a fire in your bedroom whatever the sun is doing, and I'm sitting now with a huge log fire behind me. The water is not as hot though – the bath is antiquated and Victorian. *Mais c'est à ravir.* [. . .]

à bientôt –
Michael

28 December 1953

Dearest Niouta,

[. . .] Christmas is really for me only a *crise de conscience*. I send no cards but merely receive many; and am glad when it is over. Though occasionally I am touched by the simple images of the miraculous

* Or possibly 'incubate', a Tippettian coinage from 'incubus'.

birth in a medieval carol. It is not a proper solstice at all, to my pagan mind.

J[ohn Minchinton] has been practising the piano-part of my songs [*The Heart's Assurance*] to play with his very attractive girl alto (of whom Margaret is now really jealous I should say) and though he is gone last night and the house is quiet (except for the sweep) and I pace up and down this big sunny room about to begin the work again – the sound of the songs hangs in my head as though they were someone else's. Because the mood of love and death was so signally externalised. As you know, they were written to the memory of Francesca Allinson, who had meditated a long time on Virginia Woolf before she herself jumped off the bridge at Clare into an East Anglian little river. And now, after making the really beautiful record of the songs with Peter Pears, it's Noel Mewton-Wood. [. . .]

Actually this mood doesn't have creative resonance any more, for the time being. Though there's one such (maybe the most powerful) moment in *The Midsummer Marriage*. For the time, it's the Yeatsian mood which has resonance still. That we must learn to accept the tragedy of the period as an actor playing a tragic role. But I don't think I could have come to feel that had not the compassionate notes been so strongly sounded already.

If 50 is really the older periods' 30, then I may yet do what I have to do – for I need a lot more time!

These periods of dreaming. They are part of change and growth and richness and whatever. I have been dreaming classical masculine dreams about drinking red wine in little round glasses at a round table with 3 unknown women. But maybe they were unknown men. I can't remember. The usual dubiety. But I hope you have been dreaming about cooking. That is the sure sign.

Francesca, by the way, was all almost that Priaulx [Rainier] is not: fastidious, elegant and feminine. I [would] have you to look one day with a side glance at Beate Ruhm v. Oppen who, also a 1/2 Jew, oddly resembles her – especially with a certain hairstyle.

Who should I take for a greater (modern) tragic heroine? My mind is in flux again.

Nurse Cavell? Could she not be *verdichtet* into a modern Antigone? Tell me.

Love
M.

24 September 1954

Dearest Niouta,

All you say about B.B. [Britten], Puccini, L.B. [Berkeley] and *Nelson* is *perfectly* right. Least, right to me! I thought very much the same – and I don't think I did *Nelson* an injustice by leaving after 2 acts. Berkeley imitates B.B. in his operatic technique, with every disadvantage. But Alan P.J. [Pryce-Jones, the librettist] let things go by, or go on, which poor little me would *never* have agreed to. I mean just dramatically. I come to think that a lot of the trouble with our minor English operatic attempts (including even a lot of B.B.) is timing; and insufficient struggle to solve the special problems. Those two, in *Nelson*, had a good moment with Mme Seraphin's refusal and then decision to tell Nelson's fortune. Only then to let the good witch moan for 5 stage minutes (at least 15 emotional minutes) before she actually did the job. Verdi would never have let his librettist so delude him. The gypsy would have come and gone with the inevitability of fate. But alternatively if the composer feels he *must* let such a character sing a lot, then he must resolve the technical problem.

This point interested me, because I have just the same kind of situation. It was my old Hungarian mathematician [Paul Dienes] (I think) who put me on the track of the solution – viz. [Paul] Valéry's 'La Pythie' – where she moves from woman to Pythia. So I lifted it entire – into my own language and metaphor – made it even stand for myself, the composer, slowly being dehumanised in favour of the Muse, or the God – and it's come out as the most splendid aria of the lot.

But forgive all this. My trouble is now that I can't get my own opera out of my mind. It's living me again day and night – so that I can't compose anything new – I worry everyone every day. Covent Garden wish I'd never been born (more or less!) – and the old illnesses come back.

But – it's slowly happening, and I get slowly my will and my way. Or, if I can't, I find the way round. [. . .]

Love,

M.

I expect to go to Switzerland for a première [Divertimento on 'Sellinger's Round'] on Nov. 6 – and then to take a week off in N. Italy. I'm looking forward to it wildly – for itself, and for a break before the final battles. Lucca maybe is too far. I must see just where it is.

10 December 1954

Dearest Niouta,

Back home again to find your 2 letters. So many thanks – *glad* indeed you like Divertimento – the best people did! But it wasn't a good performance. Prof. [Anthony] Lewis had such a gigantic programme on his rehearsal time, it was scamped – and that isn't, in *my* opinion, the real thing the Third should permit. It was rather unhappy for me; for even the actual players were a poor lot. However – maybe [Paul] Sacher himself can be allowed to do a radio show when he's over next year for Glyndebourne again. Meanwhile I've heard more singers – King Fisher ([Otakar] Kraus) ought to be a winner. He knows exactly what he's meant to be – and he's said apparently that he found the Walton (he sang Diomede) such pastiche of all he'd sung in Cov. Gdn before, that *now* he has at last something real and new. [. . .]

Still the Divertimento showed that one is still alive . . .

The second movement was written first, in the series of variations (by different composers) on the tune 'Sellinger's Round' for Aldeburgh Fest. last year. Mine was the best! So I took it out and back to make the Divertimento for Sacher. Have now (10 days past) sent B.B. [Britten] a score of the Divertimento and a nice letter. But at *Troilus* he cut me twice dead. So I've had it. *Er ist äusserst empfindlich!* [He's extremely touchy!]

Love –
M.

24 February 1955

Dearest Niouta,

We must be living in sympathy! I came back on Sat. and went Sun. morning to London to a rehearsal – the cold, and the horrible nausea of being back in the London professional atmosphere, made me quite ill. Needing desperately to get peace and quiet now and to work again, I've got back here at last. I didn't even enjoy Tuesday's opera performance! But I wish you had been with us after all. I'm disturbed and distressed you've had such a bad turn. Barbara Hepworth has been shut in, only allowed out in the sun, ever since the première. We all grow *old*, Niouta. That's what's happening . . .

On Sat. I have to rush to Dortmund to hear a perf., and then rush back. After that, I think, real peace and tranquillity for a while. Over the opera [*The Midsummer Marriage*] and the press and the what-have-you of all kinds, I've got now a lot to readjust myself to. I need to lie back and think and wonder and cogitate. I need always to learn afresh from what I've done and not done. I want to do a new big choral work soon and must try not to let myself go too far away into too strange worlds. Yet I can't ever be the just orthodox. I express myself badly. I mean I can't rejoin the traditional things in a conventional and orthodox manner. Please get better.

Love –

M.

2 January 1956

Niuta dear –

[. . .] the opening of the new Symphony [No. 2] has come suddenly, and is good. The better word would have been *Einfall*: more accurate. (I don't think there's an English equivalent.) And the going has been so good last week that I can only with difficulty think of Mozart [for a radio talk] at all . . . and I dare say I would never, but that I must, and because as ever I seem to be in financial need for the day to day costs of my household. (One of the reasons why I was so glad to be able to compose the new Symphony on BBC commission. That does help, in that means some immediate, if small, payment for the year's otherwise unpaid work.) [. . .]

Love –

M.

12 January 1956

Dearest Niouta,

I'm a bit depressed today by a violently active internal chill. Which corresponded (naturally!) with all the fussation of Katchen irresponsibility throwing-in his hand for the Concerto [for Piano and Orchestra] at Birmingham (so that is also postponed to the autumn) – and with the fact that I had to sit up very late to get the Mozart talk done – and I didn't like the theme at all. I have the strongest sense that I can't for the moment recapture any of the 'flair' of earlier talks' occasions – and that this is not wickedness – or weakness, but the imperious demands of the music to be written. I have incredibly stupidly agreed to do 5 minutes on *Woman's Hour* to keep out an old (eccentric) friend, Minnie Pallister. It is the end!!

I am still *very* unsure about the horn piece [Sonata for Four Horns]. But shall leave it be for the time being. So long as I am quiet and well – not writing talks or giving press interviews on the phone – the Symphony [No. 2] goes splendidly.

I shall have my usual panics about being financially insolvent, but somehow I've got to stick it out here. [. . .]

Love

M.

2 March 1956

Dearest Niouta,

I fell 'ill' after John [Minchinton?]'s party – and had to be Thursday in bed, instead of taking Webster of Cov. Gdn out to lunch. Which was a pity. I got myself home eventually, and had en route an unexpected notion for a quite different talk. I wondered, pondering on my past, if I could be allowed to 'welcome' Auden back to England. We were exactly of an age. I met him first when we were 25 or so; and he read me some of *The Orators* in manuscript. I would have liked to discuss our England of that time, and how Auden spoke for some of it – and of the decisive events that forced decisions: the sudden sharpening of the unemployment crisis; the Spanish War; Hitler; the war itself. Seen from the angle of course of one who was a composer not a poet; much later off the mark; did not go to America; was deeply engaged (in a quite different way from Auden) by Disraeli's [*Sybil: or, The*] *Two Nations* [1845]. For at 26 or so I began my adventures in the industrial north; discovery of another England – and out of which eventually came part of the temper of *A Child of Our Time*. I doubt if I've ever told you of that part of my past.

But Auden remains an extraordinary figure – and I would like you to consider seriously whether I mightn't, semi-biographically, give a gently discursive but public tribute to his return. I confess of course that it is very personal. I knew all the Auden crowd (though was never one of the 'initiates') – and to read *The Orators* now is to recapture a mood from a 'chunk' of our real past. The chief difference, as between myself and them, that I didn't go to Berlin, but had a kind of rootedness here – and my own brand of prophetic intuition developed rather later, when the decisions that broke everyone apart, were already taken.

One curious thing is that we never then came into touch with the painters and sculptors. [Graham] Sutherland, [Henry] Moore, Hepworth don't seem to have been there – though of course they were of our age.

Then I don't really mean, as you would know, a nostalgic return to a past – but to set that past, when we were in our twenties, in relation to the present of young folk now in *their* twenties.

If you took the idea and gave it Stephen Spender, I would never forgive you!

Love
Michael

15 May 1957

Dearest Niouta,

I read your letter on the train to town yesterday – I had to hear some tapes at Yalding Hse, and then pre-record (on Stravinsky) for CBC [Canadian Broadcasting Corporation]. This I decided I never want to do again – viz. music appreciation talks, however enlightened. CBC bullied me into it – as Canada seems, temporarily, rather Tippettophile. I don't think I'm interested in any talk except of my own kind . . . and I think I have a serious one for you, one day, tucked away in my mind. To call it, maybe, 'Response to the Situation' – in inverted commas – and to give an analysis of its words and meanings – movement, mavericks, commitment, serial technique in music as extreme avant-garde and no public, our one world (globular) etc. To start with an analysis of 'the' – in 'to the situation'. However, it can't happen at all till the Symphony [No. 2] is finished (October) – and that depends on my living a disciplined life here. I do that indeed, but have been in a considerable imaginative ferment about the new theatrical work [drafts for *King Priam*], after an intense and most illuminatory talk with Peter Brook on the theatrical side. At present the material has all swung over into scenes (chosen to fit my own scheme) from Homer – chiefly *Iliad* – and from something the old witch Gertrude Levy said in your room one teatime. When you come I'll tell you all again where it's got to. [. . .]

Love –
M.

26 August 1957

Dearest Niouta,

[. . .] I go on Wed. to see Peter Brook again, and put my tragic drama [*King Priam*] to him. Because (if Covent Garden in the person of Webster agree) I want to get the Koussevitzky thing [a commission from the Foundation] put over onto the new opera. So I need to have it clearly added up before I write to America in those terms.

Symphony [No. 2] is *very* hard work. It's taken a record long time. But I *think* it has good quality of imagination *all through*. That's a tremendous achievement, if I've done it indeed.

Will see you sometime.

Love –

M.

13 June 1958

Dearest Niouta,

[. . .] I have been working hard – both at finishing the girls' piece [*Crown of the Year*], which is ended, and at the dead-pan-language script of the opera [*King Priam*]. There I've reached end of one act. (There are only two [eventually three].) And I've started on a terrific scene between the 3 women. How men dare to write scenes for women, I can't imagine! Or vice versa. But one has to. And it *seems* to me that I have gone a long way further down the road to understanding.

Part of the script is rather bitter. And the general conception changes a bit. It becomes less the fate of one man, but the interwoven fate of all. My friend, David Ayerst, thought it might almost have the title (too pessimistic in the event) *Nemesis*. I am tentatively thinking of it as *Charade*. After the children's game where one guesses the word spelled out in syllables by the scenes. But that can all wait.

Yes – John [Minchinton] did *Agon* very well.* Not a breath-taking performance but very able and clear and clean. And the Mozart concerto excellent. However, on Tuesday he had a letter from Maurice Johnstone, Head of BBC music, to say that owing to his lack of technique shown in the Third Prog. broadcast and the *Agon* concert, they would not employ him again for at least a year.

* The British première of Stravinsky's ballet.

Poor John had a terrible day – and so did his nearest and dearest. But he weathered it, and Wed. saw Adrian Boult, who was marvellously encouraging. Offers to share a public London concert with him to show his rejection of the BBC decision – which he imagines is partly personal somewhere. The *Konkurrenz* is very violent. Anyhow don't do anything. John is busy with Prades and his tour in France – and a probable command concert for the dying Queen Mother of the Belgians in Brussels on the return. The BBC have it very wrong – but they are badly confused at present. Shall come to see you soon.

Love

M.

16 September 1958

Dearest Niouta,

[. . .] it's been a curious period of abrupt change outside – after a long unsuspected inner change, I suppose. That is – a young would-be painter [Karl Hawker], fresh from a broken marriage, has come to be in the house (the little old cottage part at the other end, but also much *en famille*). John [Minchinton] has had a furious and prolonged *crise de jalousie*; and it will be ages before he gets through to a fresh relationship based more on the musical common interests. (It's a long and fascinating, if sordid story, involving Jessica [later Minchinton's wife] – who now has her chance!). As for myself I seem to have flung round on to a more masculine road. I can't put it otherwise – though it's clearly not quite just that. I suddenly won't be pushed around; whereas before I have wanted to be. And by the same token I am not in any way at all now competing with the girls. It has all happened with astonishing speed. And coincides with a growing obsession with the new opera [*King Priam*]. Mixed up I dare [say] somewhere, somehow. As to that – I have shown the first draft script to [Christopher] Fry, and then in Edinburgh to [Günther] Rennert, the opera producer. I've already done a second version of Act 1. I shall go with it, and Act 2 I hope, to see Rennert again in Hamburg in a few weeks' time. Then I shall possibly start at last the music. It is powerful and good – *I* think. Rennert is more than pleased with it too. [. . .]

Love

M.

9 April 1960

Dearest Niouta,

[. . .] K[arl Hawker] and I go tomorrow to get his children from Norwich – and on Wed. we go to St Ives for a week's break. See you again soon. And – K. and I have had to decide that there ought to be a room of our own – or maybe chiefly Karl's – in London. We shall try to find a friendly household with a spare room and not in too great need to make money from it. A room to manage in – so to speak – a gas-ring maybe, and we'd furnish it according to need. We shouldn't use it very much, at least not until opera rehearsals began. It's really to enable us to be overnight in London without depending on hospitality – and also so that Karl can see pictures etc and get away from my music occasionally!

If you heard of such, let me know.

Love

Michael

18 September 1960

Dearest Niouta,

I remain faithful indeed – and have been thinking many times of you in the last months – but constant work and troubled relationships have kept me enclosed – that and the fact that London visits get so professionally booked up.

However – things sort themselves out – and I'll see you soon – or would you not visit a Sat. or a Sun.? Whichever seems easiest.

Act 2 [of *King Priam*] is finished and the last act now begun. We've had a lot of bad luck over producers, but it looks now as if it'll be Sam Wanamaker (very unorthodox for opera!) who thinks highly indeed of the text.

But all news when we meet.

Love

Michael

13 November 1960

Dearest Niouta,

[. . .] Last Thursday was a 'knocking out' day for me. Karl's analysis has swiftly shifted him again, and he told me he is going back to

373

Anne – which is wonderful for him and Anne and the children. But heartbreak for me – of less final consequences I dare say. But it knocked me off balance as it always does. We seemed at the start (and we did) to have chosen each other and loved *each other* and through a temporary transformation of us both all seemed possible.

Perhaps it seemed especially vivid to me because through the luck of the game I've never found union in a one home. So now I'm really alone in the house – though not alone *of course* in all the loved ones around. I'm trying to get back to the rhythm of work (which has been a little difficult for a while back and impossible for the last days), because that heals and holds the mind and body steady. [William] Glock doesn't know my need, but his immediate assignment brings a proper professional response. This sounds terribly stuffy and pompous – but you understand. I'm afraid at first I couldn't keep the tears back, but that's nearly all over.

Love –
M.

PS. I'm hoping to get to the Kokoschka paintings on Tuesday. M.

16 November 1960

Dearest Niouta,

[. . .] I am more riven by Karl himself now as he is – because he is really torn in two between Anne and me and is like a lost child or a mixed-up kid. So the crying out has stopped for me by sheer shame!

And so the work returns again.

I didn't get to the Kokoschka, but am going definitely next week. I'll tell you after what I thought.

Love, dear Niouta
Michael

8 April 1961

Dearest Niouta,

Yes, all is well. I work away and so well that I've taken 2 weeks off to do songs for Pears and [Julian] Bream [*Songs for Achilles*]. Now 2 weeks break away. I'll try and get in to see you when we're back, and to tell you then personally all the news. Too much for a letter! And I'm in wild haste getting ready to go – paying up bills etc, etc – copying scores . . .

My mother leaves Tidebrook for her Norfolk guest house (permanently) in a week's time. Karl and I will move to Corsham in the summer – subject to date of sale of Tidebrook (no one bought yet).

Do come and visit.

Love

Michael

2 January 1962

Niouta darling –

It was lovely to get an unexpected telegram on my birthday. Indeed I had forgotten the day it was till Karl's children gave me a pair of warm gloves. And then a letter came from my mother, and a telegram from you. Now I write to wish you return returns for your own birthday – and to say I must try and fix a time in London to meet and talk. I *think* the New Year will be less rushed – with visits to Cov. Gdn that allow time to see folk in other places.

And here and now this house is at last becoming ready – that is, workmen should be out of the house by the end of the month. And our night storage heaters come today!

I want you to see it some day some time. The music room is in many ways more exciting than Tidebrook. You will hardly believe it, till you see.

King Priam is well under control now. Libretto and vocal score will be published (!) this month. Cov. Gdn have training in hand. Sean Kenny has finished, I think, his sets, though I haven't seen them – but Wanamaker has.

Première in Coventry, as you know, is May 29, and in London on June 5th. [. . .]

Blessings and greetings – *et à bientôt*.

Michael

19 September 1963

Dear Niouta,

[. . .] Karl, I and the children had a good fortnight, in north Spain mostly – we found a tiny *pension* run by friends of Karl's, which had only 3 families – Russian-Italian, French and English, which was cheap and good in every way. Mrs Asquith, *la patronne*, was Finnish-Austrian and a marvellous cook.

Edinburgh was a great success – and we enjoyed it. The new piece

[Concerto for Orchestra] will come on in Festival Hall on Nov. 21st; also broadcast then.

I must try and see you in London as you suggest. It would be nice.

[. . .] I'm just about to begin my strange 'vision' from St Augustine. Won't be due out for a long time, if we use Fischer-Dieskau to sing, as we hope to.

All news when we meet.

Love

M.

8 December 1965

Dearest Niouta,

[. . .] all's set for [*The Vision of*] *St Augustine* now. And the new opera [*The Knot Garden*] has begun to flow. Maybe I'll try to get in some day to see you. When I can face London again! I'm somewhat buried away temporarily in order to hammer out the first musics of the new piece [*The Shires Suite*] – always difficult. Or maybe you could venture one day here again, come spring weather.

herzlichst

Michael

31 December 1966

Dearest Niouta,

It's always a pleasure – and always a surprise – to get something from you for my birthday – which I myself as regularly forget (except when I can't, as at 60 or 70!). I wish I remembered yours though in the way you remember mine. Though I do inside somewhere – as I guess you know and understand. Last year was too much of a run-around. My operation [for prostate cancer] seemed to throw everything, but mostly composition, into disarray. Now I'm trying to catch up on myself by sticking here and as solidly as my public life will allow to the new opera – which is strange and difficult – i.e. difficult to write and maybe strange to accept. It'll come out at Cov. Gdn in 3 years or so. *Priam* comes back next May, and *The Midsummer Marriage* April 68 – and then the new one 2 seasons later. M.M. is to have an entirely new production. I've stood out for this all along and have now got it. I don't say it will be the miraculous kind the Wanamaker–Kenny *Priam* was, because that's rare. But at least a theatre set that will *do* all the magic I want, and good costumes – probably Beni Montresor, who has just done [*Benvenuto*] *Cellini*. Conductor will be Colin Davis, with a good cast. Choreographer probably [Kenneth] MacMillan, brought home from Berlin.

I'll try and get to see you sometime, though London is very nightmarish to me at present. Or perhaps you'd visit here one day? I must phone and see how things are.

Meanwhile blessings and birthday greetings.

Michael

31 July 1968

Dear Niouta,

I was just considering writing or phoning you. It's been a rather hectic period during the Bath Festival. Then my mama came for a 3 weeks stay, but I had still to rush around a fair bit. We drive mama to Sussex today later. She is fantastically well, despite her disabilities. We have already deposited Karl's mother in Wales for a bit. Tomorrow we go to York where I have to do [*The Vision of*] *St Augustine* in the Minster next Monday (like BBC Music Prog.) then home Tuesday for a long Aug. at the 3rd act of *The Knot Garden*. We have 2 weeks holiday then (Ischia) with the 2 daughters and their 2 boy-friends. Lovely to look forward to – gay and amusing. So – when *you* are back in Oct. et seq. we must meet – I am here solid all the autumn. But of course a day in Aug. *anytime* it suits you to phone and make a date! The 10.45 Pullman to Bath is the obvious train, and then lunch and talk.

Yes – I do know about the strange pull of the 'inner' for some characters like your niece. Your account reads very like Francesca Allinson's diary of her last months. Heaven knows if one can ever 'have helped' in the obvious sense of carrying someone over until the real growing old and stable can begin. I was of course quite the wrong age. I did imagine *you* succeeding though.

Sorry Salomé isn't so well. Give her my love and of course to yourself

Michael

1 January 1969

Dearest Niouta,

Your telegram came in grand almost old-fashioned style to the

377

door where Karl brought it in. I was just finishing work for the day – and that goes so well that I shall probably finish *The Knot Garden* by the end of next month. One of my next jobs is to prepare a definitive libretto for printing, and you must certainly see that to begin with.

Come the spring you must arrive yourself at the door (and I could thank you in person for the cabled [birthday] wishes). I come to London as little as I dare. It's been a wonderful long spell here since September. Karl's girls and their respective boys came for a week at Christmas and it was lovely. But my mother I think is going now towards her long home. Your birthday is now or soon. All the very best wishes.

Love

M.

18 November 1969

Dearest Niouta,

[. . .] As to *The Knot Garden*, I'll send you a vocal score when printed in a month or so. The work is already cast and will come to première on 2nd Dec. next year. Colin Davis conducting, Peter Hall producing, Tim O'Brien designing. A marvellous trio in their early forties.

I overworked (conducting etc) in the summer and have had a series of nervous 'crises' this autumn (physical not mental) and have had to go very slow. Composing on the good days, resting on the bad. But now I'm beginning to get around that corner – and of course I've given up all extra, outside work to the fullest extent I can. I shall give up the Bath Festival too as soon as I have got it on its feet again and can hand over decently.

Finally, we decided to move. Partly because this place has become too public for me (local newspaper publicity etc) and partly to refind the total quiet as it was in Tidebrook, Sussex. So, come the spring, we go to Nocketts Hill Farm, about 8 miles east of here, high up on a hill and up a mile-long farm drive. But I'll tell you all about it when I come to see you, as I will, in the New Year.

By a fortuitous coincidence my mother died after a long period of speechlessness and frustration. Everything seemed to 'fall' and get 'built again'.

Love

M.

14 March 1970

Dearest Niouta,
We move [from Corsham to Calne] in 10 days! But, would you [be] at home (end of morning and lunch) on Tues., March 31st? I want to consult you about Russian names for a 4th opera [*The Ice Break*]!!
April 1 or 2 could be just as easy, if better for you.
All news then. Love
M.

21 December 1970

Just to say that Schott will send you, when they've had it made, a large copy of the photo you liked. A Christmas–birthday token – though it may not get you on time.
I'll be sending you all account of the 6 characters of the new opera in a little while, so we can meditate on names.
Love
M.

30 December 1970

Dearest Niouta,
We didn't send any cards this year – so this is a Christmas, New Year, cum birthday letter and an answer to your card with the new names. I now feel the father should be Yuri, the son L(i)ev (but possibly Ivan) and the mother, I had thought, Liubov – but maybe Zoya is nicer. I'll see you again in any case before there has to be a final decision. And I shall meanwhile try to find the English names.
Love as ever
Michael

13 July 1972

We leave tomorrow for Canada – 6 days work and 2 weeks holiday after. I *badly* need that. Have only just recovered from the experience of the Symphony [No. 3] performances – the impact and the response. As you can understand. I'll come to see you after I'm back (Aug. 7) or get you down here if the weather is fine. [. . .]
all love,
M.
I *would love* to meet Nadia [Nadezhda] Mandelstam!

September 1974

Your postcard *has* come after all – which was nice. This is to say short-ly, and *confidentially*, that K[arl Hawker] and I are separating out. I've come to my end. (He will have all security financially.) It's difficult in this interim period. Please don't comment *by letter*, because K. is still opening the post as 'secretary'. I'll phone some time and see you when I can. I'm working and well, *néanmoins*.

  Love,
  M.

Eric Walter White

Eric Walter White (1905–85) worked in arts administration from 1942 to 1971, for the Council for the Encouragement of Music and the Arts and its successor the Arts Council. He was the author of numerous books and essays, most notably on Stravinsky, Britten and English opera. The letters selected here (one of them addressed to White's wife Dodo), concerning The Knot Garden, *reveal how Tippett refined his scenario and text before embarking on the music. White appears to have negotiated the sale of a manuscript of the opera to Northwestern University, Evanston, Illinois. He commissioned* Crown of the Year *for the Badminton School centenary celebrations in 1958, and is the dedicatee of* Songs for Dov.

27 February 1963

The renaissance rose garden had always (it appears) lovers, a fountain, and music. (The negro with a guitar?) Allied, I should say, to the Shakespearean idea of 'music' counterpoised to 'tempest' – or the sea in distractive action. (Jessica and Lorenzo in the garden [in *The Merchant of Venice*], do they talk of music?) So the 'music', in this sense, forms as the garden forms – and as the lovers, or love, speaks. The whole charade could be Persian or Indian or Italian. But it'll depend finally on what the characters (in charade) force on us . . .
   herzlichst
   Michael

25 August 1964

Dear Eric,
   [. . .] I guess the names are mainly right now – the title is still fluid till we see the whole text. Act 2, oddly enough, alone has a shape and a series of 'events'. Act 1 is a vague outline. Act 3 quite unknown, as I don't see yet what the central 'celebration' is, a charade, a marked ritual, a play within the play etc. Nor quite yet the function – except that

in the end all must go their ways except Faber and Thea, left together for the first time. [. . .]

31 August 1964

Dear Eric,

Yes – I like 'The Amazing Garden' [White's suggested title]. It seems to tell us the proper things – viz. – the garden as setting to mazes and amazement, etc. I also find your threefold act titles good. I had had 1. Confrontation, 2. Labyrinth, 3. Charade. But your titles are more of the set and the stage. So far as I've got, Act 1 sets out the characters as quickly and simply as possible, with hints of the inner values of each which make relationship difficult, e.g. Faber's engineering, Thea's 'mysticism', Claire's* surgical asceticism, Mel's race, Piers' [eventually Dov's] music and so on. But these things are shown as only potentially explosive within some pattern of manners. The catalyst is Denise who brings the 'outside' in with denunciatory violence, and which provokes Mel to the blues that ends the act.

In Act 2 the maze begins to operate and in a series of meetings and departures nearly every 'coupling' is 'broken up' – though only that of Mel and Piers finally. So that when Flora and Piers are thrown clear (down stage!) of the whirling maze at the end it's Piers' heartbreak that, through comforting the frightened Flora, starts him singing the music that makes the garden flower for a moment. When the music stops the 'reality' returns. This is dangerously near to sentimentality, but maybe can be managed. Even Mel's 'Come. I taught you that'.

In Act 3 we need some surrealist goings-on (with Mangus trying to play Prospero?), or some ritual that takes the action deeper into some moment of truth, or better some absurdity which gets the characters onto some take-it-or-leave-it existentialist ground (this is what I mean by dadaist tradition) – this means, I think, that the spring or fountain is highly metaphoricised, even into some horse-play of Mangus, and the music must be equally 'dadaist' or 'absurd', where the ridiculous meets the sublime. From this point everything and everybody unwinds until Faber and Thea are alone and together for the first time and must speak directly as man and wife – which is the curtain.

Enough – till Thurs.

Michael

* The character Claire is present only in early drafts.

26 October 1965

My dear Eric,

I've been hammering away at Act 3 again. Improved I think. Though I've not yet seen the solution for Epilogue. But that can keep.

[. . .] I've looked again at the *cuts*. I see that in fact some are true *cuts* and some are really *dissolves*. This distinction helps quite a lot.

I expect I shall have to let the music start soon. But as that is always very slow in accumulating, the constant re-consideration of details in the later part of the text can go on.

Love to Dodo
Michael

27 October 1965

My dear Dodo,

I came entirely to your view that the Epilogue can't be Woolf.* So last night I hammered away at it in Blake–Whitman–[D. H.] Lawrence aphorisms. It very nearly works. But the second pair of separate lines is still the crux. I see Thea and Faber standing up from their seats, but can't quite hammer that gesture into the thought in the way the seed packets and the factory papers encompass garden and works. The thought isn't quite concrete in the right way. And maybe it's the notion of enmity (in the Woolf) which has got elided.

And writing out that sentence to you nearly gave it me, i.e. when they stand up they are certainly themselves entire but still unable to 'imagine' the other (in Blake's sense). I'll get it quite soon.

Show it to Eric for me. No need to return – it's an extra copy.

I've much improved the central bit of Act 3. Got a tough quartet for Thea, Mel, Faber, Piers [eventually Dov] which both leads to the 'trial' (Caliban and Ariel) and towards the Epilogue.

Love
M.
[. . .]

October 1965

Dear Eric,

Here is the libretto without Claire! No doubt of its improvement.

* Tippett had considered using the concluding words of Virginia Woolf's last novel, *Between the Acts* (published posthumously in 1941).

But – Richard [Hawkins?] has found, on a straight reading without previous knowledge at all, that Act 3 turns round corners he can't yet follow. [. . .] I think this significant. I've been myself worried that I catch myself out just through the possibilities that have lain hidden in *The Tempest*. Yet I still feel the charade via *Tempest* is the best to date.

My present instinct is that in any case the mime rape of Miranda is an extra. And that any successful cutting of Act 3 helps the rest. [. . .]

herzlichst
Michael

15 March 1968*

My dear Eric,

I would have written before, but I've been more or less in bed for a week, after our previous week's slog in Scotland. A very heavy flu-cold that made me so exhausted I have done nothing but rest. Now, I am coming to, and beginning to clear the way through matters left undone. So I've been looking this morning through the *Tempest* manuscript. It's more considerable than I thought. For which I'm glad. But I see that the sequence of the music is quite obscure, really because it had to be written according to a priority of the theatre's. They had to have Ariel's songs first, so that the actor could have the longest possible time wherein to learn them. And so it went on through.

I can't recall the proper order now. I made an ink score of the pieces as I finished and sent them to the Old Vic. [John] Lambert then constructed his conductor's score from these pieces of ink MS. That is what he recently told me. I have a feeling you might if interested ask the Old Vic (with my complete concurrence) to let someone search out this score from their archives (if still around) and let us photograph it, or borrow it back on permanent loan, or whatever.

I am pretty clear I don't consider the incidental music of any 'use' to me, or anyone, outside of its original use. So that the Ariel songs only, and perhaps the other song eventually (Schott have a photo of this already from your MS), will remain in general circulation. The rest is a musical record of a particular (and not very good!) production of

* Response to White's request to see the incidental music that Tippett composed for a production of *The Tempest* at the Old Vic, London, in 1962.

The Tempest – at least will be, if clarified by reference to the conductor's ink score.

Did I tell you that we saw the *Midsummer Marriage* set designs, models etc and the costumes before we went back? They are excellent. Rehearsals must have started last Wednesday. So all is set for an exciting venture.

Schott are giving a small party afterwards in the Covent Garden Crush Bar. Strictly limited, I'm afraid (cost-wise) to the cast and Covent Garden folk and the very necessary professionals and one or two very close. All to be, I hope, on a nicely unpretentious scale and no formality – with adulation for no one! Till then.

Love to you both –
Michael

16 November 1970

My dear Eric,

Many thanks for your letter. And herewith the best answers I can give.

Yes: I think I would be willing to sell an MS of *The Knot Garden*,* but seeing it will be an important manuscript it oughtn't to go for a song. Would you like to negotiate at some time? That would be kind and good.

As to performance of an opera at an American university, this has tentatively come up before. So far no project has reached substantiality. But I imagine each new operatic venture of mine (and *The Knot Garden* seems likely to [be] a winner, here) brings a break-through nearer, there. However, while I myself would be inclined to let anyone go ahead who wanted to, I must put projects up, for advice, to Mr Robert Holton, of Schott Music Corp. in New York (our new agents). (Bob Holton was before Ben's agent with Boosey's, and then mine with Argo, then he went elsewhere. The new set-up is the result of Schott's withdrawing their catalogue from AMP–Schirmer.) I am sending the relevant question in your letter to Holton in a day or two, so that he can comment. But so far as you are concerned, the composer is agreeable if the American agents don't object.

---

* White had offered to act on Tippett's behalf in the sale of a manuscript of *The Knot Garden*. The pencil score went to Northwestern University, Evanston, Illinois, where the first production of a Tippett opera in the USA took place.

Finally, I suppose if the occasion and terms and performances made sense I could become part of your general project, if that had any sense for you. I don't really seek these things, as you know, but enjoy them at times if they seem worth while and I am likely to be tolerably free at the time from compositional necessities.

Yours
Michael

F. W. Sternfeld

The research interests of the Austrian-born British musicologist F. W. (Fred) Sternfeld (1914–94) covered the whole of music history from antiquity to the twentieth century, with special focus on the Renaissance. His studies of literature and drama as they related to music chimed with Tippett's concerns about the place of music in cultural and intellectual history. Although Tippett's connection with Sternfeld and his wife Sophie was mainly a personal one, his letters touched on matters of composition – here, his use of blues patterns in the last movement of the Third Symphony.

1970/71

Dear Fred,

I shall write a finale of 4 vocal blues, interweaved with (instrumental) breaks. I shall articulate them somewhat on the lines of the groupings in *Das Lied von der Erde*, i.e. slow and sad and gay etc according to my plan – which ends with wildness rather than nostalgia. For the 4 blues I should be enormously helped instrumentally by being able to use my own version of standard formulas and procedures (which did of course grow up historically). Thus, already for the fast section of the blues in *The Knot Garden* I composed my own boogie-woogie L.H. piano bass for the 12 bars after seeing various bar sample formulas which a young chap [Meirion (Bill) Bowen] wrote down for me. Now I want others – written down in notation. These formulas could be out of primers on playing (quite naive and primitive) or instrumentation, and for piano, guitar, sax or whatever. This is what I know will set my mind working. Basic formulas, which have e.g. produced slow blues, or fast blues etc, etc. Because I shan't depart much from the 12-bar sequence (repeated) but use this primitive procedure in my own form of variation.

Secondly, I have to write lyrics. This again is assisted by reading existing blues lyrics – e.g. St Louis blues et al. So I should be much helped by any standard collection, or by good examples in a scholas-tic book (which I'd probably only use for that purpose!). There's a fine example in an appendix to [Wilfrid] Mellers *Music in a New Found Land* [1964]. I'd love to see more.

The trouble with players is that they do it all by ear, while I am much more directly assisted by formulas in notation. This will be espe-cially so when I get down to the breaks. Thus suppose e.g. a slow vocal blues, with answering 'dialogue' with say trumpet or clarinet goes over into a break, then it's the standard procedures out of which breaks are all done that I'm longing to see set out in some analytical notational form. And of course tunes might really help – in that the breaks might make use of famous blues melodies for basic variation material in cadenza form.

By this time I have the basic 12-bar movement 'in the blood' – but it's that primitive harmonic basis I must construct the often 'baroque' ensemble above. I can't help feeling that e.g. the jazz percussionist must accumulate rhythmical formulas in relation to the 12 bars (whether 4/4 or 2/4) on which he 'invents'. If I could get some or any of these formulas as tiny examples in notation I'd have what I chiefly need.

To be more precise as to the articulation: blues 1=Mahler's first 2 songs – and is slow. Blues 2=Mahler's no. 2 (Von der Jugend) and is fast. Blues 3=Mahler's no. 4 (Von der Schönheit) and is slowish. Blues 4 comes near to Mahler's no. 4 (Der Trunkene im Frühling) but 'takes off' into a wild ecstasy – accelerando somehow. Thus making a Song of the Body rather than of the Earth. Also, in tiny format, a Song of Joy.

I have no idea yet what the metaphor(s) of the lyrics can be. It's a dramatic soprano voice – and I guess each blues will 'dialogue' with a different solo instrument till all 'takes off' in jam session together.

I want to assist my natural inventiveness!

Herzlichst

Michael

Ian Kemp

Ian Kemp (b. 1931) held various positions at Schott & Co., London, in the mid-1950s and early 1960s, and it was through that connection that he met Tippett. Kemp, whose work as a musicologist has also focused on Hindemith, Weill and Berlioz, subsequently followed an academic career, holding posts at Aberdeen, Cambridge, Leeds and Manchester, but he remained in close touch with Tippett, who helped him in the preparation of his life-and-works study Tippett: The Composer and His Music, *published in 1984. He is the dedicatee of* Symphony No. 4.

mid-1966

Dear Ian,

Many thanks for your letter. Was lovely seeing you. And delighted that the mothers have met. When I was at Maldon over Xmas something someone said as to your father's progenitors seems to show that it is in fact the same family* – however, it's a long way back!

Am exhausted and washed out still by all the nervous energy over St Aug [*The Vision of St Augustine*]. But also deeply satisfied by the achievement. I am slowly, slowly getting back to the opera [*The Knot Garden*].

Incidentally (hardly the right word!) [Georg] Solti rang yesterday and seemed to say that they were reviving the M.M. [*Midsummer Marriage*] with Colin Davis. I didn't dare ask exactly when, but I think it seems fixed in principle.

Now – as to your request for 1968. The answer is 'yes' – under the conditions you offer – viz. pre-preparation, Haddo House, soloists agreed etc. Early March is better than late Feb., if merely that a week or two at that season often clears the worst winter away, and means likelier better communications. The fee will *have* to go through Howard [Hartog] (though I control him of course) – he also has lots

* Tippett and Kemp had discussed the possibility that they were distantly related.

389

of good ideas as to singers. So I'll leave you to write him in due course.

I have had to ask Howard to cancel the Camb[ridge] lectures as I can't face any more for the moment. They were in any case a hangover from a last year's decision to stop lecturing. I shall only do some conducting occasionally as it seems good. I shall give up the Leics. Youth Orch. [Leicestershire Schools Symphony Orchestra] after their big festival next year – as that is the hardest work.

Love to you all –
Michael

early 1968

Dear Ian,

[. . .] I'm slogging away very steadily at the new opera: *Knot Garden*. I hope to have it finished by spring of 69. Am 1/3 through Act 2. K[arl Hawker] has been making a clean reproducible libretto to date and when finished I'll get Schott's to send you up a copy.

As to M.M. [*The Midsummer Marriage*] we're back with a house producer – Ande Anderson – but I think it will be good. He knows his stuff concerning the house, knows the score (from Norman [Del Mar]'s tape) and the libretto intimately, has a clear idea of how to do all the 'tricks' by light and manifold projections on a fairly clear and open stage. So it will be just the other thing from the old one. And most important of all he's been at it a year or more before première and has most of the cast under his hand now already. I'm not sure where the designer has got to yet. Ande wants Jocelyn Herbert but there was some problem of her filming in Greece.

Cast was, when I last heard –
Mark [Alberto] Remedios
Jenifer [Joan] Carlyle
K.F. John Shaw
Jack Burroughs (? spelling) [Stuart Burrows]
Bella I've forgotten – but a good one! [Elizabeth Harwood]
She-A. [Elizabeth] Bainbridge
He-A. [David] Kelly
Choreographer was to have been [Kenneth] MacMillan but now is someone younger but whose name I've forgotten again. There – enough.

Love from us both to you all, especially Gill with her 5 moonstones.
Michael

mid-1969

Dear Ian,

[. . .] Through my crazy stupidity this year (since finishing *Knot Garden*) I signed myself up for so much conducting it brought on an inner crisis (from the creative side). I've got through it – after a few nasty turns – and am now buried in the *Songs for Dov*. (I must try and get a copy of the words to you.) We go on Tuesday for 2 weeks with Sarah (Hawker) and boy-friend Heinz (Kuhl) – which ought to do me a power of good, though it's a bit mistimed. Then there is only one other chore: to take the Leics. kids to Berlin and other places in Germany (Richard [Rodney] Bennett again coming to play Gershwin *Rhapsody in Blue*). But by mid-Sept. or so we settle down for a 6-month spell of composition – perhaps indeed to next May. So – if you were able in any way to shoot down this way again we'd be in residence and could house and feed you. [. . .]

Glad you listened to the Ives. I enjoyed that concert very much. The V.W. [Vaughan Williams] Pastoral (at York) in the end much less. The Elgar was the best of that lot. America meant a concert (with Zagreb Phil.) near Philadelphia: Tippett Double Conc. [Concerto for Double String Orchestra], Ives *Three Places* [*in New England*]; Purcell Dido's Lament; Stravinsky *Firebird*. Nice – but had meant a helluva struggle with the orchestra people to accept even that, and then I had to go and be a week in Zagreb to rehearse it (before Bath and York). So I've duly learnt my lesson about conducting. (But I enjoyed doing the Ives '3 Places' and in the end we did it well.)

I like your ideas as to the [*Vision of*] *St Augustine* fill-up. The Praeludium [for Brass, Bells and Percussion] in any case is to open the LSO [London Symphony Orchestra] season at RFH [Royal Festival Hall, London], I think. So we can both reconsider the piece as such and know the LSO will have learnt it.

Another possibility, I think, could be the [Divertimento on] 'Sellinger's Round' (on second side of course). But if the Praeludium holds up, then that should be seriously considered, as an opener.

I had already, in my own mind, thought of *Songs for Achilles*. But if it's these, or Divertimento, it surely must be a standard 'fill-up' *after* the main piece. Praeludium alone, I feel, might open the whole disc.

For your diary: *Midsummer Marriage* returns to Cov. Gdn July 10, 14, 17 (1970) with recording (Phillips) in between dates. *The Knot*

Garden is Dec. 2, 5, 8, 11, 14, 17. Also 1970.

I hope to finish *Songs for Dov* by Christmas. (Then I *might* complete the Leics. set of 5 pieces [*The Shires Suite*], of which 3 are done. As a break.) After 'Dov' I begin the 3rd Symphony (LSO – a hugely well paid commission) and have allowed 2 years i.e. finish by Christmas 71. Then I've accepted a commission from Solti for Chicago, for Dec. 72 – a setting of Richard [correctly Robert] Lowell's poem 'For the Union Dead'.* But I'll tell you all about that later when it gets a bit nearer.

So there's 3 years hard at 2 big pieces.

Meanwhile Colin Davis and Peter Hall have nearly finished casting the new opera [*The Knot Garden*], I believe. Perhaps entirely so. The designer is Tim O'Brien – one of the very best. The vocal score proofs are slowly coming through my hands – so you'll have a copy of the publication fairly soon now. I'll get one sent you off the free list.

Love to you all
Michael
[. . .]

11 February 1970

Dear Ian,

[. . .] I finished the Dov songs on Monday and felt *much* better – in that I actually had managed a work under these troublesome conditions. For, that being so, I can do another! But the pressure for the end did produce the 'vicious circle' you spoke of. I do very much hope to break out of it come the spring and the new house [Nocketts]. I shall certainly find eventually some regimen that matches up to the external conditions. It's just been a rather nightmare winter. [. . .]

Love to you all
M.

14 August 1970

Dear Ian,

Just a hasty note before I go off on holiday tomorrow. Suddenly feel I'm very glad to get a break and from the obsessional side of music composition.

* This piece was never completed. Instead, Tippett wrote the Symphony No. 4.

Got your letter of course – with your comments on various things. I'm sure it will all slowly sort itself out. Once some of the more biographical material is collected and collated we can work out the music influences – until the period when they become too overall. I mean, listening to *Messiah* from the Proms I realised in memory how in my 20-ies Handel was my bible not Bach. The Op. 6 Concerto Grossi especially. That lovely clear vigorous string writing! Hence of course my mounting an original *Messiah* before I was 30 – or just 30.

However, now for holiday. I enclose a *very* personal note about Symphony 3 which I've done really for Colin [Davis] – so that he could esteem what's toward. Hope to have Part I done by time we go to Toronto mid-Jan.

Love

M.

21 September 1970

Dear Ian,

If I have called the music of *Knot Garden* ironic I'm overworking the word. It's only a word that covers part of the libretto.

As to the 'surprise' on page 1: that's only a small ingredient (of the total music). It 'makes' the 3 'storms' which start the acts (and a part of the spinning of the Act 2 cage) and also the inner storm after Dov smashes his cocktail glass, i.e. the accompaniment to the string glissandi is a form of the opening page 1. Perhaps I had imagined it would prove more fruitful – but in the event it didn't.

I was also trying other possibilities with heterophony – but found that limiting also.

Since Tom the cat left us the birds have returned, and a tiny wren has taken over the terraces as his territory. Karl [Hawker] is taming him. He's hopping about outside my window now.

I *hope* to get my personal piece for Cov. Gdn done this afternoon.

Love to all –

Michael

early February 1972

Dear Ian,

[. . .] I struggle with the end of the Symphony [No. 3]. Another 5–6 weeks I guess, if nothing untoward intervenes. I'm in fact in the middle of the last song – i.e. the 'dramatic scena' one. The 'blues', slow–fast–slow, are done. Simple, rich, moving. Now comes what I call 'a burst of Nobodaddy* rhetoric' – and that's less easy. Finally the 'dream of the Peaceable Kingdom' and more difficult still. However, I don't think I've lost out yet!

Get to a TV set (colour if poss.) for Sat. even., Feb. 19, BBC-2. My *One Pair of Eyes* film. You will not be disappointed I think.

When you're all settled, and maybe I've finished at last, we can meet, here or in London.

Love to you all
Michael

9 September 1972

Dear Ian,

To get the record straight as to the papers you took:

The period of Francesca Allinson was roughly 1930–45 – when she took her own life. At first it is all London and around. At the war she took a small house in E. Grinstead to be near a small-holding for conchies she bought to help some very young ones. But in 1941, or so, her emotional and bodily problems became so acute she went to live with Cyril and Veronica Allinson (siblings) at the Red House [correctly Mill House], Streetly End, W. Wickham, Cambs. – and is buried in their garden. I fancy some time you ought to drive out to see them – they must be in their 70s. So the letters may cover all this period – but are chiefly I think, when she was at Streetly End. I used to go there to visit, but wrote frequently – phoning was too expensive and F. took really to her bed at the end. I think the letters could be tolerably sorted out from the musical references. If you find this impossible and still think it interesting I could probably sort out a bit myself from other references.

The 'analysis' period is from about say end of 37 to Sep. 39. Till Jan. 39 with John Layard; and then by myself, really seriously. I doubt if they will give you anything really germane. The true nature of the experience was probably to become existentially aware of the vast cauldron of imagery inside that in such periods breaks through. One obtains some fresh balance and relief from this experience. But of course I did not thereby solve the socio-emotional problem that had

---

* William Blake's irreverent name for Jehovah in a number of poems.

driven me into the experience, but surprisingly (to me at the time) came out better equipped to concentrate myself artistically! (*A Child of Our Time* followed the next day, so to speak.)

I found the talk anent *The Ice Break* enormously helpful. I'm pretty certain I can get the start in better progression, character- and situation-wise. Also, at least for the moment, I see the middle scene, Act 3, as the descent from the sky of the millenniary Saviour-hero with the 'message' etc. (I shall go to see *Hair* and *Jesus Christ Superstar* to watch the techniques.) I don't yet see the ironic element, disillusionary or punch-line or what. But I did *hear* the humming in the sky as the space-ship comes musically related to the airport murmur!

Was lovely to see you – and we'll meet again soon.

Hope the new house move goes easy.

Love

Michael

A PS as the opera starts to engulf all again – praise be!

All those composers' names of influence – they were, at the start, totally within an unquenchable voracity for music of all kinds and periods. I heard the 1924 Prom season probably entire. 8 Beethoven Fridays; 8 (?) Wagner Mondays – and masses of all else. (A programme book would reveal.) I can recall even now the sound of the horn solo in Brahms 2nd Pf. Conc. (I wonder who played?) Then 4 years of standing at Boult's side at every Friday 1st orch. rehearsal at RCM. A *very* great variety . . . operas – studied in depth – were *Pelléas* [*et Mélisande*], *Parsifal* and *Hugh the Drover*!

But of course, e.g. Haydn meant the 4tet. I easily got hold of a 2nd hand set of parts of the entire series and persuaded 4 students to read some – before I settled down to study of Op. 76 chiefly and others of that period. Mozart chiefly meant Pf. Concerto. I bound up the min. scores in leather (as the Haydn Qts). Handel of course meant C.G.s [concerti grossi] (heard first, I guess, at the Proms) and *Messiah* (in score only). But in my early 20ties I gave a pure, uncut performance of the Chrysander min. score (at Oxted) – one of the earliest ever, in this country, I should think. The public were given free copies of the text (Novello at 1d. or 2d.!) and I gave a short introductory lecture before each part of what the text of that part meant within the whole structure. I found all this out for myself. I never forgot it.

Beethoven meant organic form – both within movements and between them.

But I heard everything – from Dunstable with Safford Cape, to Stravinsky, [Samuel] Dushkin and that clarinettist, in an all-S. programme. I felt music to be a great and *rich* art. I feel so now.

M.

8 August 1975

To try and clarify a bit for you. Nell Tippett [married] Percy Shuter. c. 1895 say. [Their daughter] Joyce Shuter [married] McGroarty. Joyce Mc. still lives at 6 Chiswick Lane, the parents' home. [. . .]

Now – my father was her mother's (Nell's) favourite brother. So, if the meeting of my pa and ma was at 6 Chiswick Lane, the daughter (Joyce Mc.) might actually remember it! She could have been up to 10 years old?

If Nell's young husband was making eyes at Isabel Kemp (young nurse) Nell would be up in arms, at least if the husband brought his favourite nurse back home! (I find this part of Peter [Kemp]'s story difficult.) This might well be exacerbated if Isabel Kemp then 'hooks' Nell's favourite brother.

Anyhow, the real point is, that Joyce McGroarty's grand-father (maternal) is mine (paternal) – so there's a new direct source.

(Joyce Tippett, of Bedford College, is the generation younger, but has been intimate with Joyce (known as Joe) McGroarty as with a cousin since her childhood right up to last weekend.)

A missing document might well be grandfather's will. It strikes me that if my pa was executor as well as legatee then a copy might well be still in the Tippett files with his solicitors – who was a friend, Stapylton-Smith of Bexhill-on-Sea. Peter had dealings with old Sechiari of this firm right up to my mother's death and the matters of my father's marriage settlement.

Going back to the Shuters. It seems that the story of their (the wife's) *father*'s (the living daughter's grandfather's) bigamy was current in that family. (So Eirene Tippett thought on the phone last night.) Joyce Mc. *might* know some more precise detail e.g. was there a criminal charge brought?

However, for fun you and I must have some time off in Cornwall I think – when it suits.

25 March 1976

Dear Ian,

[. . .] *If* it made sense try and set aside a 2–3-week visit perhaps. Or a *long* w.e. with time to answer questions [for Kemp's biography]. But what I'm thinking about is of course to *help*, in keeping other pressures at bay, as I have to do myself when I'm home here.

Off on Sunday – back Easter Sunday middle of the night.

New work [Symphony No. 4] goes well –

Love

M.

28 February 1977

Dear Ian,

[. . .] I took the whole of Section 5 (out of the 7) [of Symphony No. 4] into Schott – and have now only 2 sections which are, in part at least, recapitulatory. So I'm really 'round the corner' 'into the straight'.

I also did at last the final corrections for libretto printing – and notes for score etc [of *The Ice Break*].

So neither Bill [Bowen] nor I have gotten down again to the biography – but we shall – and of course, say the word that it's really needed, and will do at once. Bill is madly over-occupied as ever, but can still manage priorities.

Was Thurs. night at RCM for 2nd Symphony and a 'talk-in'. The whole operation was joyous and fun; and a good performance (Del Mar) from the orchestra into the bargain.

Friday morning Bill and I tried out electric organs and chose the necessary!

Hope to be back, and refreshed, next Sunday and return to the desk and the piano.

Alles gute –

M.

9 May 1977

Dear Ian,

I seem to miss not having a phone no. for getting you. Not because I have owt special to say, maybe just because I am 'loose headed' at the moment, doing no composition. Instead a long queue of critics etc wanting copy for the new opera [*The Ice Break*]. Perhaps you could find a comfortable coin-box sometimes and call reverse. That would be nice. Also let me know if you're in London, for I can pop up very easily being so uncommitted. On the other hand am on vacation and [in] Paris May 26 to June 15.

Bill has had to do a short para. on T. and America for the exhibition [A Man of Our Time: Michael Tippett]. Quite nice and to the point. He'll show it you I guess. On my side I'd like, I think, a slightly extended sentence or so as to Francesca [Allinson], marriage, analysis and homosexuality!

I'm still a bit numbed from the Symphony [No. 4] and unable to consider the quartet [String Quartet No. 4]. But no hurry.

Love

M.

5 December 1977

Dear Ian,

Two things.

1. If you would like to be here for the coming vacation, or over Xmas, or not at all – then I am in fact on my own here and you'd be welcome.

2. Would you consider very seriously a proposition that you had a 6-month, say, 'sabbatical' at the end of Leeds, specifically to finish the book – 'sabbatical' finance of course to cover your family obligation etc. That this project be the *official* reason for your leaving Leeds. This would greatly help [Edward] Boyle and the University: would greatly help you when you apply for a new job: it would help me (quite differently).

I had entertained this project already – then found that David Ayerst put it to me as his strongest advice, within those more public fields.

If you can see *your* way to entertain this proposition for real, in some terms, then you should tell Boyle *now*, and say, maybe, that I wish it, if feasible.

In haste –

M.

Meirion Bowen

Born in Swansea in 1940, Meirion (Bill) Bowen graduated in music and English from Birmingham University and went on to study at Cambridge. He then worked in a variety of jobs, including that of a BBC radio producer, director of music at Kingston Polytechnic, and critic and journalist, chiefly on the Guardian; *he also founded a music-theatre and percussion group, the Electric Candle. It was during his time at Cambridge that he initiated contact with Tippett, writing to inform him of a misprint in the score of Piano Sonata No. 2. The two quickly struck up a friendship, during the early part of which Bowen was in another close partnership; a more serious relationship developed when he became free. At the time Tippett was still living with Karl Hawker, and although they were for the most part leading separate lives, the break was a protracted and difficult one. Tippett's struggle to balance these conflicting interests is documented in this selection, characterised by its uninhibited outpouring of emotion. After the separation from Hawker, Bowen became the composer's personal assistant and manager. His books include a study of Tippett's music (1982) and editions of his essays (*Music of the Angels, *1980;* Tippett on Music, *1995), and he has arranged and orchestrated some of Tippett's works. He is the dedicatee of* The Mask of Time.

30 September 1962*

Yes, i.e. bar 263, should be 8ve up (as bar 13 in fact). Thank you.

Yes, I hope Nigel [Fortune] fixed a meeting. You're both welcome here, outside my work hours. i.e. each weekday morning. [. . .]

Yours ever
Michael T.

---

* Response to Bowen's letter about a misprint in the Piano Sonata No. 2.

29 December 1962

Dear Bill,

Many thanks for your letter. Come sometime, whenever it suits us both. I've a rather hectic January and early Feb., as I have to go to Germany to the first German production of *King Priam* at Karlsruhe on Jan. 26. And to Brussels Feb. 8th to attend *Child of Our Time* and conduct the Radio choir. But I'm only away for the bare minimum of days necessary. So the thing to do is to suggest possible dates, as you say.

Did you want to be in the studio for *The Midsummer Marriage* either on Sat., Jan. 12, when it is taped for a later broadcast, or Sun. evening Jan. 13, when it's relayed live? This might be interesting – but maybe it is a bit far.

Not surprised you should find Cambridge mixed. It's an odd atmosphere – though why I should say that I don't know, as I was never in it either as undergraduate or musician. But I know it well and like the place.

Will be nice to meet you eventually and hear all your plans and ambitions.

Love
Michael

Oh yes – your notion of *A Child of Our Time* staged. The notion has cropped up before but never carried out. We can discuss it when we meet finally.

January 1963

Dear Bill,

I'm sorry we didn't manage more talk at the M.M. [*Midsummer Marriage*], but such occasions are notoriously difficult! Nor did we make any date for you to visit. As to that it depends very much on what your times and plans are. I mean, you are welcome when you feel so disposed. I have to stick to my work hours, which are weekday mornings. Otherwise I'm free afternoons, and evenings when anyone is around, and of course all Sunday. I go to Germany on next Wed. till Sunday, for *King Priam* there. And I have to be away in Brussels Feb. 8 to 18. Otherwise I am almost solidly here. So come when it suits, and if you want to. I think, since it's a hell of a way, you must let me pay or at least contribute to the fare. I guess it's a hefty chunk out of your pocket.

The BBC did *Midsummer Marriage* proud. Was strange and exciting to hear the score again after 6 years.

Love

Michael

The station is Chippenham.

June 1963

Dear Bill,

[. . .] Have you by any chance a set of discs of my Symphony No. 2? I seem to have loaned mine into non-existence! I want to use them to practise beating the bars of the Scherzo against a performance I'm to do in April in W. Berlin.

By the same token, I have no discs here at the moment – a friend of mine, Karl Hawker, has them all in London; as his was the record player we shared at one time. I'm afraid this won't unduly worry me. I rather like to get away from my own music in any case at the weekend and go lighthearted and gay. We might visit a young family on Sat. evening, before we see late night TV (*That Was The Week That Was*). And if it's a *Monitor* Sunday I usually ask Helen [Binyon] and Isabelle [Symonds] in.

I shall want to hear of all your doings past, present, future.

Love

Michael

[1964]

Dear Bill,

Expect you got your car alright. I fell asleep again till 8! I'd been up on the Mon. night till 1.30 at the TV party and so had sleep to make up. Hope I didn't disturb you too much during the night. I usually have an hour or two's deep sleep at the start and then wake every so often and shift around. I was glad when you turned to me in the morning of course. That's a nicer wake-up and shift around! And I doubt if I did wake-up, I sort of wake instantly according. If you need you'll see.

I've been on my own all week (and enjoyed it), but don't know how it will go ahead. Maybe the week following this coming one. And Gran Hawker [Karl's mother] will be back so you'll have to appear to sleep in the little room then because I suppose she will tell Lily [Speirs;

SELECTED LETTERS OF MICHAEL TIPPETT

Tippett's housekeeper]. But maybe I'll ask her not to, if she's amenable – so sometimes we can get away with it altogether. I mean, with Lily or Mrs Voss you must not be obviously sharing mine!

I've nearly put £2 10s in the letter against your coming on your own next. But decided it's more sensible to do that as and when.

I know that I have to be in London for Mon., Dec. 12. And clearly K[arl] will drive me up. More than likely he will then stay up and I'll return by train – having this time really managed the Br[itish] Council affair – and perhaps too the *Composer's Portrait* (?) with BBC viz. pre-recording of the talk. We could catch the Pullman again or the 18.45 and have supper on the train. But if Dec. 12 seems far away maybe there'll be a chance before on a sudden call.

Luv

M.

You'll not get this till you're back from Swansea. But I shan't be alone tonight.

[1964]

Dear Bill,

I'm still bemused, in the nice sense, by sharing a bed with you all night. Warm and comforting and intimate – with time to make love and time to sleep as it comes to us. It seems like the natural fulfilment of intimacy – to both of us I guess.

I hope Dec. 12 holds when the day comes. I think it will. But if, after driving home this Sunday, I'm left alone again next Tue.–Wed.–Thurs. (as is possible), I shall phone you on speck. But you're not to do anything special about it or not do anything you would ordinarily be doing etc. It's too problematic, and there'll be plenty of opportunities. It's rather Blake-ian – we must 'take love as it flies'.

I've been stuck in the opera [*The Knot Garden*] for the past days. Unusual for me. It'll soon pass.

John Ardoin from Dallas, Texas, has sent me a record of all Ives choral music. You probably know it. But if you don't we can try it out.

It looks as if the [Wilfrid] Mellers piece for Leics. [Leicestershire Schools Symphony Orchestra] is too complicated for us to bring off. I'm discussing it with [Norman] Del Mar this Sunday at his home.

Luv

M.

February? 1965

Dear Bill,

Half-term holidays and the Hallé seem to be mucking up our proposed weekend. Can you postpone for a week to Friday, March 5th? I hope so. Don't like postponing in this way, as it begins to seem a long time, but it's been mostly due to the un-holy gadding-about of this last January, followed by some fixed dates from of old.

And can you consider the first days of your vacation? I go on April 4th, Sunday, to fetch my aged mother from Maldon, Essex, to be here for a week. I wondered if you could manage a day or two immediately then, and I'd take off 2 or 3 days from working. This suggestion is really because April becomes completely impossible afterwards with one thing or another. And if we don't try to disentangle some time together ahead it won't happen.

Perhaps on your way to some days with your parents? But it's the *first* part of that week that works for me.

It's been wonderful to get back to composition. I've got a more or less uninterrupted 8–9 weeks, and hope to finish [*The Vision of*] *St Augustine*.

Love
Michael

April 1965

Dear Bill,

Glad to get your letter. Had been meditating writing to you. Yes – come back to Corsham with Arden [Fisher]. Will this be Sunday or Monday? Either is alright. I have to fetch my 84-year-old mama from Essex, and shall get her to Corsham about 6 p.m., I guess, on the Sunday. I'm also bringing Karl's 82-year-old mum, who is splendidly Welsh. They're both going to stay for a bit. I shall stop work while you're here – beyond learning scores for Leicester, perhaps. (I guess [*The Vision of Saint*] *Augustine* will be finished.) What will you stay, 2 nights, 3 nights?

I haven't seen the Edinburgh programme yet! I never seem to get anything till much later than most. So the news about Hungarian S.Q. is news. My best news of this kind is that Amadeus [String Quartet] have been persuaded by Aspen Festival to learn No. 3 while they're there. So with patience and hard work we'll no doubt finally get a recording, and of the best.

Sorry about the Essex Technical College. But glad Croydon [Art Institute, where Bowen had obtained a teaching post] may be helpful to you. I should have thought they should be.

I haven't seen Pf. Conc. record, or Concerto for Orchestra yet. Usual delays. But had one or two nice letters thereon – and unexpected ones.

Will be good to see you – and so soon.

Love

Michael

26 April 1965

Dear Bill,

The car idea Friday is alright. I've thought of a good place to meet. I shall put the car as I usually do in the Lex garage, which is built onto the back of Selfridges, and is run by them. I use this garage when I'm going into Schott's for some hours – as I shall be doing on Friday afternoon. Now, I reckon that if you usually can catch 5.45 at Paddington, you could manage Selfridges by 5.30 or so. Because this really would save me a rush-hour drive down to Norbury and back, and we could go off from Selfridges due west. The entrance to the garage is either right through the shop to the back, or turn out of Orchard Street itself into the service road behind the shop. The garage *office* is towards the east end of the service road and is marked clearly. Inside is a little foyer, with lifts and pay-desk. We'll meet there. I'll get confirmation the Lex garage stays open after the shop closes; and I'll phone you anyhow.

The hi-fi is working now – so we can play music – tapes or discs. With luck I *might* have stereo versions of Pf. Conc. and Conc. for O[rchestra] here by the weekend. I've ordered them.

Love

Michael

7 September 1965

Dear Bill,

I'll ring occasionally, not I guess for anything specific, but just to keep in touch, as that has to depend on me.

I had to take 2 days off work when I got back from London last week – a kind of nervous trembly-ness. So I just lazed about and read.

It's part of the price for the necessary nervous sensibility all composition demands, but a long work more so. An inner repressed impatience. I generally manage to relax easily at night in the first sleep, but now there are hints of a deeper restlessness. I think, incidentally, for a while I may sleep the first sleeping bit of our nights together, in the next room, partly I'm sure so as to be fresher when I come to you in the morning! I find our times together – warm, loving, sensual – as *you* might say, gorgeous. And I soon miss you again when you're gone.

I'm sort of coming within sight of the finale of Act 1 [of *The Knot Garden*]. So I shall begin to feel better – or less inner-ly impatient.

Not that I'm not extremely well, on the face of things, as you know – and gay and cheerful. So I only mean better or calmer, in the inner nervous system – whatever that is!

Wonder what you thought of *Arabella*. I'll hear later. Karl, who went, left before the end. Not his cup of tea.

I'll be counting the days and working hard.

Love

Michael

2 October 1965

Dear Bill,

I put a first draft libretto down of all 3 acts [of *The Knot Garden*]; but am unsure whether Act 3 hasn't gone round a wrong corner, so am waiting on outside comments and advice, and Karl hasn't had time yet to deliver me clean typed copies, as he teaches the first half of the week. So I'm held up; and occupy the time proofreading (*St Augustine* min. score, *Child of Our Time* d[itt]o, Pf. Conc. d[itt]o) and considering what kind of orchestra for the new opera. Hence the enquiry as to that tough effect Boulez got with electric guitars. It seemed to me potentially excellent for certain music out of a theatre well. But I can't remember how he did it? Just simple line? And is that the normal use of it with beat groups?

I've missed you many times since Edinburgh. I'm glad you see a way to come down over a day. And if your bisques make too short commons then maybe you can come sometimes on a late afternoon train and I'll put you on the early breakfast train next day. (But I'd at least have to share the expense for you in travelling.) Could you perhaps think of a date soon? Any Mon.–Tues.–Wed.; though next week is bad. And Mon. Oct. 18 evening I'm supposed to lecture at Oxford. Otherwise it seems clear, and the sooner the better!

Glad your BBC job's come out so well.

Luv
Michael

January 1966

Dear Bill,

[. . .] Have asked Ian Kemp of Schott's to give you necessary information as to the 1st [String] Qt, because it was one of the few extant pieces which underwent revision – 2 early mvts got replaced by new 1. The present slow mvt and finale date back further than any printed music of mine. The former is the first of the long lyrical slow mvts. A tri-partite unbroken stream of sound – each of the 3 parts in 2 rough 'halves'.

The finale was the first appearance of additive rhythm and had been stimulated by Northumbrian bag-pipe music, somewhere or other. But of course is really me, in a vein I had no experience of. It cost a lot of hard work merely to learn how to write the rhythms down. And cost the old Brosa Qt the most frightful headaches! It's easy now.

So the work is in fact nicely germinal. Have been under the weather – even bronchitis – and am staying as put as I can here. But will get along to see you in Croydon some day or other.

Colin Davis does Symph. 2 sometime in April I think. Ian [Kemp] would know – I'll try and remember to tell you when I know myself. Pf. Conc. record won't be out till the autumn.

Shan't be at the concert this Sunday – hope the boys play it well.

Love
Michael

2 February 1966

Dear Bill,

Sorry I seemed cagey last night on the phone – I was in fact (unknowing) alone in the house. I'll ring you when it's easy and mutually possible.

I'm still extremely exhausted. Partly the weather I suppose. But the chief trouble was the huge endeavour with the Leics. Y.O. [Leicestershire Schools Symphony Orchestra] in Belgium followed immediately by [*The Vision of St*] *Augustine*. I had a nervous 'bad turn' the day I flew to Brussels, as a warning of how much it was all going to take. So I am *very* slowly unwinding. I have started the music of the opera, but it's at present exceedingly slow. However – good news. [Georg] Solti rang me last week to say M.M. [*The Midsummer Marriage*] is to return to Cov. Gdn, season 67–68. (*Priam* is 66–67.) And Webster confirmed (Colin Davis). So that was a wonderful outcome of all the press notices for *Augustine*, which is clearly what set Solti off.

I thought I was due to go to London this last Tues., but got a week out! So I'm up next Tues. Might try to see you somehow. I'll try and ring you anyhow. It could only be to fetch you from Egdon House the moment you came free. My last train is really 7.45. Keep the time free just in case it works if it's alright for you.

Will ring.

Luv –

M.

16 February 1966

Dear Bill,

I'm so pleased you're willing to take all these 'risks' on my behalf. And I'm glad Alan [Ridout] spoke to you as he seems to have done. He told me roughly about it, when I rang him about something else, because he was afraid he might have acted wrongly. But it was certainly difficult for me to tell you anything. It's one thing to implicate oneself in this way and quite another to involve someone else. There's a long history behind it, but it isn't discussable to any purpose and our own relationship is somehow outside it. So let it be.

However – in practice it means always the possibility of the unforeseen. It's a lot to put up with for you, but I guess you manage.

If you can borrow discs of *Rio Grande* and *American in Paris* they'd be useful for me to hear here. I've got to learn the pieces for Leicester in March, to replace certain other older pieces.

Phone as late as you can before you go for the 4.45. Let's hope all works well – but there might be a last minute dash from the opposite side, so to speak.

Love

Michael

1966

Dear Bill,

[. . .] The point is that I feel your place [in Clapham, south-west London] is going to be the chief home we can be together in alone. So that I'd like to get to know it. Even this weekend is fraught with possible snags here. Though more likely, still, not. But if we can be together sometimes in your flat it would be a relief for me – and I believe you'd like it too. Anyway, you'd tell me if you didn't like it.

I'll phone you to see how it is, before Thurs. aft[ernoon], when I go to London.

Luv,
Michael
I'd pick you up at BBC, or meet you wherever.

23 May 1966

Dear Bill,

Thanks for the letter and the singers' names etc. But I'm always a bit scared at a letter from you, because K[arl] is in fact my secretary. I mostly see letters first even when the typing etc is being done at weekends and so forth. But not always. The thing to do please if you can is to avoid anything which pre-supposes a previous and continuing communication. And better maybe just to let me ring you every so often and see you when possible. I hate involving you in deception, but I practise it myself after due consideration because my partner is still suffering from deep-seated insecurity – which is only now beginning to pass. I'll talk it out with you when I see you. I'll ring you some time this week.

I tease myself about you know what because it sits very oddly on my shoulders!* On the other hand to get used to it is to accept the public persona honestly I dare say. Anyhow, 'tis done now.

See you're on the *Observer* again!
Love
Michael

[1966]

Dear Bill,

This is a sad letter to have to write. About the only word to describe

* Tippett was knighted in the birthday honours.

it. For the inevitable has happened – or something of the kind that I always knew was bound to happen sooner or later. Our garage gave Karl the monthly bill to give to me, and the taxi for you was itemised with your name. So we fell into a nightmare world from which we've only just gotten ourselves out again. K.'s nightmare (no quarrelling) is a terrifying fear that you are waiting so to speak to step into his shoes. He knows rationally this isn't true – but irrationally it's true enough for him and seems to echo what did in fact happen to his marriage. My nightmare was different, but terrifyingly real also. I have never had a secret relationship before, and on the face of it it's right out of character. So its positive side has a negative obverse: of a deep-seated guilt. Least I suppose that's what it is. And to practise deliberate deception in K.'s own home seems to give this irrational guilt its sharpest symbol. Maybe too there's an element of guilt towards you too. That I have somehow led you down the garden path. But I don't think either of us, you or me, regrets this.

I'm going to ring you tomorrow Friday if I can and am still alone, just to make verbal contact. Then I must try and see you in London to talk things out. I'm not rushing up to town immediately in a panic, either on your behalf or mine. It has never been thus between us. I don't feel it like that now. It must ride till the occasion comes of itself. There's never been anything forced or nightmare-ish between us, and we've managed a rather rare lightness of touch. Luckily, for me, the music flowers and I'm on the finale, Act 1 [of *The Knot Garden*]. And luckily, for you, you have also a huge life of your own. Hang on to that till I can manage a London meeting and a talk at any rate.

Luv,
Michael
[. . .]

1966

Dear Bill,

[. . .] Things are slowly settling again after the upset. Part of Karl's extreme shock was that I had promised a year ago or so when it happened before that it would be the end. The broken promises and the lies were hard to take. Also, of course hard to give. It's something relatively unknown to me as an experience – and quite frankly I'm not at all sure about it. I know I never wanted you to have to lie too, and I've always felt better on those few occasions here when no one at all knew you were present – not Gran [Hawker] or Lily [Speirs]. Karl now sees that it is partly his overwhelming 'suspicion and possessiveness', as he calls it, that prevents him moving on to a more tolerant ground. But it's one thing to recognise something in oneself and another to grow out of it. And even then, what is the nature or extent of tolerance between partners so close and fundamentally united as we are? I am myself an almost ridiculously unjealous person – possibly just complacent – though not quite, for I've had *crises de jalousie* in the past of Proustian violence. But 'sauce for the goose is sauce for the gander' is pretty unreal in actual, not mythical, relationships.

For the moment it will have to be played quite cool. Karl is in London but returns tomorrow to drive me to Brum [Birmingham] Friday, where I'm the year's President (?) of the Music Soc. and have a lunch and answer questions etc, etc. Separation is difficult for him and me at the moment. We need to be together – we feel thus safer! So he may be here all next week. In which case I couldn't telephone, but *might* write. If I'm silent for a bit just don't worry. We've had such periods before. It's pretty unclear yet how much deception I am able and willing to practise in the future – so one needs time to let things settle a bit before testing what one feels. This playing it cool is part of the quality and success of what you and I have known and enjoyed together. The price (for me) in deception has been high but worth it. But it's not to turn round now into tragedy.

Luv
M.

20 June 1966

Dear Bill,

My own doctor came yesterday – and it's clear I must now proceed to the usual and common prostate operation. (It runs very much in my family – grandfather, father, brother.) Because the 'acute retention' or temporary stoppage might happen in the American desert or elsewhere with no help available – and that would be that. So I'm going into hospital just as soon as I can fix it, and so get it over. It's 2 to 3 weeks I fancy – the hospitalisation.

I'll try and hope for a visit from you before, but it mayn't be possible. K. is deeply disturbed naturally and doesn't want to go far away while things might suddenly flare up. But if a chance comes I'll phone. In any case I'll let you know the dates of the event when I know. It's a simple operation – and extremely common. So nothing to worry about. And if we don't manage before we'll manage eventually after. You must just leave all communications to me. In hospital anyhow I shall have a private phone.

Opera [*The Knot Garden*] goes along slowly – but well. And that's the chief matter. Also casting of K.P. [*King Priam*] and M.M. [*The Midsummer Marriage*] for 67 and 68. Colin Davis, for the latter, is immensely cooperative and determined to bring it off.

Love,

M.

27 June 1966

Dear Bill,

I'm going into nursing home tomorrow [for prostate surgery] – and it'll be about 2 weeks. I'll maybe phone you later in the week from there, to BBC most likely.

When I'm back and fit and well we must hope for a flying visit on your part. Prob[ably] at short notice – and you wouldn't need to pre-pare – I can always provide – if we shared a bed for the night none would know you'd been here!

No more now.

Luv,

M.

Karl is in residence here while I'm in.

18 July 1966

Dear Bill,

I've been home nearly a week. The surgeon wouldn't let me go away – and quite rightly. It's been a week of extreme weakness, and growing exasperation at being unable to compose. It's going to be a longer convalescence than I ever imagined. For though it's a very common operation it still is a major one, and leaves one temporarily without bodily reserves. However, I feel during this coming week I may begin to gather strength at last – because by now the inner wound will have healed, which is the first great step.

When it will be time for you to seize an opportunity to fly down I don't know. Not for a while. It's no good till I'm properly myself again. I'll phone some time to find out your own movements. I think you were going down to Gowerton [Swansea, where Bowen's parents lived] and then of course later on leave. I'm assured that eventually I'll feel better than ever! And I dare say that really will be the fact. We stay put here till Edinburgh in mid-August – and then again put till Berlin early October.

Looks as if the casting of *Priam* is now complete for next May–June. *The Midsummer Marriage*, for mid-April 68, is gradually settling itself. Hope to have the main structure fixed by the autumn. If luck holds it will be good.

The poor old 3rd opera [*The Knot Garden*] waits sadly in the wings. This b[lood]y op[eration] has knocked all the fine plans for a long summer sideways. But we'll catch up somehow – and operas always take me ages.

Will phone.

Love –

M.

Leave communication meantime to me.

[1966]

Dear Bill,

Nice to have even a word or two on the phone – but I never like to prolong it when you're at work, or when I'm having to be on the alert myself at all. But as ever it matters a lot to know our pleasure at meeting when we can is mutual. And that the troubles and trials and off-the-cuff attempts don't put you down. They'll work sometimes and sometimes they won't. But I feel sure we'll be together again before long. If it has to be in Bath, or we need to try for that, I'm sure I could have a date to 'stay out late', or at least later than before, so that we could manage well if you came on the first afternoon train. But then it may work out for you as it did before without inconvenience. I just want you always to do only what is reasonable.

A long love-making in Bath is a nice dream anyway!

[. . .] It's just possible that long August weeks with no outside excitements may send K[arl] sometimes to London for a day or so – and if that happened the week you're at Gowerton it may work out fine. But

if it happens any week and I'm alone here I'll ring immediately.
Luv –
M.

3 August 1966

Dear Bill,

I rang last week out of impatience – not because I was alone in the house – I wasn't. But recovery [from surgery] seemed so long delayed. One day off one day on – and the off days I felt deeply depressed. In fact only Karl's endless kindness and gentleness really kept me on an even keel. It's what happens sometimes after big ops. But now I have turned the corner and am nearly myself again. And the scar isn't so sensitive etc, etc. So I'll phone you again sometime soon. In any case keep Thurs. evening 18th free – looking ahead. But if gone already don't phone or write – I'll phone soon.

Fidelio Qt recorded [String Quartet] No. 1 very well finally. And now they go on to [No.] 3. Issue in November.

Otherwise nothing to report beyond that I'm back at work on the opera. All the more detailed news when we meet.
Love
M.

22 September 1966

Dear Bill,

I'd meant to ask you on the phone to write out for me a possible 12-bar blues bass sequence for L.H. (piano) using a boogie woogie formula. I think I could do it myself, but would very much welcome it from an 'expert'! I can get it from you next week. I shan't be in fact putting it to final use [in *The Knot Garden*] till the new year.

I still expect Wed. will be our day for London – i.e. we shall come up by car, then Karl will stay overnight and I shall go back on 7.45 or 6.45 (the earlier is the better but not important). In that case I'd come to get you I'd hope by 4 and we'd see how you are and what's best to do. I wouldn't want to cause you pain when really meaning your pleasure!

Anyhow, let's expect Wed. If any change I can drop you a card, if phone is difficult. But won't communicate further unless I have to.
Love
M.

November 1966

Dear Bill,

Monday was fine. Have been singing away since. Also your remarks about Beethoven 3, 5 and 'Pastoral' stimulated me a *great* deal and by some means helped further clarify the shapes of the new Symphony [No. 3] that I'll start in 2¹/₂ years or so. That is; things you said, though I didn't really get all the gist of your own trains of thought, set me considering and reconsidering, as though there were something significant buried away and about to be brought out to the view by an effort. And a tremendous sense that too constant preoccupation with the immediate journalistic, stylistic matters of today wasn't finally my line – so that your remarks worked as a fresh release into my own proper more time-extended world.

That all sounds a bit pretentious but it's roughly how it was and is. [. . .]

Love
M.

January 1967

Dear Bill,

Was nice to talk to you unexpected today – and unlucky that nothing else could be arranged suddenly. As I see it the best possibilities ahead are for you to make a day of it, so to speak, and come down to Bath or Chippenham and for me to meet you as soon as you get in and then maybe again later (time in between to return to face Gran Hawker and be at the phone's end). I'm sending you a train list. Perhaps you could even manage the 13.45 as being lunch time once in a while? Chippenham has a motel I'd like to look into – because motels (at least in America) are immediately get-at-able without porter problems, and if I got hold of a car I could be tolerably late away on the second visit and so on. However I can't do anything till I'm back here for good, which looks like a morning train on Tues., 23rd, after *Priam* the night before. I *think* I shall most likely be going home Thurs. on my own. So would ring you from Padd[ington] or Corsham. And then the sooner the better!

It's frustrating being so separated. But when we do meet it's always as though for the first time anew and that freshness and excitement is part of the converse gain, in the 'profit and loss' account.

As always, going away feels like going to the moon, but in fact by Sat. week we're in London once more after a night flight.

Luv

M.

15 March 1967

Dear Bill,

The good and bad of meeting is that the pull together gets so strong and so the frustration more frustrating. Anyway – I was a bit edgy yesterday as I knew that I was being 'watched' as K[arl] felt I would be bound to use the opportunity to see you. And this compulsion, which I think he wants badly to resist, made him sick. I phoned him from a Padd[ington] call box. But after all this is still so soon after the shock of discovery that it's not settled down in him at all yet. Nor quite in me – i.e. I give away my intentions by my silence! a kind of underground intuition.

But gradually I become steadier – wickeder perhaps! – and give little if anything away just because I've got onto the more nonchalant assured intentions, when I know what's been 'arranged' is pretty fool-proof and also that the arranging has been done by a truly private letter – as now, when I'm alone in the house. So the essentials are, I'm sure, to be as fool-proof as we can, and to be ready to let go at the last moment without desperation. If you were ill or couldn't make it in anyway and I hadn't communicated, just to do nothing at all and not worry and certainly not try to leave *any* message. And if I got into some unexpected last moment hitch and couldn't communicate, to take it as it comes and go elsewhere as soon as you'd satisfied yourself that I had got held up somehow.

I do think the hotel idea is sensible. For most of the possibilities are like yesterday, when some London afternoon date (which is known to everyone, publisher, agent, Karl etc but which is for me alone to keep) is open-ended – i.e. has no fixed end, except a train at Padd. and a taxi at Chippenham. Even yesterday there was time had we been able to fix ahead in hope. If we fix ahead and then it doesn't work it won't be too terrible. You could use the room for the night or cancel and pay (expenses mine of course). The actual tele-recording for the [Bernard] Levin interview will be either next week or the week following. It *seems* that it should be just the right kind of open-ended date. So we can but try. I'll let you know somehow the moment I know the day.

The obvious hotels are the Great Western itself, the Cumberland at Marble Arch, the one at Lancaster Gate; anything near Marylebone etc, etc. Presumably your secretary could book as for some Brum [Birmingham] don or friend – in your name or an assumed name – and you may have to confirm in person or by letter. I should have to ring you on the day from the TV studio, as did yesterday, or a call box. Because I can never be *quite* certain that I'm not unexpectedly accompanied and not alone. And if on the other hand you've had difficulty in finding a room that makes sense (incidentally it can be single or double, with bath, or whatever is easily available) then that would just be that. Hotels do get very booked up in London. But within walking distance of Padd. there are quite a few – and there's one near BBC Maida Vale in the crescent going from the nearest Bakerloo underground (Warwick Ave) up towards Maida Vale itself. That would be two stations off the train so to speak. I'll have to leave it to you.

I hope this plan and date works because April–May isn't very hopeful – i.e. wouldn't have been hopeful ever. For my mama is to be here from Ap. 9 to 29. And on Ap. 29 the Leics. [Leicestershire Schools Symphony Orchestra] thing starts. On May 10, after the Fairfield Hall concert, Del Mar and wife and K. and I have 10 days holiday, getting back for the general [dress rehearsal] for *Priam* on Sat. May 20.

I feel however there *might* be possibilities hotel-wise even at this end, in the summer when I go out of the house to swim or into Bath etc. Because the summer tends to be a time when we both are rather constantly at Corsham, in the garden and so on. But I can't think this out very much just yet. And the thing is not to lay too much store by exactly this or that. And to try and keep you from any feeling of being cut off I'll write pretty often and phone. For instance, when the car is here and not in London, I sometimes drive myself (K. stays in the house) up into the downs to walk (and as I shall do on hot days sometimes into Chippenham to swim) and this could mean a neutral callbox somewhere (in the afternoon) – if I take plenty of six-pences. So that I may find a simple on the spot way of phoning occasionally even though I'm not on my own here.

Anyhow – I'll let you know the TV date the moment I can.

Luv

M.

8 April 1967

Dear Bill,

Work seems to have gone so hard and so well this week that by last night I was exhausted – and doubt if I can do anything this morning. My head is too far gone – is what it feels like. However – am virtually all set to start the blues, the finale ensemble of the [first] act [of *The Knot Garden*]. I desperately want to get that finished before we go away for the 10 days break.

Go later today to London to pick up K[arl] and to drive to Essex so as to bring my ma here tomorrow, Sunday – for 3 weeks.

It was a nice stolen meeting in the sunny town. We shall manage others as the luck comes and goes.

I'm writing in case I get 'cut off' this week. Though usually K. doesn't like being here much when my ma is staying.

The Fidelio Qt in the Purcell Room ([String Quartet] No. 3) were not very good, so he said. Rough and out of tune. I guess they can only really make it under recording conditions. They can then make enough takes to get things right. But I'm sure the disc will help towards the eventual proper players for No. 3 – who haven't appeared yet.

I shall have to come to London to talk *Midsummer Marriage* over with Colin Davis and Ande Anderson sometime after Ap. 18. But it may not work to be of use to you and me. I'll let you know though if it does. Otherwise May 2 isn't very far away.

Luv –

M.

16 April 1967

Dear Bill,

I've got the *two* 86-year-old grandmamas in bed and under the doctor now. So for the moment I'm fully engaged!

Meanwhile I've talked to Alan Ridout. He's very sympathetic to you and me, and I'm hoping he can provide a simple alibi to help me on May 2. But I haven't told him in any detail of course what we are to each other. Just that we like meeting. Though if he guesses, or knows, or you even tell him I shan't mind. But Karl always flies to him when I get 'found out' and so he already knows we (you and I) see each other. But my general inclination is to keep mum, and with Ingpen &

Williams [concert agency] I gave the idea that I never see you off my own bat. The fewer that are in the secret (on my side) the better. And in any case it's so absolutely a personal matter to us both, a curious lucky dip that has its own quality even from its secrecy. It always does me good to know that you're there when the chances conspire. I'll ring you, with luck, next week if I'm on my own (barring the mamas) which is very likely.

Luv

M.

late May 1967

Dear Bill,

Sorry if I was mumbling and tentative on the phone last night. I just couldn't be sure how you might feel yourself, coming all the way down here. But you cleared that up quickly.

I'll fix the hotel late this morning and confirm before I go to post. The trains are 12.45 non-stop, so very good, and 13.45 stopping at one or two. Although all seems set fair for certainty I guess it's better to hang on till I phone. Something might go wrong.

I shall probably have a make-believe dentist in the afternoon (I have really started such appointments in fact!) and intention to swim in the hot baths! K[arl]'s appointment in London is 3 p.m. – so it really turns on how much he leaves it till the last moment to set off – which he generally doesn't like doing.

It's a lovely thought having a long time together soon. I'll put in an extra £1 as I guess you'll need it.

Luv

M.

Will you write and confirm the single room for Monday to Pratt's Hotel, South Parade, Bath in your name. They need this they say. If you prefer a double, big bed, you can ask for that. I said on the phone for one person! Seemed silly to say anything else. For 1 night.

1 June 1967

Dear Bill,

Just a tiny note to explain, which I didn't very clearly yesterday, that we've lent K[arl]'s tiny flat in London to John Ardoin, the man from Texas, for 2 weeks as from tomorrow. So we're entering the summer period when we're both here together mostly, K. and I, and when I avoid London if I can, just to get as much uninterrupted composition done in the better weather. And I need this uninterrupted spell badly, as I'm behind hand, one thing with another.

So we'll just have to see. But I'll communicate when I can, and the silences in between won't be portentous. It's the rough with the smooth. If June 15 is possible I'll phone when and *if* I can! But I'm not going to drive it. The Oxford concert and the Bath Abbey do (and composition) are grinding up together and I may feel unable to carry off cloak and dagger arrangements. Too much complication at one go . . . So don't lay any store by it. But we'll meet soon all the same.
Luv
M.

Now for 2 *Priams*[revival of the première Covent Garden production]!!

8 August 1967

The restlessness [Karl's] is very evident, much as I expected, though still don't know how far afield it will go. I think the London flat becomes free again next week and that's the week most likely, as I see it.

I shall send you a clean copy soon of the libretto to date (though no hurry) as I've done the words for Dov's (Dov is to replace Piers; he's the musician; and Dov is David, who played the harp and loved Jonathan) 'ballad'. Then I can talk to you about it one time.
Luv –
M.

9 November 1967

Dear Bill,

I'm on my own today and can write easily – and tomorrow morning I'll phone. Remind me, if you get this letter in time, I want to ask your advice on some recordings I want to get – for study purposes and for later performances.

With Monday and Friday your free days it means that once in a while I hope you'll be able to come down to Bath. If I knew ahead that, say, through some fixed London appointment, I'd be left on my own here on a Monday as a reasonable certainty I'd write you, and phone if I could. Then I could phone the moment I was 'safe'. Fridays are likely to be in this sense easier for you because they can only be the *end* of a few days on my own and so I'd have a chance to phone you a day or two before. Tomorrow, for example, would have been such a day, but I'm dashing to London myself to get driven back late via Tunbridge Wells, to visit my hospitalised mama – and I'll go straight from train to car.

If the Monday Dec. 11th afternoon in London works out it ought to be in the Strand place [Hotel Strand Continental], as I'd theoretically be around Cov. Gdn and wouldn't have time to come to you. Whereas in the hotel there'd be plenty of time to make love and to talk just as we needed. It would be a 3.15 sort of time and I'd catch the 5.45 from Padd[ington]. I'll let you know as soon as I've fixed things for certain.

K[arl] has dentist appointments in London for a while and that means I think the next 2 weeks should leave me free some days each mid-week. So I must see tomorrow on the phone how you think you're placed, if you feel Bath a good idea.

Luv

M.

18 March 1968

Dear Bill,

[. . .] I finished my *Songs for Dov* on Monday – a great relief. I've had a struggle to continue working with these almost weekly 'nervous' knockouts – so it's tremendous to have got something written and finished. Now I've got to discover some new regimen that will carry me on till things return into balance. [. . .]

Luv –

M.

9 April 1968

Dear Bill,

[. . .] I hope you didn't get any adverse effects from our last meeting – i.e. hope I wasn't carrying some real virus. I felt as ever very warm and close to you. Mutual erotic play seemed to become very mutual – under your guidance I think.

Blessings

M.

25 April 1968

Dear Bill,

Got back from the States on Tuesday and went straight to film with the Leics. Schools [Symphony Orchestra] lot in Chippenham! It's all been pretty mad – and exhausting. But also exhilarating. The St Louis concerts were a great success. One of the best performances of 'Enigma' [Variations] in the USA ever, I should guess. The orchestra played with love and fire – and they were good as such. Concerto for Orchestra a trifle under-rehearsed, esp. the long cello line in slow mvt, but good too. Marvellous clarinet, trpt (a red Indian boy!), xylophone, tuba. A brash and brilliant perf. of Holst, *Perfect Fool* – and a weird, slow do of *Unanswered Question*. I met my agent, who came from N.Y., and is a very nice man indeed, and explained the strict limits of my availability. Because it was all in all a success, I shan't go back (for other English–American programmes) till the fall of next year, when the opera [*The Knot Garden*] is completed.

I'll ring you tomorrow morning, to see how you are and hear your news. K[arl] has just gone up to London for M.M. [*The Midsummer Marriage*] tonight, and I shall follow on Sat. That seems to have gone well. Schott's had to re-print librettos overnight. I'm still a bit over-whelmed by it all.

When we shall see each other next I don't see. I am here all next week, but probably not alone. Then the week following I have to be mostly in Bournemouth to rehearse, and on May 10 go for a 10 days holiday away, ending with 3 days (official) at the Bergen Festival. Get back May 24, and have to film with Leics. Schools again on Sat. May 25. After that life becomes normal! I want to make some Monday dates in London to see Sir D.W. [David Webster] and metronome new Act 2 [of *The Knot Garden*] at Cov. Gdn. I'd hope to dash Clapham way if you were there. It isn't really so long in fact since we were in Bath together – but it seems ages to me because of America in between. I worry for you about the kind of loneliness you were describing on the train. I know it very well. Not that *I* could solve it for you even if I were 'single'. I had though so many years of it earlier that I can only promise you it's never final.

Will ring first thing tomorrow.

Luv

M.

January/February 1969

Dear Bill,

[. . .] I expect to finish *The Knot Garden* by end of Feb. or mid-March. Première seems definitely for Nov. 70 (Cov. Gdn and Colin [Davis]). I'm using melodrama for Mangus' final speech from the footlights. Speech against background of music (echoes of earlier acts etc) and off-stage voices (like Shakespeare directs in *Tempest* for bow-wows and ding-dongs). I'm doing it now and it comes off very well.

I want to pick your brains over a concert (in Bath, 70) to include [*The Vision of*] *St Augustine*.

But most I just want to see you – grabbing at the few possible times given all our present circumstances.

Luv –
Michael

21 February 1969

Dear Bill,

I finished [*The Knot Garden*] yesterday – with Thea and Faber moving to go off together to make love. I thought of you – and felt (in a dream way) we'd have done the same had the opportunity served – and all night if we felt like it! Though we're a stranger couple than is often found. [. . .]

Luv
M.

8 May 1969

Dear Bill,

[. . .] What a jamboree of music London is now – and even elsewhere around the country. Composition, in such a whirl of a world, gets harder and harder. But of course the very word 'composition' begs the question. And to explain what I mean would take pages and not be very interesting at the end. Suffice to say I long to be settled down, come the autumn, at the new Symphony [No. 3], which has been so long in the cogitative process and is mighty ripe for making.

See you.
Luv
M.

November 1969

Dear Bill,

I've been hoping to phone but it hasn't worked – chiefly for two reasons – I've been unwell off and on; and my mother eventually died at midnight last night. This was a merciful release for her, as she'd been some months dumb from a stroke, and it was not easy living for her.

[. . .] This week I *will* manage to phone somehow. I am likely to be on my own for part of it, and will be at home except for the funeral (in Essex). If Dec. 10 is OK I'd get to you about the usual – 3 p.m. or so. I feel I need to see you and feel the need more than usual. I've been forced to be rather shut in on myself.

Meanwhile all love.

Michael

11 October 1971

Dear Bill,

There have been moments, during this 'bad' time, when I have wished K[arl] totally not there. Not as surprising, I dare say, as my seemingly unshakable loyalty. But what is to be done after 15 years of being together? or even not together! For I keep hearing the inarticulate cry for help.

These remarks aren't really addressed to you, but rather 'for the record' – to be noted away.

Being with you on the other hand . . . That needs no expression beyond itself.

Love

M.

I'll phone you when I can.

[1973/4]

Dear Bill,

The wrenching has been rather horrible – predictably – but it's kind of over.* Now there's an interim to get it actually to happen. Week and work days are OK, but the weekends alone together are *not* easy. So I'm getting out occasionally. I'm going this next Friday, 20th, to Cambridge for 'biography' – and so it's just occurred to me that it

---

* Tippett had persuaded Karl Hawker to agree to a separation.

423

might make sense to see you Sunday afternoon on the way back – but of course it may not make sense for you. I'll phone however Sat. evening from Cambridge – or even Sun. morning, if I don't get you – it can all happen or not at the last moment.

If not then, some time soon!

Love

M.

Colin Davis

The conductor Colin Davis (b. 1927) has distinguished himself equal-ly as a conductor of orchestral music and of opera. He is noted espe-cially as an interpreter of Berlioz's music as well as that of Tippett. In Britain he held important posts included at Sadler's Wells and the Royal Opera House, Covent Garden, and with the BBC Symphony Orchestra. Later he worked mainly as an orchestral conductor in Germany and Austria: with the Bavarian Radio Symphony Orchestra and the Dresden Staatskapelle, and at the Vienna Staatsoper. His most recent appointment was as principal conductor of the London Symphony Orchestra in 1995. He conducted the first performances of Tippett's Concerto for Orchestra, The Knot Garden, The Ice Break *(dedicated to him),* Symphony No. 3, Triple Concerto, The Mask of Time *and* The Rose Lake. *The following selection contains some of the last letters and cards the composer wrote, mainly in appreciation of Davis's commitment to the presentation of his music.*

27 October 1982

Dear Colin,

I'm so near the end of *The Mask of Time* and the 3 years (I shall prob-ably finish at Christmas) that the usual tension between impatience and strain of invention has been mounting. So on Monday the body took over and knocked the *Mask* dead. And the coming 4 weeks of public doings and no composition is a kind of relief. But yesterday was still 'no man's land'. Chunk of 3rd Symphony and all [*The Vision of St*] *Augustine* made me horribly aware of what crazy worlds of music I got into then – crucial pieces though they may be. At the mid-point of *Augustine* the sheer exaltation of the sound seemed ready to put me under the seat! Whatever does a stranger to the work make of it?

At least *The Mask of Time* won't have one problem; that is, it will be sung always in the vernacular (I've already agreed to 1/2 the German text, to be printed on the vocal score). So that though choirs take ages to study notes and intonation, they will eventually be able to go over into finding the colours and musical functions of the lines and harmonies that spring somewhere from the needs of the scenario. I think I oughtn't to be lazy, and I should come to see you sometime to help, if I can, before the *Mask* is premièred. *Nicht?*

Bill [Bowen] and I will be at *Faust* on Sunday. May look into green room after.

herzlichst

M.

28 October 1982

Dear Colin,

Just to explain, as it were, the way things work for me now.

I employ Nick Wright 1/2 time, as sec.–manager–promotions and whatever. He's very quiet and efficient, is a professional expert in Egyptian antiques! He has a tiny office in the Schott attics [. . .].

Bill [Bowen] looks after me for love. Though, especially since his small biography of me was published a few months back, he gets paid work as a Tippett expert – I'm delighted to say. He is very caring and generous. I won't go on any big professional trip without him, and he gives up time for that.

Now, these two alone arrange all my commitments for public life, leaving me in reasonable ignorance till the appropriate time. It's chiefly long scale, i.e. 83 and 84 are already mapped out I gather (always according to what Bill guesses my composition needs are to be) and 85 is being considered.

It works marvellously for me. Perhaps sometimes tough on others.

This isn't so much a personal letter as 'information' in case.

love

M.

7 July 1983

Dear Colin,

Clifford Caesar (Schott) will now send you (at my command!) the F.S. [full score] *notes for performance* [on *The Mask of Time*] which you should have had of course. These have both notes for voices and instruments. He is going to add now a note explicitly saying that ⌢ over a double bar means a break in the musical flow. Since Part 1 vocal score has gone to print, and with notes for voices, then this new note as to ⌒ is absent. But it's only a matter for conductors not chorus masters surely!

Clifford will also send you copy of the annotated libretto which will be printed in huge numbers for cheap availability at every performance and to all critics etc.

As to quotes: the model was 'The Waste Land'. This is printed without indication of what is [T. S.] Eliot and what is quote. E. was persuaded to make some post. notes later, which are always printed now in published copies. I was persuaded likewise, as you will see. If you would like to know further the 'interlocking' of myself and quotes, e.g. 'My new country's there, "far far beyond the stars"' ([Henry] Vaughan?) or 'Spring out the "orient and immortal wheat"' ([Thomas] Traherne?) then Clifford is ready to make up a copy for you. The 'interlocking' is so total that I've nearly forgotten myself which is what, e.g. which is me and which Rilke (my translation) in 1st song of No. 9. (Actually, so as not to fox you, Rilke is the baritone solo.)

Incidentally, even Michael Tillett hadn't noticed that the bass line to organ accompanying tenor solo towards the later part of *Jungle* is our old friend *Deus creator omnium* out of *Augustine*. So there! I might ring in a day or two to see how it all seems.

herzlichst

Michael

PS. The proofreading corrections to the F.S. (I finished No. 9 and 10 with Michael here yesterday) are minimal. A few notes, some accidentals and time signatures. There's a master copy in Schott now with all corrections marked by Michael in red ink. He's quite ready to come up to London and mark up *your* copy.

22 September 1983

My dear Colin,

[. . .] This is really to say that I've now finished a piece for solo guitar [*The Blue Guitar*] (good) and one for brass band [*Festal Brass with Blues*] (fair); both with premières before Boston. So I'm having a break, before a piece for solo piano [Sonata No. 4], which I look forward to doing. It's a marvellous instrument I think. But in mid-Jan. Bill [Bowen] takes me away for a long-planned 3-month professional trip round the world, which is scheduled to end at the *Mask of Time* première in April. So – if I can be of any use to you for that piece, it should be before mid-Jan. Being free I can come to you as suitable if that would help. [. . .]

Love to Shamsi [Colin Davis's wife],
Michael

7 May [1984?]

My dear Colin,

I didn't listen yesterday [to a broadcast of *The Mask of Time*], but some of those whose opinions I really value did. And as one of them said: 'The final number 10 was like a defiant paean of joy.' He spoke for them all. I feel curiously relieved!

Bill [Bowen] said the tape was the Saturday, and performance terrific.

I think many of the critics' problem was, as you hinted in Boston, the implication of their ignorance. It can't be otherwise probably. Those that knew knew, so to speak, just as we did.

herzlichst
Michael

26 January 1986

Dear Colin,

It was good to meet up with you in Amsterdam, both for yourself and the music making – although I may have appeared too abstracted into my inner world of the new piece [*New Year*]. And still in that world I've just finished a book which Bill got me, and that I found rich and rewarding, and occasionally, even, like a correlate of *The Mask of Time*. I've asked B. to send you a copy, you might like it – and to show my continued affection, however odd I may seem sometimes.

Lots of love to you both
Michael

17 February 1986

My dear Colin,

Of course you shall have a libretto [to *New Year*] We had one assembled around Christmas. It's structurally how it will be. The characters though will sharpen and deepen, and scenes likewise. The young ones of the 3 'of somewhere and today' have already gone by

428

this point. I'm about to start (music, that is) for the same process on the older woman. The 3 'of nowhere and tomorrow' won't be till summer, I guess.

B[ill] and I went to Copenhagen, Sat. to see the *Hamlet* ballet to 2 T[ippett] symphonies, Triple [Concerto], etc. It is in fact terrific – an extraordinary feat of choreography (John Neumayer). Symphony 2 came over marvellously fresh and strong – and dramatic. I was a bit knocked out by it all.

Hope this gets you in time in Munich.

Love to you both

Michael

24 November 1987

My dear Colin,

[. . .] today I started work again, slowly, on *New Year*. Michael Tillett was here to help me find my way back to where I had stopped – and we listened to some of the S[ymphony No.] 3 cassette. He was delighted by the extraordinary clarity of the opening music – how did you get it? I was delighted by Faye [Robinson]'s marvellous dramatic projection. The 'prologue' to Part 2 seemed a little off yet of the controlled abandon possible to make it seem 'off the cuff'. But didn't dare to hear it all. I need to forget that sound for the new sound of the opera. Bill was lucky to hear it in the hall and watch you in action.

If you do think further of *Songs for Dov* I recorded it for Virgin Records with Scottish Chamber Orch. and Nigel Robson. Due out Jan.; so the press copies should already be there. Good I think. The real find was the electric guitarist [Steve Smith?] (Cov. Gdn has signed him up for *Knot Garden* production next May). *Hauptsache* is that it must be played with *plectrum* not fingernails. That alone gives the true colour; marvellous. Try and hear it if you can.

love to all

Michael

19 October 1989

The Colonnade, Boston

Dear, dear Colin,

Here we are in the old Colonnade again (a gruelling week with NEC [New England Conservatory] students playing pieces from chamber music to Symphony 4) and with such good memories of the late nights after *Mask of Time* consuming oysters and Californian wine. (The performances still ring in many people's ears here.)

And when Bill was at the reception desk when we came in very late, I had to go and look round into the Promenade Café to see if you might after all be sitting at the corner table there!

New Year première is Friday, next week. Prognosis good.

Love to you both from

Michael and Bill

10 July 1990

Caro mio Colin,

Just a few bits of news of my doings in this rather frantic 85th year.

I am very gradually making a CD for Nimbus of Pf. Conc. and Triple Conc. (BBC Philharmonic and new, different soloists). I made the Triple half last week after a fine performance in public in Lichfield Cathedral. We did the recording in Manchester the next day.

When the master-tape cassette comes I'll get the office to send you a copy for your curiosity. But: – do you remember asking me some time back, why I hadn't written a concert piece for woman's voice and orchestra? Well, it's done. A setting of Yeats' 'Byzantium'; 23± min.; a big sing. It comes out in US next year, April 10; part of a joint centenary celebration of Chicago SO and Carnegie Hall. I gather the singer is Jessye Norman. It comes out in London next year, late Prom, with BBC SO and t'other Davis [Andrew Davis], and Faye Robinson. It's very you! I'll get the office to send you a F.S.

Be good; love to you both.

Michael

1 October 1990

Dear Colin,

The day after you rang I fell into one of my bouts of 'exhaustion', triggered off by heart fibulation [fibrillation] induced by a viral cold. Can seem at times like delayed reaction from a decade of perhaps over-intense creativity. It's gone now, so I can contemplate the Qt [String Quartet No. 5] again. I need lots of breaks home or away these days.

Despite all this I still feel an LSO [London Symphony Orchestra]

piece (not a symphony) will move gradually from possible to likely [contemplating *The Rose Lake*]. When I know I'll let you know.
love
Michael

15 November 1990
Senegal

My dear Colin,
The Mask of Time, RFH [Royal Festival Hall] Nov. 3, was *very* good, and lifted me, and the audience, up high! I've come away to find quiet. The period of bouts of exhaustion have gone now. I go back to take up the Qt [String Quartet No. 5] and other things, but at a slower rhythm altogether. Feel very close to you both.
love
Michael

22 February 1991

My dear Colin,
I *did* enjoy being with you on Wed. (and thanks from us both, B[ill] and I, for the lunch). I thought the performance [of the Triple Concerto] flowed – and so did Bill. Then, Michael Tillett, whose opinion I value, had listened on the radio and told me today he found it quite different from the first ever performance; flexible and measured like a 'standard'. He said [Nobuko] Imai, a marvellous player, was so much more on top of her part this time, the whole trio therefore better balanced. Hope you were pleased yourself, and with yourself!
Love to you all,
Michael

17 July 1991

My dear Colin,
The 4tet [String Quartet No. 5] was finished on Monday. Many times a tough struggle – 'health' mainly. Now I'm in full recoil. Never again! Compensated by a euphoria at being free. After a good rest, we shall see if creative energy returns again. *The Rose Lake* is only a hazy mirage at present. I'll let you know at once if anything transpires.
love to you both
Michael

6 May 1992

My dear Colin,

No! The section finished by Tobago was the 1st of the 5 sections of the piece [*The Rose Lake*]. Second section is due to be finished by early June. (I have to go to Sheffield May 9 for *Uraufführung* of Quartet 5; and May 16–30 a vacation in Greece, with Carlos Carter, a young Dutch computer-expert friend of Bill's, with a passion for music. He will look after me and drive us to see the sites etc as suits us.) 3rd section should be finished by the fall. 4th section by Feb. of next year; 5th and last section by this time next year, *hoffentlich*.

The 5 sections are related; kind of variation-wise. Each should be 4–5 min. long – so whole piece 20–25 min. But we haven't done any accurate timings yet. All is already in F.S. section by section; so there'll be no delay for you to see it as you wish. I read all your news in the letter, which I was glad to get. See you sometime.

love to you both,

Michael

PS. My *guess* is piece may reach 30 min. – *am Schluss*.

Biographical Appendix

The aim of this Appendix is to place Tippett's friends and associates in the context of his life and work; it includes mainly those figures on whom information may not be readily available in standard printed or online reference sources. Where a name is shown in **bold** type, fuller details will be found in the introduction to the letters to that person.

Allinson, Adrian (1890–1959): painter, brother of Francesca Allinson.

Allinson, Cyril: brother of Francesca Allinson.

Allinson, Francesca (Fresca): see p. 69.

Allinson, Veronica: wife of Cyril Allinson.

Amis, John (b. 1922): music journalist, administrator and broadcaster; worked for London Philharmonic Orchestra and sang in choir at Morley College, helping Tippett with concert arrangements there; married to Olive Zorian 1948–55.

Ardoin, John (1935–2001): music critic of *Dallas Morning News* and US correspondent for *The* [London] *Times*.

Ayerst, David: see p. 218.

Ayerst (née Fisher), Larema: wife of David Ayerst. See also below, under Fisher.

Bartlett, Ken W.: head of promotion for Schott (Mainz); translations of operas (by Tippett and others) include *The Ice Break*, for German première (Kiel, 1978).

Bergmann, Walter (1902–88): flautist and recorder player, also trained as a lawyer; forced to flee Germany after defending Jewish clients in lead-up to Second World War, escaped to England and worked at Schott (London), replacing Edgar Hunt during latter's war service; later worked with Hunt on editions of baroque recorder music; translated *King Priam* for German première (Karlsruhe, 1963); dedicatee of String Quartet No. 2.

Binyon, Helen (1904–79): artist, teacher at Bath Academy of Art, Corsham; became major proponent of puppetry as an art form.

Blom, Eric (1888–1959): London music correspondent for the Manchester *Guardian* (1923-31); music critic od the *Birmingham Post* (1931-46) and of the *Observer* in 1949.

Boult, Adrian: see p. 3.

Bowen, Meirion (Bill): see p. 399.

Britten, Benjamin: see p. 189.

Bush, Alan: see p. 120.

Caesar, Clifford (b. 1947): general staff editor at Schott (London); responsible (1980–85) for production of contemporary scores and performance materials.

Campbell, John: former professor of architecture in Munich, fellow RAF officer of David Ayerst, with whom he was billeted in London in Second World War; wrote words of hymn 'Unto the Hills', to which Tippett composed tune *Wadhurst*.

Cleverdon, Douglas (1903–87): BBC producer and director, in Features Department during Second World War, then working mainly on Third Programme productions until retirement in 1969.

Cooper, Gerald: concert promoter at Wigmore Hall in the 1940s.

Davis, Colin: see p. 425.

Dienes, Paul (1882–1952): Hungarian-Greek mathematician; Commissar for Education under Communist government in Budapest after First World War; fled during counter-revolution via Vienna and Paris to Britain; taught mathematics at University College, Cardiff, before becoming professor of mathematics at Birkbeck College, London.

Dienes, Sari: Polish-Greek painter, second wife of Paul Dienes; on outbreak of Second World War, followed her teacher Fernand Léger to the USA.

Dods, Marcus (1918–84): conductor and composer, mainly of film music.

Fiske, Roger (1910-87): BBC broadcaster (1939-59) and Talks Manager.

Fisher, Arden: son of Bryan Fisher.

Fisher, Bryan: brother of Larema Ayerst; bursar at Bath Academy of Art, Corsham.

Fisher, Stanley: brother of Larema Ayerst and fellow student at Oxford of David Ayerst.

Franklin, Colin: editor with publishing firm Routledge; oversaw publication of Tippett's collection of essays *Moving Into Aquarius* (1959).

Franks, Wilfred (Wilf): artist, Tippett's lover in late 1930s; conscientious objector in Second World War; dedicatee of String Quartet No. 1.

Gardiner, Rolf (1902–71): organiser of Boosbeck work camp and co-operative market gardens, one of three such ventures set up in Cleveland, north Yorkshire, to help unemployed ironstone miners.

Glock (Davenport), Clement: scene painter at Covent Garden; married to William Glock, 1944–52.

Glock, William: see p. 427.

Goodman, Paul (1911–72): American social critic, novelist and poet.

Grisewood, Harman (1906–97): joined BBC in 1929, subsequently becoming chief assistant to Director-General; Controller, Third Programme, 1948–52, then Director of the Spoken Word.

Grüber, Arthur (b. 1910): German conductor; musical director of German premières, in Karlsruhe, of *King Priam* (1963) and *The Midsummer Marriage* (1973).

Grynspan, Herschel Fiebel (b. 1921): Polish youth whose story inspired *A Child of Our Time*. In November 1938, while living illegally with an uncle in Paris, Grynspan shot Ernst vom Rath, third secretary at German Embassy in Paris, over persecution of the Jews and mistreatment of his family. For details of his subsequent imprisonment in France and Germany, see Appendix 1 to Ian Kemp, *Tippett: The Composer and His Music*.

Hartog, Howard: administrator; at Hamburg Radio was influential in having *A Child of Our Time* performed in Holland and Germany; worked in promotions department at Schott (London), then moved in 1962 to concert agency Ingpen & Williams, which he eventually bought; married to pianist Margaret Kitchin; dedicatee of Symphony No. 3.

Hawker, Anne: wife of Karl Hawker.

Hawker, Gran: mother of Karl Hawker.

Hawker, Karl (d. 1984): painter and teacher, conscientious objector in Second World War; met Tippett in 1940s then married and had a family; after separation from his wife, he and Tippett renewed contact in late 1950s, became lovers and remained a couple for 17 years; ended his own life; dedicatee of *King Priam*.

Hawker, Susan and Sarah: Karl Hawker's daughters.

Hely-Hutchinson, Victor (1901–47): South African-born composer, conductor, pianist and administrator; Concerts Manager at the BBC 1944–47.

Hepworth, Barbara: see p. 342.

Holme, Christopher: Assistant to the Controller, BBC Third Programme, from 1952 acting Head of Planning, Third Programme.

Howgill, R. J. F. (1895–?): joined BBC 1923 to take charge of copyright department; held various posts culminating in that of Controller of Music 1952–9.

Howes, Frank (1891–1974): joined *The Times* as music critic in 1925 and from 1943 to 1960 was its chief critic.

Hubback, Eva (1886–1949): principal of Morley College, 1927–49.

Hunt, Edgar: leading figure in 20th-century recorder revival; taught flute and recorder at Trinity College of Music, Lodon; worked for Schott, especially in collaboration with Walter Bergmann on editions of recorder music.

Ingpen, Joan: joint founder-director of concert agency Ingpen & Williams, which represented Tippett as a conductor.

Isaacs, Leonard (1909–97): administrator, teacher, pianist, conductor and arranger; held senior administrative posts with BBC, including Head of Music for Third Programme (1950–54) and Home Service (1954–63), then taught at various Canadian universities.

Johnstone, Maurice: BBC Third Programme producer.

Kallin, Anna (Niouta, Niuta): see p. 360.

Kelly, David: bass; created role of Old Man in *King Priam* (1962) and sang He-Ancient in 1968 production of *The Midsummer Marriage*.

Kelly, Lawrence (1928–74): American impresario, founder and general manager of Dallas Civic Opera.

Kemp, Ian: see p. 389.

Kemp, Peter (1904–92): naval historian, brother of Tippett; dropped the name 'Tippett' in 1923.

Kemp, Phyllis (Phyl) (1902–early 1980s): cousin of Tippett, expert in Slavonic languages and lifelong Stalinist; introduced Tippett to Marx and persuaded him to join Communist Party, but his Trotskyist sympathies led to ten-year rift between them. Taught in India with her Indian husband, Aschraf (d. 1962); both later settled and taught in East Berlin.

Kitchin, Margaret: pianist; married to Howard Hartog; gave first performance of Piano Sonata No. 2 (1962), dedicated to her.

Langford, Roy: manager of theatres in Hammersmith (Lyric) and Wimbledon; shared a flat in West Hampstead with Tippett and Aubrey Russ in 1925.

Layard, John (1891–1975): English anthropologist, Jungian analyst and author, from whom Tippett learnt to interpret his dreams.

Lewis, Ben: coal miner from Wales; lost his job in the Depression; employed as road worker in Oxted; he and his wife Miriam occupied one half of Tippett's double cottage, their daughter Bronwen and son-in-law Jack Wilson the other.

Makings, Peter W.: managing director of Schott (London) from 1961 to 1980.

Mark, Jeffrey: composer and economist; fought in First World War; fellow student of Tippett at Royal College of Music, introduced him to traditional music of north of England. Tippett's revolutionary play *War Ramp* arose from discussions with Mark. Dedicatee of Concerto for Double String Orchestra.

Mason, Eric: pacifist and conscientious objector.

Maude, Evelyn: see p. 299.

May, Fred (Freddie, Freddy): leader of the South London Orchestra, based at Morley College; imprisoned as pacifist in Second World War.

Maynard, Edric: conscientious objector; worked at Doolittle Farm, Francesca Allinson's smallholding in East Grinstead. Unreciprocated obsession with Bryan Fisher led to a breakdown; treated by John Layard with financial help from Tippett and friends.

Minchinton, John (c.1920–late 1980s): conductor and close friend of Tippett; proofread full score of *The Midsummer Marriage*; worked as Walter Goehr's assistant. Dedicatee of Symphony No. 2.

Moore, Philip: head of music, BBC West Region.

Morris, John (1895–1980): Controller of BBC Third Programme, 1952–8.

[Moule-] Evans, David (1905–88): English composer and conductor.

Murrill, Herbert (1909–52): English composer and musical director; became Assistant Head of Music at the BBC in 1950.

Newby, Howard (P. H.): writer and administrator; joined BBC in 1949: Controller of Third Programme, 1958–69; Director of Programmes, Radio Three, 1971–5; Managing Director of BBC Radio, 1975–8.

Newman, Ernest: see p. 290.

Newton, Douglas (Den): see p. 140.

Pennyman, Ruth: joint founder, with her landowner husband Major James Pennyman, of Cleveland Unemployed Miners' Association; collaborated with David Ayerst and Tippett on words of folk-song opera *Robin Hood* (Boosbeck, 1934).

Phipps, Jack: concert agent and arts administrator; one of three directors of Bath Festival, 1969; worked for Arts Council as Controller of Touring from 1985.

Piersig, Fritz: musical director of Nordwestdeutschland Sängerbund, Bremen, which commissioned *Four Songs from the British Isles*.

Pilz, Werner: authorised signatory in stage and concert department at Schott (London), 1947–60; promoted and enlarged contemporary music catalogue.

Pollard, Robert: solicitor, Quaker and member of Haldane Society of Socialist Lawyers; represented a number of conscientious objectors including Tippett.

Ponsonby, Robert: Director of the Edinburgh Festival, 1955–60, and of the Proms, 1974–86; Controller of Music at the BBC from 1972 to 1985.

Purves, Alison (d. 1991): wife of Antony Hopkins from 1947.

Pryce-Jones, Alan: writer and librettist.

Raybauld, Clarence (1886–1972): Enlgish conductor and accompanist; assistant conductor of the BBC Symphony Orchestra from 1939 to 1945.

Robeertson, Alec (1892–1982): chief producer of music talks on the Home and Third Programmes.

Ruhm von Oppen, Beate (1918–2004): German writer and translator, refugee from Nazi Germany; maintained lifelong association with Birmingham University, where she studied modern languages.

Russ, Aubrey: former schoolteacher who worked for his solicitor father; flatmate of Tippett's in West Hampstead, then shared accommodation at Chestnut Cottage, Oxted; his gift of J. G. Frazer's *The Golden Bough* greatly influenced development of Tippett's views on opera.

Sackville-West, Edward: see p. 270.

Schneider-Schott, Heinz (1906–88): joint director with Max Steffens of Schott (London) from 1958; son-in-law of Ludwig Strecker.

Schwarz, Rudolf (1905–94): succeeded Sargent as principal conductor of the BBC Symphony Orchestra from 1957 to 1962.

Seefehlner, Egon: deputy director of Vienna State Opera, 1954–61; general administrator there, 1976–86.

Shaxson, Eric: stockbroker turned farmer who, with his wife Dorothy, lived in Oxted; their four sons attended Hazelwood Preparatory School, where Tippett taught French and Latin.

Sherman, Alec: conductor of New London Orchestra; married to pianist Gina Bachauer.

Smith, Cyril (1909–74): English pianist, married to Phyllis Sellick.

Smith, Morris (d. 1967): trombonist, later orchestral director at Royal Opera House, Covent Garden.

Stallabrass, Tom: partner in Robert Pollard's firm of solicitors.

Steffens, Max: joint director with Willy Strecker 1929–58, then Heinz Schneider-Schott, of Schott (London).

Stephani, Martin (d. 1983): director of music for city of Wuppertal, 1959–63.

Sternfeld, F. W. (Fred): see p. 387.

Strecker, Hugo: son of Willy Strecker; director of Schott (London).

Strecker, Willy (1884–1958): manager from 1912 of Schott (London); moved to Germany after First World War and managed the firm in Mainz in partnership with his brother Ludwig (1883–1978).

Sullivan, John: production manager at Royal Opera House, Covent Garden.

Symonds, Isabelle: deputy principal of Bath Academy of Art, Corsham.

Taylor, Charles: leader of the Royal Opera House Orchestra.

Tillett, Michael: pianist who joined Morley College choir when Tippett was director of music; as amanuensis and copyist, prepared vocal scores of all five operas as well as choral works *The Vision of Saint Augustine* and *The Mask of Time*; dedicatee of String Quartet No. 4.

Tippett, Peter: see Kemp, Peter.

Trecu, Pirmin: Romanian dancer; created role of Strephon in *The Midsummer Marriage* (1955).

Turnbull, Rose: wife or daughter of Fred Turnbull, the signalman at Oxted and a staunch Labour supporter.

Warr, Eric (b. 1905): BBC producer, arranger and composer.

West, Christopher: resident producer at Royal Opera House, Covent Garden; directed première of *The Midsummer Marriage*.

White, Eric Walter: see p. 381.

Wilson, Bronwen (d. 1944): daughter of Ben and Miriam Lewis; lived with her husband Jack and son Ian in one half of Tippett's double cottage in Oxted; died in bombing that destroyed cottage shortly after birth of her daughter Sheila; motet *The Weeping Babe* dedicated to her memory.

Wilson, Steuart (1889–1966): English tenor, Head of Music at the BBC, 1948–49.

Wogan, Jude (Judy): actress, close friend of Francesca Allinson.

Wright, Nick (b. 1940): educated as boy chorister at Westminster Abbey, read Egyptology at Cambridge University; worked in concert promotion and artist management, first with London Pro Musica then the Electric Candle, directed by Meirion Bowen; met Tippett through Bowen and took over responsibility for management of Tippett Office during 1980s and early 90s; dedicatee of *Byzantium*.

Zorian, Olive (1916–59): violinist, leader of Zorian Quartet; also had career as orchestral leader; married to John Amis 1948–55.

Tippett's Life: A Chronology

1905 Michael Kemp Tippett born on 2 January in a nursing home at 51 Belgrave Road, Pimlico, son of Henry William Tippett (1858–1944), a hotel proprietor, and Isabel Clementina Binny (née Kemp; 1880–1969), a nurse; lives at The Stigers, Eastcote, Middlesex; the family, with Michael's brother Peter (b. 1904), moves to Rosemary Cottage, Wetherden, Suffolk

1909 begins private tuition, including piano lessons

1913 his mother is imprisoned for a fortnight in Holloway for her activities as a suffragette

1914 enters Brookfield Preparatory School (now Forres School), Swanage, Dorset (joining his brother)

1918 wins a scholarship to Fettes College, Edinburgh

1919 financial circumstances force his parents to move to France

1920 enters Stamford Grammar School, Lincolnshire, for subversion; has piano lessons with Frances Tinkler

1921 his father sells Hôtel Beau-Site, Cannes; for many years his parents have a nomadic existence in Europe, returning to England rarely

1922 expelled from Stamford Grammar School; moves to lodgings, continues piano studies with Frances Tinkler; teaches himself composition

1923 enters the Royal College of Music (30 April) and studies composition with Charles Wood, the piano with Aubin Raymar and conducting with Malcolm Sargent then Adrian Boult; teaches himself counterpoint; lives in London University lodging houses or flats with friends

1926 Charles Wood dies; studies composition with C. H. Kitson

1928 passes the BMus examinations at the second attempt (December) and leaves the RCM

1929 moves to Oxted, Surrey, where he had been conducting a successful

439

madrigal choir, and lives in Chestnut Cottage belonging to Hazelwood School; joins the school staff as a French teacher (Christopher Fry is a colleague); meets Evelyn Maude

1930 conducts Oxted and Limpsfield Players productions of ballad opera (his own editions) and 20th-century opera; conducts a programme of his own music in Oxted (5 April); enrols at the RCM again to begin rigorous composition studies with R. O. Morris (September); has private tuition in orchestration from Gordon Jacob; at the suggestion of Francesca Allinson (whom he had met through his cousin Phyllis Kemp and who becomes a close friend) goes to a Kinderheim near Lake Constance to learn German; begins friendship with David Ayerst, who introduces him to left-wing politics

1931 conducts *Messiah* at the Royal Albert Hall, London (15 November); begins lifelong interest in progressive education

1932 moves to 1 Whitegates Cottages, Oxted, on Sidney Parvin's farm; is introduced by Ayerst to Wilfred Franks, with whom he has an intense relationship; Ayerst introduces him to W. H. Auden, through whom he meets T. S. Eliot; visits the North Yorkshire work camps; goes with Allinson to the Musikheim at Frankfurt an der Oder to learn work-camp teaching techniques; starts taking a weekly rehearsal class for unemployed professional musicians at Morley College, south London; gives up his post at Hazelwood School; meets Alan Bush and begins conducting for the Education Department of the Royal Arsenal Co-operative Society; reads Marx and Trotsky

1933 conducts the first concert by his Morley College class (5 March), now called the South London Orchestra (which flourishes until 1940); conducts a performance of *The Beggar's Opera* at the Boosbeck work camp

1934 conducts a folk-song opera, *Robin Hood* (with his own music), at Boosbeck; his musical activities are now influenced by his political sympathies; adjudicates at the London Labour Choral Union competition

1935 his revolutionary play *War Ramp* is produced in London; with Phyllis Kemp he joins the Communist Party (Camden Town, London, branch) but leaves within a few months; Kemp's espousal of Stalinism causes personal rift with Tippett, who opposed the Soviet persecution of composers; première of String Quartet No. 1 in London (9 December)

1937 begins friendship with Eliot

1938 buys the whole of 1 Whitegates Cottages and has a bungalow (named Whitegates Cottage) built on the site; joins the Socialist Anti-War Front, revived largely by Trotskyists; the Nazi pogrom confirms his disillusionment with political idealism; his relationship with Franks comes to a distressing end (August); he undertakes a course of Jungian analysis; première of Fantasy Sonata (later Piano Sonata No. 1), London (11 November)

1939 conducts Jungian self-analysis, from which he feels emotionally renewed and ready to devote himself to composition; works rejected by Oxford University Press and Boosey & Hawkes; meets Willy Strecker of Schott (March) and begins lifelong association with Schott as his publisher; begins *A Child of Our Time* (4 September); returns to Hazelwood to teach Latin

1940 première of Concerto for Double String Orchestra at Morley College, London (21 April); becomes Director of Music at Morley College (October); joins the Peace Pledge Union; applies for registration as a conscientious objector (16 November)

1941 first recording of Fantasy Sonata, played by Phyllis Sellick, favourably reviewed

1942 his case is heard and he is given non-combatant military duties (3 February); he appeals; tribunal gives him conditional registration (full-time work on air-raid or fire duty or working on the land) (30 May); he refuses to comply; Fantasy Sonata published by Schott; meets Benjamin Britten

1943 broadcasts *Portrait of Stravinsky* for the BBC, the first of a series of radio talks (January); première of String Quartet No. 2 in London (27 March); Oxted Police Court sentences him to three months' imprisonment at Wormwood Scrubs (21 June); released early and taken to a performance at Wigmore Hall, London, of his String Quartet No. 2 (21 August); continues to expand and strengthen Morley College music, attracting Walter Goehr, Mátyás Seiber and Walter Bergmann to the staff and giving increasingly enterprising and wide-ranging concerts; moves in literary and musical circles and embraces pacifism

1944 première of *A Child of Our Time* in London (19 March); his father dies (July); meets Alfred Deller and conducts him in Purcell; continues to present extremely popular Morley concerts combining Tudor and Baroque music with that of the 20th century

1945 Francesca Allinson commits suicide (April); première of Symphony No. 1 in Liverpool (10 November)

1946 plays major role in the PPU, joining a deputation to the Labour government in protest at its conscription policy; première of String Quartet No. 3 in London (19 October)

1948 develops acute hepatitis; Phyllis Kemp contacts him again after 13 years; declines invitation to be a delegate at a Cultural and Scientific Conference for World Peace in New York attended by Shostakovich

1949 Eva Hubback, principal of Morley College and champion of Tippett's work, dies; begins 16-year membership of the Music Advisory Committee of the British Council

1951 resigns from Morley College; sells Oxted property and moves to Tidebrook Manor, Wadhurst, Sussex, where he lives with his mother

1953 première of Fantasia Concertante on a Theme of Corelli in Edinburgh (29 August)

1955 première of *The Midsummer Marriage* at Covent Garden (27 January)

1956 becomes president of the PPU; première of Piano Concerto in Birmingham (30 October)

1957 begins long relationship with Karl Hawker

1958 première of Symphony No. 2 in London (5 February; Boult breaks down in the first movement and starts again); publishes *Moving into Aquarius*, a collection of talks and essays

1959 made a CBE

1960 moves to Parkside, a house in the High Street at Corsham, Wiltshire

1962 première of *King Priam* at Coventry Cathedral (29 May); première of Piano Sonata No. 2 in Edinburgh (3 September)

1965 begins long association with the Leicestershire Schools Symphony Orchestra; goes to the Aspen Festival (July), the first of many visits to the USA, a country that he was to find increasingly appealing

1966 première of *The Vision of St Augustine* at the Royal Festival Hall, London (19 January); receives knighthood (June); undergoes prostate surgery (June)

1968 conducts the St Louis Symphony Orchestra (deputising for Stravinsky) in the USA (April)

1969 his mother dies (November); begins five-year contract as artistic director of the Bath Festival, widening its scope and encouraging younger audiences; conducts in Philadelphia

1970 moves to Nocketts Hill Farm, Calne, Wiltshire; onset of macular dystrophy and degenerating eyesight; première of *The Knot Garden* at Covent Garden (2 December)

1972 première of Symphony No. 3 in London (22 June)

1973 elected an honorary member of the American Academy of Arts and Letters; première of Piano Sonata No. 3 in Bath (26 May)

1974 tours the USA (February–March; American première of *The Knot Garden*); relationship with Hawker ends; he begins an open relationship with Meirion Bowen

1975 goes to Zambia for a performance of *A Child of Our Time* in Lusaka Cathedral (April)

1976 awarded gold medal of the Royal Philharmonic Society

1977 première of *The Ice Break* at Covent Garden (7 July); première of Symphony No. 4 (conducted by Georg Solti) in Chicago (6 October)

1978 visits Australia (spring), returning via Java and Bali; elected a foreign honorary member of the American Academy of Arts and Sciences

1979 première of String Quartet No. 4 in Bath (20 May); becomes a Companion of Honour; sets up the Michael Tippett Musical Foundation, a charitable trust

1983 awarded Order of Merit

1984 première of *The Mask of Time* in Boston (5 April); Hawker commits suicide (June)

1985 première of Piano Sonata No. 4 in Los Angeles (14 January)

1987 diagnosed with cancer of the colon

1989 première of *New Year* in Houston (27 October)

1991 première of *Byzantium* in Chicago (11 April); publishes his autobiography, *Those Twentieth Century Blues*

1992 première of String Quartet No. 5 in Sheffield (9 May); his brother dies

1995 première of *The Rose Lake* in London (19 February)

1996 moves to a rented house in Isleworth, Middlesex; suffers a stroke (September)

1998 dies on 8 January in Isleworth

Alison Latham

General Index

Abyssinia 125
Adams, Anthony 359
Aeschylus 245
Albert Hall, London 118
Aldeburgh Festival, Suffolk 210, 211, 277, 329, 367
Alison, Flight Lt. 39
Allen, John 304
Allinson, Adrian 98–9, 152, 153
Allinson, Cyril 87, 110, 179, 204, 394
Allinson, Francesca xii–xiii, xiv, xvi, 120, 140, 158, 173–4, 175, 187, 236, 239
    air raids 150
    Boyhood's End 146
    financial help for MT 24, 185
    folk music 302, 306
    health problems 176
    letters to 69–119, 256–7, 394
    memorial to 203, 205
    on MT's health 148
    and Rose Turnbull 162
    The Source and *The Windhover* 147
    suicide of 179–81, 184, 242–3, 254–5, 277, 365, 377
    taking MT's appearance in hand 160
Allinson, Veronica 74, 110, 180, 204, 394
Amadeus String Quartet 403
Amis, John xviii, xix, 80, 101, 103, 113, 129, 130, 156, 163, 171, 184, 299
    attractiveness to MT of 153
    concert arrangements for MT 193, 250
    holidays with MT 116, 152
    and London Philharmonic Orchestra 103, 104, 108, 150, 249
    meets MT on his release from prison 308
    MT's instructions from prison 302, 304
anarchism 133, 135, 220
Anderson, Ande 341, 390, 417
Anderson, Marian 282
André, Franz 10
Aprahamian, Felix 150, 308
Ardoin, John xxiv, 67–8, 265, 402, 418

Ashton, Sir Frederick 43, 284, 285, 320–1
Aspen Festival, Colorado 403
Atherton, David 68
Auden, W. H. xii, 146, 181, 206, 227, 325, 369
Avshalomoff, Jack 30–1
Ayerst, David xii, xviii, xix, 4, 74, 78, 79, 84, 90, 98, 156, 182, 398
    advice to MT on ENSA job 83
    and Douglas Newton 187
    early draft of *The Midsummer Marriage* 176
    family of 109, 153
    letters to 218–46
    and MT's conscientious objection 89, 95, 96, 144, 150, 237, 239
    MT's visit following his prison release 301, 305, 308, 310
    on the suicide of Francesca Allinson 181, 243
    and Wilf Franks 121
Ayerst, Larema xix, 109, 153, 231, 237, 305, 307

Bainbridge, Elizabeth 390
Balkwill, Bryan 334
ballet 97, 429
Barbirolli, Sir John 6, 18, 207
Barker, George 16
Bartlett, Ken 64–6, 68
Bartók, Béla 12, 41, 52, 54, 244, 248, 258, 270
Bath Academy of Art xx
Bath Festival of Music xx, 66, 67, 217, 247, 267, 268, 269, 339, 377
Baumgartner, Paul 50
Bax, Arnold 5, 23, 101, 130, 195
BBC 26, 75, 79, 128, 371-2, 368-9, 430
    attitude to MT's conscientious objection 106, 251
    A Child of Our Time broadcasts 52, 77, 80, 133, 293, 360–1

444

Music Index